Collateral Damage

The Daily History of a Blog

MSNBC WEBLOGS/ENTERTAINMENT & THE ARTS/THE JUICE

Jan Herman

Latest entertainment and arts news from the Web

With a Foreword by William Osborne

Impromptu Editions

FOREWORD

By William Osborne

IF THERE IS A SINGLE ETHOS that defines this collection of blog entries, it is that the arts do not exist in a vacuum, that culture is holistically connected to every aspect of society. Through this remarkable, wide-ranging cultural diary, Jan Herman shows us that the art we so often take for granted is intimately interconnected and explicable only in the context of the culture that produces it. Art is viewed through the forces that shape it including politics, business, philosophy, spirituality, social mores, and technology.

This holism serves as a welcome complement, and even a palliative, to the narrow reductionism that often defines the specialized views of academia, and even much journalism. Herman brings art down to earth and embeds it in our daily lives — an approach made possible because there are few writers who more strongly play down their cultural erudition and high level of education. Pretense is replaced with witty, incisive, and often pungent observation of our daily cultural follies.

The wide range of Herman's commentary also makes for lively and informative entertainment. One day we are reading about Brittany Spears and Michael Jackson, and on others about Quentin Tarantino and the founders of small literary magazines like Daniel Pinchbeck. From Noam Chomsky to Bugs Bunny, from peep shows on Times Square to Donatella Versace, Herman writes like a David Carr on steroids. By January of 2003, his blog already had well over half a million hits per month, a large following by any standards, and especially impressive in those days when the web was still finding its place in the American cultural landscape.

There are three areas where Herman is especially adept. The first is film, one of his beats during his long journalistic career which included a parade of America's most prominent newspapers in New York, Chicago, and Los Angeles. As part of this interest, he wrote the definitive biography of the film director William Wyler. The second is his insider takedown of the media industry in which he has worked for more than a quarter century — a love-hate relationship that is very informative, and one I suspect many journalists secretly appreciate. The third is his sophisticated knowledge of the literature of the Beats, a focus not of his graduate work at NYU during the 1960s but of his experience as a book clerk both at the Eighth Street Bookstore in New York and at City Lights Books in San Francisco, where he was also the poet-publisher Lawrence Ferlinghetti's editorial assistant. This led to an interest in small alternative publishers and literary bohemians that makes him a fascinating conversationalist.

This book is also valuable because it provides a detailed snapshot of a wide cross-section of American culture during a pivotal time in our country's history. Written in Manhattan during a 14-month period between May 2002 and July 2003, it captures the American cultural zeitgeist in the immediate wake of 9/11. We see that much of the collateral damage was of our own doing. Herman observes the hypocrisy and greed embodied in the plans for rebuilding. We see his discomfort with the growing surveillance state and his portrayal of Americans entertaining themselves to death like lemmings taking their last leap into a delusional freedom. And as always, he speaks with the modest, direct language of a man who grew up on the streets of New York.

Herman also impresses with his fair-minded tolerance. He embraces a balanced and inclusive view nurtured during decades as a professional journalist. He invariably lets you know his view is only one of many. Even when dealing with highly contentious people and topics, his tone remains open-minded and self-ironic. At heart, he loves people, and he loves a world where everyone's voice is heard. And above all, he loves the city in which he works. I'll close with just one of countless quotable passages from this remarkable blog:

"In a reprieve from rain, the skies cleared above Manhattan and roughly 100,000 people came last night to the Great Lawn in Central Park for a free concert performance of the Metropolitan Opera singing Puccini's "Turandot." The lush beauty of the music, the cool breezes and the grandeur of the New York skyline in the distance made the world seem right. Stretched out on blankets as far as the eye could see, we were more than a band of brothers. We were polyglot humanity. We had gathered there for pleasure, not for combat. It was a huge picnic with a sublime soundtrack under the stars, a reminder that life can be civilized even in a time of turmoil. The harsh realities of war and terror were not lost on us. Their presence beyond the park underscored our luck. We seemed to have entered a safe zone, where conflict was banished from our minds. Thank you, Puccini. Thank you, Met Opera. Thank you, City of New York."

Author's note

The text appears in chronological order. When posted online, it ran in reverse order –
latest date first – which is the customary sequence for blogs. Furthermore, many of the
illustrations have been deleted due to limitations of the print format. And of course none
of the links work, although they are identified by underlined text.

Jan Herman

Latest entertainment and arts news from the Web

Entries from May 16 to May 31, 2002
(Some links may be nonfunctional.)
Back to 'The Juice'

LATEST UPDATES

May 16 / 10 a.m. ET

"I am so tired of critics analyzing the crap out of movies. I go to a movie for entertainment, not life lessons." **— From the mailbag**

Remedial physics for critics: Is there anyone worse than a movie critic who gives "Star Wars: Episode II — Attack of the Clones" a nuanced review instead of a simple-minded rave or an equally dumb pan? For most George Lucas fans, probably not — unless it's a critic who doesn't understand basic physics.

David Elliott, who reviewed "Attack of the Clones" for MSNBC.com, remarked that the original "Star Wars," which opened 25 years ago, "is probably now a big hit 25 light years away."

Boy, was he wrong.

"Unfortunately, this statement defies the laws of physics," Steve Flippo writes from Prattville, Ala. "The first episode ... was not available to inter-galactic viewers until the film was broadcast on television, thus enabling the radio waves transmitting the film to escape our planet and start their journey at the speed of light to other destinations."

Since "Star Wars" didn't air on TV until the early '80s, "at best the first 'Star Wars' is only reaching an audiences within a 20 lightyear distance from Earth," Flippo writes. "Hopefully this has not significantly harmed its revenue generating potential."

The case of the missing director: Has Quentin Tarantino gone underground? That's the question being asked at Bright Lights Film Journal, probably the best Web-only movie magazine around. It's been five years

9

since the cinema wunderkind of the '90s made his last film, "Jackie Brown" and even longer since the release of "Pulp Fiction" and "Reservoir Dogs."

Getty Images file

Jane Mills, the Australian cineaste and author, writes that Tarantino's "silence creates an eerie vacuum after the loud howls of outrage and euphoria that greeted almost everything he did, most of which stomped loudly and bloodily on mainstream cinema." Above all, indie film is "about attitude," she adds.

Well, nobody had more 'tude than Tarantino. Yet his outsider status seems to place him beyond even the indie reservation. When he surfaces again with his long-delayed "Bill Kill," scheduled for release in 2003, maybe he'll answer the question.

May 16, 2002 / 2 p.m. ET

Attack of the critics: Now that "Attack of the Clones" has opened, we've received so much mail from viewers complaining about David Elliott's review of it for MSNBC.com that I thought you might like to see what other critics have said. It shows, if nothing else, that taste is inexplicable.

"It's not what's on the screen that disappoints me, but what's not there." — Roger Ebert, *Chicago Sun-Times*

"An exhilarating two hours of serious fun." — Richard Corliss, *Time*

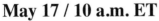
LucasFilms Ltd.

"It's too dull, it's too long, it's too lame." — Stephen Hunter, *The Washington Post*

"A decidedly mixed bag." — David Ansen, *Newsweek*

"Only a teenage boy could find this kind of stuff continually diverting, and only a teenage boy would not notice flimsy emotions and underdeveloped acting. It seems George Lucas, like Peter Pan, has never really grown up." — Kenneth Turan, *Los Angeles Times*

You get the picture.

May 17 / 10 a.m. ET

Just your friendly news: So Rachel gave birth, and Ross helped with the delivery, and they named their baby Emma, and Joey proposed to Rachel, sort of, and then Monica and Chandler thought the baby was so cute they decide to make a baby themselves. You needed to know that, right?

Apparently The Associated Press thought so. It reported Thursday night's season finale of "Friends" at 5:47 a.m. Friday, as though it were nearly a war bulletin from the Middle East.

I saw the finale myself. It was cute, but not that cute. And even if it was the cutest, cuddliest TV show on Earth, which its No. 1 Nielsen rating for the season seems to prove, I don't think the plot details rated a "news" story. Just the way the phony competition in "Survivor" doesn't rate a news story. Just the way the breathless developments of "Who Wants to Be a Millionnaire" don't rate a news story.

The rotten truth, though, is that I'm as complicit as anybody in this chain of "news' decisions, because I help edit these stories when they're produced for MSNBC.com. More important, as senior editor-producer for Entertainment & Arts, I decide whether they're newsworthy or not — and I can't count the number of times I put them out there.

This is not a big moral dilemma on the order, say, of genetic cloning, but help me out here anyway. Let me know whether I'm helping to pollute the Web, passing off mindless junk as needed information, or whether I'm just spinning my wheels wondering if I am.

May 19, 2002 / 3 p.m. ET
Just your friendly e-mails, a representative sample:
"You're polluting." — Joe Brooks

"Keep the news serious (that doesn't necessarily mean morbid, violent or vapid). Entertainment should be given its own time and place." — David Bixby

"Most of the HYPE on the finales are a lot more interesting than the actual shows, otherwise why would all the networks be trying to revive all the old shows?" — Shirley Park, Owasso, Okla.

"Don't be too holy, your job is to provide info and let the 'viewer' decide what is important." — Mark Davis, Somerville, Tenn.

"Some people need to know these kinds of things. ... I'd only really worry if that ever ended up being the ONLY news story and to find out about the war on terrorism you had to click 12 times to find the story on a website." — [Someone called] Nobody

NBC via AP

"Did I care if they had a baby? I don't think so. ... I was even more appalled when one of the 'Survivors' cast was a judge at a recent beauty contest; and who wants to be a millionaire? We all do, but

11

is it newsworthy? I don't think so." — Jannie Kiser, Benton Harbor, Mich.

"You really are just cluttering up the web. But then, the web is designed to be a source of 'information' of every sort. Just make sure it's easy for me to see that you're talking about mindless plots of worthless TV shows, so I can skip it and get to coverage of the Middle East or biomedical advances." — Shelly Perry, Littleton, Colo.

"Does TV entertainment cater to an audience with a bubble gum mentality? It seems so. Are soaps relevant to reality? Never. Do these ersatz dramas provide a vicarious escape for passive viewers? Of course. Are producers pandering to the audience for profit? Need I ask?" — Patricia Eileen Lewis, Port Charlotte, Fla.

May 19, 2002 / 3 p.m. ET

Shut up and look at the numbers: When I asked whether the plot details of the "Friends" finale were worth a news story and whether I was helping to pollute the Web by spreading that information, the Nielsen ratings for the episode had yet to appear.

Now they have — and it looks like 35 million Americans tuned in, making it the most watched, prime-time episode of the season and second only to the record 52.9 million who watched the post-Super Bowl "Friends" special that aired in January 1996.

That's not as many Americans as voted for George W. Bush for president (50.5 million to Al Gore's 51 million), but it's too large a number to ignore. Although I didn't get as many replies to my question, I still think they're worth reading.

May 20, 2002 / 2:15 p.m. ET

Attack of the bloopers: So George Lucas and his crew of high-tech space jockeys spend years making "Star Wars: Episode II — Attack of the Clones." Then the flick opens big at the box office, and what happens?

Hard-core fans begin catching bloopers — mistakes in continuity from scene to scene, illogical story leaps and other peculiar errors.

For instance, one eagle-eyed film-goer points out: "When Yoda and Mace listen to the Senate voting Palpatine emergency powers, Yoda starts on the top ledge nearest the Senate chamber. When the shot changes he has moved down onto

Getty Images file

a different ledge which wasn't there before." Why can't Lucas get the details right? And is he Hollywood's bloopmeister?

Nope. It turns out that Andy and Larry Wachowski's "The Matrix," is the all-time King of Bloops, according to Movie Mistakes.com, with James Cameron's "Titanic" and Sam Raimi's "Spider-Man" solid runners-up. The original 1977 "Star Wars" only ranks ninth.

May 21, 2002 / 9 a.m. ET

Does Anne Heche have something to prove? Seems so. She'll not only make her Broadway debut on July 2 in "Proof," the hit play that won last year's Pulitzer Prize and Tony Award, but she'll be following two critically acclaimed actresses in the role of the central character — Mary-Louise Parker, who won a Tony for her performance, and Jennifer Jason Leigh.

Getty Images file

Closer to the bone, Heche will be measured against Gwyneth Paltrow, who just received wild raves from the London critics for the same role in the West End production. (The play took a battering, though.)

Heche will be playing Catherine, a sort of surly post-adolescent who happens to be 25. Given her looks, Heche, 32, shouldn't have trouble playing younger than she is. The problem may be projecting the image of the alienated daughter of a crazy math genius who is herself a quirky genius. Somehow the idea of Ellen DeGeneres' goofball ex solving mathematical equations doesn't compute — even if the goofball part does. But then it's hard to imagine Paltrow, Leigh or Parker dealing with higher math, either. To my surprise, Parker managed that miracle when I reviewed her on Broadway.

May 22, 2002 / 11:45 a.m. ET

Gallows humor for our time: People of a certain age may recall the satirical newspaper Not The New York Times. An occasional publication that mimicked and ridiculed The New York Times, it deflated the pomposity of the nation's newspaper of record by taking deadly aim at the content of its reporting, the style of its writing and the manner of its self regard. It preceded a similar newspaper parody, Off The Wall Street Journal, and was in some respects a forerunner of that deadpan chronicle of the ridiculous, The Onion.

Now comes a satire much funnier and more acute in my estimation: The CNN Splash Page of Terror, a cheeky piece of gallows humor for our time that imitates the front page of CNN.com.

It is the brainchild of Daniel A. Mahoney, whose Web page, 0 (zero) format, is a smart, even brilliant smorgasbord of offbeat literary and cultural insight. Mahoney understands the way CNN.com and — correct me if I'm wrong — MSNBC.com jump on the news story of the day and fan its flames with single-minded enthusiasm.

In this case, Mahoney has rightly chosen terrorism as his subject. It is not just the story of the day but the story of the year and, if things continue as they are, the story of the decade. Mahoney's brainchild is, as Homer Simpson says, "funny because it's true."

May 23, 2002 / 2:40 p.m. ET

Broadway torture chamber: Few theater folks hold out much hope for this year's Tony Awards, to be broadcast from Radio City Music Hall in New York on June 2.

There are lots of reasons. One, which might as well stand for all of them, is the fact that "Sweet Smell of Success" has been nominated for seven Tonys. The prospect that it could even win for Best Musical — small as its chances may be — diminishes still further the idea that the Tonys stand for excellence.

"Sweet Smell of Success," unlike the movie it's based on, was so awful that I chose not to review it when it opened. The experience was a form of Broadway torture. Everything felt wrong — a show trying its damnedest to fulfill pathetically outmoded theatrical conventions; seats so small and aisles so tight that the ushers should have handed out shoehorns with the programs; and a ticket price so high ($96) that to call it highway robbery would be charitable.

There's no point in reviewing the show now. When it opened, the critics panned it almost unanimously. But given its nomination for Best Musical Score, I feel duty-bound to claim that the score offers the single, most laughable romantic lyric ever sung by one lover to another on a Broadway stage: "I offer you me." Mind-boggling. I guess you hadda be there.

Meanwhile, Ann Hornaday, a film critic for The Washington Post, is working on a book about the making of the classic movie. It's called "Match Me, Sidney," and she's looking for a publisher.

May 24, 2002 / 11:30 a.m. ET

Message from a French philosopher: Though I like to bash The New York Times as much as the next guy, what other daily newspaper would publish an essay on its editorial page that delves into the real meaning of Hollywood's love affair with digital technology and virtual reality? Brent Staples' piece, headlined "A French Philosopher Talks Back to Hollywood and 'The Matrix'" goes way beyond the usual clichés. It tells us why the filmmakers behind movies like "Spider-Man," "Attack of the Clones" and "The Matrix" are more of a cultural threat than we realize. It's essential reading.

May 24, 2002 / 3:45 p.m. ET

The man with no madam: We have enough cop shows already. So I'm not really bothered by hearing that Michael Mann's "RHD/LA," about the LAPD's robbery-homicide division, could be dead before its fall premiere on CBS. But the byzantine byways of the tale are intriguing.

One reason the show could die on the vine, I'm told, is that its star, Tom Sizemore, has just broken up with Heidi Fleiss, the fabled Hollywood Madam. Fleiss' attempt to keep her nose clean since getting out of the slammer following a parole violation for using methamphetamine may have helped keep Sizemore away from one of his favorite former diversions: substance abuse.

Without any restraining influence, my little birdie says, there's no telling what kind of havoc Sizemore could wreak on "RHD/LA."

On top of that, Universal, the mother ship for the show, has been so wary of Mann's well-known spending habits that it has assigned an exec full-time to keep watch on the director. Mann is a brilliant creative force, but if he wants to buy so much as a pencil, he must have the bean counter's approval.

May 28, 2002 / 9:40 a.m. ET

Disney-fying Dr. Seuss? Theodor Geisel, aka Dr. Seuss, traveled an imaginary world before he died. Now, a decade later, he's being brought back to his very real hometown of Springfield, Mass. The city is about to open a park and sculpture garden featuring Horton the Elephant, the Cat in the Hat, Yertle the Turtle, the Lorax and, of course, The Grinch (minus Jim Carrey).

Besides paying tribute to Dr. Seuss, the monument (a national memorial to be unveiled Friday) is supposed to "spark imagination and creativity." A nice sentiment. What goes unspoken is the touristic Disneyland aura that's bound to creep in — if it hasn't already.

May 28, 2002 / 5 p.m. ET

Seeing black on the Web: You don't see many black arts critics in the media. Not in newspapers or magazines — and not on the Web, either. Even BlackVoices.com uses a white movie critic (Kenneth Turan, of the Los Angeles Times). But then there's Esther Iverem and seeingblack.com, the site she founded in April 2001.

When it comes to reviewing films or commenting on culture and the arts, Iverem lays out views about issues of race and ethnicity that no white critics can.

"Jennifer Lopez is able to 'pass' on film," Iverem writes, "in a way that at least one award-winning Black actress wishes she could ..."

Would a white reviewer write that, even if she thought it?

Iverem points out in her review of "Attack of the Clones" that "many Black folks ... are ambivalent toward the 'Star Wars' phenomenon." Or writing about Samuel L. Jackson in "Changing Lanes," Iverem jokes about stereotype: "He's chucked the crazy 'fro from 'Unbreakable' and the locks from 'The Caveman's Valentine' to look like an insurance salesman, corny eyeglasses and all. If we didn't all look alike anyway, Jackson could play a secret agent!"

Agree with Iverem's black perspective or don't. It's great to have her shooting from the lip. Which is not to say she doesn't use her head. Iverem is no slouch at slinging intellectual phrases.

Her review of "The Black Female Body: A Photographic History," by Deborah Willis and Carla Williams, serves as a prime example. She writes about "the discomforting gaze that seeks to consume or 'objectify' [women of color] for prurient entertainment or derogatory judgment;" and she draws a parallel between "Saartjie Baartman (the Venus Hottentot), who was displayed in 19th century Europe as a sexual freak" and "rapper Lil' Kim, who uses the sexual freak badge as a modern marketing tool."

Big words. Big thoughts. Big-hearted site.

May 29, 2002 / 12:40 p.m. ET

Better than movie stars: Rich Cohen, the young author of "Tough Jews," "The Avengers" and "Lake Effect," recalls: "Like a lot of people just out of college, I was a little resentful that I had a job I thought I really shouldn't have to do. I felt like I should be put in charge of something big immediately ..."

Cohen's remark, in an interview on Beatrice.com, may not be dazzling, but it reminds me that interviewing writers is more fun than interviewing movie stars (except for Robin Williams or Dustin Hoffman or Bill Murray). I know because, for many years during my print career, I averaged a movie star or two a week.

So I always jumped at the chance to interview writers whenever they came along: William Burroughs, Norman Mailer, Paul Theroux, John Cheever, William Styron, Allen Ginsberg, Nelson Algren, James Michener and many others who held me in thrall, each for different reasons.

The names of these writers dates me. Most of them are now dead. None of them is young.

At Beatrice.com, however, Ron Hogan has interviewed just about any current, news-making writer you'd care to meet — there's an archive of roughly 150 at the moment — and all of them in the full flush of their careers: Carl Hiaasen ("Basket Case"), Jennifer Weiner ("Good in Bed"), Jim Crace ("Being Dead"), Ann Packer ("The Dive From Clausen's Pier"), Richard Russo ("Nobody's Fool"), and on and on.

Hogan says he has been running author interviews online since 1995. He's striving to maintain a pace of at least one new interview a week. If you want advance notice about them, email him.

Beatrice.com has been a steady fixture of his own writing career, he adds. It's a personal project that he's kept at while freelancing for a variety of dotcoms and during a two-year stint as the current events editor for Amazon.com.

Are voracious book readers as interested in authors as I am? I hope so, but I have no idea. Let me know. Meanwhile, Bookmagazine.com is another great book-and-authors site to keep in mind.

May 30, 2002 / 2:15 p.m. ET
For technophiles or technophobes? If artists are society's leading edge, Net artists are its leading technophiles. That's a far cry, though, from poets, who, Shelley once claimed, are the "unacknowledged legislators of the world."

Maybe they're more like the fictional Stephen Daedelus. James Joyce described him as "the uncreated conscience of his race." I think of Daedelus because, while Net artists are by definition technophiles, many express technophobic ideas through their works: They feel conscience-bound to warn us of technology's dangers.

For instance, "Open_Source_Art_Hack," currently at New York's New Museum of Contemporary Art, is an interactive group show of "artists who openly undermine the programming of everyday software tools."

The show even includes a walking tour of New York City conducted by the Surveillance Camera Players, who have mapped the city's more than 10,000 strategically placed surveillance cameras, a number said to be climbing in the wake of 9/11.

To protest against "unreasonable searches and seizures," the players put on satirical performances for these cameras. As described by the leading Net Art site on the Web, rhizome.org, the show's artists "are co-opting existing means of surveillance or surveillance-culture indoctrination to make new comments about life in network culture."

The trouble I have with Net art, though, is not the ideology behind it — whether technophile or technophobe. My problem is I can't stand the awfully pompous language surrounding it.

Consider the third round of Net art commissions just announced by the Walker Art Center's Gallery 9 in Minneapolis, which describes itself as "an online platform for project-driven exploration, through digitally based media, of all things 'cyber.' "

The theme of the commissions, worth $9,000 each, is the "translocal."

The what? OK, I have to quote here. Bear with me.

"There is, potentially, an important difference between what has been termed McGlobalization and the translocal," Gallery 9 explains. "If one version of globalization is the transnational ubiquity of global brands and the dominance of global capital, can the translocal be a counter-example, specifying an individual, local environment yet situating it in a global context? If the topology of the network is one of connected nodes, every node is global. Is any node local? No node is the center. Is every node a center?"

Is your brain pixelized or pixilated? Mine is both.

Maybe this will help: The commissions encourage proposals "that broadly explore and interpret translocal, particularly in relation to issues of situatedness, embodiment, and agency in a connective, global context."

The heck with it. But don't give up yet. To see some different kinds of Net art, check these out:

Antiwargame
Carnivore
Times Square Cam
TraceNoizer

May 31, 2002 / 7:30 a.m. ET

Will they never shut up? Everybody's writing about Thursday's silent ceremony of grief and remembrance for those who died at the World Trade Center. It WAS silent at the site. But if, like me, you were one of the millions who watched it on NBC or ABC, all you heard were words, words, words. Dull, repetitive, unceasing words from anchors who almost never shut up.

This is no place for a TV review. But the worst offender, by far, was NBC, followed by ABC. At least CBS had the good taste to keep silent for long stretches during the ceremony — so that we, too, could meditate with the mourners at Ground Zero without having to listen to the drone of superfluous commentary. I don't know about you, but I did what anyone with half a brain would do: I finally muted the sound. It was the least I could do to say good-bye.

Let me know how you felt.

This just in from the mailbag: I enjoyed your article on TV Newsanchors' tendency to fill the void with verbage. This compulsion toward perpetual pontification seems to arise either from habit or from the fear that a bit of silence might give rise to something horrific ... like actual feelings, or even thought! Oh, the horror! God, I love the "mute" button! — Forrest Lee Horn, Kernersville, N.C.

MY SENTIMENTS EXXXXXXXXACTLY! — dinaghan

I, like you, was appalled at the amount of "chatter" during what was meant to be a respectful ceremony. ... Why did the networks feel they were above showing respect? Overall, it was a beautiful service, with the exception, of course, of the people on TV. — Michelle Neglia

I just wanted to say that I was there at the WTC, with my brother, (his girlfriend was on Flight 11), her mother and her little brother. I had been down several times since September and I couldn't get over how QUIET it was, until the very end when the Ironworkers started chanting USA. Too bad the reporters & media have to overexploit everything. — Kristy Gray

Too bad TV doesn't understand that we sometimes don't need talking heads to [tell us] what we can see and hear (or not hear). — Bill MacKay

I watched the coverage on MSNBC and not a word was spoken during it. Well done!! — Victoria Stephens

Thank you, thank you, thank you!!!!! I too got very tired of listening to the commentaries going on during the ceremony. I would have much rather viewed it in silence as the people attending did. I get very tired of anchors thinking we can't figure things out for ourselves unless they lead us step by step thru the process. — Carpenter

My morning show in Seattle (the buzz, q13, fox network) was actually pretty quiet, they would speak about every 7 minutes. — Kristina L Cline

I agree 100% with your assessment of the chatter going on during the silent ceremony at Ground Zero. I was appalled at the meandering banter the anchor subjected us to during such a solemn moment. Thanks for putting into "not so silent words" what I was thinking and feeling. — LeeAnn C. Schaff

More from the mailbag: Did you say the language surrounding Net art and artists is pompous? Don't you think you understated things? [See May 30 item below] ... Thanks for the laughs and the links. [Here] are a couple of links for you — one to my publisher, W.W. Norton, the other one to my personal site: ddmartinez and nortonpoets. Or is that transpersonal? See what you've done? My brain is having a seizure caused by an illegal search in relation to issues of situatedness. May the topology of the network be with you — even in these nodeless times. — Dionisio D. Martínez

We have created a new human; part bureaucrat, part businessperson, part technophile. Would that be a biznophile? — Marty Heesh, Lake Como, Pa.

Also from the mailbag: Your slant on the Dr. Seuss memorial [see May 28 item below] is as steep as the last pitch up Everest. ... The great thing about this monument garden ... is that the city and the community [are] actually showing some pride and moving in a deliberate fashion to display that pride, for once. The city is wrought with problems, but in two areas — the Seuss monument and the Basketball Hall of Fame ... it has the right to be proud. — J. LeDuc, formerly of Springfield, Mass.

Share your perspective on entertainment and the arts with Jan Herman. MSNBC is not responsible for the content of Internet links.

Entries from June 1 to June 28, 2002
(Some links may be nonfunctional.)
Back to 'The Juice'

LATEST UPDATES

June 1, 2002 / 6 p.m. ET

Touching a nerve: Mail has poured in over my criticism of the TV news anchors for their incessant remarks during Thursday's silent ceremony at the World Trade Center. I guess I touched a nerve. But which nerve?

With a few exceptions, including someone who flamed me as "a shallow jerk," everyone who wrote agreed that they were as disturbed as I was.

My outrage about the TV anchors' compulsion to talk apparently tapped into a disgust with TV news in general. I can't say that I blame people for feeling that way. But I hadn't intended to touch that nerve, though I suppose I should have expected it.

TV anchors can't resist the urge to play the nation's nursemaids. They were holding our hands, ushering us through the ceremony in hushed tones reminiscent of (but more talkative than) golf sportscasters. Why they felt the need to play nursemaid is a separate subject for another day. Suffice to say, their sense of obligation is misguided. It treats us like a nation of children, which is a bad idea.

On Sunday, there will be another ceremony at the WTC — this time for all the families of the thousands who died there, not just to mark the end of the recovery effort or to mourn the loss of hundreds of firefighters, police officers and rescue workers. And this time it will not be nationally televised, which is a good idea.

June 3, 2002 / 11:55 a.m. ET

Enough with the awards already: Tonys, shmonys. Pulitzers, shmulitzers. Oscars, shmoscars. Nobels, shmobels. Awards for so-called excellence in arts and entertainment have spread like a plague. They've been so devalued by poor choices, commercialism, politics, showbiz — you name

21

it — that nobody really believes in them except egotists and their mothers and their publicists and their publicists' mothers.

What Jeannette Walls says in this morning's Scoop about the MTV Awards — that they've become stunts — applies to all sorts of awards, high and low. (The notion that last night's Tonys honored Broadway's best and brightest is a sweet fiction. Just ask Special Theater Event Tony-winner Elaine Stritch, who actually did deserve her praise but was cut off in mid-speech even though she was one of the few — maybe the only one — worth hearing.)

The Oscars? We won't even go there. The Nobel Prize in Literature? Marcel Proust never won it for the epic "Remembrance of Things Past." But Carl Friedrich Georg Spitteler received it "in special appreciation of his epic, 'Olympian Spring.'"

There may be more justice in the Mythopoeic Fantasy Awards, or the Nebula Awards.

And in music, do you think they give out enough awards? We've all heard of the Grammys, with its 100-plus categories, and the Country Music Awards and the American Music Awards and the World Music Awards and the Soul Train Awards and the VH1 Music Awards.

But how about the Dove Awards, with 61 categories? And what are the Juno Awards?

Let's not even talk about the Pulitzer Prize , which is sporting a black eye these days, because of the controversy over Doris Kearns Goodwin, who sat on the Pulitzer board and who was accused of plagiarizing many passages in her 1987 book "The Fitzgeralds and the Kennedys." (Though she hasn't been accused of plagiarism for her 1995 Pulitzer-winner "No Ordinary Time: Franklin and Eleanor Roosevelt: The Home Front in World War II," she has resigned from the board.)

Where I work the powers-that-be go ga-ga over awards. Thank God they don't know about all of them. Maybe I'll try for the Spiffy Entertainment Award. That might impress them.

The Spiffys are mindful of devaluation. "Are the merit awards just an easy-to-win door prize for applying?" the Spiffy creator asks, and answers: "Nothing could be further from the truth."

Maybe the Spiffys will make an exception for me.

June 4, 2002 / 3:55 p.m. ET

Man with a cause: What happens to artists who don't "make it"? If they're lucky, they have someone like Daniel Pinchbeck to remind the world of their work. Pinchbeck has written a beautiful, affecting memory piece in the current Artforum about his father, the painter and sculptor Peter Pinchbeck.

Peter Pinchbeck died two years ago, leaving 40 years' worth of abstract paintings and sculptures in his rent-controlled SoHo loft, where Daniel grew up in Manhattan during the '70s, before the invasion of the boutiques.

"My father's art went ignored, essentially unseen during his lifetime," he writes. "There were no career retrospectives, no solo museum shows, no fanfare. His artist friends were his only audience. In the aftermath of his life, I find myself compelled to fight his battle for him."

The world will also be hearing more from Daniel Pinchbeck as he continues his own cultural-political battles.

His forthcoming "Breaking Open the Head," due Sept. 17 from Broadway Books, takes up the theme of globalization and spiritual crisis from a psychedelic perspective. It's both a cultural history of mind-altering drugs and a personal adventure. He chronicles his "transcendent and terrifying" experiences with iboga, yagé, peyote and other botanical substances in West Africa, South America and Mexico.

And on another front: Pinchbeck is also one of the founders of Open City, a literary magazine and book publisher that has just brought out Michael Brownstein's "World on Fire," a book-length poetic rant against corporate globalization and environmental meltdown.

Publisher's Weekly gave the book a starred review "but no other mainstream media source has touched it yet," Pinchbeck says. "Left-wing books such as 'World on Fire' are finding audiences while being ignored by the media. There is obviously a great hunger for these perspectives now."

Supporting evidence? How about: Michael Moore's best-seller "Stupid White Men," Noam Chomsky's "9-11," which has sold 110,000 copies according to The New York Times, and Greg Palast's "The Best Democracy Money Can Buy," which is selling well without many reviews.

June 5, 2002 / 9:56 a.m. ET
   The Woodman's not-so-lucky day: Woody Allen has a problem. Did you know that while he was in court on Tuesday claiming he was cheated out of $12 million in earnings from his films, only eight people showed up to see his latest, "Hollywood Ending," at a matinee in Times Square? At a discount movie house, no less.

And do you know what happened? The screening was canceled.

And do you know how I know that? Because it's on the front page of The New York Times this morning, in the print edition. The front page, no less. (Here it is online, consigned to regional news.)

Now, I'm as ready as the next guy to bash the Woodman. I used to love his shtick, and I don't these days. But is bashing the Woodman what Times executive editor Howell Raines had in mind when he told his editors he wants more pop arts coverage in the newspaper of record?

Or was The Times' front page just thumbing its nose at the tabloids?

June 6, 2002 / 10:01 a.m. ET

Rock and roll is over: I'm not sure it's true — in fact, I seriously doubt it — but I do know that Michael Wolff, the media columnist for New York magazine, has come up with an ingenious theory. It's a clever metaphor, really, that not only explains why music replaced books as "the engine of popular culture," but why the music business has now gone down the tubes and will become just like the book business — with pop stars taking on the cultural valence of authors.

At mid-20th century, Wolff writes, "Hemingway had rock-star status. ... Steinbeck was Springsteen. Salinger was Kurt Cobain. Dorothy Parker was Courtney Love. James Jones was David Crosby. Mailer was Eminem." Then, in the '50s and '60s, "rock and roll took over fiction's job as the chronicler and romanticizer of American life."

Eventually the music bubble burst, at least as a business. Wolff details the paradigm shift to the Net (free music downloading 'n' all). But everybody knows that already. What's fascinating is his prediction that rock and roll itself won't last, that it's "just an anomaly" and that as the youthquake fades: "Alanis Morissette becomes Grace Paley. Bono becomes John Hersey. Fiona Apple is Joyce Carol Oates. Moby is Martin Amis."

Wolff doesn't say, though, what tunes we'll be listening to when that time arrives. Meanwhile, "The Eminem Show" is booming.

June 7, 2002 / 9:33 a.m. ET

After the Holocaust: I have just witnessed something more chilling than poet Paul Celan's "Death Fugue," more frightening than Primo Levi's "Survival in Auschwitz." I have just seen, under a banner that says New England's Art & Entertainment Authority, the Boston Phoenix's linked Webcast of the video of Daniel Pearl's execution.

No work of art depicting murder or the breakdown of civilization that I have ever seen — not Goya's "The Third of May, 1808," not Picasso's "Guernica," not any of Anselm Kiefer's somber, monumental canvases — has left me feeling more bitter, terrified or angry than this ugly piece of hate-filled propaganda, this epitome of non-art, this anti-Semitic, anti-American monstrosity.

I realize many people have already seen bits and pieces of this video on television. But this is different. They haven't seen this. This is off the scale.

There is a debate raging over whether the Phoenix should have shown the video. (See Voyeurism or principle?)

The execution itself is unspeakable. Thank God we see only a brief glimpse of it. What is equally horrifying, however, is the lengthy prelude to Pearl's death: He describes his Jewish lineage, declaring that his father is Jewish, that his mother is Jewish, that he is Jewish, that his family has visited Israel, that a street in Israel is named for his great-grandfather — all of which is topped off by a denunciation of the United States.

A journalism teacher, who thinks the Phoenix should not have shown the video, has told The New York Times: "I can understand the execution of an individual without having to see it. I couldn't necessarily understand concentration camps without seeing them. The scope is so much larger." Others feel the same way.

I beg to differ. For the first time in my life, after seeing that video I understand in my gut what I have always thought I understood in my head, what I thought I understood by reading Levi and Celan and Eli Weisel and Daniel Goldhagen and all the rest.

After seeing that video I now tremble with the same foreboding that two weeks ago two Holocaust survivors told me they were feeling: "It can happen again. It has already begun."

That is why I originally provided the link to the video at the top of this page. I had thought about it long and hard and felt it was my moral obligation. But it has since been taken down because (I've been informed) I am not to link to anything that MSNBC.com would not itself show. I don't think anybody should be forced to watch this video, but I don't see why it should be suppressed.

If you want more eloquent reasons than I can give, have a look at this e-mail message.

June 10, 2002 / 9:27 a.m. ET

Lessons in art: OK class, listen up. The question for today is: How come there is so little Bad Art in museums throughout the world and so much Good Art? We know Good Art is harder to make. We know it requires greater skill. Logically, there should be less of it.

At least one institution is trying to rectify the situation: The Museum of Bad Art, which takes for its credo "art too bad to be ignored." MOBA (not to be confused with MoMA, New York's Museum of Modern Art) has already put on several exhibitions. Here you can see "four of the most distinctive pieces" in the MOBA collection from its first show on the Web. And here are highlights of its second show.

We would be remiss if we did not also mention Documenta11, the Olympics of the art world, currently taking place in Kasel, Germany — although its organizers would hardly like being lumped in with MOBA.

A little background is necessary. More than 2,500 years ago, Plato categorized all art as bad. The world's greatest ancient Greek philosopher has a well-deserved reputation for banishing artists from his utopian Republic. As any half-educated college graduate can tell you, the reason all art is Bad Art is that by creating images that are, in fact, illusions even so-called Good Art is the enemy of Truth. "Painting or drawing ... when doing their own proper work, are far removed from truth, and have no true or healthy aim," Plato warned.

Recently we learned the New York State Board of Regents has allied itself with the world's greatest ancient Greek philosopher and, needless to say, with MOBA. On statewide regents tests for high school students, the board sanctioned the idea that all art is Bad Art by sanitizing excerpts from the literary works of Chekov, Annie Dillard, Isaac Basshevis Singer, Frank Conroy and others.

The board's stated goal was to keep the excerpts from giving racial, ethnic, religious, sexual or linguistic offense. Plato would have understood that. The former mayor of New York, Rudy Giuliani, would have understood that. So why can't Anna Quindlen understand that?

FROM THE MAILBAG

I've received so many thoughtful, anguished e-mails in response to "After the Holocaust" and the video of Daniel Pearl's death that I will be putting them up as the day goes along. A lot of them are angry as well as anguished. Some express prejudice as well as patriotism. Some will make your hair curl. I've put up a representative sample with as little editing as possible. So be prepared. Here's the first batch; here's the second; here's the third and the fourth.

June 11, 2002 / 2:15 p.m. ET

Once more, with feeling: They're finally getting around to making the umpteenth film about der Fuehrer's rise to power. This time it's CBS backing a four-hour, prime-time mini-series based on Ian Kershaw's best-selling Hitler biographies "Hubris" and "Nemesis."

"I'd be lying if I said we aren't a bit nervous about attempting to examine one of history's most heinous characters," the executive producer told Variety.

And I'd be lying if I said I believed him, especially when he explains why he and CBS have bucked up their courage to do it: "[In] this age of megalomaniacal terrorism, we feel it is all the more important and relevant."

Right. And so was "Life with Judy Garland." The same producer did that melodramatic mini-series last year on ABC, starring Judy Davis in one of the most godawful Emmy-winning performances ever. He also did the boring "Joan of Arc" mini-series that starred Leelee Sobiesky in 1999.

But heck. From Joan of Arc to Hitler with a stopover at Judy Garland — that's a nice spread. Very relevant in a time of terrorism. What's next, Red Buttons?

June 11, 2002 / 2:15 p.m. ET

More on the Pearl video: The Wall Street Journal's chief television and media critic has weighed in today on the Boston Phoenix's use of the Daniel Pearl video. Tunku Varadarajan objects to showing it for many reasons. Chief among them is this: Pearl's widow, Mariane, has said it defies comprehension that his family "should have to relive this horrific tragedy." He writes, too, that watching the video "won't add a layer of understanding, but only one of repugnance."

I still think the video needs to be seen to truly appreciate what Pearl's loathsome execution means. But Varadarajan's piece has given one of my readers — Jim Philips, of Atlanta — second thoughts. He'd agreed with me but hadn't realized Mariane Pearl objected to showing the video.

June 12, 2002 / 11:40 a.m. ET

A kiss is still a kiss: The last time I looked the American Film Institute rated "Casablanca" the second best movie of all time, behind "Citizen Kane" and ahead of "The Godfather." Now it tops a new AFI list as the best screen romance ever.

So who is Hollywood's greatest director of movie romances? The list doesn't say. But a count of the top 100 by cinephile Harry Haun reveals that it's none other than William Wyler, probably the most underrated great director ever to grace the silver screen. (Yes, he snuck into a scene in "Dodsworth," his legendary film that didn't make the list but should have.) Wyler has four flicks among the top romances: "Roman Holiday" (No. 4), "Wuthering Heights" (No. 15), "Funny Girl" (No. 41) and "Jezebel" (No. 79).

(A confession here: I wrote a biography of Wyler called "A Talent for

Trouble." The editor insisted on the not-so-bright idea of subtitling it "The Life of Hollywood's Most Acclaimed Director," because Willy's films earned more Academy Award nominations than any other director — the record still stands — not to mention his own three Oscars. But let's face it, most people wouldn't know who he was.)

Following Wyler on the AFI's romance roster, comes a cluster of directors with three films each: Alfred Hitchock, the last director you'd think of as romantic, George Stevens, Billy Wilder, Mike Nichols and Rob Reiner. Poor George Cukor, the fabled "woman's director," doesn't even crack this group.

Will the cup that runneth over for "Casablanca" ever draineth? Let's see ... an informal survey sent to 4,500 members of the Writers Guild of America rated the flick as one of the two best movie scripts of all time, but also as one of the two most overrated. The other was, of course,"Citizen Kane."

June 13, 2002 / 9:35 a.m. ET

More arts and technology: Another classical music event on the Web — The first annual International e-piano competition — comes this evening from St. Paul, Minn.

In this case, six finalists will play before a panel of judges in a recital hall at Hamline University. But another judge, the eminent pianist Yefim Bronfman, will be listening in a different recital hall — in Hamamatsu, Japan — where a 9-foot computerized concert grand piano (a Yamaha CFIIIS equipped with a Yamaha Disklavier®) will replicate the performances down to the smallest details.

The only thing missing from the recital hall in Japan will be the players themselves, Anthony Tommasini writes. But Bronfman will be able to see the pianists on a video hookup synced to their performances. "I thought it would be kind of neat to be sitting ... in Japan and seeing what happened in Minnesota at the same time," he told Tommasini.

The final rounds of the competition began Wednesday and run through Sunday. In tonight's round, starting at 6 p.m. CT, the finalists will play a Schubert Sonata of their choice. You can see the live performances here, according to the competition Website.

June 13, 2002 / 9:35 a.m. ET

Learning music from a distance: It's a banner day for the alliance of arts and technology, so catch it while you can. World-renowned maestro Pinchas Zukerman — violinist, violist, conductor — gives a chamber music masterclass this afternoon on the Internet. He'll be in Ottawa coaching a young string trio in New York.

How will he do that? Via an interactive video-conference hookup. You can tune into the 90-minute class — it begins at 2 p.m. ET — by logging on here. And you can e-mail questions or comments to Zukerman before, during and after the class.

The masterclass and the Webcast come courtesy of the Manhattan School of Music, Columbia University's Teachers College, Canada's National Arts Centre and the National Research Council of Canada.

All you need to tune in is Realplayer software. If you don't have it, download it here for free.

Just in case you were wondering: The trio (made up of students at the Manhattan School: Daniel Khalikov, Jaime Amador and Darin Anderson) will play Erno Dohnanyi's "Serenade in C Major, Op. 10."

June 14, 2002 / 11 a.m. ET

Identity crisis: The critics are thrilled. They're all so desperate to see a good film for a change that they've fallen in love with "The Bourne Identity."

"There isn't a dull or dumb moment in this movie," Desson Howe writes in The Washington Post. Even The Wall Street Journal's curmudgeon Joe Morgenstern agrees: "The outcome is distinctive and entertaining. There's no way you'd mistake this for James Bond."

And David Elliott, no pushover, notes for MSNBC.com: "This is the swiftest and sexiest modern thriller since 'The Thomas Crown Affair.'"

Well, maybe it is all that and the Second Coming, too. I haven't seen the flick yet, so I reserve judgment. But weren't spy thrillers supposed to have died with the death of the Cold War? Could that be why Matt Damon plays a spy with amnesia?

June 15, 2002 / 4:35 p.m. ET

The brawl in Montreal: Charles Dutoit's abrupt resignation in April from the Montreal Symphony, after 25 years as music director, still reverberates like a kettle drum in the world of classical music.

"The exit has had something of a polarizing effect on communities far beyond Montreal," Martin Bernheimer writes in Andante. "Musicians long weary, also wary, of what they regard as conductorial mistreatment hail Dutoit's departure as a symbolic step forward."

But, Bernheimer asks, does great music require great tyranny? He answers with an anecdotal essay that's as entertaining as it is illuminating.

There are all sorts of maestros, he reminds us, from "Leopold Stokowski faking his picturesque way through 'Turandot' … conducting the audience more than the participants," to Fritz Reiner, who "endured the reputation of a martinet," and George Szell, who "was feared as an often abrasive taskmaster," but who both made "glorious music."

June 16, 2002 / 10 a.m. ET

Mysteries of the Old Masters: David Hockney's theory of lenses is back in the news. Maybe you remember it. He claimed that Europe's Old Masters used optical devices as as an aid to draftsmanship. This, he said, explains why "there is no awkward drawing, none," in almost 400 years of Western art until the late 19th century.

On Sunday Michael Kimmelman, chief art critic of The New York Times, wrote in the paper's Arts & Leisure section: "Lately, one thing after another — a show, a book — has been mysteriously causing people to fret about painters, dead and alive, using 'crutches' like lenses, cameras and photographs, or possibly having used them."

In fact, they've been more than "fretting." Hockney's theory, based in part on his own experience as a painter, has sent many art historians around the bend.

When my colleague, Laura Tuchman, and I first wrote about his theory in 1999, (check out "Art and tech: an intimate, early mix," and "Seeing paintings in a brighter light"), Hockney's main focus (no pun intended) was the use of optical lenses through which artists could project an image onto a surface. This, he said, was the only way to explain how artists, no matter how skilled, could have captured certain detailed images in perspective. The details would have been humanly impossible to draw freehand, Hockney contended, even for such master draftsmen as Caravaggio, Raphael, Velazquez, Holbein or Ingres.

The use of lenses — to project images that could be copied or traced — was also particularly helpful for portraiture, because it speeds the work and enables the artist to capture fleeting or spontaneous facial expressions that inevitably go stale over lengthy sittings.

Lawrence Weschler later wrote a piece about the theory for The New Yorker, "Through the looking Glass." Then Hockney published his book "Secret Knowledge." And earlier this year, after The New Yorker declined to publish it, Weschler posted "Further adventures in opticality …" on artkrush.com.

Hockney has by now broadened his argument. Curved mirrors have entered the picture in a big way. And he has a new ally in Charles Falco, a

30

physics professor and an expert in quantum optics, who says he has incontrovertible scientific proof that Hockney is right. I believe him. If Falco is wrong, "Further adventures" still makes for entertaining (if complicated) reading. Let me know what you think.

June 18, 2002 / 10 a.m. ET

And the winner is ... : A 21-year-old Juilliard student, Mei-Ting Sun. He took first prize, worth $25,000, in the first annual International e-piano competition. He also gets a nice boost for his potential career and another $1,500 for earning the Schubert Sonata Award. Winners were named Monday night.

Second prize, worth $15,000, went to 24-year-old Victoria Korchinskaya-Kogan, who studied at the Moscow State Conservatory and Texas Christian University.

Just wanted you to know.

June 18, 2002 / 12:40 p.m. ET

Connecting Tom Cruise's dots: Do you think the futuristic "Minority Report" is getting enough hype? Tom Cruise made the cover of Time this week, with an eight-page spread telling us, in the most overused phrase of the moment, that he's "someone about whom we have never quite been able to connect the dots."

Meanwhile, Steven Spielberg talked up their sci-fi flick on this morning's "Today" show, where he spoke about the trade-off between fighting crime and giving up basic constitutional rights. (As a preventive measure, Precrime cops in "Minority Report" get to arrest people before they commit their crimes.)

The weird thing is, Time says that it was Spielberg's friend, the historian Doris Kearns Goodwin, who alerted him to the constitutional problem of Precrime. "She said, 'This would be a wonderful thing,'" recalls Spielberg, "'but what about the Bill of Rights?'" Didn't he just graduate from college? What did they teach him there? Bowling?

June 18, 2002 / 3 p.m. ET

Do you have to be dead?: Elvis Presley, who's been dead for the last 25 years, has the No. 1 hit on the British charts, "A little less conversation," putting him ahead of the Beatles (with 18 chart-toppers all told, to their 17).

Frank Sinatra, who died four years ago, has a six-CD boxed set just out, "Sinatra in Hollywood (1940-1964)," recapping all the songs from his movies.

Michael Jackson, who hasn't died, couldn't get Sony to promote "Invincible" the way he wanted and allegedly owes the label $200 million.

And now, in Los Angeles, Bob Dylan has begun shooting a film called "Masked and Anonymous," in which he plays a washed-up singer trying to revive his career.

Do you have to be a dead to be happy in the music business?

At least Dylan gets it. Variety said his flick is "set in a nameless country wracked by an endless and senseless civil war in which everyone has forgotten what they are fighting about."

June 19, 2002 / 10:45 a.m. ET

And the winners are us: I hate awards and awards ceremonies. They're always pompous, mostly predictable and often unfair. But there are exceptions, and some awards are actually useful.

Last night's 6th Annual Webby Awards, for instance, lets you in on 150 of the best sites out there. Here they are, nominees and winners, in 30 different categories.

On top of that, the Webby Awards have an unprecedented rule that sets it apart from all other prize ceremonies: Winners are held to five-words-or-less acceptance speeches. This does not guarantee protection from tears or boredom, but it helps.

Even with those restrictions, some speeches were smart. My pick for smartest acceptance: "Spielberg, give us a budget!" (Donnie Darko, winner for best film site) and "Hominids rule — thank you Lucy!" (Becoming Human, winner for best science site).

Some acceptances were unfailingly promotional, of course. Most promotional was Amazon, winner for best commercial site: "Our stock is rising." Runner-up was Salon, winner for best print + zines site: "We know deep throat is..."

Yeah, right. Check out The Scoop, which tells who deep throat really, really is.

June 20, 2002 / 10 a.m. ET

Goodbye to hip-hop? Well, maybe. Geoff Boucher makes you wonder in "Hip-Hop's Slump: A Blip or a Trend?" It's a conservative report written in the typical on-the-one hand-this, on-the-other-hand-that style favored by the Los Angeles Times — but it raises the question.

What Boucher doesn't or can't clarify is whether we're merely witnessing a huge drop in hip-hop CD sales (Eminem notwithstanding) or the fitful death knell of a musical genre now two decades old.

Ladies and gentlemen, let us pray.

June 21, 2002 / 10:10 a.m. ET

Strike up the brand: That's what Variety says, after counting <u>no less than 15 major brands</u> appearing in "Minority Report."

It's a product-placement party for American Express, Aquafina, Ben & Jerry's, Bulgari, Burger King, Century 21, Fox, The Gap, Guinness, Lexus, Nokia, Pepsi, Reebok, Revo and USA Today.

Got any others? Count 'em and let me know.

And check out this <u>Lexus promo for the flick</u>, courtesy of MSNBC colleague Christina Johnson. How's that for product placement.

June 21, 2002 / 10:20 a.m. ET

The great escape: Time to test the theory that movies are booming because people in tough times want to forget their troubles.

<u>"Minority Report,"</u> which opens today with <u>almost more raves than you can count</u>, looks to be one of the biggest openings of the summer season so far — maybe the biggest.

Even if it does just monster business, will that prove the theory? Or does it prove that people prefer Tom Cruise's troubles to their own?

Or maybe it simply proves that people prefer anybody's troubles to their own. Remember these c'mon-get-happy, forget-your-troubles hits? <u>"The Sum of All Fears,"</u> <u>"Panic Room,"</u> <u>"Insomnia,"</u> <u>"Changing Lanes"</u> and <u>"Black Hawk Down"</u>?

There must be a better theory.

June 24, 2002 / 9:50 a.m. ET

Shootout at the box office: Make that a dogfight. Disney accused 20th Century Fox of inflating the box-office numbers for "Minority Report" so it could claim the film was No. 1 over the weekend. Disney says its own film, "Lilo & Stitch," was really tops.

Later today, when so-called final figures are in, one of them will be declared the "real" winner. But if you believe any figures handed out by the Hollywood studios, final or not, you need to have your head examined.

Just ask David Shaw. He wrote a huge, devastating takeout about the film industry last year in the Los Angeles Times, "Lights, Camera, Reaction," which concluded that nobody should believe in the accuracy of box-office figures. Even in Hollywood they don't.

In fact, almost nothing the studios say about their movies can be taken at face value, including the grosses. "Virtually everyone in Hollywood agrees that most of the numbers the studios report to the media are inaccurate, if not downright dishonest," Shaw wrote.

Some folks dispute him. Mickey Kaus, for one: "Does Shaw give an example of an actual box office figure that was actually manipulated? No. But he only has 16,000 words!"

When I was at the L.A. Times, Shaw, a Pulitzer Prize-winning media reporter, was famous for writing bloated pieces. But this one hit the spot. (There's a charge to read the complete article.)

June 24, 2002 / 3:51 p.m. ET

Art find worth millions? Did a long-haul trucker buy a Jackson Pollock drip painting worth millions of dollars at a roadside thrift shop? Or did she buy an imitation worth no more than the $5 she paid for it? After 10 years of scratching their heads, the experts still can't decide.

The ones who say it's not authentic base their opinions on visual examination and point to the painting's sketchy provenance (meaning they can't trace a direct line of ownership back to the artist).

The ones who says it's the real deal also base their opinions on visual examination and point out that Pollock's style is virtually impossible to imitate.

The one art expert who conducted a forensic examination, Montreal sleuth Peter Paul Biró, analyzed the paint and the canvas and even found a fingerprint that matches Pollock's. His conclusion? "It is exactly what it appears to be: a poured painting by Jackson Pollock c. 1947-49." Here's Biró's full report.

Visual (as opposed to forensic) examination by experts is not as reliable as they would have you believe. Take a look with your own eyes (a few steps removed) here and here.

June 24, 2002 / 6:55 p.m. ET

It's Fox by a whisker: The really really honest-to-goodness absolutely final numbers are in. And the weekend box-office winner was — ta-dah — "Minority Report." It grossed $35.7 million. That's less than the estimated $36.9 million Twentieth Century Fox originally claimed for it, but more than the $35.3 million final tally for Disney's "Lilo & Stitch." So Disney was right: Fox inflated its estimate. But it turns out, Disney did, too. And don't forget, none of these figures — final or estimated — is independently verified.

June 25, 2002 / 11:45 a.m. ET

Hip-hop anthem: Power to the peeps. The entire world is outraged. OK, just some of the entire world. Fuming e-mail came in saying stuff like: "#@$&*!!!!!" and "&%$#@!!!!!"

That was last week, when Geoff Boucher wrote a piece in the Los Angeles Times asking whether the hip-hop slump in CD sales is a blip or a trend, and I quoted him and wondered if it's good-bye to hip-hop.

Today the Washington Post puts out a piece reporting that hip-hop is finding its political voice after chillin' in the 'hood for three decades, and The New York Times runs a piece declaring that hip-hop is reshaping theater. And let's not forget Danny Hoch's New York City Hip-Hop Theater Festival, running through June 29, with Will Power, Jonzi D, Sarah Jones (Surface Transit) and a whole lot of other performers.

What a backlash! Ladies and gentlemen, your prayers must have helped.

June 26, 2002 / 10:50 a.m. ET

Why can't Ethan Hawke smile? Actors who write are not such a rare breed, especially if they're British. Terence Stamp, the late Alec Guinness, Peter Ustinov and Simon Callow are among the best of them.

But actors who write fiction? Rare indeed. Ethan Hawke seems to be a breed apart. And he's not even British. Check out Book magazine's cover story.

Here's a guy who makes having it all look as easy as Tiger Woods shooting par. Hawke is rich. He's married to Uma Thurman, happily it seems. He's only 31. He's a movie star. And his second novel, "Ash Wednesday," is due out in July.

But why does he look so glum? He appears incapable of putting a smile on his face. Maybe it's the T.S. Eliot influence. Eliot always looked as dour as a banker who just swallowed a bad loan.

Hawke says he took the title for his novel from Eliot's poem, "Ash Wednesday," because he loved the lines: "Teach us to care and not to care / Teach us to sit still." It's a great incantatory poem, and it would't make anyone smile.

June 27, 2002 / 9:25 a.m. ET

More from the Osbournes: Guess what? The Osbournes' long-estranged grandfather may start appearing on their show. They've all made up. Grandpop is Sharon's rock-manager father Don Arden, the so-called "Al Capone of pop." I read that on the bus in Blender, the music mag, of which

Jay Leno says: "You know you've been drinking too much when you give an interview to Blender magazine." Too bad the interview isn't online yet.

June 27, 2002 / 9:30 a.m. ET

The pure poetry of the Pledge: Why couldn't they have left the Pledge of Allegiance alone in the first place? All through grade school, every morning without fail, I recited the Pledge of Allegiance. To my child's ear the Pledge sounded like a cool poem. We were all of us "one-nation-indivisible-with-liberty-and-justice-for-all." You know how kids are with poetry. You learned it — and recited it — by rote.

Then one morning the Pledge changed. I had no idea the Knights of Columbus got Congress to change it. All I knew was that now we were all part of "one-nation-under-God-indivisible-with-liberty-and-justice-for-all."

Suddenly the lines didn't scan. To my child's ear, the rhythm was way wrong. It was as if "Georgie Porgie pudding and pie, kissed the girls under God and made them cry." No one would go for that.

Now everybody's full of shock and outrage that the Pledge has been declared unconstitutional because of those two words. Why not just go back to the original wording? At least it scans.

June 28, 2002 / 10:22 a.m. ET

Hot-button issue: If Martians had landed on Earth yesterday, they too would have had an opinion about the Pledge of Allegiance. So I don't kid myself that the blizzard of e-mail that arrived — and is still arriving — from as far away as Japan had anything to do with me or my brilliant remarks. What did surprise me was how smart, earnest and anxious the e-mail was in general, and how relatively few rants there were. As soon as I can martial my staff of thousands, I'll put up a representative sample.

June 28, 2002 / 10:25 a.m. ET

Looking for weekend thrills: The big new release for the weekend is an Adam Sandler comedy — our critic likes it — but everybody is really waiting for next week's "Men in Black II."

If you have nothing better to do and feel like wasting your money, you could catch up on "Minority Report" just to find out what all that buzz was about. Curiosity killed the cat, and I bet it will kill "Report," too. I can't imagine anything but lousy word-of-mouth, critics' raves notwithstanding. The movie is full of hot air.

So let's shift gears to classical music.

"Was Bach an anti-Semite? Does John Adams' 'The Death of

Klinghoffer' romanticize terrorism? Is Philip Glass's 'Hydrogen Jukebox' immoral? Do you feel 'violated' by performances of Wagner or Strauss - or by suggestions that their work be banned?"

That's the way Paul Mitchinson begins his <u>provocative piece</u> in the music magazine <u>Andante</u>. Reading it is time better spent than seeing Tom Cruise in the latest Steven Spielberg opus, no matter how many tidbits Speilberg has about <u>future gadgetry.</u>

Share your perspective on entertainment and the arts with <u>Jan Herman</u>. MSNBC is not responsible for the content of Internet links.

Jan Herman

Latest entertainment and arts news from the Web

Entries from July 1 to July 31, 2002
(Some links may be nonfunctional.)
Back to 'The Juice'

LATEST UPDATES

July 1, 2002 / 8 a.m. ET

Ol' Blue Eyes' tarnished reputation: Neither rain, nor sleet, nor snow (yes, even in summer) will stay Frank Sinatra's minions from their appointed rounds — at least not in the hometown he spurned (Hoboken, N.J.), where the main post office is to be named for him.

But the reputation of the late great singer takes a stinging hit from The New York Times. The paper may have been channeling Kitty Kelley, the biographer who did everything she could to blacken Sinatra's name before he died.

On Sunday, the Week in Review section of The Times had a funny Sinatra takedown by Tom Kuntz. He rebuts every point the speechifying politicians in the House of Representatives made about what a saint Sinatra was.

It turns out The Times actually was not channeling Kelley. In fact, it had a direct line to "The Sinatra Files: The Secret FBI Dossier." Kuntz compiled that book with his brother Phil, a top editor in the Washington bureau of The Wall Street Journal. Here's a review.

Also in the Week in Review: a terrific little piece about bluegrass that talks about Luther Wright and the Wrongs. They've set Pink Floyd's 1979 rock opus, "The Wall," to a bluegrass beat.

What's really peculiar is that the Week in Review — usually reserved for a roundup of world and national news, with some analysis, some humor and the editorial pages — produced more vibrant reading on culture than the paper's Arts & Leisure section.

July 1, 2002 / 9:20 a.m. ET

For the bridge-and-tunnel crowd: They called it Transient Rainbow

— and boy, they got that right.

To celebrate the opening of the Museum of Modern Art in Queens this weekend, the museum's poo-bahs commissioned Chinese artist Cai Guo-Qiang to create a rainbow in the nighttime sky that would briefly connect the two banks of the East River in a blaze of colorful fireworks.

But the rainbow connection between Manhattan and Queens (that sadly dissed borough) turned out to be a disconnect. The fireworks, lasting all of 30 seconds, never spanned the river from bank to bank. They lit up the sky with a burst of letters, spelling MoMAQNS, and bright pom-poms in a brilliant arc. And then it was over.

Why go to all the expense for so little dazzle? Thousands who'd made the bus or subway trek to the pier on the Queens side of the river drifted back to the streets, with perhaps a murmur of admiration but not much astonishment. It was less than auspicious.

Despite the long lines that waited patiently all weekend to get into the museum, attendance is liable to fall off briskly once it opens for real. Admission was free for the opening. But it will be $12, up from $10.

(If you hadn't heard, the museum's Manhattan home will be closed for the next three years due to construction and renovation).

July 2, 2002 / 8:50 a.m. ET

For the love of books: Move over, Oprah. Whoops, she already has. Well, move over anyway.

Make room for Harriet, the online book critic who is "Amazon's most prolific reviewer." She has more than 3,000 reviews on the site and writes two a day on average, according to Wired magazine.

She also comes cheaper. Harriet doesn't get paid. You can't say that about Oprah.

July 2, 2002 / 2:11 p.m. ET

Vulgar rap hits the high notes: Conservative scold William Bennett has tossed in the towel.

"They've won," Bennett tells Washington Post rock critic David Segal, who has an excellent piece today about best-selling rap CDs that demean women and gays and praise lowlife behavior, yet have not faced anything like the rightwing boycotts and protests of old.

"They can't stand to have won, but it's over and they've won," Bennett insists. "They get to say and do anything and make billions and castigate us in the process."

Does that mean the culture wars are over? That one of the nation's most vocal scourges of leftwing liberals has surrendered? That organizations like Empower America have cried uncle?

Please. Would you bet on it? I wouldn't.

July 3, 2002 / 1:35 p.m. ET

Hurrah for 1902: Everybody in show business and plenty of others have been celebrating the Richard Rodgers centennial. The 100th anniversary of that peerless Broadway composer's birth and the the story of his career have been publicized everywhere. If you didn't know that, now you do.

Less well known is the fact that the great Hollywood director William Wyler would have been 100 on Monday. He, too, has his advocates and fans. A lot is happening to celebrate his legacy.

Although Hollywood insiders have always regarded him with admiration and frequently with awe, his films are better known to the public than he is — largely because he didn't seek the limelight.

Wyler was a witty man in private (despite a reputation for being inarticulate), the life of the party and something of a daredevil. But while he had a strong and charming personality, he was neither an egomaniac nor an egotist. He left that to his longtime producer Sam Goldwyn, who loved to hog the credit (often at Wyler's expense).

Full disclosure: I wrote a biography of Wyler "A Talent for Trouble." (You can see a review here. I don't necessarily agree with it.)

There are upcoming screenings and mini-retrospectives of Wyler's films at key venues around the country. Here are some of them:

The San Francisco Silent Film Festival will show "Hell's Heroes" on July 14. It was Universal's first all-sound outdoor picture (released in 1930 also as a silent) and helped gain Wyler his first major recognition. (I've seen it both ways and prefer the sound version. But either way it's great stuff.)

Terence Stamp will be there to present the film. Stamp starred in "The Collector," Wyler's 1965 psychodrama. "The best directors I ever worked with were Fellini and Wyler," Stamp once told me. Laurence Olivier has said: "If any film actor is having trouble with his career, can't master the medium and, anyway, wonders whether it's worth it, let him pray to meet a man like Wyler." And this from Bette Davis, who fell in love with Wyler during a tempestuous affair and later regretted that they never married: "Willy really is responsible for the fact that I became a box-office star."

The San Rafael Film Center, just north of San Francisco, will screen nine films, beginning with "The Collector" on July 13 (Stamp will be there, too) and ending with "Wuthering Heights" on Aug. 7.

It's a great lineup and a reminder of how many classics Wyler made: "Jezebel" (starring Bette Davis and Henry Fonda); "The Best Years of Our Lives" (Myrna Loy and Frederick March); a new print of "Dodsworth" (Walter Huston and Mary Astor); "Roman Holiday" (Audrey Hepburn and Gregory Peck); "The Little Foxes" (Bette Davis and Herbert Marshall); "Counsellor-at-Law" (John Barrymore).

There's also an Academy Centennial Salute to Wyler (a three-time Oscar winner for directing) on July 18 at the Academy of Motion Picture Arts and Sciences in Los Angeles, which launches a four-week retrospective at the Los Angeles County Museum of Art (click on "calendar" under EVENTS).

The Gene Siskel Film Center at The Art Institute of Chicago is planning a two-week retrospective (Aug. 12-31), which is ironic. When Gene was alive I could never get him to say anything about Wyler, who didn't register on his thumbs-up scale. All he ever said was, "I'm not interested." (Gene was a lovely guy personally, but he was always a bit of a snob when it came to his taste in films. Maybe he felt obliged not to like Wyler because Roger Ebert did.)

Shortly after, the Film Forum in New York will host a three-week retrospective (Sept. 13-Oct. 3, titles and screenings to be announced). And further down the line there will be a screening of "Best Years" at the National Gallery of Art in Washington.

In December, wrapping up the celebrations will be four evenings of Wyler films at the George Eastman House, one of the world's great film archives, in Rochester, N.Y.

Thanks to Wyler's granddaughter Amy Lehr, who has been tireless in spreading the word, and to his children — Catherine (whose own documentary "Directed by William Wyler" will be screened in San Raphael), Judy, Melanie and David — the Wyler film legacy may be gaining broader recognition.

Meanwhile, let's please not forget to salute Max Ophuls, who was also born in 1902 and who is another great film director even less well known to the public than Wyler. Anthony Lane hasn't forgotten. Here's his tribute to Ophuls in The New Yorker.

July 4, 2002 / 9:50 a.m. ET
   Virtual fireworks for the Fourth: Have a great holiday weekend. I won't be back until Tuesday.
   In the meantime, enjoy these virtual fireworks and these, or create your

own, or visit fireworks in different cities <u>here</u>.

For the more serious among us, here's <u>a history of fireworks</u>.

July 9, 2002 / 11 a.m. ET

First Anne Heche, now 'N Sync's Joey Fatone: Who's next? Nicole Kidman? Well, almost. Make it Baz Luhrmann, her "Moulin Rouge" director.

Broadway has been such a fabulous invalid lately — emphasis on invalid — that I've pretty much stopped going. But something weird is happening. The Great White Way seems to be showing signs of life-after-death.

First came Anne Heche. <u>She proved the point</u>, making her Broadway debut last week in "Proof." She replaces Jennifer Jason Leigh, who replaced <u>Mary-Louise Parker, who originated the role</u>. Now comes 'N Sync's Joey <u>Fatone</u>, who will make his Broadway debut on Aug. 5 in <u>"Rent."</u>

Come November, Luhrmann's production of "La Bohème" will arrive on Broadway with a cast being billed as "a multinational 'Olympic Dream Team' of the best young opera singers in the world." Which pretty much disqualifies Kidman.

Oh, did we mention <u>Giacomo Puccini</u>? We should have. "Rent" is Jonathan Larson's updated, watered-down, rockabye-babied, Pulitzer Prize-winning version of Puccini's 19th-century <u>"La Boheme."</u>

Luhrmann will be doing "a full, traditional version" of "La Bohème," the show's publicist says, except that it's set in 1957. But it will be sung in Italian (with English surtitles for the benefit of dummies like me).

The idea that <u>Baz Luhrmann</u> will be doing a traditional version of anything boggles the mind.

July 9, 2002 / 5:30 p.m. ET

Trailers for Potter, LOTR addicts: Hey kiddies, are you ready for your next "Harry Potter" fix? Do you need to get "The Lord of the Rings" monkey off your back? Cheer up. Here's the new movie trailer for Potter's <u>"The Chamber of Secrets,"</u> and here's the trailer for LOTR's <u>"The Two Towers."</u>

(Thanks to Gael Fashingbauer Cooper, my MSNBC colleague, for the trailer alert.)

July 10, 2002 / 12:35 p.m. ET

The Michael Jackson case: Have you ever heard of anything funnier in your life than Michael Jackson's complaint that Sony dissed him because he's black? I thought the former King of Pop was white.

I don't doubt that some black musicians have suffered from <u>racism in the record industry</u>. But it's difficult to believe that Jackson — given <u>his past success</u>, his wealth and his style of life — is among them.

<u>FREE VIDEO</u> **START ▶**

Click on the video to see Michael Jackson at Tuesday's press conference with the Rev. Al Sharpton and others.

The poor baby couldn't get Sony to pay for a world tour to promote his latest CD, "Invincible." What a shame. The poor baby couldn't get Sony to fork over $8 million so he could make a third promotional video for it. Worse than shameful: racist.

The ultimate in cynicism, though, is Jackson's "activist" stance. It's one thing to form <u>a coalition to support the rights of black musicians</u>, another to exploit the issue for personal gain in his vitriolic battle with Sony chief Tommy Mottola.

For all I know, Mottola really is a bad guy, though even <u>the Rev. Al Sharpton denies he's a racist</u>. And maybe Mottola does deserve to be depicted the way Jackson drew him, with horns as the devil incarnate.

But coming from a rich-as-Croesus rock star who was investigated by police for alleged child molestation and who made an undisclosed settlement before a case could be brought against him in court, Jackson's sense of injustice is hard to credit.

Imagine the crude drawing Mottola could make of him.

July 11, 2002 / 1:50 p.m. ET

The Jackson reaction: So many reader e-mails. So little time to put them up. (My staff of thousands is otherwise engaged.) The handful of messages below pretty much sums up the gist of them. I've divided them evenly here, pro and con, just to be fair. But the overwhelming majority was anti-MJ. I know that's hard for some of you to believe. I'd get a board of certified accountants to testify to that, but you wouldn't believe them either.

"As a black woman working in the music industry ... I'm not going to let Michael Jackson speak for me. Michael needs a reality check ..."
— Lisa, New York City

"You're a WHITE RACIST Jan Herman which is why you wrote that ignorant article about Michael Jackson — Olivia Jackson, Grand Blanc, Mich.

"Michael probably is acting like a fool, but over the last few weeks, I've decided that you are very one-sided and downright mean." — Scott, Danville, Va.

"As a black woman, I thought The King of Pop was white too." — No name

"Why are you totally bashing Michael???? YOU DON'T EVEN KNOW HIM ... and if you did you would know that now tons and tons of Michael fans want him to tour and are very disappointed with SONY!!" — No name

"What upsets me the most is he is playing the race card now that he is in need. If he really wanted to make a video I'm sure he could pay for it himself. ... It's all so stupid and self promoting it makes me sick." — Natasha, San Diego

"Michael Jackson is an amazing artist and human being, too bad you can't see that. I feel sorry for you, truly." — Nick C., Las Vegas, Nevada

"Thank you for summing up so succinctly the Michael Jackson issue. It riles me to no end that this cry-baby has to resort to such idiotic tactics to keep his name in the spotlight." — Steven J. Athanas, Toledo, Ohio

"I totally agree ... who is Michael Jackson kidding ... racist plots against him now? Please!" — Kelly Vinci, New Milford, Conn.

"I think you are full of hot air. Thanks." — O.S., Louisiana

July 12, 2002 / 11:44 a.m. ET
Michael Jackson, Elvis, and Tony Shalhoub: To judge from the deluge of reader e-mail I've received, Michael Jackson still is a remarkably potent touchstone of popular culture — especially for a star on the downhill side of his career.

This was true of Elvis. For many years his significance as a musical icon never waned, despite a career that tanked.

But Jackson's importance these days has more to do with his touchy, self-proclaimed role as a victim of racial discrimination than with his talents as an entertainer.

For instance, Drewdawg writes from the Virgin Islands:

"As a black man from birth, with no induced whitening or lightening (that probably has to be said in this day and age), I am offended by MJ's claim of racism on two fronts.

"1) It has been many years since MJ could look at the 'Man in the Mirror' and tell whether he was 'black or white' and 2) After making hundreds of millions of dollars, MJ now claims racism because his album was more 'Invisible' than 'Invincible.'

"Racism exists in all areas of society, that is just the way it is, but do I want MJ championing the 'end racism in the music industry' struggle on my behalf? I think not."

Another e-mail, from a self-described "28-year-old actor of Middle Eastern decent" living in Los Angeles, highlights the fact that racial discrimination against blacks in the entertainment world should not dominate our focus to the exclusion of other minorities:

"It would be great if you would write about the exclusion of Middle Eastern actors. Let me mention that Hispanics, Asians and Native Americans are at a disadvantage as well. ... Unfortunately, African Americans tend to be considered the only minority in the USA.

"I think it's great that black Americans, through years of lobbying and hard work, have achieved more recognition and employment in this town. However, let's not forget that there are more Latinos living in this country than blacks.

"And where are the roles for Native Americans? And last, God help you if you are a Middle Eastern actor. You are lucky if you go to one audition a month to play a terrorist, cab driver or a 7-11 employee. ... Network, studio and production executives have underestimated the diversity ... of the American people."

Which brings us to Tony Shalhoub, an actor of Lebanese-American descent who has often played ethnic types, like Italians and Jews. Still, he has long been among Hollywood's more valued actors in films ("Men in Black," "Spy Kids") and television ("Wings"). And now he moves further up the ranks, breaking out of the supporting-actor mold, as the star of "Monk," the new, sparkling detective series that premieres tonight.

Go, Tony! (We know one success does not redress all the injustices.)

July 12, 2002 / 8:45 p.m. ET

More troubles for Jacko: It looks like Michael Jackson's claim that Sony blocked the release of one of his songs as part of an alleged "conspiracy" against him has hit a road bump.

The Los Angeles Times reports that Jackson's own advisers asked Sony to bury the song after discovering its producer was involved in the gay porno industry.

The song in question? Jacko's Sept. 11 charity single "What More Can I Give." Dozens of pop stars performed on it, among them 'N Sync, Ricky Martin, Mariah Carey, Carlos Santana, Celine Dion, Tom Petty, Julio Iglesias and Reba McEntire.

It's doubtful whether the single will see the light of day. But Jackson's publicist, Dan Klores, has told Reuters that as of "three or four days ago there was still hope that this single will be released."

As of three of four days ago there was still hope that President George W. Bush was going to hold cheating corporate bosses accountable, too.

July 15, 2002 / 12:52 p.m. ET

What's wrong with film critics? They see too many movies, and they see them for free. Freeloading addles the brain and dulls the senses.

Consider the chorus of praise for "Road to Perdition." "A truly majestic visual tone poem." — Stephen Holden, The New York Times. A "resonant story with the potent, unrelenting fatalism of a previously unknown Greek myth." — Kenneth Turan, Los Angeles Times. "The passion and precision ... is staggering." — Peter Travers, Rolling Stone.

My take on "Perdition" is that like "Minority Report," which also received unwarranted raves, it's one of those coulda-shoulda-woulda films.

It's gorgeous to look at but lacks punch. It's watchable but unreal and uninvolving. And it's not in "The Godfather" league, contrary to David Elliott's praise on MSNBC. It's not even close.

Some critics did not fall all over themselves to drape this Tom Hanks-Paul Newman gangster flick in robes of glory. Roger Ebert, on the Chicago Sun-Times, was less than thrilled with its tragic dimensions: "I prefer Shakespeare." Ditto Jack Matthews, of the New York Daily News, who wrote that it's "a dreamy, poetic impression of a world ... that has no resonance for most of us."

There were other demurrals, too. But here's what you're more likely to get from critics who see too many films for free.

"I realized something halfway through," Terry Lawson, of the Detroit Free Press, wrote. "Unless fall holds unimaginable secrets, 'Perdition' will surely be nominated for multiple Oscars — best picture, actor, supporting actor, director, cinematography, screenplay."

I would never accuse Lawson of shilling for Hollywood. But what do you make of this? "In all my years of movie reviewing, I don't think I've ever spent a more satisfying summer indoors," he writes.

And how does Lawson explain the fact that movies are ringing up the cash register?

"While hits can still be bought, there is a renewed respect for storytelling, as witnessed by 'Spider-Man,' the riveting 'Sum of All Fears' and Steven Spielberg's near-classic 'Minority Report' ..."

I wonder if Lawson saw Tom Cruise's photo at the newsstands. The star of "Minority Report" was simultaneously on the cover of Time, Esquire, Entertainment Weekly, W and Premiere to promote that film. Seems to me Hollywood has more respect for marketing than storytelling. And magazines, Time especially, have too much respect for hype.

July 15, 2002 / 12:55 p.m. ET

Robin Williams does 'The Juice' on stage: Was it déjà vu? I could have sworn Robin Williams was doing 'The Juice' Monday night in his live show from Broadway on HBO.

Actually that was my editor's take. She points out that Williams went after Michael Jackson and the Pledge of Allegiance — I've been harping on both lately — and "he even sweats as much as you do," she told me.

My take on the show? I liked Williams' line about Jacko better than my own. He said that MJ has to pick a race before he can claim racial discrimination.

I thought his Pledge of Allegiance line was funny — instead of pledging to one nation under God, let's just pledge to one nation under Canada and above Mexico. But the line was cribbing. He'd used that gem earlier, in an interview.

In any case, the show was out-there-filthy-funny. Have you ever heard such a major star — Chris Rock, Eric Bogosian and several other lesser stars excepted — get so down and dirty?

I kept getting the feeling that Williams was playing to a Hollywood A-list of two: Jack Nicholson and the ghost of John Belushi.

Can you imagine Jerry Seinfeld getting that down and dirty? Not on his life.

As for the sweat, I'm not as hairy as Robin. (He joked that he's been accused of wearing fur.) But I guess you can't tell from my picture at the top of this thing. Sam DePriest of Washington, D.C., apparently couldn't even tell my gender: "I love your bitchy commentaries . . . . You go girl!"

I know my name is Jan. For the record, I am not a transvestite, and I've never had a sex change.

July 16, 2002 / 9:55 a.m. ET

Jacko in Sonnenfeld 'Black': For the first time since he made a fool of himself last week, I feel sympathy for Jacko.

Director Barry Sonnenfeld, <u>interviewed by BBC News</u>, recounts that 15 months into making "Men in Black II," he received a phone call from the former King of Pop, who had turned down a part in the first film but now wanted to be in "MIIB."

"I had a lovely conversation with Michael," Sonnenfeld recalled, "in which he told me he had seen the first 'Men In Black' in Paris and had stayed when all the other people left the theatre and sat there and wept.

"I had to explain to him that it was a comedy."

Enough said.

OK, almost enough. My colleague here at blog central, MSNBC's Gael Cooper, has let me know that Modern Humorist just put in its two cents with these <u>laugh-out-loud interoffice memos</u> between Sony chief Tommy Mottola and one of his chief henchmen.

July 17, 2002 / 9:40 a.m. ET

Virtual memorial for Ground Zero: Proposals to rebuild <u>the World Trade Center site</u> are missing a virtual component so far. But some artists are busy creating their own online memorials. Here is one, called <u>"September 11th, 2001."</u>

It "consists of motion footage of United Airlines Flight 175 striking the South Tower of the World Trade Center," preceded by a note warning that the artist's aim "is to connect those images of 9/11 to the actual lives that were lost" and that "the images themselves have been changed so that they consist of the names of the people who were slaughtered ..."

The piece is clearly influenced by Maya Lin's famous Vietnam Veterans Memorial in Washington.

I don't think it works as well as Lin's, largely because I couldn't read the names on my computer screen. But you be the judge.

And now have a look at <u>"The Sept. 11 Photo Project."</u>

July 17, 2002 / 9:45 a.m. ET

Where are the women? Let's take a breather from the Michael Jackson saga. Time to hit the high-brows with a major revelation about The New

Yorker, our national water-cooler magazine for aesthetes, semi-literate intellectuals and all-around armchair generals.

Brace yourselves: The magazine can't stand women writers.

I hadn't realized that until I saw "The Talk of the Rest of the Town." According to MobyLives, which has been keeping score, "there have even been issues of The New Yorker this year where the magazine's table of contents featured no women at all."

As Mr. Kurtz once cried in a whisper that was no more than a breath: "The horror! "The horror!"

Just kidding. I really do think The New Yorker under its vaunted, current editor David Remnick is overrated — and under its maligned, former editor Tina Brown was underrated.

July 18, 2002 / 11:45 a.m. ET

Emmys vs. Ground Zero: I don't want to talk about this morning's Emmy nominations, except to say, as Lenny Bruce once said to the prison warden, "Yadda yadda."

"This year's awards are some of the most surprising we've ever seen," said Bryce Zabel, chairman of the Academy of Television Arts & Sciences, which presents the Emmys.

So let me say it again: Yadda yadda.

Who knows, they could still cancel the awards ceremony (scheduled for Sept. 22) as they did last year, because of Sept. 11. Or will they just need black bunting?

I'd rather talk about Ground Zero.

When the six proposals to redevelop the World Trade Center site were unveiled Tuesday, officials went out of their way to say they were only starting points.

Why? Because they're leery about the proposals. Nobody seems inspired by, or even satisfied with, any of them.

In fact, they have generated so little enthusiasm that a Newsweek live vote to choose the best one had drawn a mere 172 votes by 10:40 a.m. this morning.

Maybe that's because the miniature scale models presented by The Lower Manhattan Development Corporation were too dull visually to justify picking one proposal over another.

(By contrast, the MSNBC.com live vote has tallied more than 200,000 responses. But there's no clear preference. The most popular plan is favored by just 26 percent of the voters.)

Compared to the presentation of an independent, unofficial proposal, which (colleague Will Femia tells me) was spammed to the MSNBC.com chat room, the official proposals look anemic. Anything might, though. This one looks like a proposal on steroids.

Or maybe people are still so torn up about Sept. 11 and so uncertain about how to resolve their feelings that they fall into opposite camps on a Ground Zero memorial.

Here are several e-mails (typical of the ones I received) that illustrate the point.

Carter, of Charlotte, N.C.: "Build the EXACT SAME THING BACK."

Paul, of Scranton, Pa.: "I think the WTC should be re-built exactly like it was!!! If they aren't in my opinion, the terrorists won!!!! ... Re-build them, so our children's children can see the New York skyline, the way it was. The way it should be!!!!!!"

Cathy Hapy, of Wilmington N.C.: "The area needs to have "special " buildings built. They should not blend into the rest of NYC. ... When I lived in NJ for 10 years, my favorite place to go was the WTC. I can never get that back. But no one can take my wonderful memories away."

As for the virtual memorial I pointed out yesterday, everyone agreed with me — except for Patty, of Seattle — that the names are too difficult to read.

"Well, I could read the names," she wrote, "and I think it is an astonishing piece, both closely examined and viewed as a whole.

"Art ripped from raw emotion is the most compelling of human expression," Patty added, "and one didn't have to personally know anyone who died in that holocaust to feel it. I'm quite certain that none of us will ever get over it. ..."

Amen to that.

July 19, 2002 / 9:38 a.m. ET

Gadfly on the wall: The other day I noted that women writers were overwhelmingly outnumbered by men writers in The New Yorker magazine, based on a survey by MobyLives.

So what happened? Dennis Loy Johnson, publisher of MobyLives, tells me his site was inundated with viewers and received lots of e-mail like this.

Meanwhile, this week's New Yorker has a great "personal history" by Katha Pollitt, called "Learning to Drive," about life lessons and a philandering ex-lover. It's probably the best piece in the issue (but not offered on The New Yorker Web site.)

(Pollitt is one of three women in the issue. There were two reviews by Joan Acocella and a Talk of the Town contribution by Jane Mayer. Men outnumbered women 10 to 2 in the table of contents, and among the illustrators it's 17 to 1.)

Johnson also keeps an eye on the shenanigans at The New York Times. Another MobyLives survey, "All the Reviews That Fit," found that the newspaper of record plugs books by its own staff writers once every day and a half.

Johnson counted 259 plugs from March 21, 2001, to April 12, 2002. Helluva record.

Incidentally, the name of the MobyLives site pays homage to Herman Melville by way of Charlie Parker — "Moby Dick" via "Bird Lives."

July 20, 2002 / 11 a.m. ET

WTC still on my mind: I woke up this morning and couldn't get two things out of my head.

One was an e-mail I received Friday from Stacy Wooley, of Pearl River, N.Y., about the World Trade Center and what the redevelopment plans mean to her.

I've received a lot of e-mail about the WTC. Many people say the towers should be rebuilt exactly as they were to prove that we Americans can't be cowed by terrorists.

Many others say we need to memorialize those who died, and to do that best we should not build the towers back as they were, but as thoughtfulness dictates they should be.

I'm not certain in my own mind what should be built, although I particularly appreciate Wooley's feelings.

"My Dad was killed on Sept. 11th in the WTC attacks," she wrote. "He was a Capt. in the NYC Fire Department. If the towers were rebuilt as they were, it would rip my heart out each and every time I saw them. We can't pretend this didn't happen to our country. That's what I feel we'd be doing by building the towers again.

"This event is something that each and every American needs to face, regardless [of whether] they were personally affected or not. The land where the towers once stood should be kept sacred. The victims' families are owed that.

"I think a little more time and thought needs to be put into exactly what should be built on Ground Zero. This isn't something that should be rushed into."

The other thing I couldn't get out of my head was Thursday's article in Slate, "Mall of America," by Christopher Hawthorne, a colleague of mine when we were Fellows in the National Arts Journalism Program. It's the most sensitive and penetrating story I've read so far about the meaning of the WTC proposals for Americans at large.

Hawthorne analyzes the social implications of the proposals in terms of city planning that has been so utterly commercialized, suburbanized and Disney-fied that "it is now very difficult for Americans to think about cities without thinking about shopping."

"Suburbs, meanwhile, have been returning the compliment in all sorts of ways," Hawthorne writes. "Twenty miles west of Washington, D.C., for example, sits Reston Town Center, a shopping mall built to look like an old-fashioned downtown and deposited in the midst of Northern Virginia's sprawling, centerless suburbia. Its designers claim it has 'the vitality of an Italian piazza and the diversity of a French boulevard.' It has neither, of course, but on weekend afternoons the Ann Taylor store is packed."

What has this to do with rebuilding Ground Zero, Hawthorne asks — and answers: "Everything. ..." He clinches his point by quoting Monica Iken, a Sept. 11 widow, from National Public Radio: "What is [the site] going to say to a 2-year-old ... five years from now? ... 'Your Daddy died right where the Starbucks is?' "

Which leads Hawthorne to wonder "[w]hether the 9/11 memorial will blend effortlessly into a gift shop that moves inexorably into a shopping promenade, so that before you realize it you've gone from weeping to deciding if you want fries with that."

And lots of ketchup.

July 21, 2002 / 9:45 a.m. ET

WTC on America's mind: What mattered more to Americans this weekend? The 33rd anniversary of Neil Armstrong's moon landing or the redevelopment plans for Ground Zero?

Look at it this way: Thousands of people showed up at a town meeting in New York — more than 5,000, by one count — to vent their anger and frustration over the WTC proposals.

And you know what? The officials in charge of rebuilding the site were forced to backpedal. That's how rough it got for them.

Here it is today at the top of The New York Times' front page in the print edition: "Officials ... said they would consider new options for the site, including scaling back the amount of commercial space and extending the timeline for completing a final plan."

Now read (below) what this column had to say Saturday, before the town meeting began.

Let's hand it to Stacy Wooley who made a wise plea for thoughtfulness and more time.

Let's hand it to the scores of others from all over the country who made similar comments but whose e-mails I did not post.

And let's hand it to Christopher Hawthorne whose article in Slate ripped the "blatant commercialism," not only of the WTC proposals but of lousy urban and suburban planning in general.

July 22, 2002 / 12:30 p.m. ET

A chorus of the red, white and blue: If anybody thinks that rebuilding the site of the World Trade Center is <u>a local matter for New Yorkers alone,</u> I've got news for them.

Of the 125 e-mails sent to me just on Saturday and Sunday — a remarkable number when you know the Web tends to be a quiet place on weekends — all but four came from the heartland, from places like Booneville, Ark.; Webb City, Mo.; Blackwell, Okla.; Cheyenne, Wyo., and Grand Prairie, Texas.

More stunning to me, it seems that Texans and New Englanders, Virginians and Ohioans, folks from Utah and New Jersey, Tennessee and California — and, yes, many Canadians — were all united in a chorus of concern.

Whether they wanted to reclaim Ground Zero with taller buildings or shorter buildings or no buildings at all, with commercial space or without it, or exclusively with a memorial to those who died there, they poured out their feelings with a heartfelt strength that will be impossible to ignore.

"I believe that this property now is holy," Rod Cooper of Barrie, Ontario, wrote.

Amen to that.

July 23, 2002 / 8:45 a.m. ET

Ain't Rand grand? I should have thought of it myself but didn't (probably because I'm no fan of Ayn Rand, her philosophy, or her acolytes).

It took Nick, from Wichita, Kan. — thanks, Nick — to remind me that when it come to rebuilding the World Trade Center, nobody is more likely to chime in than fans of Rand.

(Remember her 1943 novel "The Fountainhead"? Remember its uncompromising architect hero, Howard Roark, the supreme personification of egoism, laissez-faire capitalism and the virtues of selfishness?)

Anyway, in true Randian fashion, Sherri R. Tracinski, who writes for the Ayn Rand Institute, asserts in Capitalism Magazine:

"All of Manhattan is sacred ground —not because people died there, but because its bridges and skyscrapers are monuments to human life."

Oh, stuff it. Try telling that to the grieving families.

July 23, 2002 / 10:25 a.m. ET

Sex, lies and spankings: I've never played cheerleader for either of MSNBC.com's corporate parents, but let's hear it for the peacock network!

On Monday night, NBC's new reality dating show, "Meet My Folks," really did manage to pull off a "Blind Date" grafted onto the Robert De Niro flick "Meet the Parents."

It started off with the all-American Blankenship family — what's more perfect than Dad as gym-teacher-drill-sergeant? — and three flawed contestants:

Jason, who likes to be spanked (which freaked out the family so much that he was the first to get the boot);

Chris, a boxer from the Midwest who allegedly slept with an ex-girlfriend's mother;

and Kory, who cheated on his SATs to get into Penn State.

This show is so far from the tedious, drawn-out reality shows I hate that I didn't touch the dial for an hour.

OK, I missed a few lines — I am a TV multitasker, I admit it — but compared to the bickering and plotting on "Survivor" and "The Bachelor," this was like a "Mayberry R.F.D." of the 21st century.

The contestants actually got along; the daughter, unsure of which guy she liked best, shed some tears — but just a few — and that old contraption, the lie detector, actually got prime play.

It looks like the producers of "Meet My Folks" have something to teach the world of reality TV: You don't need endless, after-the-fact contestant commentary — just weave the commentary in as you keep the action going forward, as in any good story.

In the end Mom and Dad send their daughter off to Hawaii with the tadpole boxer Chris. There's just no explaining human behavior.

I wonder if tonight's "American Idol", on Fox, will be as much fun.

July 24, 2002 / 12:20 p.m. ET

"American Idol," fad or bad? James Brown, where are you? "Star Search" revisited — otherwise known as "American Idol: The Search for a Superstar" — is the "hot" show of summer television.

On Tuesday alone more than a dozen news stories appeared — not about the show, but about a news conference about the show.

The main attraction was not the finalists, who were allowed to put in their two cents, pretty much the way they're allowed to put in their two cents on the show itself.

The main attraction was the battle of the judges, with Paula Abdul ("Ms. Nice") and British nasty, Simon Cowell (rightly described by one reporter as the "Snidely Whiplash" of judges), dissing each other also pretty much the way they do on the show.

Which goes to prove that the marketing of "American Idol" is better than anything else the show has to offer, just as the snippets teasing the show are better than the whole. (Have you ever met a flakier pair than the two yo-yos hosting "American Idol"?)

What's also better is the "American Idol" Web site on MSN, which is much more involving than Fox's TV production. It has everything from "Jaded Journalist" recaps of the shows to, my favorite, Musical Performance Clips and song lists.

(Here I go again, praising another corporate parent of MSNBC [see below]. It's enough to make me sick-ish — tip of the pen to Snidely Whiplash, who described one finalist's performance Tuesday night as "good-ish.")

There's no point going into the details of the show. You can get other recaps of the episodes here, written by catty, doting fans who catch every nuance and twist.

(I particularly like the summaries of "justcallmefluff," an interior designer from Toronto. In the second episode, for instance, one performer belted out the song "R.E.S.P.E.C.T," and Snidely gave his verdict: "Sorry love, you're too F.A.T." Ms. Fluff smartly took him to task.)

By now, of course, the battle of the judges is as stage managed as the rest of "American Idol." And with more than 200 news stories on the show since the beginning of the year — read 'em here — the press is going along with it.

If you want to read more, you can feast on these sharp fan comments.

July 25, 2002 / 11:40 p.m. ET

Cell-phone flicks and The Fringe: Are you ready for movies on your cell phone? Is anybody ready for them? I doubt it, and so does Dack Ragus, a Web designer who makes them. But he hasn't given up on them.

Wired magazine reports that Ragus has "settled on a distinct genre: He draws stick figures to play the lead role in [his versions of] famous movies, and he always decapitates them."

You probably won't be able to see them, however. The image is slightly more than a square inch.

I'd say Hollywood's not likely to come calling, would you?

Meanwhile, the Edinburgh Fringe Festival, that annual summer gathering of the avant garde and other theatrical riff raff, has a more traditional delivery system — and it's booming.

Of course, not everybody's in love with The Fringe. Some detest it, Michael Billington for one.

Oh, I was kidding about the "theatrical riffraff." I just said that to see if you were listening.

July 26, 2002 / 9:40 a.m. ET

The Austin Powers theme park: Today's big deal at the movies, "Austin Powers in Goldmember," tempts me to turn the page. But to what? "The Country Bears," which is based on a Disney theme park?

Come to think of it, Mike Myers has turned himself into a tie-dyed, Day-Glo, theme-park attraction with polyester grace notes. One more Austin Powers sequel could make him a national monument.

There's always television to turn to. Television has its attractions, now that Ozzy Osbourne has pioneered "reality TV" for celebrities.

Soon to join him among the reality ranks of the famous, the not-so-famous and the retread famous:

Sean "P. Diddy" Combs on MTV

Anna Nicole Smith on E!

Liza Minnelli with her new husband David Gest on VH1.

And if you hadn't already heard: Brian "Kato" Kaelin, O.J. Simpson's former house guest, has taped three episodes of a series titled — are you ready? — "House Guest," in which, as he's told ABC's "20/20": "I knock on doors of the unsuspecting and invite myself in to spend a weekend with the family."

Can't wait.

July 29, 2002 / 9:05 a.m. ET

Beats the heck out of me: I thought I was kidding about an Austin Powers theme park. It turns out that Powers' alter ego, Mike Myers, already has one.

Larry Hall, of Santee, Calif., informs me that it's based on Myers' earlier Wayne Campbell character, from "Wayne's World," and it's a themed mini-park in Paramount's Kings Dominion, in Ashland, Va.

I couldn't find any reference to "Wayne's World" on the official Web side for Kings Dominion, but I'll take Hall's word for it that Myers, as Wayne, "does video commentary" for people waiting in line for the

"Wayne's World"-themed roller coaster, "The Hurler."

(Here's a photo of "The Hurler" fronted by a "Wayne's World" sign. Keep scrolling down.)

"So you can see, you really weren't wrong," Hall writes. "And if I had to guess, it probably won't be too much longer before Paramount eventually adds some Austin Powers-themed attractions to its parks."

Don't bet against it. "Goldmember" just broke the box-office bank, setting a July record for movie openings.

What next? A Hollywood version of Mount Rushmore? I can see it now: Myers' face carved in styrofoam above Sunset Drive, alongside box-office stars like Will Smith and Yoda.

July 29, 2002 / 9:10 a.m. ET

Bruce Springsteen, man of the moment: Today belongs to The Boss. And tomorrow. And August and September, too.

In fact, "Today" belongs to him tomorrow, when he'll perform live from Asbury Park, N.J., on the NBC morning show in an exclusive preview of his world tour with the E Street Band.

Click on the video to see The Boss on NBC's "Today" show in Asbury Park, N.J.

(Don't bother to make the pilgrimage to Asbury Park, folks — unless you're prepared to crash the gate. Springsteen's performance at the town's Convention Hall is by invitation only.)

All of this coincides with the Tuesday release of Springsteen's new CD "The Rising". (You can listen to "The Rising" and read the lyrics here.)

Meanwhile, the Boss gave "Today" show host Matt Lauer a brief tour of Asbury Park this morning. They noodled around town in Springsteen's blue Mustang convertible. (Actually, it was taped last Wednesday.)

They stopped at a few places, to plug Asbury Park's revitalization. They also stopped at the Stone Pony nightclub, where Springsteen has made surprise appearances over the years, and Sonny's Southern Cuisine, where Springsteen performed "My City of Ruins" and "I've Got a Feeling (Everything's Gonna Be All Right)."

(You didn't miss anything. Only a couple of bars of "Ruins" was televised.)

57

Fans packed the restaurant. "It was like seeing someone on VH1, unplugged," Bill ("Sonny") Wiley, who owns the restaurant, told The Star-Ledger of Newark. "I tell you, he brought tears to my eyes."

Tomorrow The Boss plugs in on TV for real. Get out your handkerchiefs.

July 30, 2002 / 10 a.m. ET

The past feels so cuddly: Has somebody turned back the clock? It seems so. There's bell-bottomed baby Austin Powers at the movies, the retro musical "Hairspray" about to open on Broadway, Bruce Springsteen reuniting with the E Street Band for a world tour.

Click on the video to see Bruce Springsteen perform the title track of his new CD, "The Rising" at the Convention Hall in Asbury Park, N.J.

And now Jacko fans, elbowing their way back into the action, have put out a press release saying: "Michael Jackson is undoubtedly one of the most talented artists to have walked this earth."

The media needs to be reminded of that modest claim, apparently because it has treated him so badly.

(One proof might be that "Today" never dedicated as much time to The King of Pop in his entire career as it dedicated to The Boss just this morning.)

Jackson "has always had to face incomprehension and scorn," the release says. "Maybe that is the price he, as the biggest star rising out of a minority, has to pay for going where no one else has been before."

I'd say Jacko's Moonwalk has gone to their heads.

July 31, 2002 / 8:45 a.m. ET

Ozzy and Mozart, birds of a feather: I can't believe I completely forgot about "The Osbournes Unf***ingauthorized," Reed Tucker's "completely unauthorized and unofficial guide to everything Osbourne," which came out last week as a children's book no less.

It's a fanzine page turner. You don't even have to read it. You can just skim the 48 pages of text and look at the pictures.

If you think Ozzy and family are vulgar, consider Mozart and family.

Mozart alone was a match for all the Osbournes taken together.

Don't believe it? Then read Aaron Retica on Mozart's "notoriously childish and vulgar" letters, "My Pen is Coarse and I am not Polite."

Remember Peter Shaffer's play "Amadeus," which some critics deplored for its portrait of the peerless composer as "a foul-mouthed, twitchy man, a disgusting imbecilic genius"?

Defending his play, Shaffer cited this rhyme which, Retica observes, Mozart wrote "in a sort of love letter" to his cousin Anna Maria: "Oui, by the love of my skin, I s * * * on your nose, so it runs down your chin."

Or how about this "excruciatingly exact" translation of a letter Mozart wrote to his mother:

Yesterday ... we heard the king of farts
It smelled as sweet as honey tarts
While it wasn't in the strongest of voice
It still came on as a powerful noise.

Retica points out that Mozart's mother wrote back "in a similar vein, though not with quite so much feeling."

Now that's a gas!

Share your perspective on entertainment and the arts with <u>Jan Herman</u>. MSNBC is not responsible for the content of Internet links.

Jan Herman

Latest entertainment and arts news from the Web

Entries from Aug. 1 to Aug. 30, 2002
(Some links may be nonfunctional.)
Back to 'The Juice'

LATEST UPDATES

Aug. 1, 2002 / 9:45 a.m. ET

Of peep shows and 'The Lion King': So they've gotten rid of Peep-O-Rama, the last sex shop on 42nd Street. It was shuttered Wednesday, the culmination of a Times Square cleanup that began even before the Giuliani era took hold.

Surely that's a milestone for a generation, just as the 2000th performance of "The Lion King" — celebrated Tuesday at the New Amsterdam Theatre, also on 42nd Street — is a milestone for the Disney generation.

What's my point? I dunno. Maybe a certain nostalgia for leering old men, junkies in doorways, hookers on the sidewalks.

Nah, just kidding.

Manhattan is still full of leering old men (they've moved to the peep shows on 8th Avenue), junkies in doorways (they've vacated Times Square), hookers on sidewalks (they've traded up to Central Park South).

Human nature is what it is, and New York is what it is (9/11 notwithstanding). Together they make a peculiar, wonderful, sad, gay, sexy, childlike, generous mix. You can't change that. At least I hope not.

Aug. 2, 2002 / 10:40 a.m. ET

'What's up doc?' Ta-dah! Bugs Bunny is the greatest cartoon character of all time, according to this week's TV Guide, with Homer Simpson the second greatest, Rocky and Bullwinkle third, Beavis and Butt-head fourth. Bart Simpson ranked 11th, if you can believe that. And the ducks? Daffy is 14th and Donald 43rd.

Taste is a sometime thing. Sometimes it's good. Sometimes it's bad. There's no way to explain it. My own runs to the great Chuck Jones characters: Bugs, Daffy, Wile E. Coyote and Road Runner (38th on the list) and Pepé le Pew (not listed at all).

I have no idea how TV Guide decided on its ranking. The magazine asked voters to choose their own favorites online. When last I looked 18,098 voters had chimed in. Their top choice? Tom and Jerry by a wide margin. (TV Guide's own list puts Tom and Jerry last.)

If you're looking for deep analysis, here's David Dale's "Thufferin' thuccotash! Another looney list."

What would we do without lists? TV Guide, celebrating its 50th birthday, didn't stop at cartoon characters. It also rated the 50 greatest shows of all time. The top five are "Seinfeld," followed by "I Love Lucy," "The Honeymooners," "All in the Family" and "The Sopranos."

More than 75,000 voters disagree. Their top five are: "Buffy the Vampire Slayer," followed by "Bonanza," "The X-Files," "Seinfeld" and "The Simpsons."

At least the magazine and the voters agree on the worst show of all time: yup, "The Jerry Springer Show." (I'll go with the voters for second worst: "Who Wants to Marry a Multi-Millionaire?"

Aug. 2, 2002 / 11:50 a.m. ET

The standing ovation? Oh sit down! Once upon a time "The Standing O" was an appreciation of excellence.

Nowadays, Los Angeles Times reporter Diane Haithman writes, it's comparable to "the 15 percent tip: no longer a recognition for exceptional service, but an obligatory payment to any waiter who doesn't drop the catch-of-the-day on your head."

Truer words were never spoken. But only the LA Times would devote 1,500 words to parsing the variations of The Standing O.

Typically, California's biggest and best newspaper reports on parochial differences between East (tougher audiences, but not by much) and West.

Gil Cates, former producer of the Oscars and now producing director at Westwood's Geffen Playhouse, tells Haithman: "People in L.A., while they are generally more jaded ... are ... looser than the people in the East."

Has he never seen "Mamma Mia!" on Broadway? Built-in standing ovations are part of the show.

Aug. 5, 2002 / 10:30 a.m. ET

Slutty behavior and the art of writing: The time has come to confess that I'm one of the guilty readers who helped put "The Sexual Life of Catherine M." on the best-seller lists, where it has been for many weeks now.

I'm guilty not because I wanted to read about "slutty" female behavior — and there's none sluttier than Catherine Millet's — but because her account turned out to be so dull.

(I much preferred the prurient interest of "The Elementary Particles," another trans-Atlantic import, not to mention the excellence of Michel Houellebecq's spare literary style. Compare excerpts: Here's Millet, and here's Houellebecq.)

Now I discover that Millet's orgy-prone life is, in any case, old news. She's just a high-end, contemporary French version (an art critic leading a double life) of the women of the Canela tribe in Amazonian Brazil, who less than 50 years ago "enjoyed the delights of as many as 40 men one after another in festive rituals."

"Slutty behavior," it turns out, "is good for the species." That's the conclusion of "a new wave of research on the evolutionary drives behind sexuality and parenting," Sally Lehrman writes.

"Fooling around appears to have helped our ancestral mothers equip their little ones for success — the sexual equivalent of reading to them every night or enrolling them in the after-school chess club."

A further thought: Judging from its stay on the best-seller lists, a lot of people have either been snookered by "The Sexual Life of Catherine M." or they really do like it.

I think Millet could have taken a lesson or two from Elizabeth Benedict, author of "The Joy of Writing Sex," a how-to guide.

Benedict, who also teaches creative writing, might have helped Millet "craft 'smashing' and 'wonderful' sex scenes" — although, as Victoria Glendinning points out in her review of Benedict's book: "The sex itself doesn't have to be any good, but the writing must be."

And while we're on the subject, there is much else to be gleaned from "The Joy Writing Sex," Glendinning notes. For example, "in the states of Georgia, Alabama and Texas it is legal to own a gun but not a vibrator."

(PS: Dana Whitmer, of Tyler, Texas, writes that "it's not illegal to own a vibrator in Texas for personal use" and attaches as proof Title 9, Chapter 43, Subchapter B, of the Texas Penal Code, which reads like somebody forgot to translate it into plain English. I'm no lawyer, but it looks to me like it's against the law to sell a vibrator in Texas. Catch-22. Joseph Heller would be proud.)

Aug. 6, 2002 / 2:20 p.m. ET
Where the media should fear to tread: In case you hadn't noticed, "the need to be constantly entertained has crossed a new threshold." So says

Toronto Star pop culture reporter Vinay Menon in <u>"Why We Like to Watch."</u>

He points to some pretty old evidence — "Channel surfing. Net surfing. Bookstore browsing. Flipping around the radio dial" — and supports his argument by quoting experts who cross an old threshold: credibility.

Here, for example, is Robert Thompson (a professor at Syracuse University and a frequently quoted media expert) explaining the, uhm, neurochemistry behind channel surfing, Net surfing, etc.:

"The complexity of the human brain is such that we are constantly doing things to try and amuse ourselves. The human brain is so sophisticated, it has this incredible ability to be amused. And entertainment is one of the ways in which human beings turn data into experience — that's an important equation."

I'll say!

It's when Menon's own cockeyed narrative sweep kicks in, however, that you wonder whether he's writing for The Onion:

"Evolution is a funny thing. And the funny thing about evolution is that we now need more funny things."

Between pet brain theories and experts out of their depth, is it any wonder <u>people don't trust the media</u>?

Aug. 7, 2002 / 11:45 a.m. ET

Welcome to Diana-land: If you think planners for a memorial at New York's Ground Zero have had a hard time pleasing the public, consider the reaction to Kathryn Gustafson's design for the Diana memorial fountain in London's Hyde Park:

"It has been compared to a puddle, a moat, a national nothing, a ditch, and — oddest of all — 'a conspiracy to forget' the most celebrated British woman of the last century," London's Daily Telegraph reports.

Gustafson, a highly regarded landscape archictect based in Seattle, has <u>a feisty response</u> to her critics: She doesn't do puddles.

"Hey," she told the Telegraph, "whoever called this a puddle is either very rich and has very rich puddles in their lives or has no sense of scale. My design is about the size of a football field."

Gustafson's design won narrowly over another by Anish Kapoor, a noted British artist from Bombay. (It took the intervention of a close friend of Princess Di and the British government to finally choose the winner.)

Meanwhile, the folks at the Gray Lady (aka The New York Times) have decided to weigh in like the proverbial 800-pound gorilla with their own vision for a Ground Zero memorial.

"The Times has assembled a crew of architectural-world heavyweights for its proposal," <u>Sridhar Pappu reports</u> in The New York Observer.

The trouble is, if you're not an 800-pound gorilla you're not likely to get a hearing.

More than 900 proposals have made their way to the Ground Zero planners, and that's not counting the ones that never got to them.

For example, American sculptor Juliette M. Cowdin, who lives in Pietrasanta Italy, asked me back in July how to submit her design "and be sure it's not just booted in the wastebasket."

I told her to contact the <u>Lower Manhattan Development Corp.,</u> which is the official planning agency for Ground Zero, via its <u>e-mail contact</u>

So far the planning agency has not deigned to reply.

Aug. 8, 2002 / 6 p.m. ET

Godawful garden in the sky: I've been traveling today. So here's a late bulletin about a tortured formula for a Ground Zero memorial that illustrates the difficulties of deciding what to build. Naturally, it comes from a professor.

Frederick Turner, who teaches arts and humanities at the University of Texas in Dallas, contends that having to choose between a garden (representing spirituality) or a commercial development (representing materialism) is dumb.

The reason it's dumb, Turner writes for <u>Tech Central Station</u>, is that the nation's founders long ago resolved the conflict between God and Mammon. They decided to make "Mammon serve God," so that "to serve Mammon is to serve God."

Turner does have one interesting idea, though: A Ground Zero memorial should somehow reflect the stylistic achievements of the "three great architectural models" that have come to symbolize New York: the Brooklyn Bridge, the Statue of Liberty, and the Empire State and Chrysler buildings.

Unfortunately, Turner's own Art Deco-ish design for a gargantuan, garden-topped Memorial Arch is godawful. (To see his garden in the sky, scroll down about midway <u>in his proposal</u>.)

Aug. 12, 2002 / 8:30 a.m. ET

The best films ever made: Whom would you believe when it comes to rating the top films of all time, critics or directors?

The British Film Institute's venerable Sight and Sound magazine has been polling critics once every 10 years for the last 50 years. Ten years ago, it wised up and began polling directors, too.

One of the best things about the Sight and Sound poll is that it asks voters to name their own films instead of giving them a list to choose from.

This year, Orson Welles' "Citizen Kane" again ranked as the best film ever made. It has topped the critics' 10-best list for the last four decades, so their choice comes as no surprise.

The directors agreed with them, but wisely ranked Francis Ford Coppola's "The Godfather I and II" second and Federico Fellini's "8-1/2" third. (The critics put Alfred Hitchcock's "Vertigo" second and Jean Renoir's "Rules of the Game" third.)

Here's the entire list of films, roughly 1,000 titles and who voted for them. Not one critic or director proposed "Titanic," the highest grossing film of all time — which tells you what they think of the public's taste.

The poll lists the 250 critics who voted and lets you see each of their top 10 choices. The same for the 106 directors. It's a great way to rate the raters.

See who voted for "Citizen Kane," for "The Godfather," for "8-/2," for "Vertigo" and for "Rules of the Game."

I'd say the directors were much less hidebound. They not only voted Martin Scorsese's "Raging Bull" into their top 10, but also included Stanley Kubrick's "Dr. Strangelove," David Lean's "Lawrence of Arabia" and two films by Akira Kurosawa, "Rashomon" and "Seven Samurai" — none of which made the critics' list.

To tell the truth, I find any best-film list suspect if it includes Kubrick's "2001: A Space Odyssey" — which is one of the most tedious "great" films I've ever sat through. The critics ranked it sixth. You won't find it among the director's top 10.

But then you won't find Stanley Donen's "Singin' in the Rain" on the directors' list either, which is too bad. (The critics ranked it 10th.)

I guess critics have to be right sometimes. They can't always be wrong. Nature wouldn't allow that, would it?

Aug. 13, 2002 / 11 a.m. ET

We take our Elvis seriously: Check out this MSNBC.com memorial package of Elvis stories on the 25th anniversary of his death. OK, three days before the anniversary.

It includes my own sensitive visit to Graceland, John Schulian's big wet kiss to The King and Lisa Napoli's heavenly tour of Elvis e-shrines.

And just so you know we're not kidding, have a look at this Newsweek piece on The King's latter-day marketing.

We take our film fans very seriously: I should have known a list of best movies ever made — especially a venerable list that comes around once a decade — would bring out the cinéaste in all of us.

Everyone has a favorite film that should have made the list or a reason why another film shouldn't have made it. Here are some of the cinéastes and their reasons.

Aug. 14, 2002 / 11:45 a.m. ET

'Idol' on my mind: The hottest TV show of the summer has finally caught up with its hype. Translation: I'm eating my words about "American Idol." Out of my infinite sense of fair play, I'm taking back what I wrote earlier.

The battle of the judges, which grabbed center stage earlier, is now just the sideshow — quippy and fun, but less dramatic. Popmeister Simon Callow (aka Mr. Nasty) has even welcomed Paula Abdul (aka Ms. Nice) "to the Dark Side."

I still don't know who was voted off the show after Tuesday night's broadcast, but now I care. Was it odds-on favorite Tamyra Gray with the golden voice? Babe magnet Justin Guarini? The talented Texan Kelly Clarkson? Not likely. They make the show worth watching.

I'd pick Tamyra to win it all, but I could live with Kelly taking the top prize. She's my dark horse. I'd put Justin third, but who knows what the voters will do?

(Is the voting fair-and-square? See Alan Boyle's Cosmic Log.)

As for the other two finalists, Nikki McKibbin and RJ Helton, they're likely to be gone soon. Right?

Here's a good take on Tuesday's show by a reporter who was there in the audience, not just watching it on TV.

Aug. 14, 2002 / 11:45 a.m. ET

Art of Adolf anyone? And now for news of the higher arts. In today's Wall Street Journal, Lee Rosenbaum is worked up about Hitler's little art show at Williams College in the heart of Massachusetts' Berkshires. What really ticks her off is the lavish, "knee-jerk praise" by reviewers.

Her own review, which appeared earlier, quotes from some of the wall texts of the exhibit and tells you what she thought of the Williams College Museum of Art's "Prelude to a Nightmare: Art, Politics, and Hitler's Early Years in Vienna, 1906-1913":

This morning she righteously takes to task The Boston Globe and The New York Times: "Both papers failed to comment upon the vertiginous spin put on this display by the show's curator, Deborah Rothschild — that Hitler 'was fueled not by the usual political motives but by the aesthetic ambition to 'beautify the world.' "

She also castigates Timothy Cahill for suggesting in the Albany Times Union "that we add Hitler to 'the list of the 20th century's great artists' for having 'choreographed World War II and the Holocaust as a mad act of aesthetic will.' "

And she hangs Martin Knelman out to dry, much too righteously, for his review in the Toronto Star, which "saw Hitler as a master at staging 'a really big show — the kind that millionaire rock stars now routinely offer their fans.' Only Mel Brooks could do better."

(Actually, Knelman does pretty well.)

The New Yorker's Peter Schjeldahl gets a special tongue-lashing in which Rosenbaum awards him "the Tony for Best Historical Comedy" for casting Hitler, the hack painter of academic landscapes, as "a modern artist" and for praising Hitler's "rather nice watercolor" of a mountain chapel.(You can see the watercolor here.)

According to Schjeldahl, she writes, "Hitler's Aryanism and anti-Semitism were developed 'in service to his artistic ambition" and Nazism "was a program to remodel the world according to a certain taste."

At that rate, Rosenbaum goes on, "we'll be soon rewriting art history to insert Nazism somewhere between Cubism and Abstract Expressionism."

But finally, there's a breath of fresh air. Only "Newsweek's painter-critic Peter Plagens gets it right," she contends, "asserting that the dull daub 'violates practically every rule of Composition 101.' " (Here's his review.)

And now for the singing arts: As of Wednesday night, they're down to four finalists on "American Idol." Voters knocked RJ Helton off the show, which didn't seem to come as a surprise to anyone.

And just in case you missed the rumor about Christina Christian, here it is in the New York Post: "SIMON HAS A HUGE CRUSH ON ME AND THAT'S WHY I LOST."

Aug. 16, 2002 / 12:50 p.m. ET

Going global for 9/11 memorial: It's time to hang out the "gone fishin'" sign. But before I do, here's the latest about the great enigma: What to build at Ground Zero.

Now that the initial designs for a memorial have been lambasted, discredited and largely rejected, officials have decided to hold a worldwide design competition.

The Lower Manhattan Development Corp., which is charged with planning the memorial and supervising reconstruction at the World Trade Center site, is to pick a winning design by the second anniversary of the attack.

The competition could begin as soon as January, when formal guidelines for the designs would be issued.

The LMDC has learned from reactions to its original WTC proposals about the need to put a human dimension into its plans. (Among other things, the victims' families are being consulted about concepts for the memorial design. Also, over the next three weeks, townhall-style meetings will be held in the city's five boroughs and in New Jersey.)

And now New York's City Council has put out a report suggesting that the site include housing and an outdoor market like Seattle's Pike Place, where vendors sell everything from organic produce and fresh fish to jewelry.

The idea is to create a street feeling that evokes a sense of community. It sounds like an excellent proposal to me, honoring the living as well as the dead.

Meanwhile, in London, a simple 9/11 memorial garden has been proposed within the garden at Grosvenor Square, where the American Embassy is located. Planners expect it to be completed also in time for the second anniversary of the attacks.

Here's a perspective sketch, looking frighteningly generic (like something thought up for a Southern California retirement community). Here's an architectural sketch, giving a bird's-eye view of where the garden will be situated on the site. And here's a photo of the site.

I'm not really worried by that generic sketch. The thing going for this unpretentious design is that it aims to create a peaceful setting conducive to contemplation. It will have an oval with two planting beds on one side, an oak pergola with a classic pavilion on the other, and a stone centerpiece with an inscription remembering all victims.

Deflated but not defeated: Remember when I mentioned (on Aug. 7) an American artist who wanted to submit her design for a memorial? Her name was Juliette M. Cowdin, and she was afraid it would just be booted into the wastebasket. At my suggestion she wrote the LMCD but never received a reply.

I have heard from her since then.

She writes: "A blurb in the International Herald Tribune ... explains WHY I have not heard from the 'powers that be' ... One must have had previous experience with at least two $400,000,000 (or more) monumental or architectural projects to even be considered.

"Well, I'm afraid that cuts out about 99.99 percent of all potentially wonderful ideas floating around out there by guess who? They're called artists.!! Even the commercially successful ones haven't worked with that kind of budget ...

"Maybe you can just post a notice — 'Hey, you forgot the artists!' I think that's what the violent public reaction and refusal was all about ... Perhaps someone with an 'in' can respectfully suggest an international contest or competition WITH an address to which to submit our plans?? ...”

Julie, I guess somebody already did.

Aug. 19, 2002 / 9 a.m. ET
Gone fishin': Back next week.

Aug. 26, 2002 / 2 p.m. ET
Ugh, what a gas: I had a great week off from work, marred only by watching that CNN video of a dog being gassed to death in a makeshift al-Qaida laboratory.

Forgive me for being late on this subject, but I have to agree with today's editorial in the Boston Phoenix: "Where are the media ethicists now? ..."

(The Phoenix was roundly attacked for linking to, and publishing images from, the video of Daniel Pearl's unspeakable murder by Muslim terrorists dedicated to killing "infidels" — namely Jews and U.S. citizens.)

Meanwhile, the CNN video has become a Hollywood rationalization for renewed violence in films (as if it had gone away in the first place).

Describing Quentin Tarantino's comeback film "Kill Bill," to be released next year, Michael Cieply writes in today's New York Times: "Privately, some Hollywood film executives speculate that the dark experiences of a continuing war against terror will pull audiences toward rougher fare. 'I mean, I just watched a dog gassed on CNN,' one Hollywood production chief said recently."

The videos are not comparable: I don't believe the Phoenix's claim that most mainstream news organizations did not air the Pearl-execution video or print images from it "because it depicted the horrific death of one of its own, a staffer for the Wall Street Journal."

But I do believe, as I wrote on June 7, that seeing Pearl's execution — a horror to behold, but swift (unlike the equally horrific, but lengthy "confession" that preceded it) — made me understand in my gut what I always thought I had understood in my head and that not even the Holocaust literature of Primo Levi and Paul Celan and Elie Wiesel had left me more chilled with bitterness, anger and terror.

What did the dog-gassing video make me understand? That CNN's decision to show it was repugnant, that by lingering over the slow expiration of a helpless dog instead of editing the tape to the bare minimum sufficient for news purposes, the network was sadistic in the extreme.

(Full disclosure: MSNBC also aired the video, but in edited form. It showed the gas going into the dog's cubicle, then it cut to the lifeless dog. MSNBC.com has a photo of a gassed dog in its news story. That, in my opinion, is responsible and legitimate coverage.)

Nobody has ever been able to defend Hollywood's sadistic glorification of violence without sounding like a panderer. The excuse has always been: "That's what the public wants." And the proof, of course, has always been success at the box office. News organizations cannot use that excuse. Though we know that's what ratings are all about, we can never admit it.

Aug. 27, 2002 / 10:55 a.m. ET

Gray Lady goes Gay Lady: In case you hadn't noticed, the wedding pages of The New York Times will now include celebrations of gay and lesbian couplings. As Rebecca Mead writes in the current The New Yorker, this could make them the paper's most romantically entertaining, not to say subversive, pages.

They used to "serve as an unofficial cultural index: once chronicling only the inbreeding of the Wasp aristocracy — noting the happy couple's lineage, club memberships, charity affiliations, and couturier," she writes.

Now "the pages have increasingly come to cover the weddings of formerly overlooked demographics, like Jews and blacks, sometimes even showing them marrying each other."

"In fact," she adds, not without a sense of humor, "gay marriage is the ultimate celebration of individualism, since it heralds a union that fulfills none of matrimony's traditional functions."

For instance, "while many same-sex unions include the rearing of children, even the most dedicated gay parents are unlikely to argue that their reason for marrying is to save their children from the shame of illegitimacy."

Timothy Noah has a different take on the subject in Slate, making the case that the Times should abolish the wedding pages altogether. He writes that "no one should mistake this reform for a meaningful victory on behalf of social justice."

His point is that gay or straight, ethnic or racial minority or not, you don't get into the Gray Lady's weddings and celebrations pages without being part of an aristocracy.

"To the extent that Times wedding notices have become meritocratic," he writes, "they reward the crudest measures of meritocratic worth — attendance at an Ivy League college, employment at the lowest rung of a prestigious investment bank, etc."

This has been true for years. Can't argue with him there.

Aug. 27, 2002 / 10:55 a.m. ET

The finer arts: Everybody has a pet peeve and maybe more than one. Among my many gripes, a hangover from being a theater critic, is the undeserved standing ovation.

Apparently it bothers others, too. The LA Times made a federal case out of it last month. (See 'Oh sit down!') Now the Toronto Star music critic, William Littler, has chimed in with an entertaining history of standing Os, "The laws of applause." It's filled with fascinating oddities, starting with Nero — you know the guy who fiddled while Rome burned.

"In order to assure a favourable reception for his own performances in the vast, open-air theatre at Naples," Littler writes, "his incendiary majesty saw to it that 5,000 brawny young men were specially trained in the fine art of clapping their hands together."

Littler doesn't say what other fine arts they were trained in, but I wouldn't count out back-scrubbing, shoe-polishing, sandal-buckling, toga-tucking and brown-nosing.

Aug. 27, 2002 / 10:55 a.m. ET

High-fiving Michael Jordan: Did you ever wonder what the man who has everything does for entertainment? The Washingtonian did.

Jordan told the magazine his favorite musicians, lately, are Jill Scott, Mike Phillips, the Phat Cat Players, and Brian McKnight. But Anita Baker is his all-time favorite singer.

The best books he read last year were "Hannibal," by Thomas Harris, and "A Lesson Before Dying," by Ernest J. Gaines.

Movies? "I just saw 'Road to Perdition,' which I didn't love," Jordan noted. "I did take my kids to see 'Spider-Man,' and I thought that it was well done."

Television? "I don't really watch a lot of TV ... so I don't have a favorite program. Lately I've been watching a lot of golf."

Jordan's favorite museum is the Smithsonian's Air and Space Museum. His favorite escape is Paradise Island, in the Bahamas. His favorite foreign city is Monte Carlo. And the historical figure he would most like to meet is Martin Luther King.

Seems to me the man who has everything plays it right down the middle of the road, at least for public consumption. That's no dis. But I do want to know: Where's the noise? Where's the funk? Where's Air Jordan?

Aug. 28, 2002 / 1:25 p.m. ET

'American Idol'-atry: Barring an invasion of Iraq, which would make me flip the channel, Wednesday evenings at my house are reserved for "American Idol." And Tuesday evenings, too. (Yes, it has come to that.)

So now it's down to three: Kelly Clarkson, Justin Guarini and Nikki McKibbin. Tonight it will be down to two. The elephant in the room that nobody can discuss, of course, is Tamyra Gray.

There I was on vacation, thinking how smart, wise and cool the American public is and bang! Who in their right minds would have voted her off the show? Boy, did I feel betrayed. It sure made me consider moving to France.

As far as 'American Idol' is concerned, Tamyra's old news. But it looks like she's no loser after all. She's already landed a management contract. And I'm willing to let bygones be bygones. (Who wants to become a Frenchman anyway?)

Now that my favorite is gone, I'm betting on Kelly to win. Like me, most handicappers had picked Tamyra — so it's hard to know whom to trust. But I defer to Sting7, whose recap and comments about Tuesday night's contest are on the money:

"Over all," Sting7 writes, "it was Justin's night. Does he have one more in him?" But Kelly is still "the likely American Idol." As for Nikki, "it was a good run ... Again, I say goodbye to Nikki. Fifth week in a row. I cannot see how she can escape from this one."

Angie, another handicapper, also picks Kelly and Justin to win tonight: "Nikki has to go."

Meanwhile, Will Young, the winner of Britain's "Pop Idol" (the model for "American Idol"), will perform on Sept. 3 with the two American finalists. And he will appear again the next night, with 10 of the 'Idol' wannabes, when the American winner is finally crowned.

That's not all. The show will wring an extra few minutes of fame out of "American Idol in Las Vegas," a two-hour special airing late next month with a concert by all 30 singers who made the early final cut.

Maybe they'll get those Vegas fixtures, Siegfried & Roy (and their big cats), to do some yodeling, too.

Aug. 28, 2002 / 10:19 p.m. ET

Bulletin for West Coast 'Idol'-ators: The vote is in. We've got two finalists. But I don't want to spoil it for you. Check back tomorrow when the glitter has settled.

Aug. 29, 2002 / 9:33 a.m. ET

Down to the 'Idol' wire: So it's Kelly vs. Justin. The voters got rid of Nikki.

Who ought to win?

Musically? Kelly, hands down.

Anyone with ears knows she's got the chops.

 Handsomely? Justin.

Anyone with eyes know he looks the way Michael Jackson wishes he looked.

Kelly gets my vote.

As judge Simon Cowell would say: "It's really as simple as that."

Here's what Simon — being magnanimous — actually said to buck Nikki up:

"Reality check. ...Out of 10,000 people you were third. ... Simple as that. ... You have a career ahead of you."

Here's a recap of Wednesday night's show. Here's another. And here's a hometown fave rave for Justin.

You can join a chat with judge Paula Abdul here at 1 p.m. ET or 10 a.m. PT.

Aug. 30, 2002 / 10:10 a.m. ET

 Stewed reality of MTV Awards: I don't even want to think about last night's MTV Awards show — what a stew! If you want to read the details, check here.

But one thing about the show does interest me: How it was "filmed" and what the cinematic, pseudo-documentary look of it means.

The telecast was aired live on the East Coast, where I watched it on television, but I felt I was seeing something not while it was happening but as it HAD happened.

It was as though the broadcast was fractionally delayed, just slightly enough to make it feel visually out of sync (bordering on the subliminal), and with a great cinematic "look," a texture that turned it into a piece of "history" in real time, as though it was already imprinted in the past.

It was, as my MSNBC colleague Tom Loftus says, "The Triumph of the Will" for pop music.

Now someone might argue that I'm making a mountain out of a molehill,

that 1) this is nothing new,

that 2) there's no difference between what I saw "live" and a delayed, videotaped broadcast,

that 3) lip-syncing (for instance) is just another form of what I'm talking about,

that 4) music videos themselves have long used the technique,

that 5) the MTV awards show was, after all, a celebration of music videos and that it merely looked like a music video — so what's the big deal?

But there's a monumental difference between presenting a video and presenting reality, even an unreal show that is meant to do nothing more than entertain.

The technique used on Thursday night's "live" show, though it looked great, is a great fraud. It pumps up the most trivial moments into an "historic" occasion. It means that the falsification of reality by television — or, as David Mamet terms it, the computer-television — is pretty much complete.

To some of us — probably to many of us — that doubtless sounds like old news. But I had to get this off my chest. The MTV telecast was a "triumph" over more than just pop music.

Share your perspective on entertainment and the arts with Jan Herman. MSNBC is not responsible for the content of Internet links.

Jan Herman

Latest entertainment and arts news from the Web

Entries from Sept. 4 to Sept. 30, 2002
(Some links may be nonfunctional.)
Back to 'The Juice'

LATEST UPDATES

Sept. 4, 2002 / 10 p.m. ET

And then there was one: The nation has voted. OK, the teeny-bopper nation has voted (15.5 million of them.) And they have decided: Big voice beats big hair. Former cocktail waitress bests former door-to-door salesman.

Kelly Clarkson, the petite, 20-year-old Texan with the rip-roaring pipes, was named the one and (for the time being) only American Idol

In "the search for a superstar" aka Fox's "American Idol," she outpolled Justin Guarini, the 23-year-old hunky hearthrob with a mass of frizzy locks and a delicately sculpted face.

It was a longshot for both of them — one-in-10,000 if you count the number of "Idol" wannabes who reportedly auditioned.

This is a spoiler for all you West Coasters, who have yet to see the show. But that's what happens when you live on the Left Coast and you can't stop yourself from clicking.

With a giant leg up on her career already, Kelly looks like a sure winner. She's got show-biz written all over her, but in an endearing, down-home way.

When she sings the national anthem at the Lincoln Memorial on Sept. 11, she's bound to break the nation's heart. Six days later, her debut CD single "A Moment Like This," will be released by RCA. And by the end of November, she will have an album out. (Here's a Kelly fan site.)

Tweedle-dum and Tweedle-dee, the hosts of "American Idol," told us the vote was a landslide: 58 percent for Kelly; 42 percent for Justin.

What was that 42 percent thinking?

More than 20,000 voters at MSNBC.com (as of this posting) had much better taste. They went for Kelly in a really h-u-g-e way: 87 percent to 13 percent. It was a moonslide. Check it out here.

A final note for the moment: Even though Simon Cowell has morphed from "His Nastiness" into "Mr. Nice," he did manage to frame the issue correctly — and with only a small bow to diplomacy.

"If America gets it right," he said just before the vote was revealed, "they are going to make the 'American Idol' winner Kelly Clarkson"

Isn't it time for His Nastiness to re-assert himself? He's much more entertaining than Mr. Nice.

Sept. 5, 2002 / 10 a.m. ET

Fans 'Idol'-ize Kelly: Now that the iridescent glow of the evening has worn off and my bleary-eyed staff of thousands has recovered from the drama of it, three minor thoughts occur to me:

1) This is the way we should elect our presidents.

2) Have we all gone nuts?

3) Kelly Clarkson for president.

And now I see that The Washington Post's Lisa de Moraes has similar thoughts. "Finally, we got an election right," she writes. "And a Texan won!"

Sept. 6, 2002 / 12:01 p.m. ET

Who's really the 'Idol' winner? Despite all the froufrou and ballyhoo over Kelly Clarkson and "American Idol," or perhaps because of it — see the interview on this morning's "Today" show — a thought has nagged at the back of my mind, prompted by many, many e-mails that seemed paranoid but which made eminent sense just the same.

Who, they asked, is the true winner of "American Idol"? Is it really the sweet, bubbly singer from smalltown Texas? Or is it some Mr. Big pulling strings, some Dark Force manipulating the publicity and the finances and the legal agreements that may control Kelly Clarkson's future career right down to the cereal she eats for breakfast?

Now, a couple of entertainment lawyers have taken a look at the "Idol" contract that she and other contestants signed with 19 Management Ltd., the company owned by "American Idol" creator/producer Simon Fuller, who is regarded as a major force in pop music.

When you recover from reading all the legalese, it doesn't look pretty.

(Thank you, Eric Olsen, for posting this on Blogcritics, a self-described "sinister cabal of the web's best writers on music, books and popular culture miscellanea.")

I especially like how the management company gains the "unconditional right throughout the universe in perpetuity to use, simulate or portray ...

[Kelly's] name, likeness ... voice, singing voice, personality, personal identification or personal experiences, [Kelly's] life story, biographical data, incidents" etc.

I guess the company is making plans for the entertainment conquest of space. But while the terms may just be standard boilerplate, that's precisely the point.

Gary Fine, the entertainment lawyer for a Los Angeles firm who dug up the 14-page contestant contract, writes politely that he "found it to be ... well ...how shall I say this ... particularly aggressive, perhaps."

Another entertainment lawyer, Kenneth D. Freundlich, is less diplomatic: "Holy Cow!" He characterizes "American Idol" and its contractual arrangements with the contestants as "a noose to stardom" not as a platform to stardom.

"A few appearances gratis, OK," Freundlich writes, "a compilation album, an Idol single, OK. But a long term contract with THEIR LABEL and THEIR MANAGEMENT TEAM, and THEIR MERCHANDISING COMPANY, is a bit much, not to mention the [mere] $1,400 fee for 'World Idol'!

"How can the Judges look Kelly in the eye and be proud of what the show has done for her? Those provisions are ridiculous. That girl ... is f - - - ed."

There is an opposite point of view: It's the one taken by John Schuch, chief executive of New Feedback Media and a former senior vice president of Artists, Repertoire and Catalog for LicenseMusic.com (which means he oversaw content acquisition activities, the unsigned artists program and strategic partnerships with that site's content providers).

"Is anyone seriously suggesting that Kelly Clarkson would have done better for herself by refusing to sign the contestant agreement and bolting the show prior to becoming one of the highly visible ten finalists to head back home to Burleson, Texas, and wait for her leverage to improve while working as a cocktail waitress?"

Schuch notes that without "American Idol," she would probably not have been discovered. "Like it or not," he adds, "media creates celebrities these days, and if being a celebrity was her dream, why would anyone seriously advise her against going down this path?"

Why should we care? Well, maybe it's because what happens to Kelly Clarkson is not just her private concern.

It's the concern of the rah-rah American public, or should be, because it was the public that made the 100 million or so phone calls throughout the series that helped decide the winner.

And it's the music industry's concern too, or should be, because what happens to Kelly and how she's treated are more than likely to be seen as an indelible emblem of its business practices.

Sept. 9, 2002 / 9 a.m. ET

New York's No. 1 tourist attraction: That's the way Katie Couric put it this morning on the "Today" show. Standing in front of the gaping canyon in Lower Manhattan, she pointed out that Ground Zero has become the city's "No. 1 tourist attraction," drawing more visitors than the Statue of Liberty.

Katie Couric takes a tour of the Ground Zero reconstruction effort with New York City Mayor Michael Bloomberg.

And New York Mayor Michael Bloomberg acknowledged that, while it's good the site is attracting so many visitors, "it's a little disconcerting. You don't want this place to be a spectacle."

The mayor's remark, mild as it was, seemed more than a confirmation of what Todd Hulin is protesting with his parody of an amusement park called Twin Towers over Ground Zero. It was a vindication.

But be warned: As pointed out here Friday, Hulin's satire is intended in totally bad taste.

Meanwhile, everybody's taking up the debate about the site's future, if they hadn't already. Here's a report in this morning's Washington Post.

Sept. 6, 2002 / 3:58 p.m. ET

What's wrong at Ground Zero: As we turn the corner of the weekend and head toward a national day of mourning on the first anniversary of 9/11, the media is working overtime preparing for it.

On Sunday, for instance, The New York Times Magazine will feature a long, fascinating history of the World Trade Center's twin towers and the visionary plans by a dream team of architects who were asked to "think big" about the future of Ground Zero and Lower Manhattan. You can see the history and the plans here.

What won't be in the magazine is this parody of an amusement park called Twin Towers over Ground Zero. The satire is intended in totally bad taste.

But before you jump to conclusions about its lack of patriotism,

78

intelligence or sanity — or mine, for showing it to you — consider this:

Todd Hulin, its creator, lived two blocks from the towers when they went down (and still lives there), and he's upset over "the cottage industry that has crept up around Ground Zero" — the sale of "booklets, pins, flags, postcards, and gold-plated crosses" — under false pretenses.

"Crass opportunists think of this flowering of blood-stained capitalism as a means of 'healing' and 'regenerating' the area," Hulin writes. "It is simply disrespectful and heartless ... A sense of the human tragedy and a respect for the astounding loss of life is the only souvenir anyone should take away."

The theme park is his way of protesting. Here's his complete statement.

Sept. 10, 2002 / 11:40 a.m. ET

Impassioned thoughts: The significance of tomorrow's ceremonies — at the World Trade Center site in New York, at the Pentagon and in the field near Shanksville, Pa., where United Flight 93 crashed — needs no elaboration from me.

I leave that to the prolific Argentine-born writer and playwright Ariel Dorfman, a professor at Duke University, who grew up in both the United States and Chile after his family was driven into exile by Argentine fascists during the 1940s.

His impassioned "Open Letter to America" in The Guardian begins: "Let me tell you, America, of the hopes I had for you. As the smoke was swallowing Manhattan and the buildings fell and the terror spread into the farthest recesses of your land and your hearts ...

"How could I not wish you well? You gave me ... this language of love that I return to you. You gave me the hot summer afternoons of my childhood in Queens when my starkest choice was whether to buy a Popsicle from the Good Humor Man or the fat driver of the Bungalow Bar truck. ..."

But Dorfman, who was driven into exile again — this time from Chile following the U.S.-backed coup against the democratically elected government of Salvatore Allende on Sept. 11, 1973 (of all dates to be reminded of) — has grave doubts and misgivings about America.

He asks: "Am I wrong to believe that the country that gave the world jazz and Faulkner and Eleanor Roosevelt will be able to look at itself in the cracked mirror of history and join the rest of humanity, not as a city on a separate hill, but as one more city in the shining valleys of sorrow and uncertainty and hope where we all dwell?"

I leave the elaboration to another prolific writer, Susan Sontag, who writes of "Real Battles and Empty Metaphors" in a closely reasoned article about "the war on terror" in today's Op-Ed section of The New York Times. She, too, has grave doubts and misgivings.

Mundane thoughts: Like most Americans, I had no relatives or friends who died in the 9/11 attacks. I do have friends who had relatives and relatives who had friends who died at the World Trade Center. (Many more Americans than you might suppose have similar, personal, if roundabout connections.)

And like many reporters covering those terrible events and their immediate aftermath, I spoke with people whose lives were, in some cases, devastated and irrevocably altered by 9/11. But also, like most Americans I would say, my life has gone on largely as before. I've made some adjustments, all minor.

The focus of my thoughts has changed more than my life — not a day goes by without me thinking about 9/11.

They are mundane thoughts that lead me to remembering small things: How I watched the clouds roll in one afternoon from the bar of Windows on the World a couple of decades ago, or how I had brunch at the top of the North Tower in the summer of 2000, or how small the Statue of Liberty looked in the harbor from the vantage point of my table in the sky.

Humbled by the tragedies of 9/11, all of us I hope — regardless of our views —will take time to reflect tomorrow. That is my "big" thought.

Sept. 11, 2002 / 12:01 a.m. ET
No Weblog entry today: Rest in peace.

Sept. 12, 2002 / 9:58 a.m. ET
Film critics' tiff in Toronto: Word comes that Roger Ebert had a "shocking outburst" the other day at the Toronto Film Festival. I suppose it's possible. But having spent a lot of time in the same newsroom with him, I'd say the notion of a shocking outburst from Roger is absurd.

Not that he doesn't state his opinions clearly, often with a smart retort. But Roger is not prone to outbursts. It's just not his style. He can be aggressive in pursuit of a point. If anything he is likely to make a straightforward declaration of ideas or principles, giving no quarter perhaps — but a tantrum? Doubtful.

Here's an eye-witness account of the incident in the Toronto Star: "Ebert was loud, arrogant ..."

Here's Ebert's rebuttal in the National Post: "Yankee bashers miss the point" — which, I'm happy to say (because it validates my judgment), I didn't read before putting in my own two cents.

Sept. 13, 2002 / 9:45 a.m. ET

Zevon, Reeve defiant together: It takes more than glib wit to say <u>what Warren Zevon said</u> Thursday about his terminal case of lung cancer: "I'm okay with it, but it'll be a drag if I don't make it till the next James Bond movie comes out."

It takes the sort of bracing defiance we've heard about so often since 9/11 and, before that, during the early years of the AIDS epidemic. It makes us forget the existential dread confronting us all as we go about our ordinary lives. It gives the rest of us courage the way Christopher Reeve does with his <u>battle against all odds</u> simply to breathe on his own again, let alone to walk.

What did the poet write more than a century ago?

"Long after the days and the seasons, and people and countries. ... Recovered from the old fanfares of heroism ... far from the old assassins ... Live embers, raining in gusts of frost ... fires in the rain of a wind of diamonds flung from the earth's heart eternally carbonized for us. — O world!" — Arthur Rimbaud, "Barbarian," from "Illuminations"

Courage to face the worst is the necessary password, the key that unlocks the future. Zevon and Reeve seem to have it in spades.

Sept. 16, 2002 / 8 a.m. ET

Hollywood crash course: There's a large <u>William Wyler retrospective at the Film Forum</u> in New York, celebrating his centenary for the next four weeks. I've got a vested interest, having written this three-time Oscar-winner's biography, "A Talent for Trouble." But I'll be going to the festival just to enjoy his great old flicks on a movie screen instead of on the tube.

I'm not the only one looking forward to the festival. (It runs through Oct. 10.) Here's <u>New York magazine film critic Peter Rainer</u>: "Fed up with what New Hollywood's churning out? Prepare to gorge on some of the best of Old Hollywood." The 33-film series "offers a crash course in Hollywood's Golden Age."

I'm grateful to Rainer for making the following point — an argument I made myself throughout the biography — and maybe with Rainer's influence, it will finally stick:

"Although he is one of the most honored of directors, with a record number of acting Oscars under his stewardship, Wyler's reputation has been dimmed somewhat by a generation of auteur critics who find his films insufficiently 'personal.' Hogwash."

There could not have been two more personal, impassioned films than the festival's opening double bill on Friday night: 1939's "Wuthering Heights" (starring Laurence Olivier) and 1941's "The Little Foxes" (starring Bette Davis).

I won't make the case for "Wuthering Heights" here, except to say that until you've seen it on screen, you haven't really seen it. Watching most films on TV that were made for the screen does them a disservice. But Wyler's really suffer, because they depend so much on subtleties of acting that are simply lost by the reduction of the image.

As for Wyler's adaptation of the Lillian Hellman play "The Little Foxes," it has to rank among the greatest movies ever made in Hollywood. (Nine Oscar nominations, not one Oscar.)

Hellman, who also wrote the screenplay, contended that what Wyler put on the screen was better than the original drama — and she was not someone easily satisfied. Thanks to her, the plot structure is brilliant, and it's supported by unforgettable characters, biting dialogue and a fabulous ensemble.

But it is the collaboration between Wyler's direction (particularly the staging) and Gregg Toland's "deep focus" cinematography — yes, before Toland and Orson Welles put deep focus to work in "Citizen Kane" — that makes the difference between the play and the movie.

I'd almost forgotten how magnificent Bette Davis was, her face smoldering beneath a mask of white makeup, as the central character Regina, or how impressed I was by Patricia Collinge as Birdie.

The scene in which Davis commits murder without so much as lifting a finger is widely celebrated. But Collinge's most affecting scene — when Birdie describes how she was fooled into marrying Oscar Hubbard in the belief that he loved her — is also among Hollywood's greatest moments, bar none.

Well, I'll stop with the details. If you live in New York, or you happen to be passing through, just go to the Film Forum and see for yourself what treasures Wyler left us.

Sept. 16, 2002 / 8:30 a.m. ET

The Beastie Boys' nasty tangle: Wrap your mind around this beast:

The rap group sampled renowned flutist-composer James Newton's 1978 musical work "Choir" and used it in "Pass the Mic" on their 1992 hit album "Check Your Head," which gave the group's career new life after the boys had been dismissed as parodies of themselves.

The Beastie Boys obtained permission from ECM (Newton's label at the time) but did not contact him or receive his permission, as required by law. The sample of 6 1/2 seconds — unchanged from Newton's composition — was looped in the Beastie Boys' song more than 40 times.

Newton sued. "Pass the Mic,'" which has appeared in CD, MP3, LP and DVD formats, presumably earned money for the group (it won't divulge figures) but not a dime for him. In fact, he never knew about the sampling until 2000 when a student of his showed him the track.

Newton lays out his case here.

The Beastie Boys offered to settle, but Newton says he found their offer insulting.

Last May, a federal judge ruled that his music was not original because the sample consists of just three sung notes (C, Db, C) and therefore was not protected by copyright.

The ruling ignored the sampled flute part notated in Newton's written score. (The judged used as a standard for comparison the system of notation employed in classical music).

Newton, who is a music professor — as well as a Guggenheim Fellow and the winner of Downbeat Magazine's poll for Best Jazz Flutist for the past two decades — says it's misguided to compare jazz notation with classical notation.

He says "Choir" is not classical European music but "a multiphonic composition and a modern adaptation of a spiritual" — inspired by his first musical memory of "four African American women singing à cappella in a church in rural Arkansas."

Newton has decided to appeal . His brief was to be filed Monday, but his attorney Alan Korn says a two-week extension was granted. The brief is now due Sep. 30.

Kick in the head: The Beastie Boys demanded that Newton pay them $492,000 to cover their legal fees. A court ruled against that, and they have not appealed.

Earlier, when they had made that demand, Newton was horrified: The "Beastie Boys have stolen my musical expression and now vindictively seek to punish me financially for trying to protect [my] work. ..."

He put out a plea to fellow artists to lend him support. He feared he could be bankrupted: "I stand a chance of losing my home and all that I have worked for through the years."

Pretty ugly. But it sounded about right for the well-named Beastie Boys, who were accused by critics and hip-hop musicians of "cultural theft" early in their career and of demonstrating "no significant musical talent." (Scroll to the biography and click Read More.)

Sept. 16, 2002 / 1 p.m. ET

In their own defense: Steve Marin, the publicist for the Beastie Boys, just sent me the group's statement about the item below.

"For the last year," the statement begins, "we've been involved in a difficult legal battle with James Newton, a jazz musician and composer whose work was included as one of several samples in our song 'Pass the Mic. ... we have no interest in taking advantage of anyone — least of all other musicians — and we made sure we had cleared the sample in question some 10 years ago. The sample is a flute sound — six seconds from Newton's song 'Choir' — which runs through the background of 'Pass the Mic' buried under our own live instrumentation as well as many other samples. ...

"We cleared the recording but did not clear the composition because what we used is three notes and three notes do not constitute a composition. If one could copyright the basic building blocks of music or grammar then there would be no room for making new compositions or books. ...

"As an aside, we slowed the sample down which changed the notes in question. So the notes that are in our song are not even the notes that are in Newton's recording or composition. This could be compared to paraphrasing.

"Newton is now appealing his case to a higher court to try to get the decision overturned. If he succeeds in his efforts it will be a huge blow to forms of music that involve not only sampling, but all musical quotation. ...

"Furthermore, it is our opinion that Mr. Newton's lawyers should be responsible for covering our legal fees, not Mr. Newton himself. If the judge had granted our motion they, and not Mr. Newton would have paid. In the UK when people are unjustly sued the claimant's lawyers are usually responsible for the defendant's legal fees. We wish that were the case in the US as well, because people would think more carefully before throwing such frivolous lawsuits around.

"Sincerely,

"Beastie Boys"

What I've printed here are mere excerpts from the group's statement. To read the full statement, click here.

Sept. 17, 2002 / 10:50 a.m. ET

Whatever happened to: . . . Kelly Clarkson? A couple of weeks ago, she was the toast of the nation. Such is fame.

I almost forgot, her first CD is being released today. You remember that, don't you? It features those two unforgettable songs with the unforgettable lyrics: "A Moment Like This" and "Before Your Love."

To Kelly mavens — and I'm at risk of becoming one of them if I write another word about her — this will be old news. For the rest of the nation not waiting with bated breath for her recording debut, it may be forgotten news. Today we'll get our first inkling of whether she's just toast.

In case you can't remember who she is or what she's been doing, you can find out here everything she's been doing lately. (Keep scrolling. You'll discover that "the Texas tornado is still a hot ticket.")

Oh, did I forget to mention that Kelly's debut album, originally bruited for a Nov. 26 release, has been postponed until early 2003? Sad, isn't it?

RCA pushed back the release, according to this fan report, so she could be part of the upcoming "American Idol" tour, and according to this fan report for a combination of scheduling and possible marketing reasons.

Not so incidentally, do you remember that Kelly was supposed to sing at the Lincoln Memorial in Washington on Sept. 11?

Do you remember how she and her handlers were criticized for poor taste? That the appearance would be seen as exploitative publicity?

Do you remember how Kelly, when she heard the criticism, declared that she had doubts about going forward?

Do you remember how her handlers said they would erase her doubts?

Of course they did. Kelly sang "God Bless America" and took a private tour of the White House. She did not, however, sleep in the Lincoln bedroom.

Sept. 18, 2002 / 9 a.m. ET

Here's what could happen to Kelly: "Hope, uncertainty, euphoria, disillusionment: This is a familiar career arc for pop stars caught in the manufacturing cogs of the star-making machine ..." Eric Olsen writes today in Salon's cover story.

Check it out. The title "Slaves of Celebrity" and the photo illustrating the story say it all. But the devil is in Olsen's details.

(Olsen is also the force behind Blogcritics, to my mind the blogosphere's most ambitious new site for creative commentary about pop culture.

Sept. 18, 2002 / 11:40 a.m. ET

Cuban music, si! U.S. State Department, no! How vindictive can the

Bush Administration get toward Cuba? Consider this: <u>The State Department has denied entry visas</u> to Cuban Latin Grammy nominee Chucho Valdés and 21 others, so they won't be able to attend tonight's televised Latin Grammys ceremony.

(The State Department now says it is <u>merely carrying out the law</u>, not denying visas.)

Valdés just happens to be <u>the jazz world's greatest living piano virtuoso</u>. Considering the range, technique and sheer brilliance of his sound, he's Art Tatum, Keith Jarret, Bill Evans, McCoy Tyner, Cecil Taylor, Erroll Garner and Vladimir Horowitz all rolled into one — with an irrepressible Afro-Cuban soul and a cheeky sense of humor.

Can refusing him a visa be anything other than the Bush Administration's vindictiveness toward Cuba? It was OK for Valdés to be in this country as recently as earlier this summer, where I caught him in a mesmerizing performance at the Blue Note in New York. But it's not OK for him to attend <u>the Latin Grammy Awards</u>? Sheeesh.

And now I'm wondering whether he'll be let back into the country for <u>his U.S. tour dates</u>.

Sept. 19, 2002 / 9:30 a.m. ET

Getting it wrong: There comes a point when taking offense at art reveals the presumed sensitivities of the public as a dangerous madness — narrow-minded, dictatorial and, worse, totalitarian.

Eric Fischl's bronze sculpture <u>"Tumbling Woman,"</u> which depicts a falling body in tribute to those who jumped to their death from the towers of the World Trade Center, was "abruptly draped in cloth and curtained off" this morning at Rockefeller Center because some passers-by complained it was too graphic.

Rick Gentilo - APTN / AP

A spokesman for Rockefeller Center apologized "if anyone was upset or offended" and promised that the sculpture "will be removed by this evening."

Have you ever heard of anything so craven? It's beyond belief to me, really. Is Fischl's sculpture pornographic? Salacious? Defamatory? Not for a second. Is it provocative? Only insofar as it depicts the horror of 9/11. Is it graphic? Yes. Is it personal? Yes. Is it tragic. Yes. Is it art? Absolutely.

You could say the same about Picasso's <u>"Guernica,"</u> to trot out the most obvious example, and a dozen works of art that represent the highest form of human expression.

The censorship of Fischl's work is disgraceful. By acting as cravenly as they have, the timid authorities at Rockefeller Center represent the sort of civic leadership that does the public welfare a disservice.

It is understandable that families of 9/11 victims are sensitive to the subject matter. It is understandable that they might protest. It is not understandable, at least to me, that this work must be censored because of such objections, if any, much less because of complaints by passers-by.

Not that it matters, except as a statement of intent, Fischl himself has declared: "The sculpture was not meant to hurt anybody. It was a sincere expression of deepest sympathy for the vulnerability of the human condition. Both specifically towards the victims of Sept. 11 and towards humanity in general."

Here's a look at some of Fischl's other artworks.

Whatever the critics may ultimately say about "Tumbling Woman" — that it is good, bad or indifferent as a work of art — the idea of hiding it from view is a large step backward for civilized discourse.

Sept. 20, 2002 / 10:20 a.m. ET

A Christmas gift from Rowling? Contrary to a rash of recent reports that there is "no sign" of the next Harry Potter tale, The Times of London told Potter fans to relax.

In an exclusive interview with J.K. Rowling, the newspaper reported this morning that the author was putting the finishing touches to the fifth book, "Harry Potter and the Order of the Phoenix."

The interview is either the truth or a clever publicity ploy to deflect Potter fans from fearing the worst. The fact that it just popped up so conveniently makes me suspicious. But I doubt that Rowling would out-and-out fake it.

She said the manuscript is stacked, "nice, neat, pristine and big" — as big, the paper notes, as "The Goblet of Fire," which came to 636 pages.

Will it be ready for Christmas? "Maybe," said the pregnant Rowling, who is expecting a baby next spring .

The author also denied she'd been suffering from writer's block, as rumored, and said it was up to her publisher to decide when to bring out the new book. But she also said she would resist being rushed.

Taking bets anyone? I'd bet there will be a twin birth next spring: One new Rowling child and one new Rowling novel.

Now comes another report: I guess The Times of London interview was exclusive for about five minutes. Rowling reiterated her remarks to the BBC, a bit more tentatively perhaps. "I really am getting there," she said, noting that "stress over a plagiarism case had hindered her work" on the manuscript.

Author Nancy Stouffer had claimed that Rowling stole words and characters from Stouffer's books. But a judge has ruled she did not and has fined Stouffer $50,000 for lying to the court and doctoring evidence to support her claims.

Sept. 20, 2002 / 10:50 a.m. ET

A note to readers: My staff of thousands has rebelled. When I asked it to post the deluge of e-mails that came yesterday in response to my sincere rant about "Tumbling Woman," it refused, citing child labor laws and calling me a Simon Legree.

I was further informed that if I so much as hinted at pursuing the matter, I would be reported to John Ashcroft's Justice Department and would be detained by the FBI as a threat to homeland security.

Did that deter me? Of course. So I have already spent many hours responding personally to several hundred e-mails. Please bear with me. I have 256 more replies to go.

Sept. 23, 2002 / 10:20 a.m. ET

The Matt & Katie Emmy Show: Emmys, Emmys everywhere. Katie Couric and Matt Lauer had them coming and going — on the Sunday evening pre-show and the Monday morning post-show.

The first signal that this year's Emmy Awards broadcast was going to be different from last year's was the spectacle of Couric and Lauer working the red carpet. You could have taken that as either a reduction in grade for the "Today" show co-anchors or as an elevation of the Emmy pre-show's tone. I took it as a bit of both, especially when fashion designer-turned-red-carpet greeter Isaac Mizrahi chimed in as their newfound chum.

Lauer in wrap-around sunglasses, shmoozing with Hollywood's finest under L.A.'s hot sun, seemed a premonition of what the future may hold for him in a worst-case scenario. Couric listening to "Will and Grace" Emmy nominee Debrah Messing talking about the "seminal influences" on her comic style seemed like a "Saturday Night Live" parody — only better.

Sept. 24, 2002 / 1:30 p.m. ET

On a lighter note: "American Idol" winner Kelly Clarkson's new single, "A Moment Like This," has moved up to No. 52 (from No. 60) in its second week on the Billboard Hot 100, which measures radio play. But Billboard's "chart beat" expert Fred Bronson is predicting that "Moment" will make "the biggest leap of all time to No. 1" when the complete sales data comes in. "She will be unstoppable," he writes. "She sold more singles in the first day of release than any recent single has sold in a week." (Scroll down to Kelly: Sam I Am.) But that doesn't cut the mustard for Entertainment Weekly reviewer David Browne. He calls Clarkson a second-rate diva, says her songs are dreary gimmicks, and gives the single a failing grade: D+.

Sept. 24, 2002 / 1:35 p.m. ET

Tell it to the judge: Was Yoko Ono just being disingenuous when she described John Lennon "as a member of a band called the Beatles" and "a good singer and songwriter and guitarist"?

Was best-selling French novelist Michel Houellebecq just baiting his critics when he said the Bible is packed with passages "so boring they make you want to s - - -" and that Islam is "the most stupid of all religions"?

If you're looking for provocative news of entertainment and the arts, apparently the best place to find it these days is in the courts.

On Monday, Ono was in court suing a former employee, Frederic Seaman, to keep him from selling family photos he took of Lennon when he was Lennon's assistant. It's part of a long battle.

According to New York's Daily News, Ono fired Seaman in 1981. He was later convicted of larceny for stealing Lennon's diaries but avoided jail by promising to return them. Many of the photos appeared in a 1991 tell-all book, "The Last Days of John Lennon."

Seaman's attorney defended his client: "This case is about the underside of the music business that you're not supposed to think about," he said. "It's a far cry from the idealized world of 'Imagine.'"

Houellebecq, currently on trial in Paris for incitement to religious and racial hatred, told the court that the while the Bible is boring, at least it offers some poetry — unlike the Koran, according to a report in The Independent.

Not that the 44-year-old author thinks much of Judaism or Christianity. He believes all monotheistic religions promote hatred.

Anybody who has followed Houellebecq's career won't be surprised by his opinions. The four Islamic groups that have brought charges against him for insulting their religion as "dangerous" and "stupid" may not have been surprised either. He's been saying things like that for years, even before his 1998 "sexistentialist" novel "The Elementary Particles" brought him notoriety.

Unlike Salman Rushdie, as The Independent also points out, Houellebecq is not under attack for what he has written. He's being sued for comments he made in a magazine interview. (Warning: The translation is poor.) Nor is he threatened by a fatwa, although he says he fears for his life.

The fact is, Houellebecq courts enemies the way flypaper draws flies. He's an equal-opportunity offender.

Consider this: In his new novel, "Platform," the hero (named Michel, like the author) says men and women of Western societies are incapable of emotional or physical fulfillment in their relationships. Their only logical solution? Sexual tourism in Third World countries. This is an "ideal exchange," he contends, since the Westerners have money and the Third World's young men and women "have nothing to sell but their bodies."

Could Houellebecq's next court date be at The Hague?

Sept. 25, 2002 / 10:30 a.m. ET

Book banning and other forms of freedom: Here's a twist. The American Library Association has many fewer book bannings to report than ever. Last year only 20 to 25 books were dropped from school reading lists or libraries, according to The Associated Press. That's roughly 10 percent of the estimated 200 or more that were dropped annually during the early 1980s.

But the ALA is hardly bedeviled by a lack of banned titles to mark its 21st annual "Banned Books Week" (through Saturday).

Topping this year's list is the "Harry Potter" series by J.K. Rowling, which has been attacked for promoting witchcraft to children. Many of the usual suspects are also on the top 10 list: J.D. Salinger's "The Catcher in the Rye," John Steinbeck's "Of Mice and Men" and Maya Angelou's "I Know Why the Caged Bird Sings." They've been cited for everything from offensive language to racism and sexual content.

"Unfortunately, any book can come under attack for any reason," Chris Finan, president of American Booksellers Foundation for Free Expression, said in a prepared statement. "Steinbeck's books have been deemed 'filthy' and 'profane,' while Maurice Sendak's popular 'In the Night Kitchen' has been challenged for nudity."

Other "Most Challenged" titles include "The Adventures of Huckleberry Finn" by Mark Twain, for its use of language, particularly references to race, and "It's Perfectly Normal," a sex education book by Robie Harris, for being too explicit, especially for children.

Consider: At least 42 of the top 100 novels of the 20th century, as defined by the Harvard-based Radcliffe Publishing Course, have been banning targets.

Some are the obvious ("Naked Lunch" by William S. Burroughs, "1984" by George Orwell and "Catch-22" by Joseph Heller), others less so ("The Great Gatsby" by F. Scott Fitzgerald, "The Sun Also Rises" by Ernest Hemingway and "Heart of Darkness" by Joseph Conrad).

In any case, Tom Minnery, vice president of public policy for Focus on the Family, takes a dim view of the ALA and its anti-censorship crusade.

"Nothing is 'banned,'" he told The Associated Press, but every year this organization attempts to intimidate and silence any parent, teacher or librarian who expresses concern about the age-appropriateness of sexually explicit or violent material for schoolchildren. What the ALA calls 'censorship,' most Americans would call common sense."

I will agree to disagree with Minnery, which is a polite way of saying: "Baloney." Apart from the principle involved, I can't imagine Maurice Sendak's "In the Night Kitchen," for example, doing harm to schoolchildren.

Admittedly, William Burroughs's "Naked Lunch" is hardly children's reading. But banning it takes us to the broader issue of censorship in general.

What do you think?

Sept. 26, 2002 / 9:48 a.m. ET

Dining out on movies: So now we have the Zagat Movie Guide. It rates the top 1,000 flicks of all time, and it's brought out by the same people who do the Zagat guides to restaurants.

No. 1 is "The Godfather." No. 2: "Casablanca." No. 3: "Star Wars." No. 4: "Gone With the Wind." No. 5: "The Shawshank Redemption"? Maybe Zagat should stick to restaurants. I liked "Shawshank" as much as the next guy. But in the top 10?

It makes me wonder whether I can ever trust Zagat on where to dine. If 5,338 movie fans voted on the film guide, as Zagat says, I hope they're not the same people who rate the restaurants.

Sept. 26, 2002 / 9:52 a.m. ET

Unfinished business: I stopped counting the e-mails for and against Eric Fischl's "Tumbling Woman." After tallying 235 messages saying Rockefeller Center management was right to hide the statue from view and 156 saying management was wrong, it was clear to me that counting several hundred more would not change the outcome unless I could include hanging chads.

But the majority of messages weren't simple thumbs-up or thumbs-down replies. Many people said they thought "Tumbling Woman" is a work of art but that public sensitivity was too great to display it now. Others wrote what Bev Cline, of Minerva, Ohio, wrote in her literal-minded objection: "No one jumped out of the WTC naked!"

Many comments simply repeated each other. One, though — from George Layburn of Eatontown, N.J. — was unique: "Artist's are all a bunch of weirdo's. This statue "Tumbling Woman" had as much taste as a Broadway musical production of "2 Nights in August" starring Harvey Fierstein in the role of Charles Manson." (FYI, there never was such a show.)

But my favorite message, for obvious reasons, came from Olivia Ash Turner, a high school teacher from Scott Depot, W. Va.: "Your editorial on the censoring of "Tumbling Woman" is the first intelligent piece I have found on the subject. ... I have spent hours tonight reviewing articles to share with my Art History class tomorrow.

"First, the students will view a photo of the work without any background information. ... Then the students will be told the intent of the work. The public's reaction will also be examined. Tomorrow's lesson may have the biggest impact on my students' long-term understanding of art — my goal is that they view art with an open mind and even if they don't like a piece they will be able to express their opinion in an intelligent manner."

I asked Turner to let me know what happened. Here's what she wrote back:

"It was a wonderful learning experience. ... A few of the students had already heard/seen something about [the statue], but I asked that no comments be made. Then we discussed the piece objectively — composition, medium, etc. At this point I explained the public reaction.

"Many of the [students'] comments were similar to the negative attitude of most folks. But as they talked, they soon found their feelings of horror and disgust, and comments such as 'It's unpatriotic,' changed when they recognized the artist's intent. Then when I read the negative editorials and quotes of onlookers, the students were able to look at the narrow-mindedness of the masses.

"They [the students] came to the conclusion that it IS art and the fact that it made people think IS good. Maybe it was too soon for New Yorkers to accept as an effective piece to keep us from forgetting, which we shouldn't. ...

"It received more recognition because of the fuss made about it than if the outcry [had been] minimal. We may never have heard about it otherwise.

"It is a depiction of a tragic event, like Goya's 'Third of May.' It depicts a moment in the history of inhumanity.

"Again, thank you for sharing your rational opinion, and know that there is hope in our future, if we educate our youth to THINK, not just react."

Ain't it great? I've got a job that's socially useful.

Sept. 27, 2002 / 10:40 a.m. ET

Sodom and Gomorrah! It's the best of both worlds in Manhattan, where the Museum of Sex opens Saturday. Hold back the crowds! Call out the cops! Is there a doctor in the house?

As Clyde Haberman nicely understates it this morning: "A claim is afoot in New York City that men and women were having sex as long ago as the 1910's, and maybe even further back than that."

Or put more bluntly: "Decades after New York introduced America to sadomasochism, legal condoms, gay liberation and the modern pornography industry, sex returns to midtown Manhattan tomorrow."

Sex is not the only attraction in Sin City. How about peeking in on some monumental portraits of Marilyn Monroe, Andy Warhol and others by "the world's most famous photographer" at a high-toned uptown arts palace: The Metropolitan Museum has a brand new Richard Avedon exhibit. For anyone interested in Avedonia, check out this Web site.

And that's not all. Now that six teams of internationally renowned architects and artists have been chosen to produce design plans for redeveloping the World Trade Center site, get a load of these 17 home-grown proposals — none of which are worth considering, I'd say.

Finally, a note of congratulations to Yoko Ono, who proved in court that even if you're rich and famous you're entitled to justice. (Did I really just say that?)

Sept. 29, 2002 / 1:55 p.m. ET

No sex. They're closed: The Museum of Sex didn't open on Saturday, after all. The world will have to wait a week to find out how New York City transformed lust in America. The museum had its wires crossed — that is, a spokesman told The Associated Press that "wiring on the floor" from ongoing construction posed a threat to safety: Opening postponed.

Sept. 30, 2002 / 8:40 a.m. ET

Connect the dots: I see that Jesse Jackson and Al Sharpton want "Barbershop" clipped because they don't like a couple of its dumb, demeaning remarks about civil rights icons Rosa Parks and Martin Luther King Jr. The brouhaha should help the box office of what is basically an inoffensive, heartwarming, family-friendly hit. Meanwhile, a few of the film's remarks about Rodney King, O.J. Simpson and Jackson himself are actually funny. Here's seeingblack.com editor Esther Iverem's take on "Barbershop."

I also see that my favorite jazz pianist, Chucho Valdez, and the Buena Vista Social Club, were among the star performers who put on a show in Havana for Fidel Castro and a trade delegation of patriotic Americans looking to sell their agricultural products to Cuba. Have a look at today's editorial in the Palm Beach Post.

And as we await J.K. Rowling's "Harry Potter and the Order of the Phoenix," here's a reminder of something worth recalling: Those ridiculous tales of the "Harry Potter" books turning children to Satanism started as a straight-faced spoof in The Onion, only to be taken seriously by Christian advocacy groups who demanded that the series be banned. Have a look here and here.

Sept. 30, 2002 / 8:56 a.m. ET

Bottom's up! Some people need a good stiff drink. Others like Daniel Pinchbeck — author of the just-published "Breaking Open the Head," an account of contemporary shamanism — need a good stiff psychedelic. I needed a good stiff dose of serious laughter.

"Medea" seemed out of the question. So I decided to take in a lecture at The New Yorker Festival over the weekend by film critic Anthony Lane, who is known for his appreciation of literary heavyweights such as Jane Austen, A.E. Housman and Buster Keaton, and whose new collection of writings from The New Yorker, "Nobody's Perfect," weighs in at a door-stopping couple of pounds.

I knew in advance from the usual tone of Lane's film criticism ("as if P.G. Wodehouse's Bertie Wooster had been given a sudden infusion of swift intelligence but had lost none of his charm") that serious laughter was possible. True to form, he titled his lecture: "Sex and Violence: The Odd Couple."

Lane is a thin, pale, transplanted Englishman who splits his time between New York and London. He never cracks a smile. But he has a fine-tuned sense of comic timing, and his lecture was filled with dead-pan quips and mildly subversive one-liners that I had no time to write down because I was too busy laughing.

I do recall, however, that he talked about Sandro Botticelli as "the Al Goldstein of the Rennaisance" for having painted "The Birth of Venus" — a lesser one-liner which I of course managed to record — and about the giant Mall of America, which is so vast that "it's a two-day journey" from the entrance to the dusty little bookshop beneath the rollercoaster where he recently signed copies of "Nobody's Perfect."

In the one serious moment that I can dimly remember — at least I think he was serious — Lane said: "If sex is the incarnation of pleasure, violence is the administration of pain." I have no idea why he bothered to point that out. It may have been a joke that went over my head.

Share your perspective on entertainment and the arts with Jan Herman. MSNBC is not responsible for the content of Internet links.

Jan Herman

Latest entertainment and arts news from the Web

Entries from Oct. 1 to Oct. 30, 2002
(Some links may be nonfunctional.)
Back to 'The Juice'

LATEST UPDATES

Oct. 1, 2002 / 11:35 a.m. ET

    Fortress America and the arts: The U.S. State Department's visa war against foreign performers and artists is wreaking havoc not just in high-profile places like New York and Los Angeles.

    Although the latest development involves the New York Film Festival and the denial of a visa to Iranian director Abbas Kiarostami, the acclaimed winner of the Palme d'Or at the Cannes Film Festival in 1997, there's been a wave of canceled appearances across the country.

    The Los Angeles Times reports that the Afro-Cuban All-Stars, an off-shoot of the Buena Vista Social Club, has canceled its 17-city U.S. tour. In Southern California alone, performances by artists from the Middle East, Cuba and Japan were dumped just in the last two weeks.

    Two weeks ago when the jazz world's greatest piano virtuoso Chucho Valdes was denied entry to this country to take part in the Latin Grammy Awards with 22 other Cuban nominees, I asked whether he would be let back in for his U.S. tour.

    Answer? No. If you look at his updated tour schedule, you'll see no dates through the end of this year. He had to cancel them all. If you want to hear Valdes in this country, you'll have to wait until Jan. 29, when he's scheduled to play in Philadelphia. But don't count on it even then.

    What's particularly ironic in the case of Valdes and the other Cubans is that he and fellow Cuban musicians were in Los Angeles last year on the day of the Sept. 11 attacks (to participate in the 2001 Latin Grammy Awards). When they heard what had happened, they rushed to give blood for the victims. This was reported a year ago in the Cuban newspaper Granma.

    (Because Granma is a Castro propaganda sheet, I checked around for independent confirmation. "I know they did because I drove them in a van to the hospital," Walter Lippmann, a Los Angeles resident, told me Monday.

"We had three vans full of Cubans giving blood.")

The intersection of art and politics even in the best of times is rarely a happy event. In times of international conflict, it gets much worse. Slogans like "My country right or wrong!" and "Love it or leave it!" tend to overwhelm rational discussion.

Arundhati Roy, a novelist and writer with strong political views, addresses that and many other issues in a two-part essay in the British newspaper The Guardian. "Recently," she writes, "those who have criticised the actions of the US government (myself included) have been called 'anti-American'. Anti-Americanism is in the process of being consecrated into an ideology. ...

"What does the term 'anti-American' mean? Does it mean you're anti-jazz? Or that you're opposed to free speech? That you don't delight in Toni Morrison or John Updike? That you have a quarrel with giant sequoias? Does it mean you don't admire the hundreds of thousands of American citizens who marched against nuclear weapons, or the thousands of war resisters who forced their government to withdraw from Vietnam? Does it mean that you hate all Americans?"

Roy believes the Bush administration is using "this sly conflation of America's culture, music, literature, the breathtaking physical beauty of the land, the ordinary pleasures of ordinary people with criticism of the US government's foreign policy" as "a deliberate and extremely effective strategy."

The visa war is just one more demonstration of that strategy. You'd think the U.S. government could distinguish between terrorists and artists. But apparently not.

Oct. 1, 2002 / 5:07 p.m. ET

More on Fortress America and the arts: From the e-mail I'm getting, a lot of people think it's not Bush administration policy making war on foreign artists but rather the bureaucratic Immigration and Naturalization Service.

Consider this: In early September the INS had already approved visa applications for the Afro-Cuban All-Stars for a five-week tour of North America, to begin Nov. 1, when the U.S. State Department's Interests Section in Havana refused to accept their application, thus forcing the cancellation of their 17-city tour.

"The reason they [the Interests Section] gave was a new policy that they require 12 weeks in advance of departure to the United States," says Scott Southard, president of the International Music Network, which represents the All-Stars, as well as Valdes and a roster of more than three dozen major artists. "And the reason they gave for that refusal is because of the backlog of security clearances at the FBI."

"The difficulty this poses for us," Southard told me, "is that without an application in the system we have no means by which to make an appeal to expedite the matter — because without an application in the system, there is nothing to appeal."

Forgetting the Catch-22, can the process be sped up? Yes, when it suits the people in charge.

"The cold fact is they can and they did," Southard says. A group called Orquesta Fantasia received an FBI security clearance in four weeks, following their visa application, also in early September. That was for one concert in Oshkosh, Wis. It's scheduled for this month.

What influence does Oshkosh have that the rest of the country doesn't?

Oct. 2, 2002 / 9:46 a.m. ET

Imitation is the sincerest form, etc.: My staff of thousands woke up bleary eyed this morning and urged me to sue The New York Times editorial page.

The Gray Lady has an editorial today that sums up the Bush administration's visa war on foreign artists: "The idea that the United States government is incapable of distinguishing between a potential terrorist and a renowned 62-year-old filmmaker ... is not flattering to America's intelligence capacities."

Yesterday this column said: "You'd think the U.S. government could distinguish between terrorists and artists. But apparently not."

My staff actually wondered whether the Times editorial page had hired Doris Kearns Goodwin. What can you do with staffers who just don't get it? I keep telling them editorial writers are copycats. It's their job. They look around for important, well-reported issues, repeat what they just read and tack on an opinion. Sometimes they tack on the same opinion.

So what's the big deal? You don't need a historian of Goodwin's stature to do that.

Oct. 2, 2002 / 12:01 p.m. ET

Connect the dots: We've heard of corporate graft. How about corporate graffiti? ... In Milwaukee, the city's anti-graffiti task force is fighting a Coca-Cola art contest that aims to have winning designs painted on urban walls there. The contest sends the wrong message, says the head of the task force, who adds: "I'm switching to Pepsi."

Meanwhile, the year 2002 will go down as the year of manufactured music. … Get this from The Scotsman: More than two-thirds of the No. 1 hits this year in Great Britain have been by made by artists groomed for stardom by record companies or promoted in TV pop contests. … "This year, only half a dozen 'real' artists have reached No. 1, and three of them — George Harrison, Elvis Presley and Aaliyah — are dead."

"It doesn't matter so much to the MTV generation if a band's members started as a group of friends and practised in a garage or answered an advert from a record company," says Linda Dryden, a lecturer in cultural studies at Napier University, in Edinburgh, who helped research the information.

One of the real artists who hasn't had a No. 1 hit in years: Prince is suing a fan who operates an Internet site for allegedly offering pirated recordings of his live performances ... The suit flagrantly contradicts the pop star's previous opinions on the subject of music downloading, Eric Olsen notes in Blogcritics. "No wonder even [Prince's] fans maintain a love/hate relationship with him," Olsen writes. He urges Prince to pick on someone his own size.

Finally, here's a little background on the latest in the Amiri Baraka anti-Semitism controversy and whether New Jersey's poet laureate bought into "the big lie" about 9/11.

Let's all chew on that for a while.

Oct. 3, 2002 / 11:38 a.m. ET

The goddess of film criticism: I too worshipped at her feet, especially after making her brief acquaintance at a screening and taking a crosstown cab with her to our separate destinations. I am speaking of the late Pauline Kael, film critic without equal.

Now, in a devastating review of "AFTERGLOW: A Last Conversation With Pauline Kael," which takes author Francis Davis apart for being a sycophantic interviewer, Susan Linfield reminds me of why I liked her so much.

Kael couldn't stand phoniness, whether it was "virtuous" middlebrow schmaltz with pretensions to art, like "Schindlers List," or a "dowdy" highbrow editor who tried to impose his prudery on her, like William Shawn, the former editor of The New Yorker, who basked in an aura of false modesty.

Besides Kael's shoot-from-the-hip honesty, I liked her not so much for her taste in movies but for what informed it. As Linfield writes: "She believed that a talented filmmaker could use lowbrow forms to create art but not that the ability to master such forms could ever make one an artist. In short, she was a democrat but not a populist."

In today's era of lousy Hollywood movies, which proliferate like fruit flies, that's not a bad prescription for current film critics.

Oct. 4, 2002 / 8:59 a.m. ET

Pricey but not prissy: Now that the Museum of Sex is really, really going to open — on Saturday, and with a steep admission price — the best quip comes from the Catholic League, an organization not known for quippiness.

"It'll be interesting to find out if anyone wants to pay $17 when they can get the same thing for a quarter on Eighth Avenue," league spokesman Louis Giovino told The Associated Press.

I say give the man a job writing dialogue for Tony Soprano.

Oct. 4, 2002 / 11:45 a.m. ET

Sex, sex and more sex: I had to let you know about Sara Rimer's story, which I read this morning with amusement in The New York Times. (You may need a password.)

To think that our fair colleges have been invaded by sex columnists is, well, thrilling. That's what I call entertainment. (I can't help it. I'm a sucker for sex — bad pun intended. See Pricey but not prissy below.)

College sexperts are writing about everything from sexual arousal to oral sex etiquette (the finer points) to bondage, Rimer reports.

In fact, she and the Times come late to the story. A beacon of news from rural northern California, Redding's Record Searchlight, had it t hree weeks ago via The Associated Press. Their story features the same information, the same central character — teen-age sex columnist Natalie Krinsky of The Yale Daily News — and some of the same sources. Here it is (and you won't need a password, either).

There's a certain je-ne-sais-quoi to Meghan Bainum's sex columns in The Daily Kansan, the student newspaper at the University of Kansas.

A recent sample: "In an honored, first-week-of-class tradition, let's start out the year with a little getting-to-know-you game. Instead of divulging favorite movies or pets' names, how about something a little more revealing — like magic numbers. You know, how many people you've slept with. I'll go first. My name is Meghan Bainum. My magic number, to the best of my knowledge, is 10. I also have three cats: Stella, Mogwei and Wayne."

Toto, I guess we're not in the old Kansas anymore.

Teresa Chin takes a less sublime approach in The Daily Californian, the student newspaper at UC Berkeley. In her column, "Sex on Tuesday: After the Goldrush," she begins: "Mmmmmhmmmm … ooh, oh oh oh oh yeah … mmm … yeah, yeah. YES, right there. Oh! YES YES YES YES YES! Whew! (pause) Uh, so, yeah … how 'bout them Bears?"

Why the blossoming of sex in campus newspapers? Competition. Circulation is down, partly due to the popularity of the Internet and partly due to the snooze factor of student newspapers. Sex columns have increased circulation — and better circulation makes better sex.

Oct. 7, 2002 / 8:57 a.m. ET

Britney's dilemma — do we care? My staff of thousands informs me I've been remiss. Not once since this column began have I mentioned Britney Spears, though I've overdosed on other passé pop stars like Michael Jackson and passé wannabe Kelly Clarkson.

And now I've been scooped by the Gray Lady, which deems Britney's problematic transition from teenybopper stardom to adult courtesan an issue of national and international significance. Yesterday it ran a front-page story about her imminent makeover right up there with news of terrorist plots, the debate on Iraq and a new missile shield in Israel.

The magnitude of Britney's dilemma was underscored by the lead paragraph: "[T]he pop star who brought sizzle to the schoolyard with glitter T-shirts and short shorts strode onto a Milan runway last Tuesday evening in a $23,000 rainbow-spangled gown by Donatella Versace" — which makes Bonaparte's march on Russia sound like a cakewalk.

You know what happened to Bonaparte. Well, it could happen to Britney if she's not careful: A scorched earth of humiliating flopsweat and failure.

Britney's advisers are so "dismayed to see insinuations in the tabloids that she's heading for a Mariah Carey-like breakdown" that one of her managers offered a flat denial. "She is not having a breakdown," he told the Times.

Is there an oops here? Should we care about Britney's dilemma? Does it really matter whether she makes the transition from midriff-baring teenybopper to rainbow-spangled diva? Will my staff leave me alone now?

Oct. 8, 2002 / 9:40 a.m. ET

Belly up, but not forgotten: The Internet's best index of high-brow articles on culture — Arts & Letters Daily, a place where intellect mattered — has folded, done in by the bankruptcy filing of Lingua Franca and its parent company, University Business LLC.

It was great news a couple of years ago when Lingua Franca bought Arts & Letters Daily for more than $1 million from Denis Dutton, an American ex-patriate professor of aesthetics who had created the site in New Zealand. That purchase was a bracing vote of confidence in an enterprise that thumbed its nose at political correctness and the dumbing-down of society.

Arts & Letters Daily tended heavily toward a neoconservative take on culture and ideas as a reflection of Dutton's gadfly attitude, and sometimes the site became so narrowly partisan as to stretch belief. Articles about the proofs of global warming, for example, were treated as a leftwing bugbear. But I always overlooked that bias because the site was so rich in aggregated content.

I suppose, given the economic climate of the Internet, that the end of Arts & Letters Daily should not have been surprising. But it's a sad shock just the same.

Meanwhile, Dutton and his co-editor, Tran Huu Dung, say they'll continue to supply content elsewhere, at SciTech Daily Review and at Philosophy & Literature.

Oct. 8, 2002 / 11:31 a.m. ET

Maybe someone should tell Rolling Stone: You love her not — by a margin of about 10 to 1. But Rolling Stone loves her anyway.

When it hits the stands tomorrow, Britney Spears will be featured on the cover with Shakira and Mary J. Blige as "Women Who Rock." And this morning Matt Lauer interviewed the three of them on the "Today" show.

Yesterday when I asked whether we should care about Britney, 200 e-mails came in saying she's not only over but please don't mention her again. Another 25 said they still cared about her. And 21 said things like: "You have a staff? Why?"

The answer to that question is classified.

Oct. 8, 2002 / 4:30 p.m. ET

I don't think I'm being paranoid: Without intending to, William Finnegan has clarified one of the mysteries of the U.S. government's visa war against foreign artists.

In the current New Yorker, Finnegan profiles Cuban-born, rightwing ideologue Otto Juan Reich, the current U.S. Assistant Secretary of State for Western Hemisphere Affairs. A Bush apparatchik virtually unknown to the public, Reich is "an anti-Castro fanatic" who was appointed to the post by the president over Congressional objections. He is seen by his critics not just as Bush's point man in Latin America but as something of an avenging angel.

All you have to do is read Finnegan's piece to realize why the U.S. State Department, under the guise of fulfilling the new anti-terrorism laws, has been so vindictive toward Cuban artists, making it difficult (and in some cases impossible) for them to perform in this country.

It's not unreasonable to surmise that because of Reich, the guy in charge of carrying out Latin American policy, a personal obsession with Castro has resulted in the idée fixe that Cuba must be quarantined to keep even positive influences from leaking out.

But it's not as simple as it looks. There's a fishy selectivity to the visa war. For instance, the Afro-Cuban All-Stars had to cancel their 17-city U.S. tour. And Latin Grammy-winner Chucho Valdez, the great jazz pianist, had to cancel his U.S. bookings. Yet the lesser-known Cuban Orquesta Fantasia has been allowed into the country to play a single concert this month in Oshkosh, Wis.

And now another strange development: Joaquim Pozo, a mesmerizing, little-known conga player who teaches jazz at The National School of Arts in Havana, has been allowed to bring five student players to Palo Alto, Calif., this week at the invitation of the local jazz society. Their visas came through suddenly at the last minute, says the Palo Alto Jazz Society's Ana Holmby, but only after Pozo and his band were forced to miss dates that had been booked for them at the high-profile Monterey Jazz Festival.

It sounds to me like a clever ploy: Keep out the best-known, most influential artists who might, after all, offer a positive image of Cuba on a large scale (in large venues and with CD sales to a large public); let in other artists who will draw smaller crowds in smaller venues and thus limit positive impact, while sending the message that U.S. policy is fair and generous.

The good news is that, for legislative reasons, Reich's appointment will not last beyond the end of the year.

Oct. 9, 2002 / 9:05 a.m. ET

Cuba disconnect: Getting flamed is one thing. I find it easy to ignore. Getting hate mail is another. That's harder to deal with. This morning I hit the hate-mail trifecta.

In response to the item below, Jose Miguel Lopez of Fort Myers, Fla., has accused me of being "pro communist," "a traitor to American values" and — because my name "doesn't sound like American" to him — "a descendant of Hitler's race."

It's e-mail like Lopez's that makes me wonder whether we're all just talking past each other.

Oct. 9, 2002 / 10:45 a.m. ET

Saved by Jesus and Harry: It's a rare thing to read. You almost think it's a put-on in The Onion: Jesus Christ and Harry Potter are being hailed as saviours of the economically challenged publishing industry.

"The industry depends on two young men: Jesus Christ on the one hand and Harry Potter on the other," says Dr. Hubertus Schenkel, who chairs the supervisory board of the Frankfurt Book Fair, the world's largest and most important international gathering of publishers, authors, agents, book marketers and salesmen.

It's a far cry from the familiar alarms raised by evangelical Christians who believe the Harry Potter series is an "encyclopedia of Satanism" undermining their religion with tales of wizardry, witches and warlocks.

And now a new booklet published by Churches Together in Great Britain and Ireland strikes another blow at that belief. According to Reuters, it says the Potter books "ask people to look again at the selfish material world and the presence within it of Christian values — truth, love and, supremely, self-giving and sacrifice."

"Christianity is not 'vanquished' or irrelevant," the Rt. Rev. Michael Nazir-Ali, bishop of Rochester and chairman of the group that produced the booklet, told Reuters.

What's next? A headline in The Onion saying: "Mary reincarnated as J.K. Rowling"?

Oct. 10, 2002 / 9:35 p.m. ET

You won't believe it: I didn't. A Monica Lewinsky opera is in the works. It's called "Monica in the Kremlin." Andante reports it's being written by Vitali Okorokov, "a classically trained musician who is well known to the Russian public for his pop hits."

Naturally it will be an opera buffa (comic opera). Although it's based on Lewinsky's adventures in the Clinton White House, the story has been changed. Masha Levinsonova is sent to Moscow by the CIA to seduce the Russian president with a love potion, thereby creating a scandal to divert attention from the Clinton affair.

Andante says the Russian president is named V. V. Krutin (rhymes with Putin and is derived from the word "krutoy," which means "being tough"). How clever.

The Saratov Opera, a regional company in the composer's hometown, plans to produce the opera next season at a cost of $1 million. Nobody has said whether Lewinsky or Clinton will be invited to the premiere.

Oct. 10, 2002 / 11:40 a.m. ET

Moving right along: Even if it seems slow and gradual, they're turning corners at Ground Zero like drivers at the Indianapolis Speedway.

Two weeks ago six design teams were chosen to submit plans for redeveloping the World Trade Center site and part of Lower Manhattan. Yesterday the teams learned they have much more leeway than the first designers whose uninspired plans were scrapped last July.

Instead of having to replace 11 million square feet of commercial and office space at Ground Zero, as previously required, the new teams are being asked to replace only 10 million square feet. More important, however, they will be allowed to rebuild as little as 6.5 million of that on the 16-acre site itself. The rest of the commercial space can be developed elsewhere within a 30-block area near the site.

This means the new designers are likely to be much more imaginative in the kinds of buildings they will be able to add to the Manhattan skyline and in their treatment of open space. It was the earlier, inadequate approach to both of those issues — largely due, it must be said, to the constraints placed on the first designers — that led to the July debacle.

No residential housing will be planned for the site, despite New York Mayor Michael Bloomberg's wishes, because it has been deemed "incompatible with a memorial" by the Lower Manhattan Development Corp. The LMDC is charged with surpervising rebuilding plans.

An international design competition for the memorial itself will be launched in January, with the winner to be chosen in September 2003. Where the memorial would sit on the site, however, will be decided by the current design teams. So far, it appears that the WTC "foot prints" (where the twin towers once stood) will be part of the memorial. But that could change.

As fast as things are moving now, the actual rebuilding will take at least a decade. In fact, the winning overall design for Ground Zero will be judged partly by how well it phases in construction. The idea is to create office space as needed and to keep the site as free of disruption as possible while the work goes on.

Oct. 14, 2002 / 8:30 a.m. ET

See ya later: They're letting me out to roam the world. I'll be back Oct. 21. So until then, as Nelson Algren used to say: "Never eat at a place called

Mom's," and "Never sleep with anyone whose troubles are greater than your own."

Johnny Carson (remember him?) claimed on the "Tonight" show eons ago that those words of widsom were old American sayings. But in case anybody really wants to know, it was Algren who made them up.

Oct. 22, 2002 / 11:40 a.m. ET

Back from abroad: Sometimes the temperature of the national mood may register more vigorously abroad than at home. Now may be one of those times.

How else to explain why so little notice was taken here of novelist Philip Roth's recent remarks about the United States in an interview with the French newspaper Le Figaro.

"What we are witnessing since Sept. 11," said Roth, a perennial contender for the Nobel Prize in literature, "is an orgy of national narcissism and a gratuitous victim mentality which is repugnant."

Maybe being away for a week enjoying the coffeeshops of Amsterdam and the theaters of London has dulled my senses. But when I returned Monday, the only detailed accounts of Roth's comments that I could find in English-language publications were in the British newspapers I was reading. Here's The Telegraph's.

Roth, never one to mince words, bristled at the claim that America "lost her innocence" on Sept. 11: "What innocence? From 1668 to 1865 this country had slavery, and from 1865 to 1955 was a society existing under a brutal segregation. I don't really know what these people are talking about."

President Bush scores no points with Roth either, especially not his declarations about 9/11, which "revolted" him. He takes the president for no more than a ventriloquist's dummy.

"Language is always a lie; above all, public language," Roth said. "McCarthy used a certain language to hunt communists. That which was used against Clinton is a bit more sophisticated. As for Bush, it's ventriloquists who make him speak."

Oct. 23, 2002 / 2:33 p.m. ET

Battle of the "über bitches": I'm always astonished by the sensitivity of the press, especially by the thoughtfulness of top editors who set the tone and make the decisions.

Take, for example, what Rosie O'Donnell says about Susan Toepfer, a former editor at People magazine and the New York Daily News, who was installed by the publisher Gruner+Jahr to run O'Donnell's now-defunct magazine, Rosie.

In her $125-million lawsuit against G+J, O'Donnell says Toepfer pressured her to ask Carol Burnett about the death of her daughter during an interview. O'Donnell says when she refused, Toepfer replied: "So you're just going to ignore the dead kid?"

G+J, which halted the magazine, filed a $100-million suit earlier against O'Donnell, contending that she basically killed the magazine herself when she quit her talk show and "...began to transform her public persona from the warm, fun-loving 'Queen of Nice' to a self-proclaimed 'über bitch.' "

The irony is that "über bitch" is a term for Toepfer that I've heard from reporters who've worked for her. I once worked for her and used it myself. Her alleged remark about ignoring "the dead kid" sounds typical.

Oct. 23, 2002 / 2:53 p.m. ET
The fierce beliefs of Oriana Fallaci: Now that best-selling French novelist Michel Houellebecq has been cleared of inciting racial hatred for saying Islam is "the stupidest religion," I am reminded of Oriana Fallaci's article on European anti-Semitism.

It is a singularly powerful indictment of Muslim-inspired violence that appeared last spring in Italy's leading newspaper, Corriere della Sera, and was apparently overlooked by the Muslim organizations who sued Houellebecq.

"I find it shameful," Fallaci begins, "that in Italy there should be a procession of individuals dressed as suicide bombers who spew vile abuse at Israel, hold up photographs of Israeli leaders on whose foreheads they have drawn the swastika, incite people to hate the Jews. And who, in order to see Jews once again in the extermination camps, in the gas chambers, in the ovens of Dachau and Mauthausen and Buchenwald and Bergen-Belsen et cetera, would sell their own mother to a harem."

The entire article is essential reading.

"I find it shameful," she continues, "that in France, the France of Liberty-Equality-Fraternity, they burn synagogues, terrorize Jews, profane their cemeteries. I find it shameful that the youth of Holland and Germany and Denmark flaunt the kaffiah just as Mussolini's avant garde used to flaunt the club and the fascist badge. I find it shameful that in nearly all the universities of Europe Palestinian students sponsor and nurture anti-Semitism."

Nobody, not even Houellbecq, states strong beliefs more forcefully than Fallaci (her writing drips with contempt for Yasser Arafat, whom she has interviewed at length); and few writers have shown as much courage when it comes to putting themselves on the line (you may recall that she faced down the Ayatollah Khomeni during an interview with him in his holy city of Qom). She makes Hemingway look like a piker.

Here's a good summary of Fallaci's career. And here's her latest book, "The Rage and the Pride," written in the aftermath of Sept. 11 and ending her decade-long silence. It sold a million copies in Italy, was a best-seller in France and is currently listed at No. 10 at amazon.com.

Despite the success of her book, Fallaci could never win a popularity contest in Europe — not given her fiery attack on Arafat, to say nothing of her disgust for the hidebound theocracies of the Arab world, and certainly not given her fierce defense of America.

"The truth is that America is a special place," she writes. "A country to envy, to be jealous of, for reasons that have nothing to do with wealth et cetera. It's special because it was born out of a need of the soul ... and out of the most sublime idea that Man has ever conceived: the idea of liberty, or rather of liberty married to the idea of equality."

Oct. 24, 2002 / 2:31 p.m. ET

Eminem meets Zadie Smith, or vice versa: Are writers the new pop stars? Of course not. It's the kind of question used in headlines to provoke the reader, as ArtsJournal does. But it's worth asking anyway, and today's New York Observer even provides a good story to go with it.

"They Might Be Authors," by Joe Hagan and Rebecca Traister, makes the case that young writers have a better chance of becoming rich and famous these days than young filmmakers. Their novels and short stories are, as the phrase goes, "central to the culture." Why else would a high school student buy a $25 ticket to a Dave Eggers reading without ever having cracked his books?

"The mark of this new literature," Hagan and Traister write, "is that it's accessible without being dumb. Literary, but also pop.

"When Vibe magazine recently sent British novelist Zadie Smith to L.A. to interview Eminem, the two hit it off — the rapper reportedly told Ms. Smith that he had enjoyed her award-winning 2000 debut novel 'White Teeth.' Ms. Smith was thrilled, declaring herself a huge Eminem fan.

"It's not surprising," they conclude. "She and Eminem are a perfect match for each other and for the moment. They share a signature style, a hopped-up blend of word-drunk verbal dexterity and manically inventive narratives."

Matched for each other? Why not. Shared signature style? That's taking the idea a bit too far. But Hagan and Traister make their point convincingly (except when they refer to Russian poet Yevgeny Yevtushenko as Yev Tushenko).

Meanwhile, the New York Observer also has big takeout about the upcoming National Book Awards, "Big Guns Go AWOL," pointing out that there's more interest in the books that didn't get nominated this year, especially in fiction, than those that did.

Missing from the short list: the new Donna Tartt novel "The Little Friend" (more than 10 years in the making and, to judge from MSNBC reviewer Don McLeese's critique, hyped beyond merit); Stephen L. Carter's best-selling "The Emperor of Ocean Park,"; perhaps most conspicuously absent, Jeffrey Eugenides' highly, widely, and according to McLeese, deservedly praised "Middlesex"; Alice Sebold's "The Lovely Bones" (debut fiction not only much praised but a publishing phenomenon as the best-selling novel of the year); and Jonathan Safran Foer's "Everything Is Illuminated" (a precocious first novel lauded as the work of a virtuoso stylist).

All of these AWOL titles have received huge amounts of publicity, so they should come as no surprise. I would add another, little-known title that has been overlooked: Steve Almond's "My Life in Heavy Metal," a debut collection of short stories from Grove Press that ranks as the best fiction I've read this year. Almond has a master's touch. His stories — about a generation caught in a whatever world — are sexy, touching, funny and gorgeously written.

Oct. 25, 2002 / 7:44 a.m. ET

Popping champagne: Arts & Letters Daily, widely regarded as the Internet's best index of high-brow articles on culture when it folded earlier this month, resumes publication today.

Founding editor Denis Dutton writes: "They were popping champagne in Washington when the phone rang this morning in New Zealand to inform me that The Chronicle of Higher Education was successful in its bid to extract Arts & Letters Daily from the bankruptcy court in New York. A little early in the day here for champagne, but the news seemed to make my coffee taste better than ever."

On behalf of my staff of thousands, I say hooray and welcome back!

Oct. 25, 2002 / 10:21 a.m. ET

Underrated but not forgotten: Wayne Robins writes that it was good to see Nelson Algren mentioned here a few days back. (See below.) He notes that Algren is "one of the most underrated American writers of the 20th century — and I'm not even from Chicago."

Robins also reminds me that I left out "the middle eight bars of Algren's troika of wisdom." What Algren actually said was: "Never eat at a place called Mom's. Never play cards with a guy named Doc. And never sleep with anyone whose troubles are greater than your own."

Oct. 25, 2002 / 10:23 a.m. ET

The feds peering over your shoulder: Can the FBI snoop into what you read? Is the sky blue?

But the question has changed. Now, Eric Olsen reminds me, four advocacy groups for citizens' rights want to know "how much the government has been snooping into people's reading habits." To find out, they've filed a request with the U.S. Department of Justice under the Freedom of Information Act.

Surveillance powers granted by the Patriot Act mean "the FBI can walk into any bookstore or library with a search warrant, demand sales or lending records for anyone suspected of 'international terrorism' or 'clandestine activities,' " Olsen writes. "The employee has no recourse but to turn the records over, then cannot discuss this activity with anyone other than his/her attorney."

(Come to think of it, wouldn't a terrorist smart enough to read stop the money trail cold by paying cash?)

For all the details read Olsen. He ought to get a medal for his watchdog service. But don't let Attorney General John Ashcraft know I said that. Under the Patriot Act, it may not even be safe to mention him.

Oct. 25, 2002 / 7:55 p.m. ET

Fallaci's rage and pride: A couple of days ago I pointed out Oriana Fallaci's singularly powerful indictment of Muslim-inspired violence that appeared in Italy's leading newspaper, Corriere della Sera.

I also wrote that her comments in the article — later expanded into her best-selling book "The Rage and the Pride" — apparently had been overlooked by Muslim organizations eager to silence critics of Islam.

In fact, Fallaci was taken to court for hate speech, according to The Weekly Standard.

I stand corrected.

On the basis of one sentence — "The sons of Allah are breeding like rats" — a fundamentalist Muslim group called the Movement against Racism and for the Friendship of Peoples tried to have her book banned, the

110

Standard reported in July. The Islamic Center of Geneva also called for banning it. Other groups "sought merely to require a warning label on the front cover."

Now comes David Harsanyi's review of "The Rage and the Pride." He describes the book as "a biting polemic against anti-Americanism, political correctness, and Islam's 'reverse crusade'," and notes that with its publication Fallaci "has managed to become a pariah in European intellectual circles."

I stand confirmed.

As I wrote, "Despite the success of her book, Fallaci could never win a popularity contest in Europe — not given her fiery attack on Arafat, to say nothing of her disgust for the hidebound theocracies of the Arab world, and certainly not given her fierce defense of America."

A final note: Fallaci, 72, has been ill with cancer. Let us hope she wins that battle not just for her sake but our own

Oct. 28, 2002 / 8:49 a.m. ET

He's sorry he tumbled: Eric Fischl, the artist who made "Tumbling Woman" regrets that he didn't put up a fight when his bronze sculpture was removed from Rockefeller Center.

Rick Gentilo - APTN / AP

You may recall that six weeks ago the sculpture was first draped, then taken away, because of complaints that it was too graphic and that to exhibit it in a public space was insensitive to the victims' families and to ordinary passers-by.

(I received a ton of e-mail at the time, after I wrote that its removal was craven and disgraceful.)

In Sunday's New York Times Magazine, Fischl was asked: "Given the outcry, would you have done things differently?"

"I wouldn't have made the sculpture differently at all," he said. "I ... regret caving in to Rockefeller Center so fast and saying: 'Yeah, take it away. I don't want to hurt anybody.' I'm sorry I didn't raise a stink over it. I hate this idea that there are some people who have a right to express their suffering and others who don't, that there are those in the hierarchy of pain who own it more than you do."

Oct. 28, 2002 / 11:36 a.m. ET

Gore Vidal and the 'Bush junta': What kind of vitamins is Gore Vidal taking? He has always been a maverick, a patrician-born traitor to the ruling class. But now, in his old age, he has outdone himself.

The 77-year-old writer has leveled a 7,000-word attack against President Bush and U.S. policy —called, provocatively, <u>"The Enemy Within"</u> — that defies even Vidal's long track record as an armed and semi-dangerous gadfly.

The Guardian Unlimited reports that in "calling for an investigation into the events of 9/11 to discover whether the Bush administration deliberately chose not to act on warnings of Al-Qaeda's plans," Vidal argues that "a 'Bush junta' used the terrorist attacks as a pretext to enact a pre-existing agenda to invade Afghanistan and crack down on civil liberties at home."

Vidal's piece is not online, due to rights problems. But the Guardian notes: "At the heart of the essay are questions about the events of 9/11 itself and the two hours after the planes were hijacked." Vidal writes that "astonished military experts cannot fathom why the government's 'automatic standard order of procedure in the event of a hijacking' was not followed" — the implication being that the omission was deliberate and not a snafu.

Vidal contends, according to the Gua that these procedures require fighter planes to be sent aloft automatically "as soon as a plane has deviated from its flight plan," without the need for a presidential order. But on Sept. 11, "no decision to start launching planes was taken until 9:40 a.m, 80 minutes after air controllers first knew that Flight 11 had been hijacked and 50 minutes after the first plane had struck the North Tower."

"By law," Vidal writes, "the fighters should have been up at around 8:15. If they had, all the hijacked planes might have been diverted" — and if necessary — "shot down" by a presidential order.

Vidal maintains that 9/11 called into question not only "much of our fragile Bill of Rights" but also "our once-envied system of government which had taken a mortal blow the previous year when the Supreme Court did a little dance in 5/4 time and replaced a popularly elected President with the oil and gas Bush-Cheney junta." The real motive for the Afghanistan war in Vidal's view, according to the Guardian, "was to control the gateway to Eurasia and Central Asia's energy riches."

Depending on your point of view, Vidal's attack is either bold or paranoid. But whichever it is, how come we have two of America's most prominent men of letters leading the attack on Bush? Last week we had <u>Philip Roth calling Bush a ventriloquist's dummy</u>. Now we have Vidal accusing him of worse. (Let's not even mention MIT's Noam Chomsky, a linguist but no belletrist.)

After seeing "The Trial of Henry Kissinger" — a polemical film based on Christopher Hitchens' book calling Kissinger a war criminal — I'd bet that somebody must already be working on "The Trial of George W. Bush."

Oct. 29, 2002 / 11:36 a.m. ET

For and against 9/11 conspiracy theory: Robyn Ess must have read my mind. She messaged from Townsville, Queensland, Australia: "Be interesting to know the statistics on those who share [Gore] Vidal's skepticism and those who don't."

My staff of thousands was as surprised as I was by the results. We figured — given President Bush's personal popularity in the polls — we'd see a landslide expressing doubts about Vidal's 9/11 "Bush junta" conspiracy theory. Boy, were we wrong.

The response was evenly divided. Of 252 e-mails, 125 said Vidal was either nuts or unpatriotic or both, while 114 said he was sane and performing a valuable public service (13 e-mails were neutral).

Here's a sample, representing both the tenor and logic of the opinions pro and con:

Glenn Stewart
Seattle
That we were asleep at the wheel on 9/11 does not mean there was a conspiracy. I love Vidal's work as a novelist — he's the best historical novelist we have — but let's face it, he's always been a little nutty. Geoge Bush, et al, couldn't organize a decent church picnic, and now we should divert ourselves from the fact that we simply elect not-so-smart people — to conspiracy theories — gimme a break.

Chuck K
Tucson
Although I am very skeptical of anything that smacks of conspiracy theory (until now that is), Mr. Bush and his junta have given me more cause for fear than even Nixon and Johnson during Viet Nam. With Mr. Ashcroft having set the tone "everyone who questions our motives is unpatriotic," the whole headlong rush to war and the nuclear abyss seems to be an unstoppable madness. The Bush junta is the most terrifying specter in my 53 years.

113

Joy Powell
Chickamauga
Vidal needs to join Alec Baldwin, Woody Harrelson, Barbra Streisand, & Susan Sarandon and form a cult and MOVE OUT OF THE USA! We don't need loud mouth do-nothings like them living here. If you don't like it, leave it! They only want publicity. That is the only way an old has-been like Vidal can get publicity!

Steven James
Houston
I have little faith in our President Select and his Privy Council. I do not believe they are acting in the best interests of the citizenry nor are their ties to the petrochemical industry completely innocent ones. Big business has raped the world and now is about to rape the public and steal our precious civil liberties. Is Mr. Gore a paranoid? I think not.

Rick Griffin
Costa Mesa, Calif.
To think our own president approved of an attack against his own country. What planet are you from? George Bush may not be the "most popular" president but he is by far a gladiator for our country and our way of life.

Tony P.
Fountain Valley, Calif.
Bold or paranoid? You forgot stupid. I bet George W. also built a time machine and killed JFK. At least those of us in the middle can rest assured that the right wing hasn't cornered the market on blindly partisan whining.

Donna
Apple Valley
The Supreme Court did us an injustice when they put Bush and Cheney in office, and I for one would like to see Bush and Cheney hauled away in chains, for what they are doing, and have done to the American people — and for what they did to Afganistan. They are in the thick of 9/11.

Beverly Buckner
Nashville, Tenn.
Thank you, Gore Vidal, for voicing what many of us have known for some time. I think Watergate will pale in comparison to what will come of out of this administration.

Roger B. Nash

Monument , Colo.

I am a retired Air Force Colonel, 24 years on active duty, former F-15 pilot. Vidal doesn't know what he is talking about. He is misinformed, obviously doesn't want the facts to get in the way of his story. ... Why give him any credibility by repeating his ridculous contentions?

Louis P. Vaira

Ayer, Mass.

Being a former military professional I have wondered for a long time why the Bushies did not give the order to launch our fighter jets to protect the airways after the flights were diverted. I think that Bush knew a lot more than is being told and ... that to do nothing and let this happen would certainly boost his standings with the American people. He has used this war to his advantage and the advantage of the Republican party and it shows that he has no shame . . .

Brandi Antram

Edgewood, Wash.

The reason we have these so-called "prominent" writers leading the attack on President Bush is because they are a bunch of bleeding-heart liberals who are so blinded by their own corrupt ideas they can't see someone of pure intentions. I thank God that Bush was Commander in Chief on 9/11, because the Lord knows if Clinton had still been in the White House, America would have been defeated.

Maggie Sinclair

Salem, N.H.

Gore Vidal knows more about the history of this nation — and how that history was made — than both Bush [mis]administrations combined. Vidal writes what he knows to be true — nothing more, nothing less . . . and I believe that history, if humanity has a future, will prove each of his carefully crafted points.

Herb Hays

Fort Worth Texas

A year ago I would have laughed at Mr. Vidal, but now, watching how the Bush Reich operates, I am afraid I agree.

Oct. 30, 2002 / 10:46 a.m. ET

Putting the boo! in books: Forget Hollywood fright flicks like "Psycho" or "Frankenstein" or "A Nightmare on Elm Street." With Halloween upon us, Book magazine has come up with a handful of "scariest" books and characters to frighten the bejesus out of anyone who still reads.

The No. 1 "scariest character in fiction"? Roderick and Madeline Usher, the twins in Edgar Allen Poe's "The Fall of the House of Usher." But Mary Shelley's lonely Frankenstein doesn't make the list, his batteries apparently weakened by too many Hollywood spoofs, and neither does Stephen King's spooky Buick 8.

Other characters who rate: Arthur "Boo" Radley in "To Kill a Mockingbird"; Bertha Mason in "Jane Eyre"; The Big Bad Wolf, Count Dracula, Hannibal Lecter, Lady Macbeth in Shakespeare's "Macbeth," Lestat from the Anne Rice books; Mr. Hyde, Dr. Jekyll's alter ego, and — just to prove that Book magazine editors read more fright fiction than the rest of us — the Narrator in Charlotte Perkins Gilman's 1892 short story "The Yellow Wallpaper."

King's "The Shining" does make the list as the "No. 1 scariest novel," and "Frankenstein" ranks in the top 10, along with Michael Chricton's "Jurassic Park," Kafka's "The Trial" and H.G. Wells's "The War of the Worlds."

Which reminds me: Syndicated talk-radio host Glenn Beck will broadcast "War of the Worlds" tonight, in an ambitious recreation of the original Orson Welles radio drama that scared the bejesus out of the nation on Halloween Eve in 1938 with its threat of invading Martians.

Beck sees scary parallels between then and now. In 1938, Adolf Hitler and his storm troopers menaced Europe. Now Americans are bracing for potential attacks by al Qaeda (and a possible war against Saddam Hussein's Iraq).

"The Martians are al Qaeda," Beck told Reuters. "It is absolutely a parable of what we're living through today." He cites Welles' introduction to "War of the Worlds," which described how "intellects vast, cool and unsympathetic regarded this Earth with envious eyes and slowly and surely drew their plans against us."

The broadcast will air on 100 stations nationwide Wednesday 8 p.m. ET and on satellite radio from the XM Satellite Radio Studios in Washington.

Share your perspective on entertainment and the arts with Jan Herman. MSNBC is not responsible for the content of Internet links.

Entries from Nov. 1 to Nov. 27, 2002
(Some links may be nonfunctional.)
<u>Back to 'The Juice'</u>

LATEST UPDATES

Nov. 1, 2002 / 1:32 p.m. ET

Boos for Al Pacino and Madonna: You'd think nobody could come up with nastier things to say about a star's performance than the recent negative notices for Madonna in "Swept Away." (<u>"Starkly amateurish,"</u> Newsweek said, and that was being kind.)

But then you may not have read the New York Observer theater critic on Al Pacino's star turn in "The Resistible Rise of Arturo Ui," a star-studded revival of Bertolt Brecht's 1941 satire on the rise of Hitler, which just happens to be the hottest theater ticket in New York — at $100 a pop.

John Heilpern is <u>asking audiences to stand up and boo the Great Shouter right off the stage</u> — along with everyone else in a show that includes John Goodman, Steve Buscemi, Tony Randall Billy Crudup, Charles Durning, Paul Giamatti and Chazz Palminteri.

"I don't mean Mr. Pacino alone, though he's bad enough," Heilpern writes. "I mean everything about this gleefully foolish, patronizing, un-Brechtian, irredeemably rotten three-hour production. ... There comes a time when the sound of lusty boos would be more than music to the ears. It would be a sign that theater audiences are actually alive and kicking."

Gee, do you think he didn't like the show?

Meanwhile, Britain's most prolific playwright, Alan Ayckbourne, says he can't stand Madonna on stage. Her recent star turn in David Williamson's "Up for Grabs" in London's West End was so bad and so "inaudible," Ayckbourne complained the other day, that <u>"she should have been regarded as a silent exhibit rather than an actor,"</u> as The Independent put it.

Maybe Madonna should be taking shouting lessons from Pacino?

Just for the record: When Ben Brantley reviewed "Arturo Ui" in The New York Times, he called Pacino's star turn <u>"the performance of his</u>

career" — not because it's his best but because he "sometimes seems to be channeling most of his more celebrated roles ... as if his entire professional life were passing before your eyes ..."

Ordinarily, this would imply a negative reaction. But Brantley actually liked the pastiche, calling it "a series of juicy, iconographic acting bites" — part monster drug lord in "Scarface," part mafia capo in "The Godfather" films, part evil attorney in "The Devil's Advocate" and, of course, part hunchback title role of "Richard III," which Pacino did in excerpted bits in "Searching for Richard."

Variety's Christopher Isherwood liked the Great Shouter, too. He wrote that the role "may just be Pacino's sleaziest gangster yet. Stooped and hollow-eyed, skulking around the stage in a soiled tanktop and garish plaid pants as he brays out orders in a high-pitched whine, Pacino's Ui suggests a mangy hyena with mild mental retardation. The effect is amusing and distinctly repellent —- and, despite its noxiousness, irresistibly watchable."

Can't wait. A distinctly repellent mangy hyena à la Pacino is my cup of tea. It sounds like a great new Starbucks drink: "Gimme a mangy hyena à la Pacino — and hold the whipped cream." (My staff of thousands is nodding its many heads in agreement. But they'll agree to anything, and come to think of it they also loved "Swept Away.")

Nov. 3, 2002 / 12: 46 p.m. ET
Doing the foursquare "crawfish": Though it sometimes gives me pleasure to thumb my nose at The New York Times for its loftiness, the Gray Lady's importance cannot be denied.

On Saturday, for instance, a news article devoid of opinion appeared under this headline: "How a Deal Creating an Independent Commission on Sept. 11 Came Undone." (If that link doesn't work, try this one.)

The article is striking confirmation of at least some of Gore Vidal's contentions about the so-called "Bush junta" — namely that, while engaging in classic Orwellian-speak tactics, the administration has done everything it can to obstruct an independent investigation into 9/11 like those that looked into the attacks on Pearl Harbor and the assassination of President Kennedy.

"Although the White House denies thwarting approval of a commission," Carl Hulse reported, "an almost completed Congressional deal was suddenly undone in October after a Republican lawmaker involved in the final negotiations received a call from Vice President Dick Cheney."

Hulse recaps how the White House at first tried to could block any investigation whatsoever. But when it couldn't, it agreed to a joint inquiry

118

by House and Senate intelligence committees that would be "more manageable," according to Congressional Republications, "because much of it would be conducted in secret and Republican lawmakers would share in lead roles."

The joint committee surprised the White House, however, by conducting "an aggressive inquiry that uncovered previously undisclosed warnings of the attacks." This led to the call for a broader, independent investigation. Finally on Oct. 10, it seemed Senate and House negotiators had hashed out an agreement on an independent commission and were about to put their stamp on it with a final vote.

Just as "negotiators headed for the cameras of the Senate television gallery" to make their announcement, however, the Florida Republican congressman who chaired the negotiations — Rep. Porter J. Goss, who heads the House Intelligence Committee — "went back to his office instead, and by the time he got there the phone was ringing."

The next thing the negotiatiors knew, Goss put the kibosh on the deal. Sorry, he told them, he wouldn't allow a vote. "A lot of us were shocked," Sen. Richard C. Shelby, the senior Republican on the Senate Intelligence Committee, told the Times.

Goss, if you can believe him, said he was not instructed to block the panel. "Rather," the Times reported, "he said he was simply encouraged to keep negotiating." What's more, he said "it was 'flat-out untrue' that the White House had asked him to derail the deal reached earlier in the day."

If you can't believe Goss, surely you can believe White House spokesman Ari Fleischer. "Mr. Fleischer said Mr. Cheney had called only to push to keep the negotiations progressing," according to the Times. Indeed, "the administration is foursquare behind the commission," Fleischer said, "and we are working very hard to make it happen."

Uh huh.

As it was put to the Times by Sen. Bob Graham, the Florida Democrat who heads the Senate Intelligence Committee: "There is a pattern of this White House announcing its support for a general principle, whether it be prescription drug coverage or No Child Left Behind. Then, when it comes down to the actual realization of that goal, they — to use the president's term — crawfish."

Or as Vidal put it: "11 September, it is plain, is never going to be investigated if Bush has anything to say about it."

Nov. 4, 2002 / 8: 28 a.m. ET

Politics and the arts: Tomorrow is Election Day, which makes it a good moment to answer readers who have asked why a Weblog column about arts and entertainment, and cultural news in general, often veers into political issues like:

Gore Vidal's contention that a "Bush junta" was complicit in the events of 9/11, or Oriana Fallaci's anger about the connection between Muslim fundamentalism and European anti-Semitism, or Philip Roth's claim that the United States is in the narcissistic grip of a post-9/11 victim mentality.

The answer is not complicated, although there are many factors. Chief among them, as the great black poet Langston Hughes has argued, is that artists and writers are obligated by their talent to engage the world, not to beautify reality by ignoring it.

To quote from Hughes' 1953 testimony, when he was hauled before Sen. Joseph McCarthy's House Committee on Un-American Activities, as reported in Saturday's Guardian:

"Poets who write mostly about love, roses and moonlight, sunsets and snow must lead a very quiet life — seldom does their poetry get them into difficulties."

Unlike Vidal, Fallaci and Roth.

"Words have been used too much to make people doubt and fear," Hughes said. "Words must now be used to make people believe and do. Writers who have the power to use words in terms of belief and action are responsible to that power not to make people believe in the wrong things."

Like Vidal, Fallaci and Roth.

In 1938, Hughes put his belief this way in a famous poem: "O, let my land be a land where Liberty / Is crowned with no false patriotic wreath ..."

Now, go out tomorrow and vote.

Nov. 4, 2002 / 11:13 a.m. ET

Eminem, man of the moment: If he's not, I don't know who is. This morning's "Today" show had him on. Both the current Entertainment Weekly and Sunday's New York Times magazine put him on their covers. And that's just the leading edge of the flackery.

For ET he's posing like a macho boxer, showing off his tattoos. For the Times he's posing like a sad choirboy, looking so angelic. Everyone loves Eminem. He's such a sweetheart.

But which is the real Eminem? Everyone wants to know. You'll never find out from the interviews in either magazine, both of which read like studio advertisements for his new flick "8 Mile."

Frank Rich, the Times' former "butcher of Broadway" once feared for his take-no-prisoners theater criticism, wrote a mash note: "We were meeting on the afternoon of the MTV Video Music Awards, in a Midtown hotel under semi-siege by those underemployed fans who always manage to find out where their icons are holed up. I was there as a sort-of fan myself. I've been fascinated by him ever since I first heard his songs at the inception of his notoriety."

Rich, who I'd say is one overemployed fan, writes up the usual Eminem blueprint: Broken home, Detroit trailer trash, nasty lyrics, hates homosexuals, insults his mother, ugly divorce, gun charges, but boy, he loves his daughter, loves the 'hood, spreads his mightiness to the suburbs, and now he's got it together, he's even OK with gays, but he's risking it all because maybe Hollywood's a trap and what if he doesn't cross over to screen stardom, maybe the 'hood will drop him and the recording industry will really tank, so stay tuned, etc.

Nobody expects a probing profile or a tough line of questioning from Entertainment Weekly. True to form, here's how the magazine's Daniel Fierman begins: "Hey, man. I know your time is valuable. So I hope you don't mind if I jump right in." Eminem doesn't mind at all. "Wow," he says to his publicist. "Why can't you be more appreciative like that?"

In fact, Eminem doesn't seem to be a good interview subject. He's not talkative, and when he is, he doesn't say much, apparently preferring to put what he has to say into his lyrics. I gleaned more revealing information and less boilerplate about him from a story by The Associated Press, which didn't interview him or the usual suspects.

AP quotes unexpected sources like Stephen King; Randy Newman, who calls Eminem a "kindred spirit"; writer Paul Slansky (a self-described middle-aged white guy, who wrote a piece last June titled, "Guess Who Thinks Eminem's a Genius? Middle-Aged Me"); and Janet Maslin, who spent time on the set of "8 Mile" and talks about "the curiosity factor" that will draw non-fans to the flick. Will you be going? Let me know.

Nov. 5, 2002 / 12:48 p.m. ET

A word to the wise: Pete Townshend, who proves to be a thoughtful critic and a first-class writer, begins his review of Kurt Cobain's "Journals" with a trenchant quote from the suicided grunge star: "I hope I die before I become Pete Townshend."

"Why?" Townshend asks. "Because I had become a bore? Because I had failed to die young? Because I had become conventional? Or, simply because I had become old?"

In the early '90s, Townshend points out, "when Kurt was struggling with himself over whether or not to do an interview with Rolling Stone magazine, I was not boring, neither old nor young, and I was not dead. I was, unlike Cobain, hardened. Tempered, beaten and subjugated by all that rock had delivered to me and via me over 30 years."

He regards Cobain's "Journals" as "the scribblings of a crazed and depressed drug-addict in the midst of what those of us who have been through drug rehab describe as 'stinking thinking'. That is, the resentful, childish, petulant and selfish desire to accuse, blame and berate the world for all its wrongs, to wish to escape, or overcome and, finally, to take no responsibility for any part of the ultimate downfall. Me? An expert? Of course. Been there, done that."

Even so, he says he mourns for Cobain and he believes the "Journals" is necessary reading, if only to see what "monumental damage" the human spirit — great talent notwithstanding — can inflict upon itself.

Eminem, who says he's turned his life around — distancing himself from the violence and gay baiting and nastiness toward women that he's shown in the past — might consider pinning Townshend's word to the wise on his bulletin board.

Nov. 5, 2002 / 12:59 p.m. ET
  Eminem as Shakespeare's Prince Hal? Early word on Eminem's "8 Mile" has some critics dilating and giving birth to raves. New York magazine's Peter Rainer calls it "one of the year's sweetest joy rides." And in The New Yorker, which aims for a tonier readership, David Denby puts a Shakespearean spin on Eminem's role in the flick.

Denby writes: "The master myth here may be derived less from pop culture than from 'Henry IV, Part I.' Jimmy is Prince Hal, a king in waiting, roistering among low company, a brawler who will eventually show his true colors. He rejects many of his friends — the movie ends in a series of renunciations — because he's headed for better things."

Whew! That's Shakespeare's Prince Hal to the letter. If it in fact applies to Eminem's Jimmy, then Detroit's Great White Rapper has turned the world upside down. I for one doubt that Eminem has ever heard of Prince Hal, let alone read the play. (OK, he's reportedly a person who reads. I still doubt that he's read "Henry IV, Part I." I'd bet only English lit majors and actors have.)

The Great White Rapper himself says: "One thing I want this movie to get across is that people who live in this world of hip-hop — how seriously we take this, how seriously we take our music and battling and the sport of it and the competition and everything."

Really, really. But it's worth remembering that for all Eminem's earnestness rap rivalries are basically marketing tools.

"Top rappers and executives, including Jay Z, Nas, Snoop Doggy Dog, Eminem and Jermaine Dupri, have advanced their careers through battles of insult," John Leland wrote the other day in the most informative article on rap rivalries that I've read. "Some of the talk is dazzlingly clever, much of it inflammatory, and all of it disseminated and promoted through the record companies. Much of the beef, or animosity, is purely promotional. ... Feuds create publicity at little or no expense."

Some feuds are as real as their dead victims. Witness Tupac Shakur (gunned down in 1996 in Las Vegas) and the Notorious B.I.G. (Christopher Wallace, aka Biggie Smalls, shot and killed in Los Angeles in 1997) — to name the best-known gangsta rappers and the most infamous rivalry.

But one New York City detective investigating the recent killing of Jam Master Jay, the DJ of Run-DMC, points out that a lot of so-called feuds are mere hype, like the one between Jay-Z and Nas: "If you listen to the songs they sing, you would think Jay-Z and Nas hate each other, but they hang with each other. I've talked to them both; they have no beef with each other."

Meanwhile, anybody who thinks rap stars are minting money for themselves doesn't know the half of it.

A music-industry accountant, whose clients include Run-DMC and Madonna said, in Leland's paraphrase, that "it's common for a performer with an album generating $17 million in sales to wind up with as little as $70,000 before taxes" and that "performers who make a 500,000-copy gold album might end up with more money working for UPS.

Yes Virginia — it's a hard, cold, peculiar, capitalist world out there.

Nov. 6, 2002 / 11:32 a.m. ET

Is the FBI bugging you? Now that the mid-term election has guaranteed the Bush administration's legislative power with a takeover of the Senate and continued control of the House, can we expect more snooping into our reading habits from U.S. Attorney General John Ashcroft's Justice Department?

The last time I brought up the issue, (see The feds peering over your shoulder), some readers wondered whether I was paranoid or just plain dumb. My staff of thousands is both, I assured them, but that doesn't deter me from pointing out the righteousness of my concern.

Now for anyone who thinks I'm trying to demonize the attorney general, oh please. Ashcroft is doing nothing that others haven't done before him. You remember J. Edgar Hoover, nyet? In the bad old days of the Cold War, Hoover was FBI snooper in chief, and he was always going after U.S. citizens he deemed threats to national security. Here's a little reminder from the Boston Globe, "Irving Howe's Excellent FBI Adventure." You remember Howe, no? He was a dangerous literary critic.

Nov. 7, 2002 / 11:03 a.m. ET

Sequels for Winona Ryder: Now that the Tinseltown trial of the 21st century has ended, the conviction of Winona Ryder on grand theft and vandalism charges has spawned a Hollywood consensus that "with the passage of time, and a dash of contrition, the two-time Oscar nominee is likely to be forgiven, embraced and welcomed back to the big screen despite her criminal record."

We can see it now. Courtesy of my MSNBC colleague Gael Fashingbauer Cooper, here are some movie sequels she might be offered: "Girl, Convicted," "Age of Innocence II: The Frame-Up," "Little Women Who Steal," "Atoning for Your Mr. Deeds" and "Reality Really, Really Bites."

Who would have thought it would come to this? (Certainly not her fans.)

In the late '60s, not long before Ryder was born, I used to visit her father, Michael Horowitz, in a tiny corner office in San Francisco's North Beach. He was a rare book dealer with a scholar's interest in psychedelic literature and the sweet disposition of a gentleman. Despite being part of Timothy Leary's circle, chiefly as an archivist of the LSD guru's papers, Horowitz was the last person one would have associated with the celebrity fast lane or the dubious glamour of Hollywood.

Traipsing down memory lane like this is an indulgence, I know. But I'm sure if I ran into Horowitz again today he would be the same kind, scholarly gentleman he was then. I suppose stranger things have happened, yet I can't think of a more unlikely life scenario than his.

Nov. 7, 2002 / 11:32 a.m. ET

Correction: Bill Olds, whose Nov. 3 column in the Hartford Courant I cited yesterday, now says he was wrong: The FBI did not — repeat, did not — install software to monitor reading habits and Internet activity at the Hartford Public Library, as he had claimed.

I regret my error in citing and repeating wrong information. So as not to continue disseminating it, I have trimmed back my quotations from Olds' column and killed the link to it. But I have left the rest of the item intact.

Nov. 8, 2002 / 11:36 a.m. ET

Election fallout at Ground Zero: Fallout from this week's midterm elections has already begun to affect redevelopment plans for Ground Zero. New York Gov. George Pataki, who kept a low profile in the process before the election, is said to be seeking big changes in the leadership of the Lower Manhattan Development Corp. The LMDC is the agency charged with overseeing the redevelopment.

Pataki reportedly avoided the process before the election, because it was controversial and anything he said might have backfired. But now that his third term as governor is guaranteed, Edward Wyatt reports in this morning's New York Times, his advisors want him to push for the resignation of LMDC chairman John C. Whitehead. Meanwhile, Whitehead wants to keep the job.

Pataki spokesman, Michael McKeon, his director of communications, did not return a phone call to confirm the report. But LMDC spokesman Matthew Higgins told The Juice: "Mr. Whitehead is committed to fulfilling his job." And Whitehead's spokesman, Ed Dovatny, said: "Only Mr. Whitehead can speak for himself, but the comment in the Times is accurate."

"I have no plans to quit, and I have no desire to be relieved of my responsibilites," Whitehead told Wyatt, who notes that when the LMDC was created a year ago, Pataki appointed Whitehead because of his Wall Street-cum-Washington connections and his political independence.

On Wednesday, moreover, Newsweek reported that LMDC president Lou Tomson might leave before the year is out.

What does it all mean? Possibly speeding up the process. Possibly separating plans for redevelopment and for creation of a memorial. But whatever happens, "the work product" of the six architectural teams now putting together their urban designs for Ground Zero and the surrounding area will be released to the public "probably in the second week of December," Higgins said.

"They will take those plans forward, making the chosen three [finalists] public in January," he said.

Meanwhile, the grass-roots memorial on the fence at St. Paul's Chapel across the street from Ground Zero is being taken down day by day.

Nov. 8, 2002 / 1:43 p.m. ET

Tying up loose ends: A juror has revealed what convinced him and fellow jurors to convict Winona Ryder in the Great Shoplifting Trial of the 21st century.

"I think that the most damaging thing was that everybody saw her walking out the door on the videotape," Walter Fox said on the "Today" show.

"And when they apprehended her, she had merchandise that belonged to the store that had not been paid for and some of which had been vandalized."

Moving right along: The nearly unanimous raves for '8 Mile' are now in, along with some purple prose for Eminem. Even the Washington Post's Ann Hornaday — in the minority because she doesn't like the movie much — swoons over the Great White Rapper.

"With his enormous eyes and the sort of aristocratic mouth that could have been painted in Renaissance Italy, he has the face of a bruised angel," she writes. "It's impossible not to watch him, which is the prime factor in making a movie star."

Pretty high-flown stuff for a film critic. She almost sounds like an art critic.

But maybe you haven't been reading art critics. According to Christopher Knight, the art critic of the Los Angeles Times, they don't write criticism, they write educational mush. Knight bases his opinion on a new study "The Visual Art Critic" released by the National Arts Journalism Program at Columbia University.

Finally, here are two eminent British artists — David Hockney and Lucian Freud — being pitted against each other, sort of, in a portrait contest.

In the Daily News: Sharon Osbourne — who recently caused a stir when she said she was fed up doing "The Osbournes" reality show — has agreed to host a talk show à la Oprah.

Nov. 10, 2002 / 12:59 p.m. ET

Hitting the "8 Mile" limit: I've just seen "8 Mile." It felt longer than it actually was — much longer — and it was longer than it actually had to be. There are too many dull, repetitive scenes and, if truth be told, too little story.

All the talk of Eminem making like James Dean is overblown. The Great White Rapper has a fine screen presence, but there's really no comparison to Dean. Eminem's reticent mood from beginning to end becomes monotonous, too.

Similarly, all the talk about Kim Basinger's knockout performance is a bit much. She's credible enough, and she helps the picture considerably, but her role is too small for a knockout. Too bad her role is so underwritten. More Basinger might have lent drama to a one-note plot.

The box-office grosses are not out yet, but it's an easy bet "8 Mile" will be No. 1. If it does skyscraper business this weekend — which it should, given the publicity and the rave reviews and Eminem's fan base — it will have "legs" because people will be eager to get in on an "event." But I don't think "8 Mile" will have terrific word-of-mouth, and without the boost of a mammoth debut, the movie could fade fairly rapidly.

I also don't know what could have prompted New York magazine critic Peter Rainer to call "8 Mile" "one of the year's sweetest joy rides," unless it was the much-bruited "inspirational" up-from-under theme — which didn't feel especially inspiring to me. The movie just laid there, an inert buildup to an "explosive" rap battle that I found underwhelming.

(Just as I finished writing this, the box-office grosses have shown up. Skyscraper business it is.)

Nov. 11, 2002 / 10:48 a.m. ET

No limit to idiocy: A lot of Eminem fans think I'm an idiot for my remarks yesterday: "Hitting the '8 Mile' limit." Many of their e-mails are unprintable. But here are two classy responses:

Jimmy
Madison, Wisconsin
"James Dean was a personification of the restless American youth of the mid-1950s and this is where the comparison with Eminem ends. James Dean led a somewhat privileged life and his character is much staged. Eminem is the opposite. Coming from a broken home and being a dropout puts Eminem in category of [his] own. James Dean represented a narrower group of American society. Whether Eminem becomes a legendary film star remains to be seen but already he's ahead of James Dean as regards debuts and is well on his way to becoming a music legend.

Rose Howard
Manchester, United Kingdom
"I admit I was curious. I wanted to see why Em was receiving such glowing reviews. He has 'it'. Whatever 'it' is, Em has it. I think the role he plays, the poor white underdog, has an appeal for many people who grew up

in such an environment, and, the fact that he is determined to 'make it', despite the odds of his poverty, elicits a certain amount of sympathy. The film was gritty, depressing, and thankfully, spiced with a bit of humour that made his character and his 'homies' all the more engaging. Not a great film but, if one can trust the screenwriter and director, '8 Mile' is a fascinating glimpse into the subculture of rappers in the inner cities of America."

Nov. 11, 2002 / 11:48 a.m. ET
Yo, dawg! He's my Eminem, too! The blistering e-mails from devoted Eminem fans continue to upset my staff of thousands. It hangs its many heads in shame. They look at me with a pitiful stare, and they ask, "Why have you risked your street cred, dawg?"   Eminem fans seem to think that only somebody who dislikes The Great White Rapper, only somebody who doesn't "get it," could possibly find fault with "8 Mile."

In fact, I have a soft spot in my heart for Em. (OK, I admit it: I sometimes think of him as "My Em.") But that probably won't make much difference to the Doubting Emmies out there. They just won't believe me.

So here are two e-mails — one from a big-city guy and one from a small-town gal — which I thought might help persuade my staff at least that I am not alone in <u>my disappointment with "8 Mile."</u> May my staff hold its many heads high at the water cooler! Amen.

Watson Sinclair
Newark, N.J.
"Being the Eminem fan that I am, I was practically first in the blockbusting line which wrapped around the theater. Expecting to be blown away with Em's notoriously witty lyrics and super sly, yet shocking rhythmic beats, I was anything but. I couldn't have been more anxious, waiting and watching for something to actually happen. There wasn't a plot, climax, or resolution. ... There were hardly any real relationships, or story-lines to follow, and in the end you were left with nothing. I had an empty feeling when the house lights came up, as I was the first to rise from my seat like I was ejecting from a fighter jet on a mission. I would think that Eminem fans like myself were left wanting more. After listening to his detailed albums describing his life, trials and tribulations, and even the voice of his daughter, Haley, a fan would expect a little more honesty. Nice try Marshall, but stick to being Shady."

Melissa

Easley, S. C.

"I went to see Eminem's movie '8 Mile' on the night that it started. I was hyped about seeing it, thinking that because Eminem was in it that it was going to be something to see. I was wrong in the worst way. Don't get me wrong I like Eminem, as an artist, I like his music and I respect him for what he has accomplished. If you are going to make a transition from music to film, make sure that it is a movie that people will want to see over and over, I didn't see it with this movie. The movie itself was too long about what I consider nothing. There was a slight message about a white boy growing up in the slums of Detroit, but that was it. The whole movie could have been summed up into about 30 minutes. I do however think that '8 Mile' will soar at the box office, only because there are a lot of young people that love his music, I am one of them, but I also think that after, or less than one week the numbers will decrease incredibly. I commend Eminem for trying to shine some light on some of what he went through growing up in Detroit, but I think the movie could have been a lot better than it turned out to be. Maybe next time."

My thanks also go to a different Melissa for this e-mail, which clarifies an earlier James Dean reference:

Melissa

Halifax, Canada

"In response to Jimmy who thought he knew some James Dean facts by saying quote, 'James Dean led a somewhat privileged life and his character is much staged.' James Dean actually had an awful home life (his mother died when he was young and his father literally abandoned him). All stars have a certain luck element with regard to their careers; I'd say Eminem owes more of his success/credibility to the fact that Dr. Dre introduced him to the mainstream audience, otherwise he'd just be another Vanilla Ice. Fans of Em should probably also realize that when a movie is 'loosely' based on someone's life, it's usually more 'loosely' than actually."

Nov. 13, 2002 / 1:58 p.m. ET

Changing the subject to bin Laden: When you get an e-mail like this, you sit up and take notice — and you blush from the sheer pleasure of it.

Mary
Nashville, Tenn.

"Okay honey. Enough of 'Em.' Yes, he's 'my Em' too. It's just I'd like you to get back to what you do best, which is change the subject matter quickly so as to foster growth in our rotting American brains and keep us on our toes. So???? What DO you think of the new Homeland Security Group that 'our Prez' is putting together? What are people saying about the new bin Laden audio tape? Etc., etc. Love you Jan! AND your staff of thousands!"

I've received a lot of e-mails asking me to change the subject (but not as well put). So here goes.

Whatever anyone makes of the latest bin Laden tape, the world-famous intellectual Francis Fukayama has already given him and Islamic fundamentalism the finger.

"It was quite revealing in Afghanistan after the Taliban were defeated," Fukayama says in the latest issue of the Australian academic journal Policy, "that the first thing the people in Kabul did was to to dig up their VCRs and television sets and watch these corny Indian soap operas.

"Like virtually every other human being on the planet, they like that sort of thing. You can't say that watching cheesy Indian movies is a universal characteristic of human beings, but beneath that there are certain tendencies that are given by nature, and if you try to restrict them too much you are going to run up against some real political problems."

You remember Francis Fukuyama. He's the former Reaganite State Department guy who wrote in 1989, when the Soviet Union collapsed: "We may be witnessing the end of history as such: this is the end point of mankind's ideological evolution and the universalization of Western liberal democracy as the final form of government."

OK, Fukayama was a little bit premature. Let's just hold the thought.

Meanwhile, here's another thought: Maybe the way to beat bin Laden is to tickle him to death with wisecracks. It's common knowledge that Islamic terrorists are humorless types who can't stand a good joke. In today's Boston Globe, for instance, Jeffrey Chase's "Critique of Pure Comedy" equates Bin Laden's sense of humor — or lack thereof — with Hitler's.

Maybe the Pentagon could turn some Jack Benny punchlines and Groucho Marx gags — or better, some Chris Rock zingers — into laser-guided weapons.

Nov. 14, 2002 / 12:27 a.m. ET

Life in a fishbowl: Performance artist <u>Marina Abramovic</u> will begin starving herself Friday night for 12 days at <u>a New York art gallery</u>, while living naked or clothed in an open-sided, three-cell unit hung in mid-air, her every waking and sleeping moment totally exposed to viewers. A telescope has even been set up for those who want a closer inspection of her daily life.

<u>Why is she doing this?</u> You'd have to ask her. It can't be fun. Her self-imposed rules include no talking, reading or writing, though she can drink water and take showers. Maybe she's an exhibitionist. But I'd say she's offering a graphic commentary on personal privacy, surveillance and <u>the bill creating the Homeland Security Department</u> that the U.S. House of Representatives just passed.

Abramovic's performance piece couldn't be more timely. Under the homeland superagency act, the Pentagon will be entitled to peek into every nook and cranny of the lives of all U.S. citizens — without a warrant — via a computer system that "will provide intelligence analysts and law enforcement officials with instant access to information from Internet mail and calling records to credit card and banking transactions and travel documents."

<u>The system is being created</u> by the Office of Information Awareness at the Defense Advanced Research Projects Agency (Darpa for short), headed by Vice Adm. John M. Poindexter, the former national security adviser in the Reagan administration whose conviction for his leading role in the Iran-contra affair was subsequently reversed on a technicality.

"This could be the perfect storm for civil liberties in America," Marc Rotenberg, director of the Electronic Privacy Information Center in Washington, told The New York Times. "The vehicle is the Homeland Security Act, the technology is Darpa and the agency is the FBI. The outcome is a system of national surveillance of the American public."

If you don't believe him because you suspect he's a liberal, <u>believe William Safire</u>: "If the Homeland Security Act is not amended before passage, here is what will happen to you:

"Every purchase you make with a credit card, every magazine subscription you buy and medical prescription you fill, every Web site you visit and e-mail you send or receive, every academic grade you receive, every bank deposit you make, every trip you book and every event you attend — all these transactions and communications will go into what the Defense Department describes as 'a virtual, centralized grand database.' "

Are you ready for that? I'm not, and I don't think Abramovic is either.

Nov. 15, 2002 / 4:05 p.m. ET

End of a long week: Is it possible that all the commotion over Gore Vidal's attack on the 'Bush junta' had an impact? Finally, after months of obstruction, the White House agreed to the creation of a Sept. 11 commission.

Like many others, Vidal had called for an independent investigation into the events of 9/11. But the wide publicity surrounding his more outrageous claims — for instance, that "the Bush administration deliberately chose not to act on warnings of Al-Qaeda's plans" — may have helped bring the issue to a head.

Pundits far and wide have derided Vidal's conspiracy theory. Ron Rosenbaum, for one, called him slippery as well as daffy and picked him apart with a microscope and tweezers (though, it must be said, the analysis was unusually tedious).

Right or wrong, however, Vidal had the guts to expose himself to ridicule. And until the commission makes its report 18 months from the time it actually begins its probe, we won't know whether he deserves to be put in a corner or put on a pedestal.

Nov. 16, 2002 / 11:34 a.m. ET

Coming up for air: I felt an unstoppable urge this morning to share this: Everybody's favorite sitcom, now that it's on its way out, has been memorialized in the lofty pantheon of the Oxford English Dictionary with the expression go commando, which means to go without your underwear.

Angus Stevenson, co-author of the latest edition of the two-volume Shorter Oxford English Dictionary, says it's his favorite of the 3,500 new expressions that have entered the language through common usage since the dictionary was last revised, in 1993.

"We got it from the TV series 'Friends,' " Stevenson told Warren Hoge, London bureau chief of The New York Times, "and then we tracked it back to American college slang in the mid-'80s, and we reasoned that that's when the writers of 'Friends' were probably at college. It could have been a private joke in a small group about commandos being too rough and ready to wear underpants ... It's turned into a phrase that is recognized by a global audience."

Hoge delivers some of the other phrases beautifully wrapped in a clever first paragraph:

"Heard the one about the fashionista and his arm candy who live in parallel universes, prefer chatrooms and text messaging to snail mail, suffer sticker shock at the cost of pashminas and like chick-lit or airport novels?

This trendy tale is nonsense, of course, but it is now Oxford-approved nonsense."

George W. Bush takes the prize, however, when it comes to Oxford-approved nonsense. This is one of the estimable "Bushisms" that just entered the second edition of the "Oxford Dictionary of Phrase, Saying and Quotation": "We are ready for any unforeseen event which may or may not happen." Or as Walt Kelly's Pogo once said: "We have met the enemy and he is us."

Nov. 17, 2002 / 12:54 p.m. ET

Saying it for the ages: Who knew the world had so many lexicologists? Yesterday's item about the '80s origin of the phrase "go commando" — later popularized by "Friends," according to the Shorter Oxford English Dictionary — has drawn them like ants to a picnic. (Pace, Safire.)

First my MSNBC.com colleague Jonathan Dube messaged: "I'm pretty sure 'Seinfeld' used the phrase on air long before 'Friends' ... and honestly, I heard the phrase long before that. I think these OED folks are living in a closet!"

Then Jim Devore, of Durham, N.C., dated the origin of the phrase to the '60s: "The term was used at Penn State in the early '60s when I was a student. I first heard it from one of my roommates from Pittsburgh, Bill "PI" Rasile, an Italian guy from the Larimer Avenue area on the East side of 'the burgh.' "

Tom Marturano, a 1988 graduate of the University of Pennsylvania, confirmed at least some of OED editor Angus Stevenson's speculations about the "Friends" college connection:

"I first heard it from a [Penn] rower and frat brother of mine named Jim Leyden, who I thought had made it up. Another frat brother had roomed freshman year with a guy named Jeff Astrof, who later went on to be a writer on 'Friends' in the early '90s. We all hung out together ... so I'm not surprised that 'go commando' made it onto the show since it was part of our everyday vocabulary. ..."

But Aaron J. Neumeyer, of Hendersonville, N.C., has news for Stevenson: "Going 'commando' has nothing to do with '80s college slang. Soldiers operating in humid, jungle-like environments often do not wear underwear. This allows air to circulate more freely ... and helps prevent what is commonly called 'jungle rot,' a really annoying version of jock itch ... Going commando has been practiced for a half century or more and is more a matter of practical necessity than [soldiers] being too tough to wear boxers."

And for good measure, someone from Cambridge, Mass., who didn't give a name, has news for the editors of the "Oxford Dictionary of Phrase, Saying and Quotation" about a "Bushism" that's really a "Quayle-ism":

"The quote that is claimed to be from George W. Bush — 'We are ready for any unforeseen event which may or may not happen' — is (sadly) not one of his own. It was originally uttered by Dan Quayle, who said, in the run-up to the Gulf War: 'We are ready for any unforeseen events which may or may not occur.' "

We've known all along that Vice President Cheney and chief political advisor Karl Rove do President Bush's thinking for him. To be reminded that his muddled language skills are not even his own — that of all things his "Bushisms' come second-hand — is downright embarrassing.

Nov. 18, 2002 / 2:37 p.m. ET

More pretzel logic: Here's an interesting take comparing Miss Cleo and al Jazeera.

Nov. 18, 2002 / 2:43 p.m. ET

The bombing in the milk bar: Between the hype for "Die Another Day," the new James Bond flick that opens Friday, and the mountain of gold that "Harry Potter and the Chamber of Secrets" raked in over the weekend, you'd think there wasn't another movie in sight. And you'd almost be right.

(Eminem's "8 Mile," a distant No. 2 to "Secrets," was a one-week wonder and seems to be disappearing over the horizon on shorter "legs" than many pundits thought probable. Hate to say I told them so. My staff of thousands is going "Nyah-nyah!")

In fact, there's another movie starring another British actor that's opening Friday — smaller in hype but more important by far than "Die Another Day" and Irish-born Pierce Brosnan. It's "The Quiet American," with Oscar-winner Michael Caine, based on Graham Greene's 1955 novel of the same name and set in Saigon a decade before the Americans took over the Vietnam war from the French.

Why is it more important? If you have to ask, you'll never believe the answer.

As Caine himself says, It's "a grownup film made by grownups for grownups, and I'm hoping it's about time. Are grownups still going to the cinema or are they stuck in front of the television? We'll find out."

Forgetting for the moment that Caine's performance won him raves when the film premiered at the Toronto Film Festival — he's already being touted for another Oscar, which is why the film is being released now — the wilder importance has to do with <u>Greene the novelist and writer</u> and the peculiar idea that nothing ever happens in reality until a writer writes it up.

Do you recall the recent terrorist bombing of the nightclub in Bali? Well, Greene described <u>an infamous bombing at a milk bar in the main square of Saigon</u> in "The Quiet American" that had repercussions around the world not unlike those of the Bali bombing. (Director Philip Noyce makes <u>the Saigon milk-bar explosion a spectacular set piece</u> in the movie.)

There was also a similar bombing in Algiers, William S. Burroughs once recalled, "about two years after Graham Greene had written this scene. ... People [had] their legs all splattered with Maraschino cherries and ice cream and blood and brains, passion fruit, pieces of mirrors. A friend of mine got to the [Algiers] milk bar ... and saw this scene. Wow! Graham Greene had written that. Writers don't want to take responsibility for these things; they have to."

When French author Michel Houellebecq's 1999 novel "Platform" comes out in English translation in the United States, American readers may discover what French and British readers already have: That Houellebecq, too, wrote the Bali bombing before it happened, <u>only he set it in a sex club in Thailand</u>.

Perhaps writers can "unwrite" events? Doubtful.

Nov. 19, 2002 / 2:43 p.m. ET

An '8 Mile' footnote: It looks like some bad news for Eminem But he's tough. The Great White Rapper can take it, right?

Estimates of ticket sales for "8 Mile" were inflated. Final weekend figures now show that <u>his flick grossed $2 million less than initially reported</u>. It still took in $19.3 million for its second outing. But that means it dropped even further from its debut than had been anticipated — a whopping 62 percent. Not. Good.

Since the public pays so much attention to the weekend grosses, it should know that Hollywood studios are not above massaging them to make their films look like they're doing better than they are. The widely reported grosses that come out every Sunday are, in fact, no more than studio estimates based upon a combination of actual ticket sales from early in the weekend and projections made for the rest of the weekend.

These estimates are then updated with the so-called final figures. Usually, the estimates and the final figures vary slightly. Variety, the entertainment trade paper, says that estimates are often "overly optimistic" — a polite way of putting it — by up to $1 million.

But when they're overly optimistic by as much as $2 million — a disparity of more than 10 percent — you should know something is fishier than usual. There's always a reasonable explanation, of course. In the case of the inflated '8 Mile' estimate, "it appeared the disparity was traceable to less Sunday business at urban ethnic theaters than had been projected." (Translation: Fewer black moviegoers showed up than claimed.)

Meanwhile, the final figure for "Harry Potter and the Chamber of Secrets" came to $88.4 million, or $700,000 higher than the estimate. That's a disparity of less than one per cent (and on much a much larger amount).

It's worth remembering, however, that none of these numbers — estimates or final figures — are independently verified.

Nov. 20, 2002 / 12:59 p.m. ET

A footnote to the '8 Mile' footnote: This e-mail came yesterday. Was it from Marshall Mathers a k a Eminem or, as I fondly call him, The Great White Rapper?

I phoned his representative in Los Angeles to find out. His rep's secretary said he'd get back to me. Famous last words. He never did. I replied to the e-mail itself. But that was a dead end. I doubt Eminem would bother. But you never know.

JUICEY FRUIT

DETROIT

"YOU ARE AN IDIOT WHO APPARENTLY HAS A PROBLEM WITH ME. IF YOU DONT HAVE ANYTHING NICE TO SAY, DONT SAY NOTHING. IM SO HAPPY YOUR STAFF OF MORONS HATE ME TOO. IM REALLY HURT, ALL THE WAY TO THE BANK!!! THE juice, MORE LIKE THE GOOSE . GO AHEAD AND FLOCK, IT SURELY AINT THE FIRST TIME. MM PS. PUCKER UP!!"

This sounds like him. You decide.

Nov. 20, 2002 / 2:13 p.m. ET

Ain't love grand? I've been avoiding "The Bachelor" like the proverbial plague. But tonight's finale has forced my hand. "Bachelor" fever is running so high that it made the front page of this morning's New York Times, not to mention a big takeout by The Washington Post and lots of attention from less tony establishments like USA Today. Oh, did I mention the multimillions of women who make up "The Bachelor" audience, outnumbering men 3 to 1?

Between that piece of drek TV and "Victoria's Secret Fashion Show" — another form of froth that's more likely to heat men up, but who knows? — tonight's tubular programming has (forgive me) an embarrassment of britches. We've come a long way from Mae West.

Some women, it seems, get their jollies from watching other women being humiliated. The Post's Paul Farhi writes, it's "a devilish entertainment" for them, and "they confess to taking guilty pleasure in [it]," which more or less accounts for the success of "The Bachelor."

But the Times's Alessandra Stanley has underscored what I think is the main issue: "More than sex, more than violence, humiliation is the unifying principle behind a successful reality show, be it 'The Real World,' 'Survivor,' 'Fear Factor,' or 'The Bachelor.'"

This has been said before, but it bears repeating. And she goes further to point out that it's not enough just to show people being humiliated, they have to be shown seeking their own degradation — what she calls "unconscious humiliation" vs. "consensual humiliation."

The former involves benign pranks, like those on "Candid Camera"; the latter involves a nasty draught of sadism. Drek TV is successful because "viewers prefer their humiliation raw," Stanley writes.

I can see my hydra-headed staff nodding off. So I'll stop preaching now. Whatever humiliations transpire tonight on "The Bachelor," just remember Mae West. The Blondest Bombshell of Them All, when asked if she believed in marriage, replied: "Only as a last resort."

Nov. 20, 2002 / 4:51 p.m. ET

Footnote cubed: It's settled — and may I never write about Eminem again (gawd willing). The Great White Rapper "doesn't e-mail." So says his spokesman, Dennis Dennehey, who also happens to be head of publicity for Interscope Geffen A&M Records. Let the record show that Juicey Fruit, a k a MM, is an imposter. Case closed.

Nov. 21, 2002 / 8:58 a.m. ET

Victimology: What a bore! Last night's finale of "The Bachelor" was the longest, windiest, phoniest romance I've ever had the pain of sitting through. If not for my professional obligation to watch it — because of this column — I would never have tuned in. The show was so unbearably dull that I'm thinking of filing for worker's compensation for headache injuries suffered on the job. I'm still medicating myself this morning.

The only thing that keeps me from filing is that I would be accused of taking victimology to new heights, of not — as they say in rehab-speak — taking responsibility for my actions. (But now I see that several teenagers are suing McDonald's for making them obese. Hmmm.) (Registration may be required for the link.)

In any case, yesterday's commentary on drek TV needs to be revised: "Consensual humiliation" applies to the audience — tearful, kissed-off Brooke notwithstanding.

Nov. 22, 2002 / 1:58 p.m. ET
And now, the one ... the only ... the sublime ... the credible ... chopped liver! You think you've seen it all on drek TV? Bugs? Snakes? Spiders? Slime? Humiliation? Well, ladies and gents, Herr Doktor Gunther von Hagens has news for you: You ain't seen nuthin' yet.

At least not until you've watched Herr Doktor dissect a corpse in public — as he did last night on British television for the edification of viewers and, he says, for the sake of democracy. In what was described as "a passionate address" before the autopsy, von Hagens declared: "I stand here for democracy ... the time is over when medical knowledge could be confined to an elite."

Hello? Herr Doktor sounds to me like that good old-fashioned spectacular ghoul, the infamous Dr. Benway in "Naked Lunch," who used to brag about performing an appendectomy with a rusty sardine can.

Perhaps you recall the scene in the operating room. Benway, watching an assistant making an incision, waxes nostalgic: "You young squirts couldn't lance a pimple without an electric vibrating scalpel with automatic drain and suture. ... Soon we'll be operating by remote control on patients we never see ... We'll be nothing but button pushers. All the skill is going out of surgery ... All the know-how and make-do ... Did I ever tell you about the time I performed an appendectomy with a rusty sardine can? ..."

Just about the only thing missing from Benway's operating room was Rembrandt's 1632 painting, "Anatomy Lesson of Dr. Nicolaes Tulip," a large copy of which was prominently on display during von Hagens' demonstration. As might be expected, von Hagens was strong on visuals. But I especially liked the picquant soundscape one spectator described as "a general sloshing about of organs." (Link may require registration.)

Who isn't in favor of democracy? I'm in favor of it as much as the next guy. I'm in favor of science and the healer's art and edgy art, too, which von Hagens claims is his provenance as well, having created a popular if macabre art exhibit called "Body Worlds," a collection of 25 cadavers shown in various positions, their anatomies exposed, all of them preserved by a technique he calls "plastination."

I also agree with the British police who decided not to arrest von Hagens for performing an autopsy in public, as he rightly predicted they wouldn't, even though it's illegal. But I wonder whether he wasn't arrested because the ban on public autopsies is almost two centuries old and the problem of body snatching that it was intended to solve has long since been resolved, or whether the police simply didn't want to give him more publicity than he already has.

And I wonder whether the author of "Naked Lunch," who died in 1997, is chuckling about all this somewhere in a parallel universe. What I know for a certainty, however, is that Dr. Benway has met his match.

Nov. 25, 2002 / 10:53 a.m. ET

In praise of Brooklyn: There was a time when Brooklyn was famous for the Dodgers and Ebbets Field, Coney Island and the Cyclone roller coaster, Rockaway beach and its boardwalk (OK, over the line in Queens), Walt Whitman and his poetry.

Ebbets Field and the Dodgers are long gone, Coney Island and the Cyclone are shadows of their former selves, the same is true of Rockaway and the boardwalk, and Walt Whitman is ancient history.

What's Brooklyn known for now? Ask Dennis Reardon, who drove all the way from Indiana to see the recent production of "Woyzeck" by Robert Wilson and Tom Waits at the Brooklyn Academy of Music. (Unfortunately, when Reardon got there, according to a letter in Sunday's New York Times, the performance was canceled at the last minute due to an actor's illness — only the third such cancellation in 20 years — so he turned around and drove all the way home to Indiana again.) That tells us something.

It tells us that these days Brooklyn is renowned for BAM. And after seeing "Woyzeck" there myself, I think Reardon's crazy enthusiasm was understandable. "Woyzeck" turned out to be the best theatrical experience I've had in years. Better than "The Producers" on Broadway. Better than "Proof" on Broadway, better than anything since Julie Taymor's "The Green Bird" was booed off Broadway by a middle-aged audience of ingrates. "Woyzek" bowled me over, blew me away, knocked me for a loop, got any other clichés?

Most U.S. theater-goers will never get to see this production. (It originated last year in Copenhagen with a fabulous, English-speaking cast of Danish performers, and this fall has toured to Belgrade, Rome, London and Saravejo.) If Reardon or anybody else wants to see the show, they'll have to drive to Los Angeles, where it's scheduled to run Dec. 3-15 at UCLA at the Macgowan Hall Freud Playhouse.

Enjoy the trip.

Nov. 26, 2002 / 11:59 a.m. ET

Guilty parties: When ABC and People magazine collaborated on a hush-hush story about the so-called "closely guarded secret conclusion" of "The Bachelor" — a secret revealed in advance to the magazine for its current issue — nobody protested.

Why not? Because the media's hand-in-glove teamwork with publicity campaigns, especially at celebrity-mongering vehicles like People, is old news. It happens all the time. As David Carr wrote in The New York Times: "The scoop provoked a single reaction: How did the magazine do that?"

But the ABC-People collaboration is a nasty reminder just the same that a relentless publicity machine powers much if not all pop culture. Promotion campaigns for movies, celebrities, TV programs, music CDs, magazines and books have replaced legitimate taste and real preferences — choice has been reduced to bogus alternatives — to say nothing of actual news. In fact, publicity disguised as news — for that is People magazine's stock in trade — undermines everything from pop culture to politics.

It's not just the soft-news media or the feature sections of hard-news media. It's a mass infection. It's e-v-e-r-y-b-o-d-y.

That includes me — why else would I be writing about The Great White Rapper instead of Louis Menand's takedown of MIT author Stephen Pinker or the literary dust-up over Michiko Kakutani and John Updike?

That includes my colleagues at MSNBC.com — why else did we have "The Business of Bond" (despite the smart disclaimer "License to shill") timed to the opening of "Die Another Day"?

That includes the alternative Blogcritics corner of the Web, where Paul McCartney comes in for fan praise: It's all Paulie all week with the CD, DVD, TV, and George tribute.

"Who would have thought the Beatles and Stones would be the biggest bands going in 2002?" Eric Olsen asks.

How about Madison Avenue, Eric.

Nov. 26, 2002 / 1:56 p.m. ET

Phony report: Talk about guilty parties. No sooner did I file an item about media publicity for "The Bachelor" masquerading as news than an eagle-eyed reader alerted me to a story purportedly by The Associated Press that is flying around the Web: It claims that three women have become pregnant "due to their participation in the show."

Ain't true. Small details in the writing style indicate that the report is a fake. And Julia Rubin, AP's entertainment editor, confirms that it's bogus. She tells me: "It's not our story. We don't know where it came from."

Nov. 27, 2002 / 11:32 a.m. ET

Peas in a pod, cog in the wheel: My staff of thousands loves this e-mail about yesterday's guilty parties. (Wouldn't you?) It comes from Melanie Luciano.

"You're right on with 'bogus alternatives' served up by a 'relentless publicity machine" that has 'replaced legitimate taste and real preferences.' I've made a career working in the movie and TV business and have reached a point where it's difficult for me to 'consume' the 'product' we are all putting out. The smartest people on the planet are contributing to the problem. I believe there has got to be a way to cure the 'mass infection.' At least you're addressing the situation, but people read it, agree, and then go about their business. Does anyone care?"

And Eric Olsen, whom I tweaked, had this to say: "Yes, I hyped up old Paulie pretty good, but I am very pleased, relieved even to have a McCartney project worth crowing about. Deep down, I'm just a fan and wish the Beatles — a miraculous, once-in-a-lifetime convergence of artistic quality, personality, culture, timing, and the alignment of the stars — had never gone away."

He's also taken the nickname "Cog," as in cog in the great wheel of the publicity machine.

Nov. 27, 2002 / 2:53 p.m. ET

The turkey that trots: It's so nice to know Eminem is being considered for Time magazine's "Person of the Year," along with Osama bin Laden, Saddam Hussein and George W. Bush. That news hit the wires last week with a pretty lame spin.

Usually, the short list is kept secret. But the magazine decided to "let some air in" on the debate, Time's deputy managing editor Steve Koepp told Reuters, "because the process itself is so interesting." He could have said the magazine wanted to drum up publicity. But that would have been telling the graceless truth.

Time's choice last year was Rudy Giuliani. There's no way on Earth Eminem will, or should, join him. Not when Rolling Stone can feature The Great White Rapper on the cover of its current "People of the Year" issue while publishing a cover story that disses him and his movie.

"[A]s he has turned the corner on thirty," Rob Sheffield writes, "Eminem remains hung up on childhood pain, and it's time he cut the cord. 'White America, I could be one of your kids,' he says on The Eminem Show. Well, not when you're thirty."

While his film "8 Mile" is certain to crack $100 million before it goes away, nobody's waiting on line to get in any more. Wayne Robins, a fan of Eminem's music, has just provided the ultimate explanation of why that is. He says the movie needs — I hope you're sitting down — a larger-than-life actor, namely Adam Sandler, in the starring role. Whew!

For very different reasons of course, you can bet the farm that neither bin Laden nor Saddam are going to be named Time's "Person of the Year," either. Which leaves — What a surprise! — George W. Bush. Maybe we could get Adam Sandler to play him, too.

Share your perspective on entertainment and the arts with Jan Herman. MSNBC is not responsible for the content of Internet links.

Jan Herman

Latest entertainment and arts news from the Web

Entries from Dec. 2 to Dec. 24, 2002
(Some links may be nonfunctional.)
Back to 'The Juice'

LATEST UPDATES

Dec. 2, 2002 / 8:57 a.m. ET

Hissy fit or Exhibit A? Now that President Bush has done what he could to justify Gore Vidal's seemingly paranoid fears that a "Bush junta" was complicit in 9/11, even the staid New York Times (which has never taken kindly to Vidal's politics, let alone his novels) has begun to sound Vidalesque.

The appointment of Henry Kissinger to head the 9/11 probe is Exhibit A. "Indeed," The Times said in a word of warning to a nation enjoying the Thanksgiving holiday, "it is tempting to wonder if the choice of Mr. Kissinger is not a clever maneuver by the White House to contain an investigation it long opposed. It seems improbable to expect Mr. Kissinger to report unflinchingly on the conduct of the government. ..." (Registration may be required.)

For Vidal and interested citizens (registration may be required) — including such Bush-friendly pundits as Weekly Standard senior editor David Brooks — the temptation is overwhelming. And now that the Gray Lady has spoken out, its equitable tones and phrases notwithstanding, perhaps Ron Rosenbaum will be tempted to cut Vidal some slack.

One thing Dr. K's appointment will do without question is lend currency to "The Trials of Henry Kissinger," a polemical, BBC-funded film documentary in which Christopher Hitchens, who specializes in nonequitable tones and phrases, calls Dr. K "a war criminal" and "a liar, responsible for kidnapping and murder."

As Maureen Dowd, another specialist in nonequitable tones and phrases, put it Sunday: "If you want to get to the bottom of something, you don't appoint Henry Kissinger. If you want to keep others from getting to the bottom of something, you appoint Henry Kissinger." (William Safire disputes that this morning — sort of — accusing "hate-Henry" liberals of having a hissy fit. (Registration for both may be required.)

But my staff of thousands believes that when mavericks like Vidal, Hitchens and Dowd see eye to eye with an institutional dowager like the Gray Lady (pace, Howell Raines) they must be onto something. Dr. K's gravel-voiced declaration ("We will go where the facts leads us") leaves too many unpersuaded.

Dec. 2, 2002 / 11:08 a.m. ET

As the girl turns: A moment of silence, please, to contemplate a pop-culture event of monumental significance: Britney Spears turns 21 today. My staff of thousands says she's been around so long they think of her as a soccer mom. I don't know whether to laugh or cry. But her birthday prompted me to re-read John Schulian's thought-provoking column from a year ago: Britney Spears: all-American 'sex babe'. Those were the days.

Dec. 3, 2002 / 1:47 p.m. ET

Mencken the übermensch: Thanks to Terry Teachout's widely praised, new biography "The Skeptic: A Life of H. L. Mencken," there's been a sudden outbreak of Mencken mania in the nation's literary pages. And there's no vaccine for it.

Everybody seems to be re-discovering the übermensch of Baltimore — his journalistic brilliancies, ideological stupidities, scholarly triumphs, moral failings, personal weirdness and, maybe most important, his paradoxical legacy as the early 20th century's "quintessential voice of American letters."

My favorite review of the man and the biography is "On the Contrary," by Joan Acoccella, in The New Yorker. But I also liked Jonathan Yardley's "The Sage of Baltimore," a personalized, informative piece, in The Atlantic. Others may prefer "A Smart Set of One," by Christopher Hitchens, a somewhat fitful, less adulatory effort in The New York Times Book Review.

The most peculiar review is Richard Brookhiser's "Bitter Sage," in the National Review. It makes no mention of Mencken's notorious anti-Semitism, one of the sage's more notable deficits, and gives him a pass when it comes to his pro-Nazi views and his contradictory regard for Hitler.

The National Review also has an interview with Teachout very much worth reading about why he wrote the book. And The Atlantic has a terrific summary of Mencken as critic with links to some of his original Atlantic pieces from nearly a century ago.

What the übermensch of Baltimore would make of our current Mencken mania is anybody's guess. (Egotist that he was, he'd love it; curmudgeon that he was, he'd hate it.) But rest assured, he would still have it in for the booboisie.

Dec. 4, 2002 / 10:02 a.m. ET

Kissy-poo with Dr. K: Here's a sweet little item from today's Los Angeles Times called the "Kissinger kiss-up," reminding us that the media is doing a lousy job on Dr. K's appointment to head the 9/11 commission.

Instead of exposing the pertinent facts that make the appointment a bad idea, Tim Rutten writes, the media have "bruised elbows and knees" from kowtowing to a Janus-faced intellectual celebrity.

Dec. 4, 2002 / 11:59 a.m. ET

Allred sticks her nose in: I've purposely steered clear of the latest Jacko madness. Ever since seeing that photo of the Masked One unmasked at trial, the one showing him with his plastered nose, I kept hearing two words in my head: "How sad!"

That was the spontaneous reaction of my MSNBC.com colleague Katie Cannon when she saw the photo, and it made me take a step back. But now that Gloria Allred has stuck her nose into the madness, demanding that a state agency — California's Child Protective Services — investigate Jackson because she saw TV footage that showed the recent baby-dangling incident, it's time to say: Enough!!

I don't have any sympathy for Jackson's game of "let's pretend I'm a victim." And I have less, if that's possible, for Jackson fans who believe he's some kind of untouchable divinity. But I do believe the tabloids have piled on him in this case well beyond their own paparazzi mandate to knock celebrities to earth. And I do believe that Allred is just hungry for publicity, an advocate trying to grandstand about child safety.

In a transparent bid for media attention, Allred went on CNN to broadcast her "concern." Unfortunately, Jackson has played right to her. Instead of ignoring her, he's told her to "go to hell." Where are his brains? In his poor, sad nose?

Dec. 5, 2002 / 10:09 a.m. ET

Off to the Moon: I've gone to see a Moon rock this morning. My staff of thousands insisted. But that does not mean I've been shipped off to the Moon. I've simply gone to the Rose Center for Earth and Space. I will be back later today to describe what the Moon really looks like, and how it feels to see a big piece of green cheese up close.

This particular piece of the Moon, billed as "never before displayed," is described as "a light-brown, coarse-grained mare basalt rock" found "28 meters south-southeast of the rim crest of Dune Crater, south of the Apollo 15 landing site." So maybe it's not green cheese after all. We'll see. ...

Dec. 5, 2002 / 12:58 p.m. ET

Back from the Moon: More laughs than "Rent," fewer than "The Producers." I know it's a snap judgment, but that's my quick "takeaway" (doncha just love corporate-speak?) from this morning's unveiling of a "never-before-displayed" Moon rock at the American Museum of Natural History's Rose Center for Earth and Space in New York.

I went to see the rock not only to discover whether, as I remarked earlier, the Moon was made of green cheese — it's not — but to find some form of entertainment that might replace Broadway musicals. (I'm a former theater critic who's pretty much given up on Broadway.)

Amer. Museum of Natural Hist.

On my way to the Rose Center in a driving snowstorm, I stopped to warm my hands at a little shop called Maxilla & Mandible. It had some pretty neat-looking steer skulls in the window that could have been from John Wayne's "Red River" country. This unexpected curtain raiser of Earth relics — along with the skeleton of a large snake that the great Harvard entymologist E.O. Wilson might have admired as a young boy before he got into ants — seemed like excellent preparaton for my Moon adventure.

I was not eager for a spectacular production, given my unhappiness with Broadway shows. All I asked for was something sublime, something to touch the soul, a symbol of the natural mysteries of the universe, a piece of Moon with the power to move me like a Shakespearean sonnet ("The mortal moon hath her eclipse endured /And the sad augurs mock their own presage").

It was not love at first sight. The "never-before-displayed" Moon rock looked dark gray to me, not "light brown" as advertised. It weighs 200 to 300 grams which, for non-metric nincompoops like me, means "less than half a pound." (I don't know why Jim Webster, the museum's curator of mineral deposits, couldn't be more specific.)

But the Moon rock grew on me as it sat in its glass case, a serene reality more than 3.2 billion years old (give or take 100 million years) rather than a

146

glittering symbol. On Aug. 1, 1971 — long after it was spewed like lava onto the surface of the now-dead Moon — Apollo 15 astronauts David Scott and James Irwin collected it near the rim of Dune Crater in the Sea of Rains. Since it doesn't have a name, I've decided to call it "Little Squirt."

Though less spectacular than the 34-ton Cape York Meteorite brought back from Greenland by Arctic explorer Robert Peary (on display here, too, in all its mightiness), I'd lay odds that Little Squirt is far more valuable. Only 842 pounds of Moon rocks have been brought to Earth, which should give you an idea of its scarcity.

The party line on Little Squirt's value is: "It's invaluable." Nobody at the museum would put a dollar figure on it. It's government property, in the first place, pretty much on permanent loan to the museum, courtesy of NASA; it's not for sale, in the second place, in fact, it's prohibited from sale; and you can't wear it like jewelry, so why would anyone pay money for it, in the third place?

No sooner asked than answered: Collectors.

It so happens that on the very day Little Squirt was brought to the Rose Center last summer, four dumbos hijacked 113 grams of Moon rocks and soil from the Johnson Space Center in Houston, where Little Squirt had just been. FBI agents, posing as buyers, subsequently arrested the thieves in a sting, and authorities said the value of the 113 stolen grams could have reached as much as $565 million on the collectors' market.

By that calculation, Little Squirt must be worth a least a billion bucks. Not bad for a lunar chip that has to be kept from rusting like an old car bumper. Indeed, Little Squirt would eventually begin to oxidize if it wasn't sealed within its glass case in an atmosphere of pure nitrogen gas.

I should mention, too, that before Little Squirt came along the museum was already Moon rich. It has three other Off-Broadway babies on display — from Apollo missions 14, 16, and 17 — preserved in amber (not nearly as effective as nitrogen, I'm told).

Other critics ought to have their say. But Little Squirt was a hit with me.

Dec. 6, 2002 / 1:58 p.m. ET

Celebrities on the Web and in memory: I see the Daily News has toured the personal Web sites of a handful of celebrities, rating the best of them for their personal touch, creativity and comprehensiveness.

It singles out Britney Spears' for praise, along with Eminem's, Lenny Kravitz's, Moby's, Michael Douglas', Tiger Woods', Jamie-Lynn Sigler's and Al Roker's. It disses Michael Jackson's. (Careful. Some of these sites are so loaded they may freeze your Web connection.)

Surfing the Web the other night, I came across <u>Artie Garfunkel's home page</u>, which didn't get a mention. But what a trip. Talk about personal and comprehensive. On his Web site <u>he lists every book he has ever read over the last 34 years</u> — from June 1968 through April 2002 — all 869 of them.

Artie doesn't read fluff, no how-to schlock or diet guides. He reads the real thing. He must be the best-read pop celebrity in America (and probably the world).

For instance, the first book listed is "The Confessions," by Jean-Jacques Rousseau, published in 1781 and weighing in at 606 pages. (Yes, Artie even lists the number of pages.) The 868th book on his list is "The Foundations of Early Modern Europe: 1460-1569," by Eugene F. Rice Jr. (No pages listed. Maybe it was a snooze?) He also lists his <u>favorite books</u>.

Artie's Web site brought back memories. He always had an intellectual take on things even in high school. We weren't what you'd call close, but we were friendly enough to consider rooming together in college. He was a smart guy. Loved math, for instance — not what you'd expect from someone who'd made a hit single ("Hey Schoolgirl") with Paul Simon in the days when they called themselves <u>Tom and Jerry.</u>

I knew Paul better. (<u>Here's his Web site.</u>) We used to hang out in his basement rec room listening to Lenny Bruce. I went with him to the Brill Building in our senior year and watched him record quick demos for other songwriters so they could show their tunes and lyrics around.

Later, during college, I'd go to the Village with Paul on bitter-cold winter nights when he needed someone to cheer him on at <u>Gerde's Folk City,</u> long before he and Artie became real stars. And I'll never forget going with Paul to a concert at Town Hall. It featured the music of electronic composer <u>Edgar Varèse.</u> (We never would have gone if a music professor hadn't insisted, and comped the two of us with free tickets.)

Paul was leery of the whole thing. We arrived late, to find a hushed audience already listening to weird, prerecorded sounds. Paul didn't seem to feel he was interrupting anything. He strode down the center aisle, and I followed. Our seats, unfortunately, were in the first row. This allowed us to watch several musicians up close as they accompanied the taped sounds. A percussionist, beating a leather pad with a stick, dropped the pad and didn't have time to pick it up. So he began beating the pad with his foot. Paul couldn't stifle his giggles. He gave me a look that said, "Did you see that?" He thought the whole thing was a musical charade.

It's been decades since I last spoke to Artie or Paul, and you won't find this reminiscence on their Web sites. Paul looked me up in San Francisco in 1968, when "Mrs. Robinson" was at the top of the charts, and we went on a weekend binge together. I ran into Artie on the street in Burlington, Vt., in 1976, and got together with him later that year in New York and, separately, with Paul.

I haven't seen them since. I sometimes talk about them. I have even dreamed about Paul. But that was in another country. I think many of us can recall a pal who became a celebrity. Do you have someone you remember?

Dec. 9, 2002 / 1:48 p.m. ET

God comes to Broadway: Just when I get through saying how I've had it with Broadway, Baz Luhrmann comes along with a Broadway production of "La Bohème" that, to believe the critics, is God's gift to the Great White Way and opera dullards elsewhere. OK, maybe it's just Luhrmann's gift. But for a less than scintillating theater season the man who put Nicole Kidman in "Moulin Rouge" might as well be God.

Or at least a genius. And if you think I'm overstating the case when I say God has come to Broadway, consider this: God and genius are pretty much equivalent, according to the great expert on the subject, Yale's Sterling Professor of Humanities Harold Bloom, who defines genius as "the God within" in his latest book, the massive, 814-page "Genius." (One reason Luhrmann doesn't make Bloom's cut, unlike Shakespeare, Plato, Flaubert and 96 others, is that he's not dead yet.)

But Lurhmann makes the cut for mere theater critics. His Broadway "Bohème" is "utterly enchanting," Variety's Charles Isherwood says, and "it's further proof of his genius." Besides, the show rates not one but two reviews from The Associated Press, in a rare departure from AP's common practice — one for theater-goers "Land of Baz" and one for opera-goers "Required viewing" — and both are raves.

From near and far the critical chorus is singing together on this: Howard Kissell, at the New York Daily News, calls the show "Puccini for the People." The New York Times's Ben Brantley calls it rapturous. And a dazzled Clive Barnes writes in the New York Post: "Opera on Broadway? Italian Opera? I mean classic Opera in Italian? Is someone crazy around here? Obviously not. The Sacramento Bee's Marcus Crowder calls the show enthralling, while England's BBC dubs it brilliant. And the critic for Melbourne's The Age, in Australia, says it's spellbinding.

The only critic singing a different tune seems to be Newsday's Linda Winer. In "'La Bohème' Shoots for the Hip," she hits this sour note: "We would have loved to really love it, thus avoiding being accused of purist priggery." But undeterred, she brands the show a "messianically hyped crusade." (Not having seen it yet, I withhold judgment. Winer could be right.

A million French have been known to be wrong.)

Hollywood, which worships at the fount of genius, turned out a gaggle of stars for the opening: Sandra Bullock, wearing a slinky black dress; Leonardo DiCaprio, who arrived via a side entrance; and Candice Bergen, who held court in the lobby, not to mention John Turturro, Marcia Gay Harden, Hugh Grant and Cameron Diaz.

Because worshipping at the fount of genius is a Broadway religion, too, Lurhmann's directorial debut on the Great White Way — a first coming, so to speak — can't be overstated. Undoubtedly, he and his co-religionists will be celebrating at the box office. But let us not forget, at $95 per seat in the orchestra pews, or $250-per for "premium seating," it's an expensive religion. Only the well heeled can share in the blessing.

Dec. 10, 2002 / 12:59 p.m. ET

Let's break the law: I'm sure (well, almost) that the U.S. State Department won't mind. Just click on "Writers on America," a propaganda site maintained by the department's Office of International Information Programs and intended by law for foreign consumption only.

You will be wonderfully rewarded, especially if you like reading Richard Ford or Michael Chabon or Robert Olen Butler and a dozen other authors and poets. Each of them was asked by the State Department to write an essay in answer to this question: In what sense do you see yourself as an American writer?

Even I have to admit the Bush administration has done something smart. Getting these luminaries to reflect on the subject — the brainchild of Mark Jacobs, who's both a U.S. foreign service officer and a novelist — has produced scintillating results. Just have a look at Ford's "How Being an American Informs What I Write," or poet Robert Creeley's "America's American," and you'll see what I mean.

The print anthology — a 60-page booklet to be given away free at U.S. embassies — is banned from distribution in the U.S. due to a 1948 federal law barring domestic dissemination of official American information aimed at foreign audiences by the U.S. Information Agency (recently annexed by the State Department).

"Technology has made a law obsolete, but the law lives on," George Clack, the State Department editor who produced the anthology, told The New York Times. As a matter of policy, Clack added, the State Department does not give out the Web address of the "Writers on America" site.

With peace warriors planning patriotic anti-war protests, including civil disobedience, for later today in the nation's capital and elsewhere, it's only right that reading warriors take patriotic action of their own. Armchair arrests are unlikely. So what the heck, live dangerously. When reading is a crime, civil disobedience is only a click away.

Dec. 11, 2002 / 11:02 a.m. ET

War and the glory of an old lie: The twain of art and politics met yesterday when "The West Wing" president Martin Sheen advised the reality-show president George W. Bush against going to war with Iraq.

"I've always believed that war is a reflection of despair, and I refused to accept despair," Sheen said. "We are the daughters and sons of God, and that means we are called to be peacemakers."

I never knew that Hollywood was such a religious place, that movie stars and other celebrated entertainers — more than 100 joined Sheen in his plea — were peacemakers. I was under the impression that Hollywood worshipped at the shrine of mayhem and violence, that showbiz liberals and conservatives alike pray to the great god of the box office and the ratings meter. But who can argue that war is not a reflection of despair? Or that going to war in the name of God and country is, equally, not a reflection of the darkest desperation? Or that giving one's life for one's country is great and noble? That it is sweet and right to die for one's country? That it isn't, rather, bitter and wrong?

People who argue for going to war — any war — ought to read the poetry of Wilfred Owen. Let them read war reporter Chris Hedges' just published "War Is a Force That Gives Us Meaning," an anti-war cry from the heart that invokes these lines from Owen's World War I poem "Dulce et Decorum est," which recalls the death of a soldier from a gas attack in the trenches:

> If in smothering dreams you too could pace
> Behind the wagon that we flung him in,
> And watch the white eyes writhing in his face,
> His hanging face, like a devil's sick of sin;
> If you could hear, at every jolt, the blood
> Come gargling from the froth-corrupted lungs,
> Obscene as cancer, bitter as the cud
> Of vile, incurable sores on innocent tongues, —
> My friend, you would not tell with such high zest
> To children ardent for some desperate glory,
> The old Lie: Dulce et decorum est
> Pro Patria mori.

Those are the words of a soldier who died in war himself, at the age of 25. They are not the words of a Hollywood star, however well meaning.

Hedges' interview with tompaine.com is instructive, too. "Patriotism, national self-glorification infects everything, including culture," he says. "Wartime always begins with the destruction of your own culture.

"Once you enter a conflict, or at the inception of a conflict ... the state gives you a language to speak and you can't speak outside that language or it becomes very difficult. There is no communication outside of the clichés and the jingos, 'The War on Terror,' 'Showdown With Iraq,' 'The Axis of Evil,' all of this stuff.

"So that whatever disquiet we feel, we no longer have the words in which to express it. The myth predominates. The myth, which is a lie, of course, built around glory, heroism, heroic self-sacrifice, the nobility of the nation. And it is a kind of intoxication. People lose individual conscience for this huge communal enterprise."

Those are the words of experience, the words of a hardened combat journalist who was himself intoxicated by war. They are not the words of some Hollywood star. We should listen well.

Dec. 12, 2002 / 9:58 a.m. ET

Frank Zappa vs. Tipper Gore, revised: And now let's take a moment to consider the latest pop-star wannabe: Koko the Gorilla. The Big Ape may never rival Eminem for clever rhymes, but she has definite musical taste in reggae, rap, blues and rock — and she has a co-writer credit for the title song on the newly released "Fine Animal Gorilla," a nine-song CD based on her life.

So how does a 31-year-old lowlands gorilla with a 1,000-word vocabulary in modified American Sign Language get a record deal that thousands of "American Idol" losers wish they had? In a word: connections.

The label, Laurel Canyon Animal Co., is headed by a pair of California neighbors, Skip Haynes and Dana Walden. They're betting that Koko's kind of music will make a fortune, according to this morning's Toronto Star.

Haynes says Koko helped them write "Fine Animal Gorilla," along with "Scary Alligator" and "Tickle Me Chase." For instance, on the title song, "there's a throwaway line that says, 'Do you think I'd lie?' " Hayne told the Star. "When Koko heard it, she signed the word 'shame,' so we took the line out."

It makes you wonder what Tipper Gore and the late Frank Zappa might have recorded together if they had collaborated on an album. Maybe you recall Zappa's reply to Tipper's claim that rock lyrics incited deviant behavior: "I wrote a song about dental floss but did anyone's teeth get cleaner?"

Dec. 12, 2002 / 4:48 p.m. ET

The Trent Lott Show: My staff of thousands has been augmented by Some Guy From Texas. He was hired for his postmodern wit and wisdom. When I asked SGFT to give me an arty idea to pass off as my own, this is what he said:

"'The Trent Lott Show' is the best comedy in town. It's an early season replacement for the 'Henry the K Show.' Our next Senate Majority Leader, in defense of his indefensible remarks at Sen. Strom Thurmond's birthday party, says in effect that he was only 8 when Ole Strom ran for president, and he didn't really know the specifics of Ole Strom's segregationist platform.

"In other words, Uncle Trent praised Ole Strom's ideas in ignorance. It turns out Uncle Trent's not really a racist, he's just grossly stupid. Aw shucks, Trent, well that's alright then. We love stupid leaders. Now don't fergit: 'Any suggestion that the segregated past was acceptable or positive is offensive, and it is wrong.' Heck fella, come on up to the back porch and set a spell.

"But see, there's this problem. Uncle Trent went through this once before — in 1980, when he made almost exactly the same statement at some other public event honoring Ole Strom. He was criticized heavily for it and apologized. So the good people of Mississippi rewarded him with a Senate seat. To get into the same mess, 22 years later, sets an indoor record for stupid."

Some Guy From Texas adds that Jon Stewart, on "The Daily Show," observed that Uncle Trent appears to praise the 1948 campaign of Ole Strom every 22 years, which makes Uncle Trent the Haley's Comet of racism.

Do you still think Uncle Trent should be Majority Leader of the Senate? Vote here.

Dec. 13, 2002 / 10:31 a.m. ET

An infinite vision for Ground Zero? New York City Mayor Michael Bloomberg has finally laid out his vision of a Manhattan "downtown for the 21st century."

The mayor's outline for a city he terms "the world's second home" precedes the public unveiling next Wednesday of new design proposals for the World Trade Center site.

Speaking Thursday at a breakfast gathering of civic and business leaders, Bloomberg said: "No matter how magnificent the best design for the 16 acres of the World Trade Center site proves to be, it must be complemented by an equally bold vision for all of Lower Manhattan.

Bloomberg's plan includes:

"A promenade lined with 700 trees" from Ground Zero to Battery Park, which overlooks New York harbor at the tip of Manhattan. It would be the city's equivalentof the Champs-Elysees in Paris.

A new waterfront park along the East River, reaching from the South Street Seaport also to Battery Park, which would embrace the skyscraper canyons of the southern tip of Manhattan in a relaxed, recreational atmosphere.

Housing, parks, schools, libraries and other neighborhood services, including direct "one-seat" subway transportation to regional airports, as well as amenities like movie theaters and neighborhood shopping.

How Bloomberg's plan will play among competing political and commercial interests — and how the $10.6 billion required to pay for it would be financed, especially when the city and state are in dire financial straits — won't be determined until the agencies with the real power to decide what is developed in and around Ground Zero make their choices.

The real power resides with New York Gov. George Pataki, as well as leaders of the various agencies charged with overseeing development of Ground Zero: the Port Authority of New York and New Jersey, the Metropolitan Transportation Authority (currently threatenend by a subway strike) and the Lower Manhattan Development Corp., along with the World Trade Center's leaseholder, Larry Silverstein.

It's a nightmare of tangled influences that won't be sorted out easily. And we haven't even mentioned the memorial, itself a challenge moving along parallel tracks toward decisions that will be made early next year.

Dec. 16, 2002 / 11:03 a.m. ET

Sean Penn, the bad boy in Baghdad: Well-meaning movie stars, and some who don't mean well, have a way of taking on real-world issues that gets them in trouble. That's why Sean Penn doesn't want to do a Jane Fonda.

"You come here on a Friday, you leave on a Sunday, and you start throwing out flamboyant and inflammatory messages — that doesn't seem to be of advantage to anyone," Penn said in Baghdad, where he held a press conference Sunday.

Depending on who's doing the reporting, Sean either "brushed off any concern that he could become the 'Hanoi Jane' Fonda of his era," <u>according to The Washington Post</u>, or "without mentioning her name" said that Fonda's Vietnam experience and subsequent apology to American vets "had been a caution to him," <u>according to The New York Times</u>.

Penn used to be Hollywood's bad boy. He played tough, spoke his mind and didn't care who heard him. He's still Hollywood's bad boy. The Times reports, for instance, that he eluded his government "minder" at one point in his tour of Baghdad, hailed a taxi and headed to the city's slums, where there's underground resistance to Saddam Hussein.

But his circumspect remarks show him to be a Hollywood diplomat, too. He did not want to be seen as supporting Iraq, and <u>he refused to criticize the U.S. government while on foreign soil</u> — even while noting he had a responsibility as a U.S. citizen to question American policy because "somewhere along the line, the actions of this government are the actions of me."

Only a few days ago I was pretty hard on <u>Hollywood stars like Martin Sheen</u>, who take a political position and promote it with all the perks of celebrity — even though I may agree with him. But if I had to pick a Hollywood star to be my mouthpiece, I'd take Penn. At 42, he seems to be a different guy from the guy who married Madonna. These days he sounds like a guy with a head on his shoulders.

Dec. 17, 2002 / 7:58 a.m. ET

Trent Lott's 'Soapdish' serum: Some Guy From Texas is turning out to be a rich source of bully-pulpit material. Here's his latest on <u>"The Trent Lott Show."</u>

"Much in life reminds me of my favorite line from the 1991 movie 'Soapdish,' but nothing so much as Uncle Trent," SGFT says.

"When the soap opera in the movie has degenerated into hilarious ad libs and awful revelations, a producer offers to pull the plug on it. But the network VP says, 'No, don't. It's hypnotic. Like a truth serum.'

"Uncle Trent's <u>slip-up at Ole Strom's birthday party</u> is the same truth serum. It exposed cornerstone Republican messages — 'states rights,' 'reverse discrimination,' 'freedom of association,' ad nauseum — as code for <u>segregation-by-other-means</u>.

"What scares the Republican leadership is that, like the soap opera in 'Soapdish,' events are spiraling out of control. The party leadership has lost control of the message. Anxious to put the truth genie back into the bottle, <u>the leadership of the Republican Party will decide</u> next month whether Uncle Trent must step down as Senate Majority Leader."

He'll be lucky to last the week. Grabbing at straws, <u>Uncle Trent held out hope</u> Monday night that he'd survive. "There's an opportunity here," he told the Black Entertainment Network, like the old pol he is. "This is a wake-up call."

Go back to sleep, Uncle Trent. You must have gotten your alarm bells crossed. <u>The sign of doom is upon you.</u> "It's an omen," SGFT reminds me. "The soap opera in 'Soapdish' was called 'The Sun Also Sets.' "

Dec. 18, 2002 / 7:36 a.m. ET
   Out on assignment: Back later.

Dec. 18, 2002 / 8:37 p.m. ET
   Visions of Ground Zero: I have seen the future and it is B-I-G. It is also tall, fantastical, memorial, ecological, symbolical, cultural, commercial, skyward, subterranean, park-like, Lego-like and — what seems most certain — futuristic, as in a long way off.

   I am talking about <u>nine visions of Ground Zero's future</u>, unveiled this morning by seven teams of architects, urban planners and artists who were chosen by the Lower Manhattan Development Corp. to create designs for rebuilding the World Trade Center site.

   For more than three hours, a torrent of <u>utopian words and images</u> filled the glass-covered Winter Garden across the street from Ground Zero. This vast marble forum, rebuilt since 9/11 and planted with towering palm trees, looks like nothing so much as a ritzy Southern California shopping mall.

   (It was an inescapable if unacknowledged irony that the presentation of these hugely innovative architectural designs was made in such a conventionally old-fashioned architectural space, a sort of Edwardian dowager with modern, shopaholic touches, embraced for comfort between the dome-topped buildings of the World Financial Center. But never mind.)

   I know you're panting to find out: How big? How tall? How fantastical? <u>Here's the lowdown.</u>

Dec. 19, 2002 / 9:01 a.m. ET
   Visionary images of Ground Zero: Without detailed pictures, it's hard to tell what the new designs are all about. Here's <u>MSNBC.com's feast of images</u>. Here's another <u>at The Washington Post</u> and another <u>at The New York Times.</u>

Dec. 20, 2002 / 11:58 a.m. ET
   Slacker Friday? Ha! So much to say and so little time to say it in, now

that my staff of thousands wants me to show up in the office. So I'll limit myself to a patriotic pep talk.

I've been taking a lot of heat for my new hire, Some Guy From Texas. But boy, he makes me proud. Right out of the gate, on Dec. 12, he gave me an arty idea: "The Trent Lott Show."

Then, this past Tuesday, on the strength of SGFT's advice, "Trent Lott's 'Soapdish' serum," I predicted right here — yeah, baby — that Uncle Trent would be lucky to last the week. And now, voila! Uncle Trent is gone.

But my predicton was not the coup de grace. I think it was Robin Givhan's stylish, blow-dried coupe in this morning's Washington Post that cut Uncle Trent down to size.

"All anyone can really see is that hair, as smooth as a geodesic dome and as old-fashioned as a white powdered wig," Givhan wrote. "It is an extraordinarily well-lacquered helmet of hair that seems not to be composed of millions of strands all trimmed to perfection, but rather one solid mass hewn from a walnut stump."

Not to be an ingrate, I can't help wondering why SGFT gave me so much advice about the truth genie and so little about Mississippi's bad-hair politics.

And for all you Republicans out there, who've written to tell me I've been unfair to the GOP, here's some balm for your wounds: "Dixiecrats Triumphant," an essay about the openly racist Democratic presidency of that great Virginia idealist who wanted to save the world from war, the Nobel Peace Prize laureate Woodrow Wilson.

Dec. 23, 2002 / 8:48 a.m. ET

Some notes: With public hearings on the design proposals set for Jan. 13-14, it would be wise to consider Newsday columnist Jimmy Breslin's point that turning Ground Zero into an extraordinarily fancy graveyard would be a mistake.

Artist-filmmaker Greg Allen tells me the giant grid of the "dream team" design by Meier, Gwathmey, Holl and Eisenman (one of the nine proposals unveiled last week) is like "a stealth deconstructivist memorial" to the shattered column fragments that remained standing in the rubble after the Twin Towers collapsed. I hadn't thought of that.

Meanwhile, Chicago Tribune architecture critic Blair Kamin makes the case for Daniel Libeskind's proposal. (Free registration required.) And The New York Times critic Herbert Muschamp writes that the new designs are so imaginative that even if none of them is built at Ground Zero, knockoffs are sure to be popping up elsewhere around the world.

One issue that must be decided, Muschamp writes, is whether New York wants to be the progressive leader of a renaissance in global world culture. The issue for many people, however, is safety.

Lots of Americans say they want the World Trade Center site rebuilt "bigger and better" than it was before. Several of the designers went out of their way to explain how safe their buildings will be. But how many people would be willing to return to work at Ground Zero, say, on the 89th floor?

I asked Meyer Feig, president of the World Trade Center Tenants Association, which represents 100 of the roughly 300 small businesses that used to be quartered in the Twin Towers. Feig is a 9/11 survivor. He was in his office in the South Tower on the day of the attacks. His office, let's note, was only on the 18th floor. Would he be willing to take an office on the 81st floor?

"Absolutely," he said, not missing a beat. "All of us would. We're advocating for the first right to be in the building. We want it to be built bigger and better. That's why these new designs are so inspiring."

Rudolph Giuliani, New York's former mayor, hasn't made up his mind yet. But for now, he says, putting the world's largest buildings at Ground Zero is "a mistake."

Dec. 23, 2002 / 8:53 a.m. ET

Think organic: There's much to be said for author Michael Abelman's proposal to put an urban farm on a couple of Ground Zero acres to reconnect the site with "a sense of the earth." (Free registration required.)

Connecting city dwellers with nature is a strong impulse in all the futuristic designs unveiled last week, contrary to the impression created by their high-tech wizardry (and to Abelman's own understanding of them). In fact, all the designs proposed parks and gardens of various kinds. But none proposed a farm.

The more I think of it, the more sense it makes. Until I spent several snowbound years in the rural reaches of northeastern Vermont, I was typical of doofus city dwellers who think milk comes from cartons, eggs from egg crates and meat from the freezer. Where I lived, the closest "town" was a village of 56 people and a gas pump on a gravel road surrounded by farms. My nearest neighbor was a dairy farmer with arthritic knuckles the size of golf balls. In his entire life he never left the farm for more than the time between milkings. Talk about unsung heroism.

Abelman, the author of "On Good Land" and the founder of the Center for Urban Agriculture, doesn't mean having milk cows and manure piles or a barnyard with chickens at Ground Zero. But he does mean having orchards, as well as growing fruits and vegetables and flowers in greenhouse environments, and selling the yield in an open-air farmers' market.

Can you think of a more nourishing memorial to those who died on 9/11? The practical value for the neighborhood would be matched by its symbolic value. A scholarship fund for families of the victims might be steadily replenished, for instance, by a small percentage of the farm sales. That seems to me a fittingly organic exchange between the living and the dead as worthy as a monument in stone.

Dec. 24, 2002 / 8:42 a.m. ET

Best wishes for 2003: 'Till then. Or as Monty Woolley said in "The Man Who Came to Dinner": "If you're ever in New York, try and find me."

Share your perspective on entertainment and the arts with <u>Jan Herman</u>. MSNBC is not responsible for the content of Internet links.

Jan Herman

Latest entertainment and arts news from the Web

Entries from Jan. 2 to Jan. 31, 2003
(Some links may be nonfunctional.)
Back to 'The Juice'

LATEST UPDATES

Jan. 2, 2003 / 10:58 a.m. ET

Starting with the grotesque: As U.S. troops mass for war in Iraq, I can't help thinking of two Georg Grosz drawings — "Fit for active service" and "Angel of Peace." I was tempted to send them as New Year's cards, but didn't. Maybe I should have.

Jan. 6, 2003 / 9:48 a.m. ET

Is Dubya a TR wannabe? It's dangerous for a sitting president to read the biography of a predecessor, especially if it's as good as "Theodore Rex," the second volume of Edmund Morris' biography of our 26th president. A good book gives people ideas.

So here's a crazy theory: George W. Bush, who read "Theodore Rex" after he moved into the Oval Office, wants to be the new Teddy Roosevelt. The theory may be expressed by this equation: $W = tr^2$ (where "t" represents the variable of world terrorism and "r" is the Rove constant). I told you it was crazy.

But Some Guy From Texas, the new hire for my staff of thousands and the author of this theory, insists he's onto something.

He writes: "It has occurred to me that, despite their enormous differences in personality, style and accomplishment, there exist some fascinating similarities between Dubya and TR.

"Both were born to wealth and influence and became Republicans closely identified with the interests of the wealthy (TR's trust-busting reputation notwithstanding);

"Neither enjoyed particular success in the business world (compare TR's failed cattle ventures with Dubya's failed energy ventures and other business flops);

160

"Neither was actually elected to his first term as president (TR took office upon the assassination of McKinley and Dubya ... well, we know that story, don't we?);

"As president, both appear to have searched for a defining historical event by which their administrations would be remembered.

"Roosevelt found his historical hook with the Panama Canal. 'The canal,' he said, "was by far the most important action I took in foreign affairs during the time I was President. When nobody could or would exercise efficient authority, I exercised it.'

"Is war with Iraq President Bush's Panama Canal? Consider his options: The economy's in a mess, and the so-called war on terrorism has stalled. In this context, war with Saddam has major appeal. It's a war our Defense Department hawks say we can win with little loss of American lives.

"TR was enormously popular during his administration and is still well regarded by the public. What do we all remember about Teddy Roosevelt? His charge up San Juan Hill in Cuba and the Panama Canal. I'll bet President Bush remembers that, too.

"Your obedient servant,

Some Guy From Texas"

Memo to SGFT: Sheesh. All that may be true, but the differences between TR and Dubya are much more noteworthy than their similarities:

TR was an ebullient polymath ("a many-sided man, and every side was like an electric battery"), while Dubya is lucky to put a grammatical sentence together;

TR championed conservation, setting aside 230 million acres for preservation by creating five National Parks, 150 national forests and other pristine areas; Dubya has allowed drilling for oil on public land near two National Parks in Utah and, among other places, at the Padre Island National Seashore in Texas, along the longest stretch of undeveloped beach in the United States; helping to diminish TR's legacy still further, Dubya also favors opening the Arctic National Wildlife Refuge to drilling and is rightly regarded as an enemy of environmental conservation (except when he's clearing brush on his Texas ranch);

TR took on the railroads, toughened the antitrust laws and tamed the robber barons of Wall Street, which is why he was dubbed The Trustbuster (though it's something of a misnomer); he also strengthened other federal regulations, for instance, pushing through the Pure Food and Drug Act; by contrast, Dubya has done nothing about corporate malfeasance except pay lip service to corporate justice, and he believes in nothing so much as

161

eliminating federal regulation wherever he can; <u>TR spoke softly and carried a big stick</u>; he was <u>a master of diplomacy</u>, helping to mediate the end of the Russo-Japanese War, <u>which earned him the Nobel Peace Prize</u>. Dubya talks tough, witness his famous ultimatum about <u>"the axis of evil,"</u> then has to back off when <u>put to the test by North Korea</u>; his disdain for its leader, <u>Dr. Evil</u>, is justified; but his contempt for diplomacy has already alienated even longtime U.S. allies.

George W. Bush might like to be seen as the new Teddy Roosevelt. If only ...

Jan. 7, 2003 / 9:59 a.m. ET

He doesn't work for peanuts: That's pretty much why America's most celebrated architect, Frank Gehry, chose not to submit a design plan for Ground Zero.

"I was invited to be on one of the teams," <u>he told Deborah Solomon</u>, "but I found it demeaning that the agency [charged with developing the design plans] paid only $40,000 for all that work. ... When you're only paid $40,000, you're treated as if that is your worth."

Total reimbursement for the seven teams came to $280,000, a tiny fraction of their combined costs of about $4 million.

So why would even wealthy architects foot such a large bill? The prestige and the publicity, of course. Some teams have even ventured the notion that they felt a pro bono obligation as Americans.

If Gehry had put his hat into the ring, what would he have designed? A park of five or six acres "with a lake in it and a place you could picnic" — all covered by a soaring roof, he said.

That's not so different in concept from a combined version of two of the THINK team's three separate proposals: <u>The Great Hall</u>, a 13-acre plaza that would be "the largest covered space in the world" (30 stories high under a glass roof, a sort of "vestibule to the city") and the Sky Park, a 16-acre rooftop garden that floats above the street grid.

But after you look at <u>some of Gehry's buildings and furniture designs</u>, you can't help being disappointed that he didn't take his shot at Ground Zero.

Jan. 7, 2003 / 2:59 p.m. ET

The Grammy game: Everybody's taking bets. <u>"It'll be the Boss versus the Brat,"</u> as rock critic David Segal notes. I'm betting it's the Brat. But the real Grammy game is gold stars for all: "This year, <u>there are 104 categories</u>, up from 101 last year."

With so many hair-splitting categories already — Best Rock Gospel Album and Best Pop/Contemporary Gospel Album or Best Pop Instrumental Performance and Best Pop Instrumental Album — you have to wonder who won't win a Grammy?

Would it be surprising if the Grammy folks in their wisdom were to come up with another hair-splitting category? Say, Best Rock Performance By A Left-Handed Duo Or Group With Vocal to distinguish it from Best Rock Performance By A Right-Handed Duo Or Group With Vocal? I don't think so.

The reason for all the categories is transparent. As my MSNBC colleague Paige Newman says, "This is just a way for as many people as possible to slap a 'Grammy Nominated' sticker on their CDs." It's a matter of marketing, not excellence. And now that we're moving full bore into the silly season for awards, we should keep that in mind.   In this month alone, we've got the People's Choice Awards (coming Sunday); the Golden Satellite Awards (also coming Sunday); the American Music Awards (coming Monday); the American Film Institute awards (Jan. 16); the Golden Globe Awards (Jan. 19); the Directors Guild of America nominations (Jan. 21); the Screen Actors Guild Awards nominations (Jan 28).

And that's just the beginning.

Jan. 8, 2003 / 2:14 p.m. ET

Gold rush with silver lining? Humiliation television can now boast a record-setting performance by "Joe Millionaire," a show that critic Tom Shales terms "mean and venal" and not worth a plugged nickel.

The Fox network had so many viewers tuning in to see lovelorn females and gold-diggers compete for the studly affection of a purported bachelor heir to $50 million that it drew the largest audience ever for the premiere of a so-called "unscripted" series.

But "Joe Millionaire" is also drawing some intriguing Weblog commentary and even some real soul searching. So, if you can believe it, maybe it's doing something constructive for the culture?

More on the silly season for awards: In the abject Grammy spirit of how not to market artistic excellence, a friend of mine suggests a new category be added to the upcoming Golden Globes: "Most Shameful TV Performance by a Has-Been." That way the entire cast of "Celebrity Mole Hawaii" — debuting tonight — could be nominated sight unseen.

Jan. 9, 2003 / 4:40 p.m. ET

Shining light on Danny Pearl: Although Wall Street Journal reporter

Daniel Pearl did not die at Ground Zero, his death at the hands of al-Qaida-linked terrorists in Pakistan was as much a part of the 9/11 attacks as anyone's.

I suppose it's possible that Pearl will be honored at the World Trade Center memorial. But it's not likely.

The preliminary guidelines just issued say that the memorial should recognize every person who died on 9/11 at Ground Zero in New York, at the Pentagon in Washington, and in the Pennsylvania field where United Flight 93 crashed, along with those who died in the WTC bombing of 1993.

Even if he is not honored at Ground Zero, a Daniel Pearl Memorial Sculpture will pay tribute to him across the street at the World Financial Center, where The Wall Street Journal is headquartered. Created by John Corcoran, a 53-year-old sculptor who lives in Tivoli, N.Y., the memorial is to be unveiled and dedicated Jan. 23 in a 9th floor elevator lobby (which looks, unfortunately, like a gloomy airport waiting room but without any seats).

Journal senior writer Robert Frank, a close friend of Pearl, says Corcoran's piece was chosen from a half-dozen proposals largely because it used light as a medium to reflect "Danny's radiance as a person" and because Corcoran, whose photo-journalist father died before he was born, "felt a close kinship with Danny's story."

The sculpture will have three slabs of polished and brushed aluminum embedded with fiber optic lights. The slabs will jut perpendicularly from the wall and will stand at a raked angle like so: / / /, training their light beams on three plaques. One will say: "Daniel Pearl, Wall Street Journal Foreign Correspondent, 1963-2002." Another will say: "They may have blown out a candle, but the light is still on."

The third will pay tribute to "the idea that Danny stood for," Frank says, "the idea that the meaning of journalism is 'to shine a light on the dark corners of the world.' It's intended to inspire other journalists."

The trouble is, Corcoran's sculpture will be more or less buried from public view and its symbolic light hidden in the dark — unless the Journal decides to let visitors up to the 9th floor uninvited. Right now, for security reasons, it doesn't.

Why not place the sculpture in the main lobby of One World Financial Center, also called The Dow Jones Building, where it could just as well inspire the journalists and the public alike? Placing it there, where 9/11 history was also made, would allow all Americans to see it, not to mention tourists from all parts of the globe who come through that lobby in droves everyday to get to Ground Zero.

Jan. 10, 2003 / 1:58 p.m. ET

Woman aboard! The 161-year-old Vienna Philharmonic — among the world's highest-paid orchestras and historically the most important in terms of symphonic music — has just hired the first female musician ever to sit in its midst as a full-time member: 27-year-old violist Ursula Plaichinger.

But the exception proves the rule — that in the case of the VPO, testosterone rules as always. For 155 years the orchestra had been an all-male bastion that believed — and still believes — in white, male supremacy. Then, in 1997, it was forced to hire a female harpist due to pressure from feminists who'd mounted an Internet campaign led by an American expatriate composer, William Osborne, and a New York trombonist, Monique Buzzarté, that drew worldwide ridicule to the orchestra's hidebound ideology.

Humiliated though not humbled, the orchestra's leadership fought tooth and nail to preserve its privilege and dignity, and claimed that by hiring the harpist it was turning over a new leaf and opening its ranks to women. In fact, it was putting on a fig leaf to cover up its continuing exclusion of women.

A harpist, for example, sits at the edge of the orchestra and is present only when the score calls for a harp, which isn't that often. Indeed, the VPO's female harpist had played with the orchestra for more than 20 years as an anonymous permanent substitute, earning lower pay than members.

When she was voted into the orchestra, her name (Anna Lelkes) was allowed to be printed in the VPO programs for the first time. But even as a member, she was not allowed to be seen in the VPO's popular TV broadcasts. Cameramen were instructed to show only her hands, never her face or figure.

Women make up roughly a third of the musicians in leading American orchestras like the New York Philharmonic or the Los Angeles Philharmonic. Many top European orchestras, too, have a similar percentage of women filling their ranks, especially the Berlin Philharmonic, which rivals the Vienna Phil in stature. So it's something in the narrow spirit of the VPO, not in mere old-world values, that prizes an exclusionary ideology.

One interesting sidebar to all of this is that The New York Times, which is the only U.S. newspaper that the VPO takes seriously — mainly because it can affect attendance for the orchestra's annual U.S. tour to New York's

Carnegie Hall — has tended to pooh-pooh the issue even as it rips the exclusionary policies of all-male business clubs and all-white golfing establishments.

Given the VPO's unusually extensive U.S. tour this year (beginning Feb. 26 and including stops in Chicago, Detroit, Boston, Philadelphia and Washington), Osborne's cohorts are sure to be out picketing and protesting. We'll see whether the Times bothers to cover that.

Jan. 12, 2003 / 3:57 p.m. ET

Women overboard! When you write about the Vienna Philharmonic as an institution, you inevitably get into a welter of contradictions, misinformation, disinformation and issues of sexism and cultural chauvinism — to say nothing of objections from people who couldn't care less either about classical music or women's rights.

Friday's item, Woman aboard, for instance, stated that the orchestra had hired a female violist as a full-time member. This was my interpretation — and the interpretation of others more expert than I — of the news in London's Guardian that the Vienna Phil had "appointed its first female musician, signalling the fall of another of Europe's all-male bastions."

Though I explained that one of the world's top orchestras was not, in fact, turning over a new leaf but rather applying a fig leaf to its shameful exclusion of women, I shouldn't have assumed that being "appointed" meant being accepted into the club.

In fact, violist Ursula Plaichinger, who was hired in February, is the only non-harpist woman hired by the Vienna Philharmonic since they agreed to admit women in 1997. But due to tenure requirements, she will not be able to apply for membership in the Philharmonic until 2004. In the meantime she's allowed to play in the orchestra as a substitute.

The stir over the issue in classical-musical circles resulted from 27-year-old violist Ursula Plaichinger's appearance in the orchestra for this year's New Year's concert, which The Guardian described as causing "a sensation."

In a message to the International Alliance for Women in Music, William Osborne writes: "This was the first time in the orchestra's history that a woman other than a harpist had performed with the Philharmonic during one of its New Year's concerts, which are broadcast to a potential audience of over one billion people by about 47 broadcast corporations worldwide. (The New York Times recently listed the actual public at 50 million people.)"

The reason for all the fuss is precisely because the Vienna Phil has such a huge audience. But it's also because the orchestra is considered the pride of Western culture, and its behavior — not so much its musical performance, which continues to draw raves — tells an awful lot about the values that Western culture represents.

For a fuller treatment of the subject, check out Osborne's latest essay, "Music, sexism and war" my own "Taking on the Vienna Philharmonic" and his update of more recent developments, "Measuring testosterone in Vienna."

Jan. 13, 2003 / 8:23 a.m. ET

Let's go to the videotape: The fact that Tony Danza was the host of the People's Choice Awards tells us how important Sunday night's awards show was. How lame was the show? Let us count the ways: The Dixie Chicks didn't turn up in person to collect their trophy; neither did Creed, nor Mel Gibson, nor Eminem. Julia Roberts didn't turn up either. We witnessed, if you can believe it, videotape of Roberts accepting four of her trophies from past years. She now has nine. It's no wonder she didn't turn up. Here's the show's Web site. Next case.

Jan. 14, 2003 / 11:32 a.m. ET

People want to know: What do I think of Pete Townshend's predicament? What am I supposed to say, I'm proud of the guy? I'd rather let Ryan McGee say what I think for me: "I haven't been hit this hard since I found out Billy Dee Williams was beating up his girlfriend."

OK, so McGee can't spell. Apparently they didn't teach him that at Harvard. And he hasn't learned since they let him out. But he sure knows his Townshend.

Meanwhile, since spelling is not a requirement of the job, McGee has applied for the position of CEO of America Online, which he claims to have seen advertised as a "job opportunity." "I was sort of surprised to see it listed on Monster.com this morning," he writes.

AOL must have been more surprised.

Jan. 14, 2003 / 11:49 a.m. ET

Great moments in musical history: What can I say? Like a lot of people, I had a soft spot for Sheryl Crow before she wore the T-shirt that said "War Is Not the Answer" at the American Music Awards, which was my favorite moment of the show.

Another great moment was when Eminem gave new meaning to the phrase "phoning it in." The Great White Rapper, who won four awards, was a no-show but sent his thanks by cell phone. "Hey y'all, this is Eminem on the phone!" his "8 Mile" co-star Mekhi Phifer told us as he came onstage, phone to ear, to accept an award for his good buddy.

I wouldn't be surprised if the call was faked. That thought immediately crossed my mind. No one else took the phone to verify whether Eminem or anyone else was on the call. But who cares? It was a clever, if patronizing piece of showmanship.

We all saw those moments. And you probably have favorites of your own. But I also had two favorite moments that nobody else saw.

One was the look of embarrassment on the faces of ABC executives when Sharon Osbourne's expletives became a running theme of the show. The other was the look of chagrin on George (the father) Bush's face after he watched the videotape of himself saying how happy he was to be part of the show ("I'm very proud to be part of tonight's tribute" to Alabama). Barbara Bush probably washed his mouth out with soap just for being associated with such a bleeping telecast.

You also have to wonder what this country has come to when a former president sees fit to shill for a band. At least Bill Clinton could play the sax. (I can hear Bill Clinton haters now. So let me add: Yes, shilling for Alabama pales in comparison with ... oh, never mind.)

Following on the heels of the dopey People Choice Awards, which had so many no-shows there basically was no show, it didn't make much difference that some AMA winners failed to turn up to collect their trophies.

What really annoys me is that the American Music Awards shares the same acronym as the American Medical Association. Everytime I read AMA, I think of doctors in white coats, not rappers and rockers in tattoos and piercings. It's so uncool.

Jan. 15, 2003 / 1:48 p.m. ET

Here come the Golden Globules: Because the Golden Globes are chosen by a grand gaggle of 90 reporters (the Hollywood Foreign Press Association), I think it's more accurate to term the award the Golden Globules — even if they've become a major Tinseltown event.

Not including the fact that Pia Zadora once won one, the Globules are more about marketing and publicity than artistic excellence. I know I've said that about the Grammy game. But that's what all these awards are about.

The whole point of the Globules, set for Sunday on NBC, is to trot out the stars, show off the fashions, promote the film industry and make money for the box office and — dare I say it? — for the network. (If they actually honor art, so be it.) And let's not forget, the studios use them to influence the Oscars, the granddaddy of film honors.(Nomination ballots are due back Jan.

29 from 6,000 Oscar voters.)

As Rick Lyman points out, it's "Dance Time For Oscar (But Don't Admit It)." (Registration required.)

Of course, with more awards than you can count on both hands this month alone, critics and their best-of-the-year picks have come in for criticism and controversy, too. (Registration required.)

So in the spirit of the age, here's my top 10 flicks, based on a strict and strictly enforced standard — The Juice Enjoyment Quotient (JEQ) — and voted on by my staff of thousands. This means films made the list only if they were either seriously entertaining or lightly entertaining. I didn't see all the films out there. Maybe that's why I found it hard-going after No. 1.

1. "Talk to Her" (Far and away the best movie of 2002, foreign or domestic, and I was never a big fan of director Pedro Almodovar. Now I am. He proves what has become very rare — that a movie can have the fullness and depth of fine literature.) JEQ: A

2. "Catch Me If You Can" (Thoroughly enjoyable, and Tom Hank's comic caricature of an FBI agent with a Beantown accent is the cream on top.) JEQ: B+

3. "The Quiet American" (Serious, adult and, if it's not Michael Caine's swan song, it's a beautiful swan dive. No belly flop there.) JEQ: B+

4. "25th Hour" (A little claustrophic as in not-a-big production. But when Edward Norton and Philip Seymour Hoffman do their things in a movie as gutsy as this one, it's a gift. Kudos to director Spike Lee.) JEQ: B+

5. "Y Mama Tambien" (A kicky flick that was both fun and touching. And did I say sexy?) JEQ: B+

6. "Adaptation" (I'm not a Nicolas Cage fan. But he won me over with this one. The complicated scenario was cleanly told, which means: At least I could follow it.) JEQ: B+

7. "The Trials of Henry Kissinger" (First-class propaganda.) JEQ: B+

8. "About Schmidt" (A bit dreary in its one-note tone, but worth seeing for Jack Nicholson, who's in just about every scene and who gives a dead-wire everyman performance to Kathy Bates' live-wire nut case. JEQ: B

9. "The Hours" (Only because Julianne Moore can do no wrong in my eyes, because I was impressed by the low register of Nicole Kidman's voice, because I'm an Ed Harris fan, and because I've got to take my hat off to a movie that managed to squeeze something out of a novel I found so precious it was unreadable.) JEQ: B

10. "Chicago" (It's a lot of stylish fun and a technical marvel of filmmaking. But I prefer the Broadway original. I felt short-changed by the movie.) JEQ: B

The others that didn't make the list:

"Far From Heaven" (Gorgeous to look at, and it has the incomparable Julianne Moore, who puts on a performance that is not only Oscar-worthy but the likes of which come around once in a blue moon. Unfortunately, the film was so static that my sweater nearly got stuck to the screen.) JEQ: B

"The Lord of the Rings: The Two Towers" (Surprised me because it's far better than I expected and it looks great, but it needed a story.) JEQ: B-

"The Pianist" (It has a lot to be said for it in terms of the music, the visual canvas and the Holocaust theme. But there were some gaffes that undermined the movie's credibility — like the disappearance of the hero's family after a lengthy setup, yet not another word about them to the bitter, schmaltzy end about a noble Third Reich soldier. "Schindler's List" was better.) JEQ: B-

You're probably wondering: What happened to "My Big Fat Greek Wedding"? I'm wondering, too. It was cute and sweet, but a little too cute, sweet and kitchen-sink for my taste. JEQ: B-

Finally, "The Gangs of New York" (A huge disappointment, Daniel Day-Lewis notwithstanding. Enough said.) JEQ: C+

Jan. 16, 2003 / 10:49 a.m. ET

From a woman's point of view: I went to get a drink of water. Sure enough three women were standing at the water cooler, yammering about "The Bachelorette." They let me in on the woman's point of view.

"The men get so upset," one of them said. "That's what's most interesting. You think women take rejection badly? These guys take it worse! That's a confirmation of what women already know. It's an undercurrent of 'The Bachelorette' — more fascinating even than seeing the woman as Queen Bee. You see these guys all holding it in — resentment, disappointment, frustration, whatever it is. Of course, that could have all been faked for the camera. We don't really know."

"I'll tell you another thing," said the second. "There's no way Trista is going to pick a guy much younger than her, not when she's 29. A couple years younger, maybe. But not 24 like Jeff, the football player, even though I think he's a nice guy. At her age, a few years younger seems like a decade."

"And I'll tell you something else," said the third. "If Trista sees the scene they showed after the goodbyes, where the men are acting like disgusting frathouse animals, she'll dump Jamie, the ballplayer."

Reality marches on, but reality TV marches in, taking over far more than water-cooler chit-chat.

Jan. 17, 2003 / 8:54 a.m. ET

Worldwide child pornsters: Rocker Pete Townshend's recent arrest for downloading child porn from the Web got me to thinking: Has it occurred to anyone that the way to eliminate most child porn is to get rid of undercover government stings?

One of my sources tells me that when he was an assistant prosecutor in the 1980s as much as 90 percent of the child porn on the market was put there by governments to snare users. My source says it wouldn't be surprising if that's still the case.

Following Townshend's arrest, the U.S. Postal Service announced on its Web site that he was taken into custody by Great Britain's National Crime Squad due to the "largest global action ever undertaken against child pornographers, with over 4,000 search warrants served in countries around the world."

Not to make excuses for Townshend, but is anyone taking bets that he downloaded from an undercover government child-porn site?

Jan. 18, 2003 / 11:54 a.m. ET

Ground Zero hearings didn't add up: The public hearings earlier this week to draw a reaction to Ground Zero developments plans were so dismal that I've avoided mentioning them. With some exceptions, most people who went to the microphones delivered a litany of repetitive complaints. Their remarks tended to show that they hadn't paid close attention to the new designs or, if they had, chose to ignore them so they could denounce them.

In some ways you couldn't blame the public. The agency charged with overseeing the plans, the Lower Manhattan Development Corp., couldn't even get a slide show to work at the hearings — let alone provide clarity over the past few months, despite the best of intentions, about an admittedly complicated process to put flesh on bare bones.

Rather than rehash what happened, I'd rather let you have a look for yourself (if you can stand it). Here's an archived Webcast of the meetings. If you prefer to read the gory details, here's an article, "Trade Center plans gain zero ground," by Lynn Duke of The Washington Post.

Since then, Edward Wyatt has reported in The New York Times that three designs have emerged as the public's favorites — Norman Foster's (favored by 25 percent), Daniel Libeskind's (18 percent) and Peterson/Littenberg's (18 percent). The hitch, though, is that the conclusion is based on "a review of 834 comments or queries sent to the development corporation's Web site" this past week — hardly a representative or scientific sample.

In fact, that sample had to be pried out of the LMDC via a Freedom of Information Request, Wyatt reports, and represents "only one-third of the 2,500 responses submitted to the site since the plans were released." (Given the widespread reporting about the plans, you'd think the agency would have received more than 2,500 responses. Maybe people can't find the LMDC Web site?)

By comparison, more than 101,816 votes at MSNBC.com have registered the top three preferences in this order: Peterson/Littenberg's (23 percent), Foster's (22 percent), United's and THINK's (tied at 15 percent), with only eight percent favoring Libeskind's. In any case, as Wyatt (and many others, including me) reported: "While rebuilding officials have sought public opinion, they are not bound to follow it." Which probably has a lot to do with the disappointment voiced at the hearings.

Jan. 20, 2003 / 8:26 a.m. ET

Elvis the King and the real Dr. King: While everybody under the sun seems to believe that Elvis Presley is an undying pop icon, Greil Marcus thinks just the opposite: Presley's significance has become more myth than reality.

Why bring up the subject now? Because today is Martin Luther King Day — and Marcus makes the essential connection between King's lasting importance and Presley's dying fall.

"It seemed to me," Marcus writes in the current issue of the Three Penny Review, "that in 2002, twenty-five years after Elvis Presley's death, and more than two years after the last interesting Elvis impersonator, Bill Clinton, had left his stage, the real story was the evaporation of Elvis Presley in American life."

If this heresy were coming from anyone other than the author of "Mystery Train," "Lipstick Traces," "Invisible Republic" and "Double Trouble" — a critic who is one of Presley's biggest fans and who is arguably the greatest cultural historian of rock 'n' roll — you could dismiss it as blasphemous hogwash.

Marcus points out that on April 8, 1968, four days after Martin Luther King Jr. was assassinated, Coretta Scott King was photographed leading a procession of mourners down Main Street in Memphis. With her were civil rights leaders Ralph Abernathy and Andrew Young, her own children, and thousands who walked behind them.

"They were passing under the marquee of the State Theater, which was playing Elvis Presley's latest movie," Marcus writes, "and the irony of the title of the movie could not have been contrived by a vengeful god: 'STAY AWAY JOE.' The title screamed: Where was Elvis? In fact he was in Hollywood, getting an electric gate installed at his house, having just returned from a weekend in Las Vegas."

But Memphis "was still his home — and there is no reason to think it even occurred to Elvis Presley to be present on this day, the most solemn day in the history of his city, or that, even if he sometimes recited the end of Martin Luther King's 1963 speech before the Lincoln Memorial, it occurred to Elvis that the assassination in Memphis had anything to do with him. He was elsewhere."

That is why The King's story — contrary to the story of Martin Luther King — "may cease to travel with the story of his country," Marcus argues. "That is why, in times to come, Elvis Presley may signify mostly as a joke (as he does today, appearing in so many stupid editorial cartoons sharing a cave with Osama bin Laden), a joke the content of which no one will be able to really explain."

Jan. 21, 2000 / 10:01 a.m. ET

'American Idol'-atry, torture by song: Despite the TV teases that show him on the rampage, I don't know whether Simon Cowell has the courage of his "convictions." But they will be tested tonight by this season's two-hour premiere of "American Idol."

I hope he is not ready to put up with torture by song. If he's in a foul mood, it will be entertaining. If he's in a really foul mood, we may be witness to death by murder. Paula Abdul will be there either to administer artificial respiration or to perform last rites.

Compared with last night's "Joe Millionaire," which gets my vote for lamest excuse for a TV show, anything — even Randy Jackson — would be entertaining.

The relationship between the level of national stress — imminent war, a flailing economy — and an escape into fantasy has been demonstrated time and again by Hollywood movies. The same is true of TV programming.

To paraphrase Stephen Sondheim: "Tragedy tomorrow, 'American Idol' tonight!"

Jan. 22, 2003 / 9:10 a.m. ET

Kooks and wannabes: I'd forgot how many kooks were out there. I'd forgot that America's cities teemed with show-biz wannabes, their empty heads filled with stardust. I'd forgot how many deluded exhibitionists, narcissistic cranks and the just plain untalented would show up to audition for the first "American Idol" of the season. I'd forgot how dismal it was to watch a freak show.

But "Idol" reminded me with its motley parade of dreamers and crackpots. It was ugly to see their foolish, desperate hopes exposed, not by the judges who spent the evening impersonating themselves, but by the producers who exploited them all and by viewers like me.

Some critics enjoyed what they saw. The TV critic of the New York Daily News, for example, says it was swell. Some were mixed. Here's a well-considered take by Eric Olsen. And some people never give up wanting to play the fool. One is suing the show for being "ageist."

Jan. 21, 2003 / 8:58 p.m. ET

Libeskind, Gaudí and Buck Rogers: With officials soon to choose two design proposals as templates for Ground Zero reconstruction, the editorial page of The New York Times has thrown its weight behind Daniel Libeskind's — variously described as futuristic, dignified and thoughtful.

"One of the two design finalists should certainly be Daniel Libeskind's soaring garden tower and ground-level memorial that uses the slurry wall holding back the Hudson River as a backdrop," a Times editorial said this morning. It also said: "Neither [of the proposals] should hark to the past to recreate the twin office towers." Which is certain to outrage from some sky-high patriots.

Along with others, Chicago Tribune architecture critic Blair Kamen had already beat the drum for Libeskind's design with a Dec. 23 article, "One plan for WTC site stands above the rest."

Lebiskind established a reputation "as a poet of tragedy" with his best-known project, the Jewish Museum in Berlin. "Shaped like a fractured Star of David. [it] packs such an emotional punch that it drew thousands of visitors before it was filled with objects," Kamen wrote. "This latest design firmly cements that reputation."

Meanwhile, a building designed by surrealist Spanish architect Antoni Gaudí in 1908, but never built, is about to be entered in the separate memorial design competition, according to the Times. You've got to see it to believe it. (Registration may be required.)

It rivals the Empire State Building in height and looks like "a Buck Rogers rocket ship." If that's not weird enough, it reportedly was conceived as a hotel for "the very site where the World Trade Center was eventually built a half-century later.

Here are some of Gaudí's buildings in Barcelona: the Holy Family Church, the Colegio Teresiano, the Casa Milà Barcelona — La Pedrera and

174

the Sagrada Familia School. When it comes to a Ground Zero memorial, though, I have the feeling that Gaudí is still ahead of his time.

Jan. 23, 2003 / 1:48 p.m. ET

Bulletin from the arts front: Peace posters and protest signs, long a people's art, are out in force these days. As marches against war make their way through the streets here and abroad, it is a reminder that "good political art makes deep logical and emotional points in an eye blink, sometimes trumping other modes of discourse," as my friend the poet George Mattingly says.

The best of it, like this protest poster (subtitle: "A Message From the Ministry of Homeland Security") from Saturday's San Francisco Peace March, can even turn the iconography of totalitarian propaganda on its head. Not all of it is that artful. But Peter Tannenbaum, the president of Tenny Press, has posted a great slide show that displays various kinds of homemade antiwar propaganda seen at the march.

John Ashcroft IS WATCHING YOU

A Message from the Ministry of Homeland Security

tennypress.com

"I was blown away by the creativity expressed in the handmade signs," Tannenbaum tells me. "It is rare in our prefabricated mass culture that people actually take the time to produce their own messages."

Slide show:
- SMALL PICTURES
- LARGE PICTURES

See images from demonstrations both for and against military action against Iraq

Artful or not, they invariably expressed real feelings — like one that says in huge letters: "I'm so sick of U.S. foreign policy that I made this sign!" Or the one that says: "Draft the Bush twins" with caricatures of two helmeted women and a pair of cocktail glasses. Or how about this one? "Impeach the dim son." which plays on the "dim sum" breakfast delicacies in San Francisco's fabled Chinatown.

Not incidentally, the San Francisco march was estimated by police and media reports as being in the tens of thousands. But people who were there say those estimates vastly underestimated the turnout, which filled the entire Embarcadero and all of Market Street up to and including the entire Civic Center Plaza — and which they put at no less than 100,000 and maybe as much as 250,000.

Here are some photos from the San Francisco march. I recall that during '60s, protestors claimed that the park police or highway patrol — and the media — routinely divided the real number of people in protest marches against the Vietnam War by a factor of five and sometimes more.

This just in: Ken Brownlow, of Winston-Salem, N.C., messages me that the poster above was lifted from the poster, "John Ashcroft's Watching You," by the Propaganda Remix Project. (Scroll down, or use their slide show.) Propaganda Remix looks like it has enough posters to supply protest marches from now to the end of the 21st century, if we get there. And here's the guy behind them all, Michah Wright, artist-propagandist extraordinaire.

Jan. 24, 2003 / 10:19 a.m. ET

The weird, the satirical, the dignified: Since we were speaking yesterday of protest posters, here is some equal-opportunity propaganda art aimed at the music industry, sexual-abstinence advocates, the American Library Association, the California Public Utilities Commission ("Turn up the juice, California, I like it!") and, leaving no stone unturned, the enemies of Microsoft. (MSNBC is a Microsoft-NBC joint venture.)

I also can't let the week go by without noting that the Daniel Pearl Memorial Sculpture was unveiled yesterday in a 9th-floor elevator lobby at the Wall Street Journal. But while the Pearl family and the newspaper's staff and top execs crowded into that drab anteroom to honor his memory, nothing has come of the idea of placing sculptor John Corcoran's spare, dignified work of art in a place where the public can see it — in the building's main lobby, for instance, across the street from Ground Zero.

One reason for that may be the Pearl family's desire for privacy. (The unveiling was closed to the press and the public.) But another may be, according to insider speculation, that the Journal might move from the building in the not-too-distant future. Placing the sculpture in the main lobby and then having to move it could then become an issue.

(I've got a call into the Journal spokeswoman to confirm or deny that, but haven't heard back yet.)

Finally, I must point to Louis Menand's essay, "Honest, Decent, Wrong," about George Orwell. Menand explains in The New Yorker why the author best known for "Animal Farm" and "1984" has been taken to heart by all sides in the polemical wars. "Orwell's army is one of the most ideologically mixed up ever to assemble," he writes. "It has included, over the years, ex-Communists, Socialists, left-wing anarchists, right-wing libertarians, liberals, conservatives, doves, hawks, the Partisan Review editorial board, and the John Birch Society."

Menand is not surprised. Orwell was brilliant but, among other things, inconsistent. He also had visceral personal reactions to historical figures that influenced his writing but could be peculiar. For instance, "Orwell took a particular dislike to Gandhi," Menand writes. "Gandhi was, after all, just the sort of sandal-wearing, vegetarian mystic Orwell had always abhorred." Worse, as far as Orwell was concerned, he smelled bad. At the same time, Orwell admitted in 1940, "I have never been able to dislike Hitler" — even while being opposed to Nazi Germany.

Face it: Great writers are weirdos.

Jan. 27, 2003 / 11:55 a.m. ET

Bread and circuses: With "American Idol" again topping the Nielsen charts — more than 50 million TV viewers watched a two-show premiere last week focusing on humiliation as much as talent — the Fox network and all the other major networks are planning more shows of that ilk. What had been a trend will be an avalanche. (Registration may be required.)

"The audience is never wrong," Sandy Grushow, the chairman of the Fox Entertainment Group, told The New York Times. "They have a huge appetite for this, and we've got a responsibility to satisfy that appetite."

So now we are to understand that Grushow feels duty-bound to offer this sort of entertainment, not unlike the Roman emperors who provided bread and circuses to the plebian rabble. Since the other network chiefs agree with him, think of TV as the modern equivalent of ancient Rome's coliseum.

Which brings us to President Bush's State of the Union, scheduled for tomorrow night at 9 p.m. ET, immediately following the second week of "American Idol," which probably guarantees the largest, youngest, lead-in audience ever for a televised State of the Union speech.

Advance word is that the speech "will not be eye-popping revelatory." The president will not issue an Iraq ultimate, nor give definitive evidence as the reasons for going to war. He will focus instead on the "bread," spending the first half of his roughly 50-minute speech "trying to show he is chastened by the economic and health care worries facing his administration and the country." Meanwhile, an American marine's deployment to the Gulf has been postponed so he can continue to compete on "American Idol." (The story has since been denied.)

Given "Idol" judge Simon Cowell's praise of 21-year-old Lance Cpl.

Josh Gracin, for his performance of a Sinatra classic last week, we may soon witness a new sort of star — the "American Idol" fighting man. Even if the "Idol" audience's eyes are guaranteed to glaze over when Bush makes his speech, patriotism demands that bread and circuses prize its gladiator.

Jan. 28, 2003 / 5:48 a.m. ET

Subtract one from Ground Zero: Skidmore, Owings and Merrill — one of the seven teams in the urban-design competition to rebuild Ground Zero — has been eliminated in a move that disappointed some of its members. It happened last week. (Registration may be required.)

The team's lead partner wanted to continue working with the leaseholder of the Twin Towers, Silverstein Properties (which has feuded over who will really get to set the new Ground Zero template), and so withdrew. It makes you wonder what's going on.

Architecture critic Herbert Muschamp thinks it's possible that officials will choose a design or two as early as tomorrow. If it were up to him, he writes, one of them would be the THINK team's pair of latticework towers.

"It is a work of genius, a towering affirmation of humanism in modern times," he writes in this morning's New York Times. He likes their "Jack and the Beanstalk quality" and the prospect that they would restore "the totemic image of the twin towers" to the Manhattan skyline. (Registration may be required.)

The Times itself has already come out in favor of a different proposal, the one by Daniel Libeskind.

Jan. 28, 2003 / 6:52 a.m. ET

Why can't 40 million Frenchmen spell Irack? In case anybody is wondering what makes France tick, consider this: 500,000 would-be stars auditioned for its most popular TV talent show, "The Golden Dictionaries," to determine the French dictation champ — far more than the 11,000 wannabes who auditioned for "American Idol."

Just as amazing, the finale of "Dictionaries" replaced the usual Sunday soccer game over the weekend and drew a larger national TV audience to boot. Can you imagine a talent show — even "American Idol" — replacing football in this country? Can you imagine a show that prizes dictation skills being broadcast in the first place?

("The presenter Bernard Pivot read a text containing grammatical traps and complex spellings to 176 finalists," The Times of London reported. "The winners were those who made the fewest mistakes.")

Now do you understand why France doesn't want to go along on Irack?

A nation of dictation-takers probably figures that we dumb Americans ought to be able to spell the name of a country we're threatening to invade.

Jan. 29, 2003 / 9:32 a.m. ET

Notes on an American idol: The White House rolled out the talent last night. ... Outstanding delivery ... Good looks ... Hit the high notes ... A little fuzzy on the details ... But listen to this: "The liberty we prize is not Amerca's gift to the world; it is God's gift to humanity." Such a great aw-shucks moment. As Simon Cowell would say: "Mr. President, you're going to Hollywood."

So maybe Nicki can belt a stronger "Lady Marmalade." Dubya's a better crooner, though maybe not in nerdy Clay's class ("Always and Forever.") So what if Stephanie has blonder hair and whiter teeth. Didn't Simon say it's all about talent this time? And correct me if I'm wrong, but that was Randy Jackson standing next to the joint chiefs, saying: "Awesome, dude!" Wasn't it?

No question: It's on to the next round for our great prez. One of my sources tells me that Paula Abdul was seen backstage dabbing her eyes with a tissue, waiting to tell him: "That was really nice." She's such a sentimentalist.

Jan. 30, 2003 / 2:04 p.m. ET

Be not afraid of greatness: What would William Shakespeare have said about George W. Bush? Nobody can know that. But after Sept. 11, White House insiders claimed the president was transformed into a leader with a galvanizing sense of purpose. And many observers said, quoting Shakespeare probably without realizing it: "Some are born great, some achieve greatness, and some have greatness thrust upon them."

They meant, of course, that Dubyah fell into the third category: The mantle of greatness had descended upon him through the accidental circumstance of history, which gave him the chance, tragic though it was, to prove his mettle — a fluke that had eluded Bill Clinton.

What they probably also didn't realize is that Shakespeare's words of wisdom were intended satirically, not in approbation. The statement comes at one of the comic high points of "Twelfth Night" in a forged letter designed to gull the social-climbing Malvolio, a preening royal steward with delusions of grandeur, into believing the Countess Olivia has fallen for him.

After reading the letter (scroll down), supposedly written by Olivia, Malvoli goes into a ludicrous swoon, envisioning himself with typical smugness as the dominating figure at court. It is sheer fantasy, and the folly of Malvolio's self-regard proves his downfall, ultimately making him a laughingstock.

I was reminded of all this the other night at the Brooklyn Academy of Music, where the Donmar Warehouse's recent London production of "Twelfth Night" has come to call in all its glory. Directed by Sam Mendes (who took Hollywood by storm with his Oscar-winning "American Beauty" and who wowed Broadway by getting Nicole Kidman to shed her clothes on stage in "The Blue Room"), it stars Oscar-nominated Emily Watson ("Breaking the Waves," "Angela's Ashes") and Simon Russell Beale, who's been called the greatest British stage actor of his generation.

The production, not incidentally, is magnetic, charming and even sublime. More than its two stars, the company features an acting ensemble so gorgeously talented that players in key supporting roles pretty much steal the show. David Bradley, as Sir Andrew Aguecheek, is the chief burglar.

Also, Anthony O'Donnell, as Feste the fool, helps raise this production above all other "Twelfth Nights" I have seen — more because of his musicality than his foolery. O'Donnell sings Shakespeare's song lyrics (exquisitely set by composer George Stiles for voice, piano, cello and guitar) with such naturalness that the production's beguiling musical atmosphere haunts you long after you've left the theater. (At BAM through March. 10.)

Jan. 31, 2003 / 11:32 a.m. ET

Them's fightin' words: Laura Bush, the White House's resident literateur, has called off a poetry reading she'd arranged for Feb. 12 because it appeared to be turning into a war protest. Newspapers are buzzing today about the postponement — more properly described as a cancellation, since it hasn't been rescheduled.

Thanks to Mobylives.com, here's a quick roundup of reports from The Boston Globe to The Toronto Globe & Mail, from The Guardian in London to a wise editorial in a small Indiana daily, describing how a symposium on Walt Whitman, Emily Dickinson and Langston Hughes became the focal point of political opposition to President Bush's war policy.

Apparently, poetry really does count for something these days — when it comes out fighting.

Poet Lawrence Ferlinghetti — the original City Lights publisher of Allen Ginsberg's "Howl" (probably the most important protest poem of the 20th century), who has published some pretty good anti-war poetry himself — has long insisted poetry is news. Ferlinghetti went about proving it in a weekly column he wrote for the San Francisco Chronicle.

But his own prescient lines from "A Coney Island of the Mind" — now almost a half-century old and, with more than a million copies in print from New Directions, his most famous book of poems — make the point more strongly than ever in its description of Spanish artist Francisco Goya's war etchings:

> In Goya's greatest scenes we seem to see
> the people of the world
> exactly at the moment when
> they first attained the title of
> "suffering humanity"
> They write upon the page
> in a veritable rage
> of adversity
> Heaped up
> groaning with babies and bayonets
> under cement skies
> in an abstract landscape of blasted trees
> . . . all the final hollering monsters
> of the
> "imagination of disaster"
> they are so bloody real
> it is as if they really still existed
>
> And they do

Share your perspective on entertainment and the arts with Jan Herman. MSNBC is not responsible for the content of Internet links.

Jan Herman

Latest entertainment and arts news from the Web

Entries from Feb. 2 to Feb. 28, 2003
(Some links may be nonfunctional.)
<u>Back to 'The Juice'</u>

LATEST UPDATES

Feb. 2, 2003 / 2:13 p.m. ET
  Columbia's picture from the Holocaust: I've seen all kinds of references to "Moon Landscape" — a pencil drawing made by Peter Ginz in Theresienstadt before he perished, at 16, in Auschwitz — that Israeli astronaut Ilan Ramon carried with him on the Columbia's tragic flight.
  It depicts what Peter (reportedly a fan of Jules Verne) imagined the moon to look like, with planet Earth visible in the background. Ramon was carrying a copy of the original, lent him by the <u>Yad Vashem Memorial</u> in Jerusalem, which has posted a picture of <u>Peter's drawing</u> on its Web site.
  (My thanks to "Juice" readers Jess Bravin, R. Lynn, Miron Kaufman, Mike Guthrie, Sheryl, Elizabeth and Chad for pointing it out.)
  Here are also two of Peter's <u>watercolor drawings</u>, "Interior of Living Quarters in the Theresienstadt Ghetto" and "Street in Thereseinstadt," which show him to have truly been a budding talent who might well have devoted himself to art had he survived the Holocaust.
  Also shown is a photo of Peter with his younger sister, Eva, who did survive and who became an artist herself. She now goes by the name Chava Pressburger. Some of her works on paper were <u>exhibited at the Jewish Museum in Prague</u> in 2000.

Feb. 3, 2003 / 3:45 p.m. ET
  Robert Hughes' strange light on Ground Zero: With officials expected at any moment to narrow their choice of Ground Zero proposals to two — <u>one by Studio Daniel Libeskind, the other by the THINK team</u> — the art critic Robert Hughes reminded us this weekend in London's Guardian that of all the arts, <u>architecture "is the supreme expression of politics and ideology."</u>

He writes, "It marshals resources and organizes substance in a way that music, painting and literature cannot. It is an art that lives from power."

Hughes might have been referring to the competing factions jockeying to decide the outcome of the Ground Zero template for the future, especially now that the World Trade Center leaseholder has asserted that officials are "ignoring his right to rebuild the site as he sees fit." (Registration may be required.)

In fact, Hughes was writing about Albert Speer, Hitler's favorite architect, who was chosen to turn Berlin and other German cities into a landscape of monumental architecture for the Thousand Year Reich. Speer's grandiose designs came to nothing, of course.

But that doesn't mean they weren't good enough to swipe, according to Hughes. He asserts that Speer's "most successful piece of architectural theatre" at the Nazi Party's Nuremberg rallies of the '30s was copied by the popular, temporary "Tribute in Light" that shined at Ground Zero to commemorate the destroyed Twin Towers.

Speer announced Hitler's arrival "by training hundreds of searchlight beams into the sky, like Doric columns of light," Hughes writes. "It was a magnificent conception, which, 60 years later, would be plagiarized by the Americans to mark the disappearance of the World Trade Center. ... No credit was given to Speer, who was dead by then."

It's a provocative assertion meant, I think, to disturb anyone who might take it seriously. I don't take it seriously myself. Though "Tribute" deployed a similar technique, the intent at Ground Zero was so far removed from anything Speer intended that Hughes' strange connection is strained at best. I'm just glad he didn't argue his case earlier, or the "Tribute" might have been caught up in an unnecessary, divisive debate.

Feb. 4, 2003 / 3:41 p.m. ET

Think Libeskind, and think THINK: Yesterday's "any moment" meant today's press conference. As anticipated, officials named the proposals by Studio Daniel Libeskind and the THINK team as finalists in the urban-design competition for Ground Zero.

I've reported the news separately.

All the public officials went out of their way to say their decision represented a unanimous consensus, but they acknowledged that it has been a contentious process. We'll see how contentious, or not, down the line.

In the meantime, they're to be congratulated for a helluva lot of hard work. One official even claimed that over the weekend he had read each and every one of 6,000 e-mails from the public about the designs. I'd like to believe him. But he was neither blind nor cross-eyed at Tuesday's conference, which makes me wonder.

Feb. 5, 2003 / 9:43 a.m. ET

The U.N.'s 'Guernica' art cover-up: When high muckety-mucks don't like what a work of art looks like, or what it signifies, they do what privileged imbeciles would do: They make believe. Which is exactly what U.N. officials have done. They're pretending that a tapestry reproduction of Picasso's anti-war masterpiece, "Guernica," doesn't really hang at the entrance to the U.N. Security Council.

As Maureen Dowd reminded me this morning — and everybody else who reads her column — U.N. officials "began covering the tapestry last week." (Registration may be required.) After all, U.S. Secretary of State Colin Powell, who today laid out evidence of Iraq's transgressions, couldn't "very well seduce the world into bombing Iraq" against a backdrop of "shrieking and mutilated women, men, children, bulls and horses."

It's not just Powell who's being protected. It's also the U.N.'s chief weapons inspector. Officials were "nervous that Hans Blix's head would end up on TV next to a screaming horse," Dowd writes.

Art cover-ups happen all the time. John Ashcroft had the statue "Spirit of Justice" covered up because it showed a naked breast, which was seen behind him at his press conferences in the Great Hall of the Justice Department.

Rockefeller Center officials draped Eric Fischl's sculpture, "Tumbling Woman," a tribute to 9/11 victims who jumped to their death at the World Trade Center, and then had it removed from the Rockefeller Center premises.

And can anyone forget former New York mayor Rudolph Giuliani's attempt to close down the Brooklyn Museum of Art by withdrawing city funding because he didn't like "Sensation," its controversial exhibit of British artists?

Feb. 6, 2003 / 9:43 a.m. ET

Phil Spector's classical-music psyche: It's mind-boggling to think that Phil Spector identifies with Mozart and Beethoven. But he does. And classical music is all the tortured "Wall of Sound" svengali listens to these days. It's just plain weird.

A few weeks before the famously reclusive pop producer was booked for suspicion of murder that's precisely what Spector told a reporter from London's Daily Telegraph.

The svengali of '60s pop told Mick Brown he switched from performing and songwriting to producing, in emulation of those masters: "I knew that Mozart was more important than his operas; that Beethoven was more important than whoever was playing or conducting his music. That's what I wanted to be."

Spector reached for Mozart and Beethoven and came up with some pretty nice hits: "Be My Baby" by the Ronettes; "You've Lost That Lovin' Feelin' " by the Righteous Brothers; "River Deep, Mountain High" by Tina Turner; "Imagine" by John Lennon; "My Sweet Lord" by George Harrison.

But it's cockeyed to think that mastery of a recording technique could possibly put him in the same league as Mozart or Beethoven, or that, were they alive today, they would have been record producers instead of composers. (And let's not forget: Both Mozart and Beethoven were among the greatest virtuosos of their time, not artists who gave up playing because they weren't getting anywhere.)

Still, reading Brown's extraordinary interview (free registration required) — the first Spector has given in 25 years — I couldn't help feeling sympathy for "the man who changed the face of pop music forever," to use Brown's effusive description, and for the man's agonizing, cockamamie self-regard.

Music by Sibelius, Bach, Beethoven and Brahms played continuously throughout the interview, says Brown, who spoke with Spector in his replica of an 18th-century mountain chateau overlooking the L.A. suburb of Alhambra.

Despite a music room filled with hi-fi equipment and an antique jukebox loaded with his old hits, the hi-fi "is silent" and the jukebox "is never played," Brown writes. "Instead, Spector subscribes to a satellite service that feeds classical music into his home, on tap 24 hours a day; balm for his troubled soul."

Apparently, it was not balm enough.

Jane Robison, a spokeswoman for the Los Angeles District Attorney's office, told me yesterday that Spector is expected in court March 3, and the D.A. has until that time to file charges. "The [Robert] Blake case took a year to file charges," Robison said. "I doubt this will take that long. It's just going to take days or a week. But there is no statute of limitations on murder."

Feb. 7, 2003 / 11:48 a.m. ET

Get him a personal shopper: I will never again put the words Wacko and Jacko together to refer to Michael Jackson. After seeing "Living With

185

Michael Jackson," last night on ABC's 20/20, I won't be putting the words "journalist" and "Martin Bashir" side by side, either.

That's how shabby Bashir's so-called documentary was. As for his post mortem with ABC, it stunk to high heaven. He belongs in the sleaze league with Howard Stern, Jerry Springer and the rest of the dregs.

I don't much care for Jackson's Peter Pan self-indulgence. But I care even less for ABC's posturing. And I'm glad Jackson's lawyers have filed a complaint against Granada Television, which produced the program, though it's hard to claim an invasion of privacy after volunteering to be interviewed.

In the end, Bashir's gross insincerity — the way he baited Jackson, the leering repetition — made the King of Pop look human to me. Jackson let a 12-year-old sleep in his bed while he slept on the floor? So what. He's built himself a huge playground to replace his lost childhood, a childhood given over to money-making performances? So what.

The conclusion I draw is not that Jackson needs advice on plastic surgery or therapy for his Peter Pan complex: He needs a personal shopper. Without one, he might outspend his wealth and have to auction off a merry-go-round, or worse. Instead of buying the perfect pair of urns, he buys nearly all the urns in sight. Instead of buying a significant icon for his Neverland ranch, he buys whatever amusement ride catches his fancy. A personal shopper might have tipped him to the historic Ferris Wheel from the great World's Columbian Exposition of 1893.

Wouldn't that be neat, having the world's first Ferris Wheel in your back yard? I've got the perfect personal shopper for him, MSNBC.com's own Teri Goldberg. I know she tuned in last night because she'd heard the program was to include a multimillion-dollar shopping spree. If that Ferris Wheel is still around somewhere, she'd find it for him. Michael, here's her e-mail: personalshopper@msnbc.com.

Feb. 10, 2003 / 8:57 a.m. ET

In the meantime: Jackson says he will make his own film with video footage to prove that Martin Bashir's ugly British TV protrayal of his private life was misleading, unfair and hypocritical. Jackson's own cameraman recorded the footage during the 8-month Bashir shoot.

A press release on Sunday said, the footage shows Bashir not only praising Jackson as a father who treats his chidren well but "making statements about how he feels it is a pity that the world is so quick to criticize Michael."

Feb. 10, 2003 / 8:57 a.m. ET

Sweet Valentines for the King of Pop: If anybody's wondering whether Michael Jackson took me up on the suggestion that he hire a personal shopper, I haven't heard yet. But the loves notes are pouring in. My bleary-eyed staff of thousands is still combing through a ton of e-mails — more than 2,000 at last count, almost all wishing Jackson well.

I'd suggested that he find a great antique, the world's first Ferris Wheel, for his back yard. But I've since learned it's unavailable.

After a successful run at the World's Columbian Exposition of 1893 in Chicago, it was dismantled and erected again near Lincoln Park as a tourist attraction — no mean feat. The wheel was HUGE. It weighed 2,079,884 pounds and could carry 2,160 passengers at a time. By 1903, however, the venture went bankrupt and the wheel was sold at auction.

The buyer had it dismantled again and took it to St. Louis for the Louisiana Purchase Exposition of 1904. Within two years what had been "the rival of the Eiffel Tower in Paris" lost its appeal and was purposely destroyed by "a monster charge of dynamite." As Patrick Meehan has written, "Chicago was glad to get rid of it and St. Louis is said to have witnessed its destruction with satisfaction."

Meehan's account of the great wheel's sad demise has been posted by the Hyde Park Historical Society. My thanks to Harley Hill, of Ventura, Calif., for pointing it out. It saves all of us a wild goose chase. But could I interest Jackson in the chocolate Venus de Milo or the 22,000-pound cheese that were also featured in the Columbian exhibit? (Free registration may be required.)

Feb. 11, 2003 / 7:57 a.m. ET

Another media oopsy-daisy: Martin Bashir, who sucker-punched Michael Jackson last week on ABC, is not the only one to give himself and the media a black eye. How about Beverly Lowry, a novelist and creative writing professor, who recently drubbed Susan McDougal in The New York Times Book Review?

Read what Gene Lyons had to say about Lowry's review of McDougal's best-seller, "The Woman Who Wouldn't Talk."

Admittedly, the Book Review is a daintier arena, and the sucker-punching more delicate. But Mobylives.com reports that Lyons' account of the Lowry-McDougal match had the publishing industry buzzing.

Lyons alleged that Lowry's review was both fraudulent and incompetent. It gave a dead-wrong summary of the central facts of the book, missing the climax so totally that he doubted she read the text. And it misunderstood the Whitewater case at the heart of the story. Her "summary of what Whitewater was supposed to have been all about is filled with preposterous errors."

"According to Lowry," Lyons explained, "Kenneth Starr's Whitewater investigation 'came up with pretty much of nothing, beyond a felony conviction for McDougal on charges of obstruction of justice and criminal contempt.' " But in fact, "Starr's failure to convict Susan on precisely those charges provides the book's triumphant climactic scene," Lyons pointed out.

I'd hate to be the editor who let that review out of the house. He or she is liable to be busted and shipped to Redbook magazine for a remedial course in fact-checking.

Feb. 12, 2003 / 7:53 a.m. ET

The Miramax Awards: That's what they should call this year's Oscars. What else is there to say? Win or lose, Miramax owns the contest. Just look at the numbers. Three best-picture nominations: "Chicago," with 13 nods, "Gangs of New York," with 10, and "The Hours," with nine. (OK, so Paramount shares "The Hours.") Add another eight nominations here and there, and Miramax's grand total comes to 40. It's embarrassing.

Feb. 12, 2003 / 12:39 p.m. ET

Rent your forehead at a protest: I know I'm coming to this late, but it's too good to pass up. "London marketing whiz kids have hit upon a new advertising medium: the human forehead," Reuters reports. They dreamed up the idea of tattooing foreheads with ads after seeing how much media coverage student protests get,

Today, nationwide poetry read-ins against war are being staged in bookstores, churches, libraries and community meeting places, in what the Los Angeles Times calls a coordinated grass-roots action unseen since the Vietnam era. It's made for forehead advertising.

The marketers told Minnesota Public Radio's "Marketplace" they're trying to help poor students supplement their income. (Scroll down to listen.) But the pay rate for allowing your forehead to be tattooed is now only $6.75 an hour, capped at three hours walking-around time. That's not so promising.

If those London whizzes want the U.S. market, they'd better raise their pay. I doubt that even hard-up, poetry-loving, American anti-war students willing to have their foreheads tattooed with semi-permanent logos would come that cheap.

Feb. 12, 2003 / 12:43 p.m. ET

Even bin Laden hates 'Joe Millionaire': American intelligence agencies haven't yet done an advanced analysis of the new Osama bin Laden tape, but David Letterman has. The late-night funnyman had the terror monger's tape fully translated, and it blasts the U.S. for misleading the world.

"The treachery of the infidels has reached new heights," the tape said. "We had been led to believe that last night would be the finale of 'Joe Millionaire,' but now we were told to tune in next Monday to see what woman Evan chooses. What kind of bull****is this?"

Letterman's expert translation tapped into the mind of every American who tuned into last Monday night's episode. With its lack of action, boring repetition and false promise of a climax, "Joe Millionaire" has achieved a new low for an already low-life form of TV. Will bin Laden — and America — stomach two hours of it next week?

Feb. 13, 2003 / 11:32 a.m. ET

The 'Joe Millionaire' spoiler: It looks like Osama bin Laden was not the only one venting about last Monday's purported "Joe Millionaire" finale. The Fox network's hype had given the impression that it would be. But when viewers tuned in, it wasn't. They say they were tricked. Fox's chat board is smoking. And rumors about the "big surprise" for the "true finale" are flying on the Internet.

"We got duped. We totally got duped," one viewer, Cynthia Wiggin of San Carlos, told the Associated Press. She dismissed the episode as "Total filler. A whole filler night."

"It's possible we were a little over the top with our promos and we're sorry if people felt misled," a Fox spokesman said. But that didn't cut much mustard.

"It just shows how low it can go," said executive producer Rob Silverstein of Access Hollywood, which had published an erroneous report based on Fox's promos. "I thought it was pretty blatant and I think it upset quite a number of people. It upset us."

Meanwhile, some people are just not buying the promised "big surprise." But rumors about it are flying on the Internet. Here are a bunch of them. (Scroll down).

One that rates a special mention, though, was posted by the blogger Moxie. I can't find it on her site this morning, however. So I'm posting "the real secret behind the whole show," written by an anonymous e-mailer who claims to know Evan's family.

I don't believe it myself, but it's one helluva dubious theory that Fox can only hope is true: "Evan is not alone on the show! His identical twin brother Ethan is also on there! Basically, they each had an equal say picking girls right down to the last two. They split up the dates at first, and then dated the girls they themselves had picked.

"Evan picked the wild Sara, while Ethan loves the quiet, gentle Zora. SOOO…on the last episode, Evan sees Zora first, rejects her, then leaves. Then you see Ethan (who u think is Evan) talking to Sara and reject her. Now youre thinking what the heck! THEN, they bring both girls in together and both brothers come out and explain the whole mess.   "They tell them they are not rich, and of course, Sara isn't impressed but Zora is relieved. THEN, Paul comes in and tells ALL of them that he IS a millionaire, and that both boys will be receiving 1 million each!!! Too bad Sara already walked out!!!!"

Feb. 14, 2003 / 12:53 p.m. ET

Will the real MJ please stand up? TV viewers who are not fed up with "Joe Millionaire," and plenty who are, still want to know what the "big surprise" will be on Monday's finale. The real deal is this: Evan is not gay, and he doesn't have a twin.

The big surprise is that Evan is really Michael Jackson. I have it on good authority that Trista will reveal on "The Bachelorette" finale that she, too, is Michael Jackson. In fact, all the TV shows next week will feature Michael Jackson.

ABC will re-run Martin Bashir's "Living With Michael Jackson." "Dateline NBC" will "investigate" Jackson's face for two hours. CBS hopes to pre-empt them both by getting Jackson to appear as himself, live, on "60 Minutes." (If I'm not mistaken, Ed Bradley has been spotted hanging around the entrance to Neverland.)

Not to be left out, Fox grabbed the rights to Jackson's anti-Bashir video, outbidding NBC's $5 million offer. (Free registration required.) And if you haven't seen Bashir's Jackson bashing, you can see it even before ABC's re-run. VH1 will air it five times, starting Saturday.

But the biggest surprise — I have it from a senior official of the Bush administration — is that U.N. chief weapons inspector Hans Blix is Michael Jackson. (If you must know, Colin Powell assured me it's true.)

Feb. 18, 2003 / 1:19 p.m. ET

Culture from the closet: It sounds like "The X-Files," but it's "The Z-

Closet." That's right, Harvard's Houghton Library has a Z-Closet where they keep weird things hidden behind a locked door, things you can't just put out on the shelves.

They've got Harry Houdini's handcuffs in the Z-closet; Charles Dickens' screw-tipped walking stick, the one he used to protect himself from escaped convicts on the Romney Marshes; T.S. Eliot's straw boater; a lock of William Wordsworth's hair and Nathaniel Hawthorne's, too. Really. I've seen them.

And behind another locked door, they've got Emily Dickinson's pinky ring and the wax sealing device she used to seal her letters; they've got her entire room with the desk she wrote on and the piano she played and the family portraits she looked at on the walls.

I hope that caught your attention. Because "Lifting the Lid on a Treasure Chest: From Artworks to an Author's Socks at the University of Texas" (registration required), caught mine — especially when it mentioned Marlon Brando's lost address book and D.H. Lawrence's beaded moccasins.

"I think it's fair to say that libraries are often ambivalent about this kind of material," Houghton's librarian, Bill Stoneman, told me. "While it can be evocative and memorable, it's also the kind of material that libraries are not meant to deal with."

Then why collect artifacts? "Because they're meant to be complementary to the written materials we have," Stoneman said. "An artifact gives context and is often meant to be iconic in its value. It makes things more real. The mere physicality of an artifact makes history more present."

Dickinson's ring is there, "because we have her papers," he said. "You're meant to put the two together and get a sense of what her life was like." (The ring is so tiny it makes you realize just how small she was.) "Even more interesting than the pinky ring is the sampler she cross-stitched as a child," Stoneman pointed out. "You see her struggling there with line ends and trying to make what she wants to say fit a piece of paper."

Houghton also holds the papers of Ralph Waldo Emerson (as well as his personal library and that of Herman Melville), the James family (including Henry, William and Alice), Wallace Stevens, James Laughlin (the publisher of New Directions), John Updike, Gore Vidal and dozens more. But you don't just walk in and get to see that stuff. You've got to have a good reason. As a research collection, Houghton serves a scholarly audience.

The library does have exhibitions open to the public, however. Its current exhibit, Borges: The Time Machine, puts many manuscripts of the great Argentine author Jorge Luis Borges on display. The next major exhibit will celebrate the bicentennial of Emerson's birth with a display of his papers, tracing his life from the early years as a Harvard student to the later years as "The Sage of Concord."

Though we will all turn to dust — and though the universe may expand so far that it, too, eventually disappears — we can at least take pride until then in these treasures of the human enterprise.

You might even want to check out the modest <u>Jan Herman archive</u> at the Northwestern University Library. It has 15 catalogued boxes of stuff from yours truly's salad days — manuscripts, collages, films, correspondence and what-not by those bad boys of American literature: Charles Bukowski, William Burroughs, Allen Ginsberg and Lawrence Ferlinghetti, plus scores of gems I'd forgot about. If nothing else, their value once paid my way to Europe.

Feb. 19, 2003 / 1:03 p.m. ET

Proud to be a mutant: A Stanford University anthropologist contends that human <u>creativity is the result of a genetic mutation</u> that occurred 50,000 years ago, when "modern-looking people suddenly began to behave in a modern way, producing art and jewelry... manufacturing styles and different cultures."

The theory does not account for <u>the rise of rock 'n' roll</u> or <u>rap</u>, however, or — more important — the tube. Another mutation must have occurred perhaps 50 years ago that led modern-looking people to develop 20th-century television. The resulting <u>rise of 21st-century "reality" shows</u> like "Survivor," "Joe Millionaire" and that bastion of creativity and fine taste, "Fear Factor," seems to me to provide anecdotal evidence of another, yet-to-be-discovered mutation.

British researchers have already identified the gene <u>foxp2</u> as "vital to human language" and that "slight changes in it result in 'animal talk'." It was proved that modern-looking people with a mutation of this gene "cannot manipulate language, or apply the normal rules for grammar, even though many of them were intelligent in non-verbal ways."

You couldn't invent a better definition of "TV executive." But television is so slimey these days, and so lacking in creativitiy, I would suggest that the modern-looking people who run the networks have a subvariant of the variant which led to <u>this week's observable decline</u>.

Feb. 20, 2003 / 12:56 p.m. ET

Why the music is dying: Despite the blockbuster lineup for Sunday night's upcoming Grammys, music critic Jim Washburn wonders whether it might be more accurate to call them the Grimmys. Given the dismal state of the recording industry, the term is more than just a clever catch phrase: It has the ring of truth.

The industry is tainted, and not only by declining sales. Artists say they're treated like chattel. They claim they're cheated of royalties. That's old news, yes, but just this morning Brent Staples has an editorial in The New York Times about an associated disease: corporate ownership of radio stations.

"With a few exceptions," he writes, "the disc jockeys who once existed to discover provocative new music have long since been put out to pasture. The new generation operates from play lists dictated by Corporate Central."

While Staples focuses on a lack of air play for protest music — taking a cue, it would seem, from Dan Epstein's recent LA Weekly piece, "Where are the new protest songs?" — his larger point is that corporate radio "is killing popular music" period.

In fact, the issue of corporate radio is not new either. Eric Olsen has been on that case for some time at blogcritics.org. He also disputes Epstein about why today's protest music is not resonating.

And here's Ann Power's take, with interviews of Boots Riley of the Oakland hip-hop duo the Coup, Eddie Vedder of Pearl Jam, Tom Morello formerly of Rage Against the Machine, and Amy Ray of The Indigo Girls.

I'll leave it to them to argue the finer points. My own reason is simple, and doubtless simple-minded: This generation has no Bob Dylan. He was peerless in his time, and nobody has shown up since to take his place.

Here comes the e-mail:

Shane Hockin
Tallahassee, Fla.
WHAT!? NO BOB DYLAN!? What about EMINEM??? I jest. I think it is a circular problem: There is no Bob Dylan because of the corporate playlists. There are corporate playlists because there is no new Bob Dylan. All I know is I switched out my radio in favor of a CD player, because the radio is a waste of my time. "Highway 61 Revisited," here I come! And I am proud to say that I wasn't even born when "Highway 61 Revisited" came out.

Tammy Crawford
Seal Cove, Maine
Nobody has shown up to take Bob Dylan's place because the music industry laughs them out of town. The talent exists, but talent is not all you

must have to be heard in todays world. God forbid you should be a little more focused on your music than your looks.

Kate Lupson
Brooklyn, N.Y.

Indie artists are doing protest songs, but they're not on major labels and don't have the same amount of money put into promotion and marketing. Ani DiFranco's albums are full of protest songs (check out the opening track from "To The Teeth," a release from just a few years ago, which suggests we "open fire on MTV") about the industry. The Indigo Girls tackle various social issues on their discs. Both artists have cult followings but receive very little mainstream press.

Here's a great site that also gets no press: listen.com, where you can download music LEGALLY; the artists still get paid. The major record labels and many indies have signed on with listen.com. Their player, Rhapsody, comes with album reviews, graphics, release dates, trivia about artists, and over 90,000 CDs to listen to. It costs less than $10 a month for all that access. To burn a track costs an additional $.99 (tracks are all streaming). I very rarely ever see any press on this, and that's a shame, as it's something that could help bridge the gap between the internet-savvy consumers and the seemingly stodgy recording industry.

Feb. 21, 2003 / 11:42 a.m. ET
Will Britney Spears pull a reverse Michael Jackson? Of course not. But it's a funny idea: Spears darkens her skin and hair to look black, so she can sing and dance better. Before anyone calls me a racist, let me explain.

It's been a lousy year for Spears. She needs a boost, and she has seen what turning white has done for Michael Jackson. It has not only put him back in the limelight, it has made him a sympathetic figure. Witness last night's two-hour broadcast of "The Michael Jackson Interview: The Footage You Were Never Meant to See," which, in another reversal, turned out to be the least sensationalized of the recent Jackson "documentaries." (That in itself was a complete surprise, given the show's tabloid TV host, Maury Povich.)

Anyway, the idea of Spears pulling a reverse MJ comes from shmater.com, one of the many satirical Web sites spawned by the Internet. The satire is clearly intended to let the air out of both Spears and racial profiling. That's not a bad thing.

As The Shmater Times put it (scroll down to the second item): "In a world where fame can be cruelly fleeting, Ms. Spears had decided to go with conventional wisdom. Given the fact (not exactly proven, but generally accepted) that black people are 'cooler' than white people and that black people can sing and dance better than white people, Britany [sic] has done Michael Jackson one better. She has recently gone through a process to make herself more African-American." Accompanying the item are two photos. One is Spears as her usual self pictured in a Pepsi ad. Another is Beyoncé Knowles, supposedly Spears, who is black and is also pictured in a Pepsi ad.

Meanwhile, another site that goes in for satire — Wading in the Velvet Sea (subtitled: One man's struggle for truth, justice, and Jennifer Garner's home phone number) — has turned briefly serious with a commentary about the "fairy-tale nature" of "Joe Millionaire" and "The Bachelorette."

Both shows represent "a seismic shift from 'Embarrassment TV' which marks shows like 'Temptation Island' and 'The Real World,' " Ryan McGee writes. "The fundamentally cruel nature of [embarrassment TV] seems to be shifting ... with 'Joe' and 'Bachelorette' paving the way." Except when the ending wasn't a fairy tale and when it may not be.

Also, McGee himself is not above suggesting some embarrassing would-be reality shows such as:

"Trading Races" (Two couples decide to switch ethnicity with their neighbors over the period of a weekend. Hilarity and racial prejudice ensue.)

"Who Wants to Take a Hit from Grandma's Bong?" ($25,000 to the person who convinces Congress to legalize medicinal marijuana.)

"The Weakest Mink" (50 members of PETA hunt supermodel Giselle, who's been left alone and abandoned in the woods. The first person who finds her gets to skin her alive and offer her carcass as a sacrifice to the Animal Gods in a pagan ceremony to be held during Sweeps Period.)

Speaking of sweeps, the funniest thing on the Michael Jackson footage that we were never meant to see was the part about his chimp Bubbles who — we were told — used to help Jackson dust the house and do the dishes. Jackson with a dust mop in his hand? I don't think so. Besides, as Kate Borysewicz e-mails from Newark, N.J., "How DO you train a chimp to do housework, anyway?"

Feb. 24, 2003 / 11:37 a.m. ET

Grammys' magical migraine: The morning after the Grammy Awards has me wondering how to cure my musical hangover. I could use some "hair of the dog." Given so much off-key, backyard yowling last night, I'd have to call it "fur of the cat."

But that would fail to acknowledge the yodeling, versifying, nostalgifying mush — and, yes, the occasional fine performance lost in the howling dullness — which inevitably turns the Grammys into a headache-making trance. If you were lucky enough to miss last night's show and don't get my meaning, try this minute-by-minute account and see if it doesn't give you a throbbing migraine.

Here's a sample that made me smile through the pain:

8:30 pm: Hey, check it out, it's Marc Antony. I heard he's living in a 2BR walkup with Ricky Martin in Astoria now. Marc's working nights at Subway, Ricky's playing Swing in "Man of La Mancha". (OK, fine. YOU tell me where they've been for a year. I am personally at a loss.)

8:32 pm: Marc spends 2 minutes talking about Tito Puente and … then introduces a performance by Faith Hill. Huh? If a ninth grader made this kind of segue in a book report, they'd be sent to after-school tutoring.

8:33 pm: Camera pans to Faith, who is doing a great impression of a Marilyn Monroe impersonator down at Flashdancers.

8:35 pm: The number ends with her being consumed by a large ball of flame. OK, that's just wishful thinking on my part.

8:40 pm: His Royal Velvetness, Paul Schaffer is onscreen and has completely lost control over his right arm. God, he might hurt someone.

8:41 pm: Did he just call Vanessa Carlton "funkifily delicious"???? Is that how you spell "funkifily"??? So many questions!!!! Head…hurting….

8:42 pm: It's everyone's favorite poster child for scoliosis, Vanessa Carlton. She's apparently part of a singer-songwriter triptych.

8:45 pm: Triptych part two, John Mayer. He gives this unmistakable look to the crowd that says, "You all want to lick me, don't you?"

But if you're looking for some, shall we say, serious-minded analysis, I'd suggest more "fur of the cat."

Feb. 25, 2003 / 1:32 p.m. ET

Real important stuff: Let's leave Michael Jackson, Britney Spears, Norah Jones, the Grammy Awards, "Joe Millionaire," "The Bachelorette" and all other forms of pop kulcha to their own devices today, so we can focus on real issues in the arts.

Like how do book reviewers get away with reviewing books without actually reading them? Or why such rancor about the winning Ground Zero design to be announced Thursday? Or why is arts funding so important, yet writing about it is so boring?

Except that we do have to take care of business, don't we? So let's address the Simon & Garfunkel reunion at the Grammys the other night and get it out of the way. Face it: The duo's return was a bad joke.

The critics pretty much gave them a pass. In The New York Times, for instance, Jon Pareles tiptoed around their performance, calling it "somber" when, in fact, it was stiff and off-key. Even our own Jim Washburn, a witty curmudgeon who never panders and is not easily fooled, praised the duo as splendid. He thought they sounded "little the worse for having been mothballed for 10 years."

I plead guilty, too. I wrote that "a nostalgic Simon-and-Garfunkel reunion ... held the crowd in thrall." True, the crowd was thrilled. But I didn't really believe the reunion was "nostalgic" or that their performance was any good at all. So I fudged, noting that they were "in fine, sober spirit, if not in finest voice."

In fact, my editor Laura Tuchman, a Simon & Garfunkel fan from way back, kept pointing out how cold they seemed toward each other, as if they couldn't stand being on the same stage together. I should have listened to her. The New York Post's Page Six reports this morning that the two of them "bickered like ex-spouses at the sound check" just before show "and almost didn't make it onto the stage."

As they were rehearsing, Garfunkel apparently complained that Simon wasn't paying attention to him: "You don't play for me — you play for yourself! We have to play in sync." Then they "went at it," according to Page Six, and everyone else was cleared from the stage, "while the former partners went to their respective dressings rooms to cool off."

Their spokesman denies the report, of course, calling Page Six's unnamed sources "liars," and claiming "the fight never happened." But the item sounds convincing to me. One unnamed witness reported: "It happened. I was one of the people cleared from the stage."

Hmmm, looks like time's up. I'll have to address the real important stuff another day.

Feb. 26, 2003 / 12:40 p.m. ET

The gloves come off at Ground Zero: The gentlemen architects went into battle with idealistic statements and high-minded blueprints. They armed themselves with well-coiffed publicists and made the rounds of the talk shows. They gave interviews. And then they took off the gloves.

The two finalists not only dismissed each other's plans, but one of them — Rafael Vinoly, the apparent winner of the competition if officials go along with the site-planning committee's recommendation — allowed himself to be profiled in The New York Times as a poverty-stricken hero who fled its mightiest buildings.

Vinoly, of the THINK team (which he heads with Frederic Schwartz, Shigeru Ban and Ken Smith), outraged some former Argentine dissidents when he was described as persecuted and poverty-stricken, effectively a political dissident, in flight from the Argentine military junta of the 1970s. (Registration required.) In fact, he did leave Argentina — but only after a successful career there. (Registration required).

As the Wall Street Journal reported this morning, one of South America's most brutal regimes chose Vinoly for such impressive projects as its 1978 World Cup soccer stadium and the national Chamber of Deputies. (Registration required.)

"For the junta, a diplomatic pariah because of its ruthless repression of political dissent, the World Cup was a propaganda opportunity to claim international legitimacy," Jess Bravin writes. "For Mr. Vinoly, it was the opportunity to showcase his talent before a world-wide audience."

(Vinoly told Bravin he hasn't hidden his past, which is true. But he also did not register any complaint about the misleading impression given of him in the Times, which stated he fled "with little more than a suitcase." Bravin reports: "He now says he arrived [in the United States] with more than $40,000 and had properties in Argentina.")

Daniel Libeskind, the other finalist, orchestrated an e-mail campaign at one point in the Ground Zero competition, for which he has apologized. And he has called his opponent's pair of lattice-work towers "two skeletons in the sky," dismissing a design concept that's been described (rightly) as inspired by the Eiffel Tower and (wrongly) as reminiscent of the molecular structure of DNA, the ultimate symbol of life.

Vinoly, for his part, has denigrated Libeskind's plan, which would expose the original foundations of the World Trade Center, as comparable to the Wailing Wall in Jerusalem. It's an unfortunate reference that could be misconstrued as anti-Semitic (given Libeskind's best-known project, the design for The Jewish Museum in Berlin, and even though Vinoly's wife and child are Jewish).

Meanwhile, the debate rages on about the relative merits and demerits of both Libeskind's and Vinoly's visions for Ground Zero — not to mention alleged betrayals and conflicts of interest — even as:

The site-planning committee unexpectedly chose the THINK team's proposal over the Libeskind proposal, which had been seen as the favorite, and made its non-binding recommendation on Tuesday to the Lower Manhattan Development Corp., the agency charged with overseeing the plans.

A broader group will decide today whether to go along with that recommendation or override it. The group includes officials from the

LMDC, New York Gov. George Pataki's office, New York City Mayor Michael Bloomberg's office, and the Port Authority of New York and New Jersey, which owns the trade center site — each of whom have their separate agendas, some overlapping others but all ultimately having to negotiate with the private leaseholder of the site, real estate magnate Larry Silverstein.

Let the games begin.

Feb. 26, 2003 / 7:31 p.m. ET

Late-breaking surprise: Officials chose Daniel Libeskind's design proposal for Ground Zero redevelopment on Wednesday afternoon, rejecting the recommendation of a key site-planning committee that had picked the rival plan of Rafael Vinoly and the THINK team.

The Associated Press reported that Libeskind was named winner of the international design competition. His proposal had been regarded as the favorite of many officials. But a report about the site-planning committee's unexpected recommendation surfaced Wednesday morning at the 11th hour, further heightening tensions and clouding the outcome until the final decision came down for Libeskind.

Feb. 27, 2003 / 11:09 a.m. ET

Readers react to Ground Zero design: Besides its 1,776-foot spire with hanging gardens at the top and its stylish, jagged towers of glass and steel, the winning design for Ground Zero is distinguished by several key ideas:

An open pit, 30 feet below ground (scaled back from 70 feet), where a memorial will go in the footprints of the Twin Towers. Known as "the bathub," the pit exposes the original foundation "slurry" walls of the destroyed World Trade Center site — which withstood the 9/11 attacks and still hold back the Hudson River — and is intended as a symbol of strength representing the foundations of democracy.

A "wedge of light" created by precise positioning of the future buildings that are to surround Ground Zero, so that every year on Sept. 11 a shaft of unshadowed sunlight will fall onto the area of the footprints from 8:46 a.m. ET (when the first plane crashed into The North Tower) to 10:28 a.m. ET (when it collapsed, after South Tower went down.)   If you want to know why officials had a hard time deciding on the winning design — created by Berlin-based architect Daniel Libeskind, who was born in Poland in 1946 , grew up in The Bronx and became an American citizen in 1965 — you can see why from reactions below. They reflect the wisdom, compassion, sorrow, incomprehension and, unfortunately, ignorance of the public at large.

From readers:

"The Wailing Wall, The Vietnam War Memorial in Washington, September 11 — walls make good memorials." — *Matt Filler,* Downey, Calif.

"You are kidding, right? I find it absolutely amazing ... no wait, appalling, that one would even think of considering this design as an option. As an employee in lower Manhattan, even better, as an employee 1 block south of the WTC, and a resident of Manhattan for 7 years, the fact that this site isn't even being considered to be rebuilt as it WAS, is comical." — *Rene Allende,* East Village, New York City

"I like the idea of Libeskind's design. It is postmodern, yet the plans he has will make the towers recognizable anywhere. The design is perfect. My father was part of the relief effort and went up the day after. He is also pleased with the design made. Making the new towers just like the old isn't a good idea and making a lattice frame for it is to retro." — *Matthew C. Heffner,* Biglerville, Penn.

"I am pleased with the decision." — *Glorian Rodel,* Fort Worth, Texas

"I am crying inside at the ugly design finally chosen at Ground Zero. It could have been made a beautiful park." — *Pam Richards,* Cottonwood, Ariz.

"Libeskind's stuff is truly tasteless. His renditions look like what the WTC looked like after the collapse." — *Todd,* Troy, N.Y.

"Both finalist designs are so horrid it brings tears to my eyes." — *G. Mart,* Atlanta

Reader responses continue:

"The idea that we can boldly rebuild ground zero with buildings higher than before is truly ignorant and disrespectful to the victims and their families." — *Louann Little,* Joplin, Mo.

"The designs for this site have been evolving way to fast. Whether Libeskind's or Vinoly's, these designs do not match the integrity of New York, period." — *Roman Heczko*

"I hate the new plan. Awful awful awful. To think those beautiful towers are going to be replaced with futuristic-looking techno crap just breaks my heart." — No name given

"Frankly, I didn't like any of the designs presented." — *Fran,* Pittsburgh

"Big mistake, these plans are bland and uncreative." — *Rick Blackburn,* Ripley, Ohio

"Selecting a German company to re-design the WTC is a slap in the face of all Americans. Especially in light of the anti-American rhetoric in Germany and France." — *Mary Lou Norris,* Vero Beach, Fla.

"I think that rebuilding new buildings, while it is a loving tribute, is the wrong idea. ... It's just too soon." — *Joal Gustas,* Buffalo, N.Y.

"My friend Nancy Morgenstern died at the WTC. Please focus on what's important, the remembrance of innocent people, THEIR memorial. To hell with egos and churlish arguments." — *Brett Weshner,* Folsom, Calif.

"I much prefer the Libeskind proposal. It has an elegiac yet transcendental quality, which I think captures perfectly the meaning of the site. — *Maryanne Conheim,* Philadelphia

"Daniel Libeskind is a talented architect, and his work dealing with tragic historical events reflects this. However, his design, which pierces the sky, does nothing more then remind me of a sharp pain I felt on 9/11." — *Anthony Lauro,* Palmer Township, Penn.

"Libesbkind's design — YUK." — *Madelyn Bryson,* Delray Beach, Fla.

"Shouldn't the designers of 'Ground Zero' be AMERICAN?" — *Keith,* Cincinnati

"As an architectural designer, I feel ... the Think proposal is far too direct, far too much like what was lost." *T.R. Hendricks,* Grand Junction, Colo.

"To go along with the THINK design would be to eternally weep for a past tragedy and not show strength in recovery." — *Ryan Girvin,* Hamilton, Ontario

"Are both of these gentlemen born Americans? And why in the world must the Jewish Wailing Wall or anything of that kind have to come into play here? This is America's tragedy not Israel's." — *Katherine Scott,* Canada

"The Think plan is great! It has majesty, message and utility!" — *Dan Levine,* N.Y.

"I think all the designs are tasteless!" — *John Lauper*, Sugar Land, Texas

"I think the new designs are distasteful and are too artsy fartsy to portray the depth and meaning that should be represented out of respect for our 9/11 heroes." — *Nancy Liggett,* Martin, Tenn.

"Forget the politics, Libeskind's design is simply better. It speaks N.Y.

sophistication, it honors the dead, and it exalts the living. What more could a city want?" — *A. G.,* Los Angeles

"No Zionist occupation of Ground Zero." — *Arik,* Boston

"I don't think either design is a fitting replacement." — *Annie,* Miami

"You would think that the people of New York would use a native American to build what they have pictured as a city striving to show the best the U.S. has to offer." — *Bobby King,* Decatur, Ala.

"Both designs are lame." — *Dan Keefe,* Bethlehem Township, N.J.

"I have always preferred [Vinoly's] latticework buildings." — *Rosalie Emerson,* Cold Spring, N.Y.

"Vinoly's design was one of the least attractive I've seen. Libeskind's was superior in physical design as well as in the essence of his project." — *Kathe Hocum,* Rochester, Minn.

"I work on Wall Street and was here on September 11th. I think it is so sick that a contest has been created over which UGLY design will win." — *Jen,* Yonkers, N.Y.

Feb. 27, 2003 / 9:02 p.m. ET

More reactions to Libeskind's design: I've received such a deluge of e-mails — more than 1,000 in less than an afternoon — that it would be unfair to post only this morning's responses. So here are a few, just a handful, that caught my attention this evening because of where they came from and what they said:

"I'm thrilled with the design. I find it bold, progressive and optimistic in it's own right even as it reminds me of the chaos and destruction of that September morning." — *Bryan,* Los Angeles

"I think the plans of what the city of New York wants to do at Ground Zero is terrific. Don't let lame, cowardly terrorists stop you from living life the way you want. America is a great country and anyone who says otherwise is a fool." — *Anonymous,* Lusaka, Zambia

"What a cold looking design. I am usually a big fan of modern buildings, but seeing this gives me the chills." — *Deniz G.,* Chappaqua, N.Y.

"Nothing will ever take the place of the World Trade Center." — *Maria Reyes,* N.Y.

"Brilliant! Beams of light to remember the past and shine light on a hopeful new future!" — *Warren Stickney,* Seattle

"The design itself did not 'take my breath away.' However, I do think the concept of the 'wedge of light' passing through to the WTC footprints at the same time every year is beautiful and amazing ... very symbolic for rememberance and hope."— *Vina,* Liverpool, England

"It is fitting that Libeskind's design won. He is an immigrant who became an American citizen. What is more New York than that?" — *Teresa,* Grand Marais, Minn.

Feb. 28, 2003 / 4:58 p.m. ET
'Six Feet Under' or 'Up in Smoke'? I got hooked on HBO's "Six Feet Under" in its maiden season, but not because of the story or the characters or all the reasons it became a hit. What hooked me was the musical tease. The word "haunting" was invented for it. I watched early episodes just so I could hear the tease.

It didn't take long, however, to get hooked for <u>the right reasons</u>: The series was a miracle of counter-programming. The setting was unheard of — a family-run funeral home — and the gallows humor had zing. All the characters were "real," offbeat or not, and they multiplied like fruitflies. The social commentary was smart, the dialogue sharp, the plotlines unpredictable.

Then came the second season. According to the critics, <u>the series blossomed</u>. But I began to have my doubts. "Six Feet Under" had turned into a hydra-headed soap opera. The entertaining foibles, the tragic obssessions, the indulgent philosophizing were becoming quaint.

I started calling the series "Up in Smoke." I fantasized that the Fisher brothers lose their battle with the corporate bullies. They still refuse to be taken over and turned into a funeral-business franchise. But this forces them to become "cremationists." They get out of caskets and into urns. There are no more dead bodies waiting for their makeovers. No more mortician scenes. No more viewings.

The fantasy didn't end there: The boys' desperate new venture happens to be an excellent business move. It's even visionary. With cemetaries running out of space, people are having themselves cremated in ever larger numbers. The Fishers tap into this booming alternative market. They become multimillionaires. They put the corporate bullies out of business to boot. Everybody in their family gets rich and happily married.

Ugh. Reality sets in. Without the dead bodies and the makeovers and the viewings the series becomes utterly bland. It might as well be called "On Top of the World." Alan Ball flips. The cast resigns. HBO cancels. End of fantasy. The third season gets under way Sunday night.

Share your perspective on entertainment and the arts with <u>Jan Herman</u>. MSNBC is not responsible for the content of Internet links.

Entries from March 3 to March 31, 2003
(Some links may be nonfunctional.)
Back to 'The Juice'

LATEST UPDATES

March 3, 2003 / 1:43 p.m. ET
     Oh, how the culture wars have changed: The culture wars used to mean the battle of left and right, between liberal and conservative. Then it became the battle of high-brow and low-brow, between sophisticated and vulgar.

     Now it means something else, an internalized settlement between substance and sensation.

     "The very same conditions that prompt a surge in seriousness also promote an escapist impulse, even in the same people," Cullen Murphy, managing editor of the high-brow magazine The Atlantic Monthly, tells David Carr. "I spent last Monday editing a serious piece about the Middle East, and then went home and watched 'Joe Millionaire.'"

     One could argue that it was ever thus — that the mix of sweet and sour, serious and frivolous, is nothing new; that the cultural divide between left and right has not changed, that it just gets less attention and makes less noise.

     But when the celebrity-mad magazine Us Weekly increases newsstand circulation by 55 percent at the same time that the ultra-sober-minded Atlantic increases it by 52 percent, or when Oprah's Book Club is coming back, this time sticking to the classics, while hip-hop turns to book publishing, or when home-video technology shapes professional television, it seems undeniable that the culture wars have changed.

     The issues have been fused like an alloy and the divide internalized. The result, for the moment, appears to be a compromise within each of us as the real war — the shooting war — begins to surround us.

204

March 3, 2003 / 7:24 p.m. ET

   A serene Pentagon memorial: Now that the urban template for Ground Zero has been decided, attention has shifted. Choosing the actual Ground Zero memorial begins soon, but the decision is many months away. The Pentagon memorial design has just been selected, however.

   Called "Light Benches," it was created by Julie Beckman and Keith Kaseman, two young architects from New York (scroll down), and will be built on a "memorial field" of almost two acres near the spot where the Sept. 11 attack on the Pentagon occurred.

   Here's what their design looks like.

   Last October, Beckman told Newsday that she and Kaseman wanted to contribute to a design for Ground Zero but were too overwhelmed by the size of the site.

   "I wouldn't know where to start [at Ground Zero] because it's too close to home and so grand in scale," Beckman said. "The Pentagon memorial ... was much more manageable. Not being from Washington allowed us to focus on the issues at hand." (Scroll down.)

   The design comprises 184 cantilevered benches made of a composite aluminum, with the name of each victim engraved into the face of each bench. Fifty-nine will face one way, while 125 face the other way to distinguish between the victims on board American Airlines flight 77 and those in the Pentagon.

   Each 16-foot-long bench is to be accompanied by "a red-purple, broad-leafed tree and a glowing light pool" and will be positioned along a timeline according to the age of the victim, progressing from the youngest, age 3, to the oldest, age 71. The benches will be placed in a parallel pattern to the flight path of the plane. The illuminated reflecting pools will enable the memorial to be seen at night.

   I'm somewhat confused about the "timeline positioning" of the benches. It's supposed to be decided by a "randomization technique," which sounds like throwing dice and is one way of considering fate. But technique aside, the memorial looks like it will encourage contemplation. The "broad-leafed" trees will be maples, in fact, so that sitting on the benches will be like sitting in a maple grove.

March 4, 2003 / 10:43 a.m. ET

   Nifty book titles for children: Madonna has a brand-new bag. As reported yesterday, she's writing children's books. The first title in a series of five, "The English Roses," will be published in hardcover in September.

   This does not sit well with some people — Malene Arpe, of The

Toronto Star, for example. She's fearful that Madonna is <u>setting a scary precedent</u> for celebrities and public figures who also might want to explore the children's market. Arpe wonders whether we'll be seeing these titles soon:

"Little Girls Are Nifty" by R. Kelly

"My Big Gun Goes 'Boom'" by George W. Bush

"Chemistry for Toddlers" by Saddam Hussein

"Mommy Has Gone Away" by Robert Blake

"Look at You! You Forgot Your Pants" by Pee-Wee Herman

"The Little Girl's Guide to Shopping Like a Grown-up" by Winona Ryder

"Drugrats" by Whitney Houston and Nick Nolte

I think she forgot at least two others:

"See My Merry-Go-Round" by Michael Jackson, for one,

and "How to Make Friends for Life" by Paul Simon & Art Garfunkel, for another.   Here are a few from readers:

"Hey, Kids! Let's Have a Pool Party" by Tommy Lee

"And the Empire Fell Happily Ever After" by Martha Stewart

"I Do! I Do! I Do!" by Jennifer Lopez

"You Can Be President, Too" by Martin Sheen

"Dress Your Best" by Britney Spears

"It's OK to Get Dirty" by Christina Aguilera

"I Can Read! Yes I Can!" by Evan Marriot

"Let's Play Hide-And-Go-Seek" by Osama bin Laden

Some more from readers:

"Counting is Fun" by Arthur Anderson

"It's Nice to Be Nice" by Simon Cowell

Any more suggested titles are welcome. The publishers can't wait.

March 5, 2003 / 11:34 a.m. ET

Is Dan Rather's face red yet? The famously hard-working CBS news anchor got an interview with Saddam Hussein, one of those mega-exclusives that his rivals would have given their right arm for — and now it turns out that CBS used an actor who apparently faked an Iraqi accent for Saddam's "voice."

<u>The Los Angeles Times reports</u> this morning that CBS hired Steve Winfield, a translator who has "a particular flair for foreign accents" and who is listed as a member of the Screen Actors Guild, to read Saddam's answers in English translation to Rather's questions.

The Times reports that "the accent ... was meant to provide 'a voice compatible with the piece,' " according to a CBS statement, and "didn't violate CBS News standards and practices." In fact, it's not even unusual. CBS has done this sort of thing before, a network spokeswoman told Times writer Elizabeth Jenson.

What's more, CBS maintains that the translation itself was "100 percent accurate."

Some observers — maybe even the 17 million TV viewers who watched the interview last week — might have considered this poor practice just the same. The news media are not exactly above suspicion when it comes to the public's trust.

Richard Wald thinks it's all hunky-dory, though. Wald is a professor at Columbia University's Graduate School of Journalism, and a former head of standards and practices for ABC News. As long as CBS didn't pretend the speaker was Saddam, "there's nothing wrong with having done it," he said. But "it would have been better if they had simply told [viewers]. It's always nicer to be straight with the audience."

Gee. That would be nice, wouldn't it?

(No wonder Columbia University President Lee Bollinger is trying to figure out what the heck they teach at the journalism school.)

Could Dan Rather clue us all in, please?

March 6, 2003 / 11:23 a.m. ET

The cover-up, not the crime: Ever since Daniel Libeskind's design was picked as the template for redeveloping Ground Zero, the experts have all chimed in to analyze, speculate and in some cases actually report on why it came up the winner.

The basic conclusion, despite all the twists and turns, is that it all came down to one man's opinion — George Pataki's. As the governor of New York, Pataki ultimately controlled the decision. Presented with a choice between the Libeskind design and the design by the Rafael Vinoly-led THINK team, he favored the former.

But did the Wall Street Journal's unflattering piece about Vinoly, which appeared on the day the final decision was to be made, have any influence?

The piece revealed that Vinoly had fudged his past, letting himself be portrayed as having fled persecution in Argentina when, in fact, he'd had a successful career during the 1970s designing major buildings for that country's military junta.

Most of the reaction to the Wall Street Journal piece has been overseas. The London Sunday Observer said it "torpedoed" Vinoly's chances. The piece also was cited in Corriere Della Sera, Italy's leading newspaper, in the

Zurich daily Neue Zürcher Zeitung and, without credit, in the Australian Financial Review.

But there hasn't been a word about the Journal piece in The New York Times, the Los Angeles Times, The Washington Post or USA Today — effectively a U.S. press blackout. The blackout ended with this week's New Yorker magazine, however, in "Eyes on the Prize," a postmortem by Paul Goldberger.

Goldberg repeats points made in the Journal but takes issue with them: "The criticism seemed to some to be not unlike attempts to discredit German architects who worked briefly for the Nazis in the nineteen-thirties before fleeing Germany." In fact, the piece itself did not make that criticism but instead tried to hold Vinoly accountable for not clarifying distortions reported about him.

As we've learned over and over again — it's the cover-up, not the crime. And as we've also learned — this is an instance — sometimes it's not even a crime.

March 7, 2003 / 11:23 a.m. ET

Canned music, from Bush to Broadway: After President Bush's press conference last night, why should anybody care about getting canned music on Broadway? They shouldn't — at least no more than they should worry about getting a canned president.

Bush sounded like someone on downers trying to persuade anyone who will listen that he's really awake. That's no different, in fact, from theater producers trying to convince audiences that computer-generated music is really live. What's canned is canned, and no amount of listening will make it otherwise.

Broadway's theater producers, faced with a musicians' strike, would like nothing better than getting rid of those pesky horn-tooters — not because producers are meanies who have no taste, but because they're businessmen who need to cut costs.

If Broadway audiences would stand for it — as ballet audiences often must, because ballet companies lack funding — theater music would be delivered straight from the sound factory.

But the producers — unlike President Bush, who talks as though using smart bombs and other precision tools of war does not depend on pleasing his audience — will have to settle for a negotiated compromise.

Without live musicians in the pit, Broadway is likely to see mass defections. Why pay $95 to tune into a musical without an orchestra? (Considering the state of the theater these days, why pay $95 for a musical with an orchestra?) Heck, given Bush's depressing rhetoric, why pay $95 billion to tune into a war?

March 10, 2003 / 9:10 a.m. ET
Who cares about the Oscars? This year's Academy Awards should be a more glittering occasion than the usual run, if only because it's Oscar's 75th anniversary. But the expected glitter of rental diamonds and designer gowns notwithstanding, the upcoming star parade may not sparkle at all — and it's not just because <u>war in Iraq may steal its spotlight</u>.

If you believe screenwriter and author Bruce Feirstein — and I do — there's "a definite lack of enthusiasm" in Hollywood "bordering on disinterest, during what is normally a frenzied run-up to the awards ceremony." His diary column in the New York Observer, <u>"Letter from L.A.: Writing Off Oscar In the Year of Harvey,"</u> tells why.

Apart from the prospect of war, there's the Miramax factor. With three out of the five best-picture nominations in Miramax's pocket ("The Hours," "Gangs of New York" and "Chicago") and an assocation with a fourth as its distributer ("The Lord of the Rings: The Two Towers"), the foregone conclusion is that the studio has already come away the night's big winner. So why tune in?

And now that <u>"Chicago" has swept three top Screen Actors Guild awards</u> — Renee Zellweger for lead actress, Catherine Zeta-Jones for supporting actress and the cast for <u>best ensemble</u> (the SAG equivalent of best picture) — the only question is: How did Miramax chief Harvey Weinstein let "The Pianist," the fifth best-picture Oscar contender, get away?

But Feirstein's piece raises a more important issue, namely the good vs. the popular. "The concern," he writes, "is that what's considered 'good' is no longer popular, and what's popular isn't any good." In the past, despite a "benignly corrupt" voting system — when studios largely controlled the ballots — there was much less discrepancy between the good and the popular.

Since then, however, prestige pictures are almost by definition not popular with the moviegoing public, which is made up overwhelmingly of teenagers; the democratization of the Oscar-voting process has been corrupted by massive marketing campaigns; and the Oscars themselves have marginalized the money-makers who "drive the business and connect with the audience." For example, Steven Spielberg.

Lower-ranking studio executives regard the Oscars as passé, Feirstein writes. "I work for a giant media conglomerate," one told him. "We're interested in sequels, and video games, and international box office. Sure, I liked 'The Hours.' But any day of the week, hands down, I'd rather have 'Spider-Man' on my resumé."

At the upper reaches of filmdom, executives point to the so-so ratings for this year's Golden Globes broadcast and worry that "there's a real lack of enthusiasm for the nominees, both inside the business and out." Or as Sam Goldwyn is once supposed to have said: "Go see that turkey for yourself, and see for yourself why you shouldn't see it."

March 11, 2003 / 9:38 a.m. ET

Off the main stem: Just when the main-stem tourists were beginning to discover that Off Broadway has musicals, too, Broadway goes and ends its strike. So the little boost that the smaller productions deserved probably won't come to much.

Off Broadway musicals (with real live musicians who have to pay the rent, too) played right through the strike, and they're still playing. And maybe you'll remember them. These are some: "Forbidden Broadway," "Radiant Baby," "My Life With Albertine," "I Love You, You're Perfect, Now Change," "Little Fish" and, now in previews, "Zanna, Don't!"

March 11, 2003 / 11:13 a.m. ET

An American speak-out: Roger Ebert ran into trouble with a reader when he expressed a political opinion in a movie review. Some people believe politics and art, let alone criticism, don't mix.

"I was offended by your remarks about Trent Lott, which were totally unnecessary and irrelevant to a review of 'Gods and Generals,' " the reader wrote. "Please stick to reviewing movies, not giving political statements." (If you click on the link, scroll down.)

Why am I not surprised? Because just this morning I got this e-mail: "I think your comments about President Bush are entirely inappropriate. Who do you think you are anyway that you have the right to judge a great man. This is the last time I will read anything you write."

I often get e-mail like that, and I'm tempted to say, "Good riddance!" But I won't. I'll quote Ebert's reply instead. "Where did so many Americans get the notion that there is something offensive or transgressive about expressing political opinions? Movies are often about politics, sometimes when they least seem to be, and the critic must be honest enough to reveal his own beliefs in reviewing them."

Ditto for this column.

So without further ado, here's a link to a very funny, four-star agitprop

Web comedy for your viewing pleasure: "THE ADVENTURES OF HERCUBUSH," a political satire by a team that includes Jay Martell, who worked with Michael Moore on both "The Awful Truth" and "TV Nation." (Martell asked in the kind of e-mail I like: "Ever wonder where President Bush got his insatiable need to kick butt?" The answer is hilarious.)

And if you're looking for political opinions in poetry, City Lights Books, which is celebrating its 50th anniversary, sent me this poem by Lawrence Ferlinghetti.

SPEAK OUT!

And a vast paranoia sweeps across the land
And America turns the attack on its Twin Towers
Into the beginning of the Third World War
The war with the Third World

And the terrorists in Washington
Are shipping out the young men
To the killing fields again

And no one speaks

And they are rousting out
All the ones with turbans
And they are flushing out
All the strange immigrants

And they are shipping all the young men
To the killing fields again

And no one speaks

And when they come to round up
All the great writers and poets and painters
The National Endowment of the Arts of Complacency
Will not speak

While all the young men
Will be killing all the young men
In the killing fields again

So now is the time for you to speak
All you lovers of liberty
All you lovers of the pursuit of happiness
All you lovers and sleepers
Deep in your private dream
Now is the time for you to speak
O silent majority
Before they come for you!

I realize this is the second poem I've printed by Ferlinghetti. But he's an old boss of mine who I'm proud to call a friend. Besides, I like his poetry. Also, in case you didn't know, here's what happens when they come for you.

March 12, 2003 / 8:57 a.m. ET

The Beastie Boys join the protest: They've just posted an anti-war song, "In a World Gone Mad ..." on their Web site, free for downloading. Five months ago I trashed the Beastie Boys. I take it all back. (OK, I'm easy.)

Cynics would say, "Sure it's free. It's free publicity for them." But I'm no cynic. (My staff of thousands says it, too: "He's no cynic.") You can't buy the song, which is being distributed to disc jockeys, at least not yet. (It will be on their next CD, which is still being recorded.)

Here are the lyrics, hard-hitting doggerel that sounds better sung than read. A sample:

Now how many people must get killed?
For oil families pockets to get filled?
How many oil families get killed?
Not a damn one so what's the deal?

The Beastie Boys have also posted declarations to ensure that their protest is not misunderstood:

"This song is not an anti-American or pro-Saddam Hussein statement. This is a statement against an unjustified war." — *Adam Horovitz*

"We felt it was important to comment on where the US appears to be heading now. A war in Iraq will not resolve our problems. It can only result in the deaths of many innocent civilians and US troops. If we are truly striving for safety, we need to build friendships, not try to bully the rest of the world." — *Adam Yauch*

In case you're wondering why I trashed the Beastie Boys, <u>here's why</u>. And here's <u>what they said in response</u>.

March 13, 2003 / 12:59 p.m. ET

The case for war branding: Selling war to the public depends on branding. åWell-branded wars include the American Revolution, the Civil War, World War I and World War II. Poorly branded wars are losing or less-than-winning propositions. They include the War of 1812, the Korean War, the Vietnam War and the Gulf War.

Is this nutty thinking or what? If you answered "or what?" you would make Tracey Riese, 46, a happy branding warrior.

"As we move daily closer to war in Iraq, President Bush might benefit from examining how America has branded major wars in the past — and how each branding strategy contributed to the outcome," says Riese, whose corporate clients have included Revlon and RJR Nabisco, Scholastic Inc. and Schwab.

Her notion of war branding sounds like commodified propaganda. And in our society, commodification is the way to go. But Riese says "the process of branding is the opposite of commodification. It's the opposite of sloganizing. It's finding the true meaning of things. It's not about <u>finding a snappy slogan for war.</u>"

She says, "Really great branding connects the product, if you will, with some very powerful emotional need on the part of the people who must pay for it or who you want to pay for it."

For instance, <u>the War for Independence</u> was transformed from a contest between a colony and a great power into a struggle for "liberty" by enlightened citizens. The brand went global as France picked up the idea and went to war in 1789 for "liberté, fraternité, égalité." That's strong branding.

"<u>Give Me Liberty or Give Me Death</u> was a fancy rhetorical point," Riese says. "But it was not just sloganizing. It had an underlying meaning. In the face of war, citizens are asked to pay the highest price. And so they need to make a fundamental connection to the purpose of any war."

<u>The American Civil War</u> began as a struggle between two economic systems over constitutional rights. But it took on new meaning — and vigor — when Lincoln was able to characterize it as a battle for the soul of a nation <u>"conceived in liberty and dedicated to the proposition that all men are created equal."</u> Strong branding.

World War I, the tragic outsized result of petty miscalculations, was redeemed when Wilson transformed it into the "War to End All Wars." Strong branding.

World War II became a moral test of humanity. So pervasive was that brand that it was reflected even in the post-war peace, when the victors revitalized their former enemies and laid the foundation for the modern global economy and the growth of democracy. It's later characterization as "the good war" was strong branding, too.

By contrast, she says, calling the Gulf War Operation Desert Shield and then Desert Storm was "just creating a name or logo. That's an expression of the brand that isn't the brand itself. The underlying meaning was that it was not really war, that it was nothing for anyone to worry about. It was just a military operation. The administration wanted to create the sense that it would all be over in no time." Weak branding.

So what about President Bush's "axis of evil" slogan? And what about the expensive set now being built in the desert by the military for branded TV press briefings? A no-brainer.

"Right now the brand the administration has established in the minds of Americans and in the global community — whether it meant to or not — is that war in Iraq is an American prerogative," Riese says. "We are threatened, and we do not have to be threatened, and so we are going to eliminate a threat to us, regardless of how it affects others. That's the brand."

Full disclosure: Riese also gives branding advice to the World Wildlife Fund. In some quarters that would mean she's a tree hugger.

March 14, 2003 / 1:28 p.m. ET
George Bush and Humphrey Bogart: I've been trying to find the apt movie metaphor that evokes the reality of President Bush, and now I've finally got it: "Capt. Queeg." I wish I had thought of it myself, but it's Paul Krugman who came up with it this morning for the title of his column: "George W. Queeg." (Registration required.)

The reference, of course, is to Capt. Philip Francis Queeg, the tough-talking, ship-shaping, mind-boggling, nervous-making Navy martinet that Humphrey Bogart played so perfectly against type in the 1954 movie "The Caine Mutiny."

"Aboard the U.S.S. Caine," Krugman writes, "it was the business with the strawberries that finally convinced the doubters that something was amiss with the captain. Is foreign policy George W. Bush's quart of strawberries?"

If you've never seen the movie, you must. It's based on Herman Wouk's Pulitzer Prize-winning novel, and it gives us Bogart's last great role. (He died of cancer three years later. He also lost the best-actor Oscar to Marlon Brando in "On the Waterfront," which aced "Mutiny" for best picture.)

You've got to read Krugman's column, too. It's the best summary I've read about the U.S. commander-in-chief's strange command. By his account, Bush is a Capt. Queeg for our time.

And just to be even-handed, here's a very different sort of opinion: the rambling but impassioned Oriana Fallaci's thoughts on the eve of battle. Which is not to say that she's confident of Bush's leadership either.

Finally, a poem by Robert Creeley, called "Help!" It reads like rap, which is totally uncharacteristic of his poetry. This is the way it begins:

Help's easy enough
If it comes in time.
Nothing's that hard
If you want to rhyme.

It's when they shoot you
It can hurt,
When the bombs blast off
And you're gone with a squirt.

Sitting in a bunker,
Feeling blue?
Don't be a loser,
It wasn't you—

Wasn't you wanted
To go kill people,
Wasn't you caused
All this trouble.

I can't say, Run!
And I can't say, Hide!
But I still feel
What I feel inside.

March 17, 2003 / 7:43 a.m. ET

Norman Mailer nails it: Just when critics like Michiko Kakutani pretty much dismissed him as an old cuckoo (registration required), calling him a writer full of "wacky mumbo jumbo" who could barely cobble together his latest book, the old cuckoo has shined a clarifying light on the <u>American dilemma and the "liberation" of Iraq.</u>

In a powerful speech he gave recently in San Francisco, now published in the New York Review of Books, Mailer asserts: "Behind the whole push to go to war with Iraq is the desire to have a huge military presence in the Near East as a stepping stone to taking over the rest of the world. That is a big statement, but I can offer this much immediately: At the root of flag conservatism is not madness, but an undisclosed logic."

Read the article and see if you don't agree. Mailer offers straightforward thinking in plain language. His diagnosis of the dilemma as the Bush Administration's dream of an "American empire" may be more frightening than ancient Rome's worst nightmare, but it doesn't sound like "mumbo jumbo" to me.

(By the way, a note to all the folks who prefer to think of George W. Bush as Capt. Ahab rather than Capt. Queeg: That's giving Bush far too much stature.)

March 17, 2003 / 4:53 p.m. ET

Turning the Chicks into Chickens? It took a lot of guts for the Dixie Chicks' Natalie Maines to say she was ashamed of the president of the United States. Foolish guts. And it would have been surprising, given the stakes for a group of platinum-selling superstars, if she hadn't apologized.

But the backlash against them — <u>pulling them from radio playlists</u> — is more than mere patriotic outrage. The indefatigable Eric Olsen, who's been following <u>the latest pro- and anti-war stories from Nashville</u> with keen attention, points out that there's been a concerted e-mail campaign orchestrated by <u>"a radical right-wing online forum"</u> to stoke the anger, manipulate the radio polls and pressure the Lipton company to drop its sponsorship of the Dixie Chicks' upcoming U.S. tour.

Do celebrities have a right to speak out on political issues? Should they? Do the media trivialize antiwar messages by providing a forum for celebrities? Media reporter David Shaw of the Los Angeles Times believes so. <u>"We've paid too much attention</u> to celebrity opposition to the war," he writes.

To correct the balance, my staff of thousands and I have taken a solemn vow to report on all the celebrities who favor war. Please help us carry on. Let us know when you hear of celebrities as famous and foolish as the Dixie Chicks going out of their way to praise the Bush team and war in Iraq. There's Charlie Daniels, Bruce Willis, Kid Rock and Dennis Miller. Do I hear more?

March 18, 2003 / 4:43 p.m. ET

Martin Sheen strikes back: "The West Wing" star who plays fictional President Josiah Bartlet has written an Op-Ed piece, "A Celebrity, but First a Citizen," in the Los Angeles Times. (Free registration required.) With eloquence, he defends his right to speak out against war in Iraq.

"I am not the president; instead, I hold an even higher office, that of citizen of the United States," Sheen begins, in reply no doubt to a story the paper carried by LA Times staffer David Shaw that said the media pay too much attention to celebrities who oppose the war. (Free registration required.)

Sheen notes: "Although my opinion is not any more valuable or relevant merely because I am an actor, that fact does not render it unimportant. Some have suggested otherwise, trying to denigrate the validity of this opinion and those of my colleagues solely due to our celebrity status. This is insulting not only to us but to other people of conscience who love their country enough to risk its wrath by going against the grain of powerful government policy."

Yesterday, my staff of thousands and I took a solemn vow to report on all the celebrities who favor war — just so we could right the balance that Shaw complained about.

Well, it turns out to be a burning issue. I've received hundreds and hundreds of e-mails, pro and con, about celebrity rights and the Dixie Chicks and famous people who've said this or that. I realize now that even with a staff of thousands I don't have time to fact-check the allegations. So here's a site where you can see for yourselves what some of Hollywood's famous have said, pro and con, about the war and about President Bush and his policies.

March 19, 2003 / 10:37 a.m. ET

And now for the petitions: We've heard of famous Hollywood actors against the war (Susan Sarandon, Richard Gere, Sean Penn, Jessica Lange, George Clooney), and we've heard of famous pop stars against the war (Sheryl Crow, Natalie Maines of the Dixie Chicks and Barbra Streisand, of course), but what about famous writers against the war?

Well, writers tend not to be famous. But some of them are — Stephen King, Russell Banks, Amy Tan, Richard Price, Jonathan Franzen — and they, along with about 150 others, have signed a petition that says to President Bush:

"Iraq, while led by a tyrant, represents no clear and present danger to our shores. We therefore see no sufficient moral or historical justification for a pre-emptive war. ... As you yourself have noted, there are evildoers in this world. Let the United States not be one of them."

Of all people, writers who depend on precise language should know better than to use the term "pre-emptive war." Perhaps they can be excused because everybody's been using it, including President Bush, news reporters, pundits and even foreign-policy experts.

But the proper term is "preventive war." A "pre-emptive war" is undertaken to thwart an imminent attack. A "preventive war" is what we're about to see in Iraq. (I notice that Tom Friedman at last uses the correct term this morning in his "D-Day" column. (Free registration required.)

Bush has promoted the wrong term precisely because he has had to justify the urgency of an invasion. (It's also why Bush has always made clear that Iraq is a threat to other shores and wants to depose Saddam for that reason.)

Meanwhile, there's another online petition out here in cyberspace. Called "Support of the Dixie Chicks," it endorses the group's right to dissent from President Bush's style of diplomacy. Not many have signed it, only 126 people so far. Many more Dixie Chicks fans have e-mailed me in support of the group. I suspect the reason so few have signed is that they don't know of the petition or can't find it.

Postscript: Whaddya know. At this time — 5:54 p.m. ET — many more people have signed: 1,697 ... and counting.

March 20, 2003 / 8:27 a.m. ET

When Bush comes to shove: The number of people who have signed the online petition supporting Natalie Maines of the Dixie Chicks and her right to dissent has climbed to 2,642. When we first posted the petition's address yesterday, the number was 126. So we may have helped people find the petition. We also may have flooded Hollywood on the March, a rightwing site that's been listing what actors have been saying for and against war. At the moment, the site is down. Possibly can't handle all the traffic.

A quick note: Amen to this morning's column by Bob Herbert. (Free registration required.) He writes: "Now that the U.S. strikes against Iraq have begun, we should get rid of one canard immediately, and that's the notion that criticism of the Bush administration and opposition to this invasion imply in some sense a lack of support or concern for the men and women who are under arms."

March 20, 2003 / 1:17 p.m. ET

The Scorsese-Wyler connection: One seeming certainty of the Oscars, if Sunday's show goes on as scheduled, is the "Chicago" juggernaut. The movie is not only a strong favorite in the best-picture category, it's likely to take home an armload of prizes.

"'Chicago' is going to win," film critic Roger Ebert, for one, predicts in a fascinating interview. "And Harvey [Weinstein, head of Miramax, which produced it] is going to be up there clutching those Oscars. After that terrible profile of him in The New Yorker, he'll have complete revenge."

But the Oscar race for best director, if it goes to "Chicago" director Rob Marshall (the likely winner), would be a paradoxical victory for Weinstein, who has been touting Martin Scorsese to win for "Gangs of New York" instead.

Scorsese is a sentimental favorite for two reasons: He has never won an Oscar, despite four previous nominations — for "Raging Bull" (1980), "The Last Temptation of Christ" (1988), "Goodfellas" (1990) and "The Age of Innocence" (1993) — and he's acknowledged throughout Hollywood as one of the two or three best directors working today. (Some consider him among a handful of the best directors ever.)

But being overlooked at the Academy Awards is not unusual. Consider William Wyler. (I've written his biography, "A Talent for Trouble.") Wyler's 1941 movie "The Little Foxes" was his sixth film in a row to receive a best-picture nomination without winning. (The others were 1936's "Dodsworth," 1937's "Dead End," 1938's "Jezebel," 1939's "Wuthering Heights" and 1940's "The Letter.")

"The Little Foxes," which starred Bette Davis, earned nine Oscar nominations and is, by any measure, one of Hollywood's greatest films. It didn't win a single Oscar. It also represented Wyler's fourth best-director nomination in six years without winning.

When he finally did receive his first Oscar — the first of three on a record-setting 12 nominations — it was for 1942's "Mrs. Miniver," a war movie he made for propaganda purposes (to promote U.S. opposition to Nazi Germany). Though extraordinarily popular — it ranked as the second highest-grossing movie, after "Gone With the Wind," for many years — "Mrs. Miniver" was no match in artistic terms for any of those six other nominated films.

It pleased Wyler that "Mrs. Miniver" had rallied opinion to a cause he fervently believed in. But after enlisting in the Army Air Force and seeing the war firsthand, he felt somewhat embarrassed that he had offered the public a sugarcoated myth. With its prettified hardships and saccharine nobility, the movie had "only scratched the surface of war," he said, "I don't mean that it was wrong. It was incomplete."

By the same token, if Scorcese were to win the Oscar for directing "Gangs of New York" (which I doubt, because it is far from his best work), he may one day look back on it and say that in spite of its vast size and ambition it only scratched the surface of the history he wanted to tell.

March 21, 2003 / 9:58 a.m. ET

Will they or won't they? I'm talking about the Oscars, of course. There have been some defections. Will there be massive defections? Will the Academy Awards regime even be able to hold the Oscars as scheduled on Sunday? Is there a more pressing issue at the moment?

B. J. Sigesmund reports for Newsweek online: "Several possibilities have been floated: the awards could be outright cancelled, with statues handed out at a smaller ceremony in the future. ... It's also foreseeable that the awards could happen on Sunday evening, but not be televised by ABC."

But a top ABC executive appeared to shoot down that possibility in this morning's New York Times: "While it is theoretically possible for the Oscars to proceed without being broadcast on ABC, that is not likely to happen," he said. "I think a decision will be made one way or the other." (Free registration required.)

The academy also reportedly feels a decision could comfortably be made as late as this evening to postpone the awards and, in an emergency, it could decide as late as Sunday. One issue that the Oscar regime has not yet addressed is whether stars who feel uncomfortable appearing at a wartime ceremony would be allowed to send doubles instead.

Meantime, Oscar honchos have laughed off "rampant rumors" that many stars won't be turning up. They say most will be there. But honchos always laugh off rampant rumors, nyet? If I were part of the Oscar regime, I'd be sure to have the CIA's face-and-voice-print analysts at the door.

March 21, 2003 / 9:04 p.m. ET

The Oscars are on: It looks like all systems are go for the Academy Awards. But officials still haven't clarified whether actors can send doubles in their place. At least one person from California objects to the idea, however.

"I think sending an actor double is ridiculous!" this person wrote in an e-mail, wisely leaving out a name. "If the actor is fearing for his or her own life what makes the life of the double worth less than that of their own?"

Such messages are priceless.

March 22, 2003 / 10:01 a.m. ET

Oh, baby! First it was Sony. <u>Remember its bogus critic?</u> Now it's Miramax. And what a whopper! I guess they took my advice: "When faking movie reviews, at least show some spunk."

Miramax has outdone even David Merrick, the Broadway showman who hyped one of his musicals by taking a full-page ad in The New York Herald-Tribune with raves from people he found in the phonebook who had the same names as the real critics who had panned the show.

As part of its Oscar campaign for Martin Scorsese, Miramax had a publicist write an article heaping praise on Scorsese's "Gangs of New York" and got the renowned director Robert Wise to sign it, then had it placed in two regional southern California newspapers and, in a final touch of genius, had it reprinted a half dozen times as a paid advertisement in the Hollywood trade papers as well as major newspapers under the headline: "Two time Academy Award winner Robert Wise declares Scorsese deserves the Oscar for 'Gangs of New York.'"

All this and more — like the fact that the publicist works for the Academy of Motion Picture Arts and Sciences, which gives out the Oscars, and the fact that the 88-year-old Wise, who won his Oscars for "The Sound of Music" and "West Side Story," is a former president of the academy — was revealed by <u>John Horn in the Los Angeles Times</u>. He's the same reporter who first revealed the phony Sony critic, while at Newsweek.

Will the revelation affect the Oscar voting? Nope. Ballots were already in. What an embarrassment for Scorsese if he were to win Sunday night. Actually, what an embarrassment if he were to lose, which is more likely anyway.

Speaking of fake: Here's <u>what the Dixie Chicks' Natalie Maines really, really said</u> in her apology for disrespecting President Bush.

March 24, 2003 / 9:52 a.m. ET

Oh! What a lovely Oscar war: The real suspense of <u>Sunday night's Oscars</u> was when or even whether the show would be interrupted by news of the invasion of Iraq and what, if anything, the stars would say about the war rather than what they would say about winning an Oscar.

For a long while, you might never have known there was a war at all — except for Steve Martin's opening monologue. The Oscar producers ought to get down on their knees and thank him. As good as the show became — only in part because of the classy production — it would have died without him.

And let us all thank Adrien Brody for his stunning, unprepared remarks

221

about the "sadness and dehumanization" of war. But let's also thank him for his sense of humor, not to mention his wonderful grace under pressure. Before Brody ever got to his serious remarks, he reacted with charming wit to his surprise at winning the best-actor Oscar. "There comes a time in life," he said, "when everything seems to make sense, and this is not one of those times."

Now, about Michael Moore's outburst. I'm all in favor of tasteless outbursts at the Oscars. They lend spice. <u>Tom Shales disagrees.</u> What I wonder, though, is whether the boos his remarks provoked were the result of anger at his lack of taste or disagreement with his political views. Or was it both?

(Full disclosure: I agree with Moore. I wasn't crazy about his Oscar-winning "Bowling for Columbine," though. Too strident.)

March 25, 2003 / 9:47 a.m. ET
Cheers, jeers and Michael Moore: Many readers hated <u>my remarks</u> about Michael Moore's remarks about President Bush. They would like me to take a hike (preferably off a high cliff). Of hundreds of e-mails, this one was typical:

Kelly Evitts
Atlanta
"Of course you agree with Moore. I only hope that when we get attacked, you and he are the first to go. Why don't you communists go over and join your 'human shield' friends. ... God bless our troops, our president, and if there is any justice in the world, let God turn his back on you, and your fat friend."

Here's one of the more pleasant jeers:
Jeff Curran
Oklahoma City
"Michael Moore? Michael less, please."

Some flat-out cheered:
Eduard Itor
Tampa, Fla.
"What Michael Moore did was brave and right."

One cheered with an explanation:

Sarah
Cleveland, Ohio
"Politically, I agree with Moore, too, but in terms of PR value, he's 'our side's' version of Rush Limbaugh: a self-congratulatory clown who behaves like a braying jackass in front of an audience."

Here's an e-mail exchange of March 20, as the U.S. invasion of Iraq began, with a thoughtful reader who doesn't like my views about the war:

Air Force TSgt. Gary J. Kunich
Kenosha, Wisc.
"I'll take it as a small victory for me that you allotted at least one paragraph to give a nod of support for the troops, even if you don't support the action in Iraq. Still think you're wrong, and your column really ticks me off, so begrudgingly, I guess that means you're doing your job.

"Speaking from my personal experience during Desert Storm, public support was very important to us. We were afraid it would change once that war started, and were grateful that the support for us — and the war — never wavered. But not everyone fighting this fight is able to see the 'support' through the smoke and noise of the protest. There definitely was no support for the troops when several celebrities and pseudo-politicians signed that full-page ad in the New York Times comparing our military to the terrorists.

"I — and the majority of Americans according to several polls — believe this to be a war to ensure our security. The war on terror cannot be summarized by just the face of Osama bin Laden. There are many facets, and this is but one of them. This isn't Vietnam. This isn't a gray area, or a murky quagmire. This is our only option. If you can add just one line in your column, add this on behalf of the U.S. military."

This was my reply: "I appreciate your point, especially since you are speaking from personal experience. I worry about the safety of U.S. troops. I want them to win — swiftly and with no loss of life or limb, if that is even possible — because I, too, am an American who believes in the ideals this country was founded upon. But I fear the motives of our president. I do not believe that this nation should be ruled by Christian fundamentalism or by the imperial mandate of corporate power, both of which I believe is at the heart of the president's beliefs."

223

And here are words of warning: Though they were never intended as such, they ought to remind us of the perils we face not only from enemies who would destroy us but from leaders who would destroy our enemies.

"Why of course the people don't want war. ... That is understood. But after all it is the leaders of the country who determine the policy, and it is always a simple matter to drag the people along, whether it is a democracy, or a fascist dictatorship, or a parliament, or a communist dictatorship ...Voice or no voice, the people can always be brought to the bidding of the leaders. That is easy. All you have to do is to tell them they are being attacked, and denounce the pacifists for lack of patriotism and exposing the country to danger. It works the same in any country."

Who said that? Hitler's accomplice, Hermann Goering (commander of the German Air Force and president of the Reichstag), at the Nuremberg trials of Nazi war criminals in 1946.

Postscript: For all you folks who think I'm making an implicit comparison between Hitler or Goering and President Bush, please put that out of your minds. I don't believe that for a minute. I'm merely using Goering's words to point out that people are too easily manipulated by leaders who are "good" and leaders who are "bad." People are too easily led, period.

March 26, 2003 / 8:59 a.m. ET

The makings of a movie star: If you've been watching any of the daily press briefings at U.S. Central Command, you must have noticed Brigadier General Vincent K. Brooks. How could you not? Tall, handsome and remarkably articulate, Brooks radiates such calm intelligence and natural good will that it's impossible to doubt his honesty. If he weren't a career soldier, I'd say we were witnessing the birth of a movie star. He has more charisma than Denzel Washington.

So who is this guy? A source of mine tells me Brooks comes from an uncommon military family. His father retired from the U.S. Army as a brigadier general. His brother, Leo Brooks, is also a brigadier general, serving as the Commandant of Cadets at West Point. And Brooks himself, at age 44, is the youngest general officer in the U.S. Army. He was also the first black man to serve as First Captain of his battalion at West Point.

Just thought you'd like to know.

And by the way: Many readers have sent e-mails challenging me to prove that President Bush is motivated by Christian fundamentalism. (Some

224

like the idea, too.) I suppose the ultimate proof would have to come from his lips. But I'd say that Jack Beatty's essay, "In the Name of God," offers some pretty convincing evidence. If that doesn't persuade you, try Howard Fineman's "Bush and God," in Newsweek. That should do it.

Postscript: From some of the e-mails I'm getting, it looks like I have to bring in bigger guns. How about this salvo from the president of the Chicago Theological Seminary, Susan B. Thistlewaite? (Free registration required.)

She writes: "It is not a clash of civilizations we face, but a 'clash of fundamentalisms' a conflict between a zealous Christianized worldview of President Bush and an increasingly fundamentalist Islam. The theology of Bush has been described as a rigid Christian evangelicalism. This theology produces its own kind of premodern zeal for pursuing evildoers, even by violent means."

And here's another salvo from Andrew Greeley, the best-selling author and Catholic priest. He writes: "The New York Times quotes presidential staffers as saying that the president sees the world as a 'biblical struggle of good vs. evil.' The name of that is fanaticism."

March 27, 2003 / 10:43 a.m. ET

Rock the protest: The war on the song front has heated up again, and it's not a confrontation over the Dixie Chicks. Lenny Kravitz has joined the battle with a song titled "We Want Peace." You can hear it or download it free at a get-out-the-vote Web site Rock the Vote.

One major critic describes the song as reaching down deep "for a funky, Middle Eastern-flavored ode to peace." What bothers this critic though, is that "it's by far the best song to address" the issue of war in Iraq. So why does it bother him? Because, he writes, it's "anti, and people, I am way pro!"

Critic Eric Olsen, who is also a radio DJ, a music historian and a relentless blogger, further objects that Rock the Vote — which is dedicated to getting young people to participate in democracy — is perverting its mission by taking sides on Iraq. He wonders whether the site would give equal time to "equally heartfelt, pro-liberation" songs by — let's say — Clint Black or Toby Keith, Darryl Worley and the Warren Brothers.

Olsen contends that the issue dividing Americans on Iraq should not be characterized as "pro-war vs. anti-war." His point is that both sides are pro-peace. When Rock the Vote's executive director states: "We hope the war will come to a swift conclusion with a minimum loss of human life and that we can move on to build a better future for the Iraqi people," Olsen counters: "Who doesn't agree with this?"

His formulation — "pro-liberation vs. anti-war" — smartly frames the issue with more nuance than "pro-war vs. anti-war." If it ignores the deeper issues dividing American public opinion, well, you can't expect a music critic-radioDJ-blogger to do what our clever leaders — Bush, Cheney, Rumsfeld and the other geniuses leading the administration — haven't done themselves, can you?

Meanwhile, Olsen is not the only blogger seeking some sort of middle ground in the war debate. Here's Ryan McGee, a Harvard smart aleck, prompted by a support-the-troops rally at Yale.

March 27, 2003 / 12:36 p.m. ET

What is patriotism? Are we born with love of country? Is it written into our genes, having proved useful for survival from earliest times like a trait expressed through natural selection? Is it hard-wired into our brains like a universal grammar theorized by Noam Chomsky, simply waiting to be applied in specific languages? Is it wholly learned?

Writers, artists and philosophers have grappled with the issue of war and patriotism for centuries — as a theme in poetry and novels (Tolstoy's "War and Peace"), as a pictorial force (George Washington Crossing the Delaware or The Flag-Raising on Iwo Jima), as a subject of academic inquiry and just this morning as a topic of debate in the media.

The secret of Rome's success, according to the Roman historian Livy, was its belief in the supremacy of country over family and — just as important — its ability to inculcate that belief in its citizens. "This, without question," Lee Harris writes in Policy Review, "was the steady drumbeat of Roman pedagogical legend, the unquestioned primacy of one's ethical obligation to the team, the origin of the specifically Western concept of patriotism."

Before that, the ancient Greek philosopher Diogenes had challenged the idea of a narrow, that is to say, national patriotism. Reputedly, when anyone asked him where he came from, he said: "I am a citizen of the world."

The noted contemporary philosopher Martha Nussbaum writes: "Diogenes knew that the invitation to think as a world citizen was, in a sense, an invitation to be an exile from the comfort of patriotism and its easy sentiments, to see our own ways of life from the point of view of justice and the good. The accident of where one is born is just that, an accident; any human being might have been born in any nation.

"Recognizing this, his Stoic successors held, we should not allow differences of nationality or class or ethnic membership or even gender to erect barriers between us and our fellow human beings. We should recognize humanity wherever it occurs, and give its fundamental ingredients, reason and moral capacity, our first allegiance and respect."

Where does that leave us today as American and British soldiers fight and die in Iraq and as Iraqis fight and die? Basically nowhere. Certainly not with definitive answers, not even with tentative ones.

March 31, 2003 / 10:33 a.m. ET

This is patriotism: It's no secret that my staff of thousands and I receive a lot of e-mail messages. Some are more heartfelt than others, but I'd say that with few exceptions they're all sincere. On Friday, we asked the question: "What is patriotism?" Below are a dozen replies. Some are frightening, others reassuring, and still others fall in between. Which are which? We leave that to you.

Jim Nabors
Baltimore, Md.
"Patriotism is being WITH one's country, right or wrong, especially if the overwhelming majority of its citizens are in favor of the government's actions. It is NOT being a minority rebel-rouser who uses 'free speech' as a pretext for one's fringe political leanings against one's country or its leaders. The 'free-speech' argument is a crock, and is used by today's anti-government newspapers, news shows, and 'unpatriotic' low lifes who have no life."

R. Guerrero
San Lorenzo, Calif.
"I believe patriotism is developed and attained by the way in which the government of a nation treats its citizens."

David Maddux
McKinney, Texas
"I firmly support our president and our efforts to remove Saddam Hussein and his oppressive regime. We live in the most loving, caring country on the face of the earth as we have given billions of our tax dollars to help suffering humanity. I respect dissent done in a civil manner but when celebrities or anyone else start getting personal with our leaders, they cross the line of being 'un-American' in my view. For example, Michael Moore's comments at the Oscars. He was disgusting. My forefathers fought and died for his right to be 'disgusting' and my right to call him 'un-American.'"

Sandra Isaacs
Oak Park, Illinois
"I am not in favor of any government that chooses violence. I am a citizen of the world. I wave the flag of Mother Earth."

Brian Kiser
Macon, Ga.
"You quote Martha Nussbaum saying, 'We should recognize humanity wherever it occurs, and give its fundamental ingredients, reason and moral capacity, our first allegiance and respect.' Should we not also recognize inhumanity in the same way? Wherever it occurs, should it not be worthy of our disdain and efforts to remove it from this world? Surely Saddam and his Baath party are guilty of some of the most inhuman crimes against his own people, yet those opposed to this war want to look away believing that the United States and its allies should not get involved. Thank God for President Bush and our brave military men and women who are willing to be true citizens of the Earth!"

John Smith
Heathsville, Va.
"Patriotism is loving your country and being willing to defend it. Our country was found on the principle: 'Don't tread on me!' Liberals would change all that. Liberals would allow terrorists and tyrants to overrun us in the name of peace. They prove that by insulting their president at a time of war, and protesting in the name of peace while throwing rocks at service men, beating up policemen, and collaborating with the enemy by not having enough sense to find out who is bankrolling their noble effort."

Michael Anthony
Calgary, Alberta, Canada
"True love of country — especially a democratic one — should embrace the concept of keeping that country true to its ideals, and holding its leaders accountable for upholding its founding principles. It is our patriotic duty to blow the whistle on an unprovoked, illegal and shamefully 'manufactured' war. If we love America we will try to keep her hands clean. If we cannot do that then at least we should remember we have dual citizenship — we are also citizens of the world."

Daniel Hendriks

Chico, Calif.

"I think patriotism is good when you are rooting for your team in the World Cup, but when it comes to a war without support from the U.N. I question my love not for this country as a whole but I question my trust in the government. This whole situation is too fishy for me. ... I will be able to vote come next election and if George Bush gets re-elected I will move to Holland and not come back until a Democrat is in office."

Letitia Little

Bartlett

"We are as one. That's why we are in Iraq. Justice and Freedom for all, is the key. We cannot stand back and allow a government destroy innocent people. And the manner that these people murder is like nothing I've ever heard of before and everything I've ever feared. While I do believe we should have done this long ago (1991) we are where we are. Let's get the job done and get our boys and girls home."

Bob Johnson

"We ARE recognizing humanity as it occurs in Iraq. And we are also recognizing man's inhumanity to man and trying to stop it. After World War II, Harry Truman said, 'We need to build a better world.' We can help to build a better world for the oppressed people in Iraq. That is something that makes a lot of us proud to be Americans."

Tanya D. June

Troy, N.Y.

"Are we going to war with North Korea — because of lack of disarmament? NO

"Are we going to war with Saudi Arabia — because of connections to terrorists? NO

"Are we going to war with Iraq — because he tried to kill our president's daddy? YES

"Have we secured our homeland from future terrorist attacks? NO

"Have we left our men in Afghanistan more vulnerable? YES

"I am a proud Trojan. Because I am an African-American I see our country's values much differently. We are a 226-year-old country trying to tell countries that existed for thousands of years how to live their lives — when our civil rights movements is barely 40 years old.

"Did we get freedom from the Revolutionary War? NO.

"Did we get freedom after our Civil War? NO.

"Did anything change after we fought in both World War I and II? NO.

"I think our government is so hypocritical. Thank you for giving me a forum to express my views."

Linda C. Strain
Tucson, Ariz.

"I am an American Citizen. Bred, born and reared here in this country. Some of my people were here to greet some of my people on the Mayflower. I love my country, and, yes would give my life for this country and it's people. But I also consider myself a world citizen, and care greatly what happens to my sisters and brothers in other parts of this world.

"The Iraqi leadership was not only a threat to it's own people, but to all of us everywhere. We need to be there, and the rest of the world needs to be there too. It's not about Islam, and it's not about oil. It's about the right of everyone to be able to live and speak freely about their own country and government without fear of reprisal. We are getting rid of a world threat.

"Do I like war? No indeed. Everyone in my family has always served this country from the Revolution to the Gulf War. I considered it an honor, even if I couldn't be sent to the front lines [at that time] because of gender. I still felt obligated to wear the uniform — for my country and my people, not the government. I still feel that way, and wished I were younger so I could join up. I am flag-waver, tree-hugger, and I break for butterflies."

March 31, 2003 / 2:41 p.m. ET

This is satire: We've heard anti-war songs from Lenny Kravitz ("We Want Peace") and from The Beastie Boys ("In a World Gone Mad"). Here, direct from England, is the latest entry: a Bush-Blair duet, "Read My Lips." It's also the funniest.

Share your perspective on entertainment and the arts with Jan Herman. MSNBC is not responsible for the content of Internet links.

Jan Herman

Latest entertainment and arts news from the Web

Entries from April 1 to April 30, 2003
(Some links may be nonfunctional.)
<u>Back to 'The Juice'</u>

LATEST UPDATES

April 1, 2003 / 8:53 a.m. ET
   April Fools' Day: Name the real tune that the Bush-Blair duo is singing — to listen, click on <u>"Read My Lips"</u> — and win our <u>booby prize</u>.

April 3, 2003 / 10:59 a.m. ET
   Material Girl to Patriotic Girl: I'm so happy to hear that Madonna is doing what she can for the troops in battle.
   In case you didn't read about it yesterday, <u>she pulled the video for her latest single</u>, "American Life," because, she said, "I do not want to risk offending anyone who might misinterpret the meaning of this video," especially "due to the volatile state of the world and out of sensitivity and respect to the armed forces, who I support and pray for."
   That's so nice of her. But I think her sensitivity is misplaced. In the video, Madonna is reported to be "wearing military garb next to dancers in camouflage on a fashion runway." Surely nobody could misunderstand that: It means that war is fashion hell. Why would anybody be offended?
   OK, maybe some sensitive types would take offense at a model <u>"wearing a thong and a gas mask and another [wearing] a camouflage chador against a video backdrop of war planes."</u> (Free registration required.)
   As <u>The Scoop reported</u> yesterday, the video has been available at various sites on the Internet. But it's been pulled at http://www.madonnainter.net/. In its place is an announcement that today <u>Warner Bros. Records demanded its removal</u>.
   The site still offers a Madonna interview under: Hot! Hot! Hot! (which has glimpses of the video). She says the war in Iraq and other wars around the world are "a manifestation of our collective consciousness" and that the chaos in the world results from the chaos in our lives.

She says she has "earned the right to have a political view." She says she's against the war in Iraq, but now she supports the American and British troops. At the same time, she supports Michael Moore and his right to dissent. And she says, "I want people to hear what I have to say more than I want to sell a lot of records."

That's covering your ... bases. What a gal.

April 4, 2003 / 11:43 a.m. ET

'American Idol'-atry instead of war: I've been asked to change the subject. Kerrie Kuhne, a reader from Allen Park, Mich., writes: "It's been two weeks since your column was about anything NOT related to the war, to protests [and] patriotism ... It is understandable that the media is paying such attention to the war and everything, but can we have a break once in a while? Please??"

She's got a point.

The last time I looked the war was still on — but so was "American Idol." The show continued to do its thing Wednesday night between commercials and filler, while collecting 15 million votes, too — all because a syrupy gaggle of would-be pop stars are trying to alienate us with their sweetness.

(For those who need a recap of Tuesday night, here it is.)

"Idol" long ago became predictable. Now that it's well into a second season, it has turned wearying . Old scold Simon Cowell is still rolling his eyes at the awfulness of things. Paula Abdul has become den mother to another group of finalists. And Randy Jackson is still dawgin' his way through the muddle. (Notice how I didn't mention Ryan Seacrest?)

Oh, let's not forget: "Idol" has added guest celebrity judges who invariably feel inspired by the contestants — but not as inspired, I'd bet, as they are by the show's promos for their own projects.

One unexpected twist that offers real promise this season is "Idol's" most wanted. It's old news, but let's recap:

Semifinalist Franchelle "Frenchie" Davis was kicked off earlier this season because she once posed topless for a porn Web site (lucky for most of the contestants still in the race that she's gone). Finalist Cory Clark was dumped this week for not revealing that he'd been charged with three misdemeanors, including the battery and criminal restraint of his 15-year-old sister (lucky for viewers he's gone).

Trenyce, aka Lashundra Cobbins, who's still in the "Idol" finals, was once busted on a felony theft charge in Tennessee, but her record was later expunged. Jaered Andrews was kicked off 'Idol" a while ago, after the producers learned he'd been involved in a fight that led to the death of a bar patron. (This happened while he was celebrating his selection as a semifinalist.)

But instead of doing a show — called, say, "Un-American Idol" or "American Joke" — what are the "Idol" producers about to do? A new thing called "Junior Idol." They're looking for wannabes between the ages of 6 and 13. Never too young to get started toward stardom or trouble.

April 4, 2003 / 11:56 a.m. ET

The books they read: I don't know about you, but I like my novels with characters who live on the page, who speak like people and not like abstractions. Among other reasons, that's why I prefer reading Richard Russo to Don DeLillo or Richard Ford to Salman Rushdie. Russo's 496-page "Empire Falls," for instance, was a breeze compared to DeLillo's 336-page purported early masterpiece "White Noise."

I don't know how many times I got halfway through Rushdie's 552-page debut novel "Midnight's Children" — a reputed masterpiece that set the stage for his later fame — before I gave up. (Well, yes I do know: twice.) Even the "novels" of William Burroughs, which are not easy reading, put caricatures of people on the page who speak or rant like living creatures. They emit nasty vapors, but they breathe.

Why do I bring this up? Because I was reading the other day that James Wood, author of "The Broken Estate: Essays on Literature and Belief" and "the most influential critic of his generation, has attacked what he saw as the trivializing tendencies of modern fiction." (Yes, it's Friday — so let's get serious.)

He has written that the contemporary novel has become "overburdened with information; cultural reference — the accumulation of 'stuff' — [is] in danger of eclipsing character as its central preoccupation." He's not thrilled by what he calls "irrelevant intensity" in novels by Zadie Smith, Thomas Pynchon, DeLillo and Dave Eggers. Wood claims that "novelists should concentrate on people rather than 'the way the world works.' "

So what happens when the critic makes his debut as a novelist. He flubs it. As one reviewer puts it, Wood's first novel, "The Book Against God," perfectly embodies its author's stipulations." But — and it's a huge but: "Although the novel is set in the early 1990s, one would hardly know it. Cultural references are conspicuous by their absence. The characters are like relics from an earlier age, one in which couples address each other always as 'darling' and life is an endless round of cups of tea and choir rehearsals."

It makes you lose faith in vaunted critics. In any case, books are in the news. Here for example is a survey of the books they read — "they" being the important people, politicians all, in this instance Democratic presidential candidates, who naturally want to impress reporters with their reading lists.

Brent Kendall reports in The Washington Monthly: "Richard Gephardt and Bob Graham both opted for David McCullough [biographies], 'Truman' and 'John Adams,' respectively. (Graham is also a fan of Marquez's 'Love in the Time of Cholera.') John Kerry chose an image-softening volume of poetry (Pablo Neruda's 'Twenty Love Poems and a Song of Despair') along with a standard-issue 'safe' book, Stephen Ambrose's 'Undaunted Courage.' ... Joe Lieberman, too, picked what would seem to be the ultimate safe choice: The Bible."

Neither Al Sharpton nor Dennis Kucinich wanted to impress Kendall, though. They never answered his survey requests. Carol Moseley Braun more than made up for their reticence. She's "a closet bookworm who insists she has no fewer than four favorites": Lewis Carroll's "Alice's Adventures in Wonderland," Lewis Thomas' "The Lives of a Cell," Katharine Graham's "Personal History" and Umberto Eco's "Foucault's Pendulum."

But, Kendall writes, "the prize for the most interesting favorite book has to go to former Vermont Governor Howard Dean. His choice of Ken Kesey's novel 'Sometimes a Great Notion' is surely the bravest. After all, in this poll-tested, consultant-driven age, how many other candidates would confess — much less volunteer — to reading the work of an acid-dropping '60s counterculture hero?"

The prize for goofiest — though not among current candidates — goes to Michael Dukakis. Kendall reminds us that his choice of vacation reading during the 1988 campaign was a book entitled "Swedish Land-Use Planning" (not as I had thought, recalling Dukakis' tank-driving photo, the Clausewitz classic "On War.")

Postscript: Reuters reports that a woman lion tamer in her late 40s has run away from a circus in Germany with eight lions, two tigers and the circus director's 20-year-old son." Not only that, "she is believed to have developed a close relationship" with the son, who she's been training to become a lion tamer.

Why do I bring up this breathless tidbit? I have no idea, except that it's Friday and people say they need a break from war and a member of my staff of thousands said: "Come on, you can work this in somewhere." Now that I have — not too well, either — he whispers: "Seamless." I'd fire him. But that would not be collegial.

April 7, 2003 / 11:43 a.m. ET

Love it or joke about it: Are we still allowed to make fun of George W. Bush? Are the comedians entitled to their jokes? Are the cartoonists entitled to their satire? Given the nation's ramrod patriotism — what some would call rampant, unquestioning, love-it-or-leave nastiness — it's not an idle question.

The best joke I heard on television, probably the least offensive to ramrod patriots but also the smartest, was Jay Leno's on <u>"The Tonight Show"</u>: "President Bush said today he has a new plan to provide everyone with health care, a decent education and it also includes the rebuilding of roads and fixing of bridges ... And if it works in Iraq, he's going to try it here, too."

More straightforward, and a heckuva lot braver, was Andy Rooney's commentary last night on <u>"60 Minutes."</u> Maybe it's because he's in his 80s and the powers-that-be can't do anything to him that matters at this stage of his career. Or maybe it's just because he has the courage of his convictions. But Rooney's closing monologue was not only refreshing, it was funny.

He aired a little montage of U.S. military spokesmen repeatedly mentioning "coalition forces" without ever letting the words "U.S. forces" pass their lips. It stuck a sharp pin in the inflated notion that America has many allies in this war. I would say that Rooney's remarks, spoken from the heart, were inspiring, if that word weren't so overused that it had no meaning left in it.

You have to go beyond mainstream network television, of course, to find satire with the blunt force of a hammer. One place is the Internet. Shortly after 9/11, clip-art cartoonist David Rees started posting his comic strip, <u>"Get Your War On."</u> (Foul language warning: It wasn't pretty then and it's even less so now.)

What began as "a personal joke," <u>according to Mother Jones</u>, became so popular that Rees' Web site was inundated by millions of fans. Rolling Stone magazine put the 30-year-old Oberlin College graduate on its "Hot List" (along with "The Matrix" sequels and Jennifer Love Hewitt), then signed him to publish "Get Your War On" in its pages.

One of the more recent expressions of angry satire — if you can call it that — was Eddie Vedder's at a Pearl Jam concert in Denver, where <u>he impaled a mask of the president on a microphone.</u> (He'd used the "Bush mask" before — in Australia and Japan to perform the song "Bushleaguer," from the band's latest album, "Riot Act." The song's lyrics say, "He's not a leader, he's a Texas leaguer.")

Pearl Jam has taken issue with <u>how the incident was reported</u>. The band claims that only two dozen or so people got up and left the stadium show out of the 12,000 people who were there: "It just made a better headline to report otherwise."

Maybe, maybe not. But one music critic was struck by the "asymmetry" — in other words "the outrageous disparity" — between the reaction to Pearl Jam's anti-Bush statement (which he describes as a "gesture of grandiose contempt" that likens the president to head-on-a-pole imagery in "The Lord of the Flies") and Dixie Chick Natalie Maines' statement (for which she apologized).

"Pity the poor Dixie Chicks," he writes. "It says reams about the diverse sociology of country and alt-rock music fans that the Chicks have been vilified, burned in effigy, boycotted, denigrated, debated ad nauseum for one member making an anti-Bush statement from the stage in London, whereas Eddie Vedder impales a mask of Bush on a mike stand and it gets barely a ripple: 'Oh that's just Eddie, you know how these rock stars are.' "

Yes, we do. We know, for instance, that they don't have degrees in international relations any more than clip-art cartoonists or Hollywood actors and actresses do. Why do I bring this up? Because readers keep asking why they should listen to actors who protest the war. They want to know: Do these actors have expertise in foreign policy? It's a steady refrain: Do they have degrees in international relations?

Some of the smartest people I've known are actors. (You realize what comes next, of course: "Gee, you must've known some really dumb people.") I'd say actors, as a group, read more than a lot of people. I'd say they understand human motivation better than most people. They may have relatively little formal education, but in my book formal education is way overrated. Personally, I wouldn't trust someone with a degree in international relations to make foreign policy any more than I would trust my plumber.

Postscript: For all the patriots who feel left out by the war protests, here's a place to protest, too. It's an online petition posted by Lori Bardsley, a mother of three: Citizens Against Celebrity Pundits. So far, by the site's own count, it has 118,514 signatures.

PPS: Coincidentally, the Durham Herald-Sun just dropped Aaron McGruder's syndicated Boondocks comic strip because of a March 29 Special Boondocks Protest Strip. The editor of the North Carolina newspaper writes that the strip stepped over the line not because of its content — nah, not a chance of that — but because it was the wrong place for McGruder to air his political views. (He also doesn't object to McGruder's conflation of those views with a funny yet racially tinged

236

criticism of Hollywood and Cuba Gooding Jr.'s latest awful movie, "Boat Trip.")

April 8, 2003 / 10:33 a.m. ET

A short history of haiku, aka war relief: The land of the rising sun (more recently, the land of fluorescent lighting), once a warlike nation, has many civilized traditions. One of them, haiku, is the art of the 17-syllable verse form consisting of three metrical units of 5, 7, and 5 syllables.

This tradition goes back centuries to Basho Matsuo (1644-1694), who is pretty much regarded as the father of haiku. Modern poets of the form write less about nature's seasons than Basho did, and more about mankind's computers.

Now that computers and the Internet are as common as grass, many peace-loving Japanese people have replaced the confrontational Microsoft error message "Your computer has performed an illegal operation?" with haiku.

Here, in the interest of relief from news of war, are some actual Japanese error messages. As always in haiku, they are expressed through the poet's first, fresh impression:

You step in the stream,
But the water has moved on.
This page is not here.

Out of memory.
We wish to hold the whole sky,
But we never will.

A crash reduces
Your expensive computer
To a simple stone.

Serious error.
All shortcuts have disappeared.
Screen. Mind. Both are blank.

Program aborting:
Close all that you have worked on.
You ask far too much.

Windows NT crashed.
I am the Blue Screen of Death.
No one hears your screams.

The Web site you seek
Cannot be located, but
Countless more exist.

Your file was so big.
It might be very useful.
But now it is gone.

Chaos reigns within.
Reflect, repent, and reboot.
Order shall return.

Three things are certain:
Death, taxes and lost data.
Guess which has occurred.

We welcome haiku error messages from the peace-loving American people.

April 8, 2003 / 2:33 p.m. ET

Haiku war relief: Wrong! Wrong! Wrong! Those haikus I thought were "actual Japanese error messages" are no more Japanese than I am. It turns out that all of them were submitted to salon.com in February 1998 as part of the site's 21st Century Challenge No. 4. Apologies to Salon.

Still, the item wasn't a total loss. We said we would welcome haiku error messages from the peace-loving American people, and we got a bunch of them. Here are two of the better ones, one from Canada:

I search for my file,
Frustration mounting inside.
Where's that sledgehammer?
— Mary Anne Brager (Camrose, Alberta)

The file that you seek
Has left for greener pastures
Namely, the trash bin
— Ryan McGee (Cambridge, Mass.)

Anyone for sushi, another fine Japanese tradition?

April 9, 2003 / 12:23 p.m. ET

Let the memorial competition begin: It is 19 months since that blue-sky morning turned black with the death or disappearance of 3,021 innocent victims. They are etched in memory from Ground Zero, from the Pentagon, from the field in Shanksville, Pa.

Finally, what has been etched in memory of that catastrophic day will soon be etched in a 9/11 memorial by the winner of an international design competition to begin on April 28. And the public will have a say — at least at first.

The memorial, to be placed at Ground Zero, "should honor as one nation all those who were murdered" in all three places, Kevin M. Rampe, the top official overseeing the competition, said yesterday. "The program also calls for individual recognition of every victim … to make the footprints visible [where the twin towers stood] … and to make provisions for a final resting place for all of the unidentified remains."

To encourage design entries from "anyone, anywhere, who is 18 years of age or older, without regard to nationality or professional accreditation," there will be "a global outreach campaign," Rampe said. "Although the attacks occurred on U.S. soil, 91 nations suffered losses on Sept. 11. The outpouring of support following the attacks confirmed that freedom is not an American idea — but a universal ideal."

We each have our memories of 9/11. Mine are of TV images of two hijacked airliners knifing into the twin towers of the World Trade Center like flung daggers, of the human hailstorm of bodies pelting the ground as jumpers tried to escape the inferno nearly 100 stories up. Like millions of others, I recall the thundercloud of smoke and powdered rubble that mushroomed through the streets after the towers' collapse and the ash that coated everything for miles around. And like my Manhattan neighbors, I remember the smell of char that hung in the air for weeks.

How all or any of that will be incorporated into a memorial design within architect Daniel Libeskind's overall redevelopment plan for Ground Zero remains to be seen. But the public will be asked to offer its "hopes and aspirations" for the memorial in future forums. Once five finalists are selected, however, a jury of experts will make the final decision without further public input. "We felt it was critical to impanel a distinguished jury and entrust them with that responsibility to ensure the integrity of the design," Rampe said.

Advertisements for design entries will be placed in newspapers and magazines around the world, and a press release announcing the competition will be translated into 22 languages. A new Web site also will be launched on April 28 to enable participants to download the guidelines. A nominal entry fee of $25 will go toward building the memorial.

The competition itself will occur in two stages. In the late summer and early fall, the jury will review the submissions. The entries will remain anonymous as the jury narrows them down to a group of finalists. The finalists will receive funding to develop their concepts further, and the jury will select a winning design in the fall of 2003.

Postscript: It's no secret that Libeskind's overall development plan has irked the Ground Zero leaseholder, mammoth mall realtor Westfield America. The company's chairman minces no words: "We don't think [it] works." His objections have been presented to public officials. But he says they've stiffed him, without even the courtesy of a reply.

April 10, 2003 / 11:31 a.m. ET

This just in: The baseball Hall of Fame has canceled a 15th anniversary celebration of the film "Bull Durham" because of antiwar criticism by its co-stars, Tim Robbins and Susan Sarandon, the Associated Press reports. The festivities on April 26 and 27 at Cooperstown, N.Y. (coincidentally the same date as the brigade tribute) have been called off. Nice timing. Maybe Robbins and Sarandon will do their thing for the brigade instead.

April 10, 2003 / 11:33 a.m. ET

Will Iraq war liberate great literature? The joy in Baghdad has put a smile (some have said a smirk) on many Bush administration faces, Rummy's and Cheney's especially. You can't blame them for feeling like country singer Toby Keith. He said he feels "vindicated" by the three video awards he just won for his hawkish anthem "Courtesy of the Red, White & Blue (The Angry American)."

We'll soon see how much great art and literature comes out of the Iraqi war. Will it compare with the Spanish Civil War, which pound-for-pound may have produced more great books and paintings than any of the last century?

George Orwell, Pablo Picasso, Ernest Hemingway, W.H. Auden, Dorothy Parker, Arthur Koestler, Martha Gellhorn, Langston Hughes, André Malraux, Stephen Spender, Ilya Ehrenburg and Jessica Mitford were just some of its more famous participants. And many of them created masterworks of literature, art and journalism either inspired by the heroism of that war or in reaction to its horrors — often both.

To name a handful: Orwell's "Homage to Catalonia" (1938), Hemingway's "For Whom the Bell Tolls" (1940), Picasso's "Guernica" (1937), Malraux's "Man's Hope" (1937), Koestler's "Dialogue With Death" (1942).

The most celebrated U.S. involvement in that war came from the 2,800 or so volunteers of the American Lincoln Brigade, which fought for the Spanish Republic against the fascist forces of Gen. Francisco Franco's rebellion in 1936. To this day, although they fought on the losing side in that war (and doubtless because they did), interest in veterans of the Lincoln Brigade remains intense.

Richard Dreyfuss, for example, will headline a special reunion program honoring them later this month at the Tribeca Performing Arts Center in New York. The show (April 27) is to feature members of the San Francisco Mime Troupe performing, "Which Side Are You On: Sounds of Protest and Resistance." (For tickets: 212-674-5398 or exemplaryone@aol.com.)

Dorothy Parker once wrote of the Lincoln Brigade: "For what they stood for, what they have given to others to take hold and carry along — that does not vanish from the earth. This is not a matter of wishing or feeling, it is knowing. It is knowing that nothing devised by fat, rich, frightened men can ever stamp out truth and courage and determination for a decent life."

The sentiment is eerily familiar today, given Saddam's toppled regime in Baghdad. But were she alive today, Parker, with her ardent leftwing views, would not be on the side of the Bush administration. "These are the days of miracles and wonder," as the Paul Simon song has it. More prosaic than that, we live in paradoxical times.

April 10, 2003 / 4:59 p.m. ET

High-powered jury: Many had hoped Maya Lin would be entering the 9/11 memorial design competition. But she won't. That's because 43-year-old artist/architect, who became world-famous for creating the Vietnam Veterans Memorial while still a Yale undergrad, has agreed to sit on the competition jury.

Others named Thursday for the 13-member jury include: Vartan Gregorian, president of the Carnegie Corporation, the renowned artist Martin Puryear and, as an honorary juror, David Rockefeller. Paula Grant Berry, whose husband died at Ground Zero on 9/11, will serve on the jury as well. The rest are all high-powered scholars, architects, business folks and political appointees.

April 11, 2003 / 4:43 p.m. ET

My kind of museum: Unless you grew up in Brooklyn, chances are you never went to the Brooklyn Museum of Art — not until it threw a big show called "Sensation" a few years ago for all those nasty-minded, British-based artists like Damien Hirst and Chris Ofili. That brought the museum worldwide notoriety, largely because New York's then-Mayor Rudy Giuliani was so upset by the art that he tried to close the show and cut off the museum's funding.

Happily, Giuliani lost that one. I doubt that even he would object to the show opening tomorrow at the museum, "Egypt Reborn," which will put on display many rarely or never-before-seen antiquities from its collection. We all know the ancient Egyptians were into the art of preserving dead bodies. But I don't think they ever went as far as Hirst, whose art consisted of sawed-up animals (mainly sharks, lambs and cows) preserved in sealed, formaldehyde-filled glass cases.

I did grow up in Brooklyn, and I do have childhood memories of the museum — forbidding ones. (Maybe I'm recalling some of those Egyptian antiquities.) I much preferred spending the day at long-gone Ebbets Field, not far away on Bedford Avenue, or at the main branch of the Brooklyn Public Library, which is still there, across Eastern Parkway at Grand Army Plaza. I didn't think of the museum as haunted so much as desolate and vast.

But that's all changed. The last time I was there it had the feel of a vibrant institution. These days it is under renovation and throbbing with life. They even throw free parties on the first Saturday of each month. The last one drew 10,000 people. And why not? The music was free. The movies were free. The dancing was free. That's my kind of museum.

April 11, 2003 / 4:43 p.m. ET

All worked up: I really am trying to stay away from the war in Iraq and patriotism and Bush and the stuff that gets everybody all worked up. Just look at my last item: It's about a museum. You can't get further away than that. And the item before the item before that was about the Spanish Civil War, which happened so long ago that Saddam Hussein was an infant in swaddling clothes at the time.

But the war and patriotism and Bush and the stuff that gets everybody all worked up just can't be ignored. Yesterday, for instance, I mentioned (only in passing, mind you) that the baseball Hall of Fame had canceled a screening of "Bull Durham" because of antiwar criticism by its co-stars, Tim Robbins and Susan Sarandon.

Wouldn't you know it? Suddenly my staff of thousands and I were overwhelmed by a flood of e-mails. Here's just a taste:

Matthew Celis
Charlotte, N.C.
"The baseball Hall of Fame is a joke if it demands everyone must swallow and follow the party line and never criticize the government. Freedom to express one's opinion is as American as...baseball."

A. McNeeley
Dallas, Texas
"Congratulations to the baseball Hall of Fame for having the courage to stand up to the celebrity of Robbins and Sarandon. In times like these, the voices of celebrities are often heard so much louder than the average American's. However, it has been uplifting to see so many Americans demonstrate their support for our troops and our president."

Shawn Welling
Winnipeg, Canada
"I don't think it is right to cancel anything because of one's beliefs. It is anti-American to do so. I think Susan Sarandon and Tim Robbins should be celebrated and commended for their fierce beliefs. It takes courage to voice them."

Barbara Mills
Eustis, Fla.
"I hope that all the war protestor's so-called 'careers' go straight down the toilet. They all deserve to become 'has-beens' and boycotted and ignored by the patriotic American citizens of the U.S.A. I am compiling a list of war protestors and also French and German products. I will boycott these people and products forever and will encourage anyone who will give me the time of day to do the same."

Kathleen Smart
"I think it's a very sad commentary for our nation that anyone who feels the war was immoral ... is either branded unpatriotic or unsupportive of our troops, both of which are totally incorrect. It is indeed a very troubling concept that a country which prides itself on freedom of speech for everyone brands those who disagree as un-American and [that], in fact, some are punished for their ideas. Now, folks, that is what is truly wrong. Shame on

243

everyone who feels we must all agree or be branded."

Anonymous
"Good for the baseball Hall of Fame. Everyone is entitled to their opinions, but that doesn't mean they are entitled to our support."

Rachel Elena Post
Wellesley College
"To announce that there must be no criticism of the president, or that we are to stand by the president, right or wrong, is not only unpatriotic and servile, but is morally treasonable to the American public." — Theodore Roosevelt.

"It's amazing that the words of one of our greatest presidents can be ignored. If TR were alive today, it's good to know that he'd be as 'un-American' and 'unpatriotic' as myself just for questioning what Bush is doing."

And let's not forget, TR was a Republican. (OK, a Republican of liberal ilk.)

April 12, 2003 / 10:55 a.m. ET
Where truth and humility reign: Have you ever read a Weblog that didn't say, "I told you so?" Not wanting to be left out of that humble tradition, my staff of thousands and I modestly submit <u>"Cooperstown Muffs One,"</u> an editorial in this morning's New York Times (free registration required). We realize that 'Juice' readers like <u>Matthew Celis</u> are actually the ones with the right to say, "I told you so." But we don't mind taking the credit.

April 14, 2003 / 10:53 a.m. ET
Where Hollywood meets Cooperstown: Is there a movie genre more celebrated than the baseball picture? Don't answer that. But the fact is that Hollywood has romanced America's national pasttime more than any other sport.

Now that the Baseball Hall of Fame at Cooperstown has <u>called off a "Bull Durham" celebration</u> because of the antiwar views of two of its stars, Susan Sarandon and Tim Robbins, may we suggest a gazillion baseball pictures that will doubtless satisfy the hall's rah-rah sense of patriotism?

Today show

FREE VIDEO START ▶

Tim Robbins talks about the Baseball Hall of Fame "Bull Durham" cancellation.

But first there are the questionable films that treat darker themes, which the hall president, Dale Petroskey, might not want to celebrate.

Here are three:

"Eight Men Out" (1988), about the World Series betting scandal involving the 1919 Black Sox and "Shoeless" Joe Jackson;

"The Natural" (1984), about a farm boy with dreams of baseball stardom, played by Robert Redford, and the demonic intrusion of a spiteful sports writer;

"Bang the Drum Slowly" (1973), a tear-jerker starring Robert DeNiro as a terminally ill catcher.

And now for the obvious films that aren't likely to offend Petroskey's red-white-and-blue sensibilities or his love-it-or-leave-it politics:

"Pride of the Yankees" (1942), with Gary Cooper as Lou Gehrig;

"The Babe Ruth Story" (1948), with William Bendix as Babe Ruth;

"Take Me Out to the Ballgame" (1949), a Busby Berkeley musical with Gene Kelly, Frank Sinatra, and Jules Munshin in the infield;

"The Jackie Robinson Story" (1950), starring himself;

"Fear Strikes Out" (1957), with Anthony Perkins as Jimmy Piersall battling mental illness on his way to major league stardom;

"Damn Yankees" (1958), the great Broadway musical about a Washington Senators fan who sells his soul to the devil for a winning team;

"The Bingo Long Traveling All-Stars & Motor Kings" (1976), an up-from-under story with a knockout cast of Billy Dee Williams, James Earl Jones and Richard Pryor;

"The Bad News Bears", (1976), a comedy starring Walter Matthau and Tatum O'Neal, about a team of misfits waiting for a miracle;

"Field of Dreams" (1989), with Kevin Costner as the ultimate baseball fantasist.

If you list them, they will come. Got more?

Postscript: As you might imagine, we've received lots of e-mail about Robbins and Sarandon's right to their political views and the right of the Hall of Fame to disinvite them. These two seemed to best express wholly opposite opinions on the subject:

Deanna Valkingburg
Wiesbaden, Germany
"I am so happy that Susan Sarandon and Tim Robbins are finally getting what they deserve! They sound like idiots when they talk about American policy, and I wasn't aware that they work at the State Department or the Pentagon. I am a proud military spouse and I hope every American boycotts these so called activists! We need to give the troops all the support they deserve! I hope they understand that many men fought and died so that they could be given the chance to be 'famous!'"

Andrew Turso
Auburndale, Mass.
"As a veteran of Desert Storm, a baseball fan, an ardent supporter of all of our troops at home and abroad, and someone who thinks this war was necessary, I was appalled by the actions of the Baseball Hall of Fame. While I don't agree with Mr. Robbins and Ms. Sarandon's views on this subject, I whole-heartedly support their constitutionally guaranteed right to express their opinions without fear of reprisal.

"Now, however, it seems that Dale Petroskey has decided that I, as a baseball fan, don't get to celebrate a fantastic baseball movie. Not only has he squelched Mr. Robbins and Ms. Sarandon's right to free speech, he's also made it impossible for me to travel to the Baseball Hall of Fame and show my enthusiasm for a movie that so wonderfully captures the spirit of the game I love. Shame on him, and shame on the others in charge of the Hall for letting this happen."

Turso also suggested that we list this baseball flick, "Major League,", which he describes as "a hysterical look at a team of loveable losers, akin to 'The Bad News Bears,' but only as adults."

More suggested baseball flicks:

Marie
Modesto, Calif.
"'Rhubarb' — old-school flick about a cat who inherits a team, then is their good luck charm.

"'It Happens Every Spring' — can't remember all the details, but about a guy who leaves his loved ones and assumes a different identity to play ball.

"'A League of Their Own' — cute slice of girl-power nostalgia.

"'Major League' — The first one only (for good reason). Although, would the ties to Martin Sheen (through his son) be too scandalous for Cooperstown?"

Shane Hockin
Tallahassee, Fla.

"Wow. Some of those baseball movies were pretty darned good. Then again, some of them ... An old friend of mine would have thrown a fit that you did not include "Major League." It is definitely not art, but I guess it is a baseball movie nonetheless.

"I just wish that there would be a hockey movie that captured the spirit of hockey [the way] 'Field of Dreams' and 'The Natural' capture the spirit of baseball. I will never forgot the feel of the cold, icy wind on my 10-year-old face as I glided over the hardened lake trying to beat the ghost of Terry Sawchuk high, glove side. 'Slap Shot' and 'The Mighty Ducks' just don't do it for me."

J. D.
St. Louis, Mo.

"'The Pride of St. Louis' — the Dizzy Dean story — as 'aw, shucks' as they come."

April 15, 2003 / 2:33 p.m. ET

Spoils of freedom: The looting of Iraq's antiquities has been going on for years, particularly since the end of the first Gulf War, but it didn't make banner headlines until the Iraqi National Museum was sacked last week.

The astonishing greed and desperation of the crowds running wild in Baghdad's streets were not unexpected. But the sheer number of ancient treasures stolen or destroyed — 170,000 artifacts "worth billions of dollars," according to various news reports — is as mind-boggling as U.S. Secretary of Defense Donald Rumsfeld's response: "It's untidy. And freedom's untidy. And free people are free to make mistakes and commit crimes and do bad things."

Some commentators have agreed with him. In yesterday's Slate, for instance, Steven Landsberg made the case for looting. He argues that, compared to the billions in oil revenue routinely expropriated by Saddam and his gang, what happened amounted to petty theft.

But he doesn't address the sacking of the National Museum. And needless to say, the heavy-duty plundering of more than two dozen museum galleries and vaults protected by huge steel doors was not Winona Ryder-style shoplifting.

It's hard to get a sense of these ancient treasures from verbal descriptions — or even from some of the fine news photos of the pillaged items, although the monumental quality is unmistakable in these panels — so have a look at the Ancient Near Eastern Art collection of the Metropolitan Museum of Art in New York. Here's a 10-foot-tall, human-headed winged bull and winged lion from the neo-Assyrian period. (Met director Philippe de Montebello cites it as one of his 25 favorite pieces out of 2 million in the museum's total holdings.)

The British Museum in London, which will be sending experts to Iraq to help restore that nation's treasures, also has one of the world's finest Near East antiquities collections. It includes many reliefs that decorated passages leading from Sennacherib's Palace at Nineveh. (You can explore both collections from the links above.) How its own collections were amassed is a story for another day.

The two most imposing Babylonian and Assyrian antiquities I ever saw were in Berlin, at the Pergamon Museum — the reconstructed Ishtar Gate of Babylon and the Processional Way of Babylon (both from the 6th century B.C.).

The Ishtar Gate must be seen in person to be appreciated. Its stunning size — the 45-foot walls are thought to be only half of their original height — is one thing. Its artistry — gorgeous animal reliefs, for instance, on glazed bricks of cobalt blue and ochre — is quite another. Here is a detail. And here is the gate in its original location. (None of these photos reproduce the brilliant cobalt-blue or ochre colors.) As for the Processional Way, the monumental reconstruction at the Pergamon is about 90 feet long. The original was probably 750 feet long.

Colossal artifacts like these would have been hard if not impossible to haul away, whole or in pieces. Among items reported missing were "a solid gold harp from the Sumerian era ... a sculptured head of a woman from Uruk, one of the great Sumerian cities ... and a collection of gold necklaces, bracelets and earrings, also from the Sumerian dynasties and also at least 4,000 years old."

But if the Iraqi National Museum had the world's finest collection of ancient Near Eastern treasures (as the experts have said) and if the museum is now totally sacked (as reported), the loss is unimaginable. One aspect of the story that has not been reported and could yet unfold is how many of these treasures may have been stolen from the secretly kept museum vaults by Saddam and his gang long before the fall of Baghdad.

April 16, 2003 / 5:58 p.m. ET
   Rumor madness: It's bad enough when Iraqis call U.S. troops "the

modern Mongols," believing "the rumors on the lips of almost all Baghdadis" that the looting of both the National Library and the National Museum was inspired by the Americans.

It's worse when Americans believe that 1) "most of the antiquities there are merely reproductions," that 2) "British experts have already been to the museum and documented" this because 3) "Saddam looted them himself," as John Smith, of Heathsville, Va., claims in an e-mail message, and that 4) liberal journalists like me have refused to print this "fact" because of their bias.

The Iraqi rumor-mongers must be in a serious state of denial. The American rumor-mongers must be nuts.

(It was only yesterday that I wrote: "One aspect of the story that has not been reported and could yet unfold is how many of these treasures may have been stolen from the secretly kept museum vaults by Saddam and his gang long before the fall of Baghdad." But that's different from believing the museum was filled with reproductions.)

Unfortunately, the ludicrous notion that U.S. troops were in cahoots with the Iraqi looters gains a certain purchase when the Glasgow, Scotland, newspaper the Sunday Herald accurately reports that wealthy American art dealers have been accused of planning to loot Iraqi antiquities, or when The New York Times reports that American antiquities experts and scholars made "repeated requests to the Pentagon" as early as January that the museum "be protected when American troops entered Baghdad," and that they believed "the military had understood the need to protect the buildings against looting as well as bombing."

Additionally, Americans who have no idea what's going on in Baghdad beyond news reports have read that American forces secured oil wells, dams and other significant sites and even kept looters at bay at the oil ministry but did not do the same to protect irreplaceable antiquities of earliest human civilization at Iraq's National Museum and National Library.

And then you come up again a reliable eyewitness report like this: "When I caught sight of the Koranic library burning, flames 100 feet high were bursting from the windows [and] I raced to the offices of the occupying power, the U.S. Marines' Civil Affairs Bureau," Robert Fisk wrote yesterday in the British newspaper The Independent. "An officer shouted to a colleague that 'this guy says some biblical [sic] library is on fire.' I gave the map location, the precise name in Arabic and English. I said the smoke could be seen from three miles away and it would take only five minutes to drive there. Half an hour later, there wasn't an American at the scene and the flames were shooting 200 feet into the air."

Which pretty much lets you know how the Baghdad rumors were fanned. But how did Smith's claim get started? Anybody know?

The most notorious instance of cultural plunder, of course, is the 2,500-year-old Elgin Marbles — a 480-foot-long section of the frieze of the ancient Greek Parthenon — which Lord Elgin, the British ambassador to the Ottoman Empire, bought in 1803 from the Turks who were occupying Athens at the time. The frieze was dismantled, shipped to London and sold to the British Museum, where it became the most treasured antiquity in its collection as well as a source of longtime contention between Great Britain and Greece.

Greece is now presenting its case for the return of the Elgin Marbles. With Iraq's looted treasures about to join the Elgin Marbles in the annals of antiquities theft, the world's art police are bound to be well employed.

April 17, 2003 / 11:59 p.m. ET
Random thoughts at midnight: Such bad PR over the looting of antiquities in Iraq's National Museum: See "U.S. under fire." Maybe the best way to avoid it next time is to invade a country with weapons of mass destruction but without an ancient heritage. Coolest reason I've heard to restore the museum's collection: It will bring the tourists back to Baghdad. Not even a chuckle? Then try this: Jonathan V. Last's summary of why the CENTCOM briefings were so valuable. He actually means it.

April 18, 2003 / 3:43 p.m. ET
Electro-shmektro music: You can't say they didn't warn us. They're hip. They're cool. They're hot. They're fake. They're Fischerspooner. And they're not the only "name" act on the electroclash scene.

But they are the only one to release a CD called "# 1" that sold just 25,000 copies in England even after getting major promotion and TV appearances and pointing out, falsely, that their record deal came to more than $3 million.

It's not surprising that they were pelted with food at London Royal Festival Hall. Musical virtuosity is not their thing. They don't really play instruments, and they lip-synch everything.

Frontman Casey Spooner told Wired, "Once you put that aside and don't worry about these issues of musical integrity — this illusion that people are manufacturing the music up there [on stage] — you have all this time and energy and space and freedom to do lots of other things. ...You don't have to worry about playing the guitar."

It's the other things that count for Spooner and his partner Warren

Fischer, like the visual spectacle. Which makes sense — sort of — for two guys who met at the Chicago Art Institute and decided their "artform" was making dance music and putting people on.

I guess it's possible to appreciate all the wigs and the makeup and the let's pretend dress-up and, oh yeah, the music, more by watching their video for the single "Emerge" than by listening to the drone of their clippety-clop, electro-shmektro music. If you can believe it — I can't — some people really love the synthetic Fischerspooner style.

Adrien Begrand, a music critic at PopMatters, is one of them. His opinion of "# 1" goes like this: "It's shallow, pretentious, flamboyant, catchy, and just plain freaky at times, but unlike all the empty pop music you hear on mainstream radio today, this is one pop album that gets it right for once, and what a pure blast it is."

I get the "shallow, pretentious and flamboyant." What I don't get is the "pure blast." Anyone?

Postscript: Mike White, of Katy, Texas, has just summed up my feelings about Fischerspooner better than I did. White writes: "Various pop artists have nothing in common with real musicians. Or artists in general. It's all just lemming music for the masses." I love his description: "lemming music."

Jay Thompson
Chapel Hill, N.C.
"Unfortunately, Mike White is dead on ... most people ARE lemmings, whether it comes to music, clothes, TV shows, or politics. The difference between them and 'non-lemmings' is that they are so totally driven by the need for external validation that what they do, say, wear, or listen to is irrelevant in any objective sense; they'd eat live palmetto bugs (with a dash of cilantro) if they thought that the people at the next table over would think they were cool.

"On the other hand, worrying about that reality and how the 'lemmings' could be enlightened is roughly as futile as trying to build a replica of the great pyramid using grains of sand and a hot-glue gun. If the lemmings make it past the age of say, 21 with no sign of understanding why books by Locke and Borges are still on the shelves, well, they're probably going to spend the rest of their lives breathlessly awaiting the incredibly important developments coming out the the latest Parisian fashion show."

And for the defense:

Matt Odom

Atlanta, Ga.

"I can't identify at all with your electro-shmektro review of Fischerspooner. I attended their concert this past Tuesday, and was overwhelmed with the power (and pomp) of the performance. It was refreshing to see an actual 'show!' I haven't seen an Atlanta crowd whipped into that kind of dance frenzy in some time. We already have an over-abundance of guitar-driven acts that would rather stand and amaze us with the power of a brooding countenance, DJ's who remix the same tired beats, and pop groups attached to the puppet strings of an unseen "let's-see-if-they'll-buy-this-crap" Pop Gestapo. We need more bands/artists who are willing to give more energy and creative thought to a stage show, and kudos to Fischerspooner for stepping out of the mainstream and doing something that makes me both laugh and dance. No complaint here!"

April 21, 2003 / 1:08 p.m. ET

Paul McCartney's deep pockets: I see that a bunch of pop stars have united to raise money for Iraqi children. They've contributed tracks to "Hope," a special CD released today. The profits will go to a charity called War Child. Paul McCartney, one of the contributors (along with David Bowie and 16 others), has acknowledged that his is a "small contribution."

What I'd like to know is why doesn't Sir Paul just dig into his very deep pockets and make a big fat contribution? I know "The Concert for New York," which he organized at Madison Square Garden after Sept. 11, raised $30 million for the Robin Hood Foundation. But that wasn't money he gave. It was money the public gave.

Sir Paul can afford to give more than a pittance out of his own pocket, can't he? It would be nice to think he's given privately — say, $10 million at least — but that he's too modest to let anyone know. Or am I giving him too much credit?

April 22, 2003 / 8:47 a.m. ET

Unshaved armpits and stinky cheese: He kind of likes it there in France — piano man Joe Kerr, that is. He's booked for "a night of enticing songs from and about France" with vocalist Midge Woolsey and their band at New York's BAM Cafe, one of the cooler venues of the Brooklyn Academy of Music (Saturday, April 26, 9 p.m., no cover, no minimum).

Kerr points out: "We took this gig way before the war in Iraq. So we're not making any kind of political statement." While BAM is not a den of flag-waving, love-it-or-leave-it patriots, it still takes a bit of courage to sing the praises of the French in the U.S. of A. these days.

If anyone can pull that off, though, it's Kerr — bluesy jazz pianist, lyricist, composer, teacher, bon vivant extraordinaire and, full disclosure, a friend of mine. He's written songs for BBC radio, National Lampoon and Sesame Street. He's also that unique native Texan, born and bred in San Antonio, who splits his time between New York, where he lives, and Fontainebleau, near Paris, where he administers the legendary classical-music program at the American Conservatory. (But that's another story.)

Kerr's cabaret songs are mainly comical. (Think Dave Frishberg or Bob Dorough.) Here's one cult classic he'll be doing at BAM: **[AUDIO]** "I Kind of Like It Here in France."

"The song sounds like a jab at the French," Kerr says, "but it's really a jab at the narrator, who's sort of stupid. At least that's how I explain it to my French friends. Most of them laugh. Some don't."

You can understand why from the lyrics:

I kind of it like here in France
Where everything is real advanced
And all the dogs are well behaved
And all the armpits are unshaved
And all the cheese is really stinky
And all the sex is really kinky
I kind of like it here in France

Coming from Texas, Kerr also knows a lot about cows. He doesn't hesitate to write about them, either. Another of his cult classics, **[AUDIO]** "Bessie," is about an American farmer with a deep affection for his favorite cow.

Kerr says he won't be doing that one at BAM, though. He keeps it for gigs with his down-home American swing band, The Western Caravan, another musical experience not to be missed. The Caravan usually plays downtown at Manhattan's Rodeo Bar & Grill, but this week — Thursday, 9 p.m. — it's at a regular uptown haunt, the Caffe Taci.

Oh, did I mention my favorite Austin, Texas, swing band, The Hot Club of Cowtown? That's Kerr playing piano on their latest CD, Ghost Train, also not to be missed. The guy gets around.

Postscript: These lyrics came via e-mail, inspired by Kerr's paen to France. How could we resist?

Jim Friedland
NYC
By Brooke (age 12) and her mom (age withheld)

We kind of like it in New York
Special interests, lots of pork
Wine flows easy, pull the cork
With hotdogs you don't need no fork
And all the cats are perched on sills
And all the men pay all the bills (editor's note: they do?)
The Yankees give you many thrills
The Mets are simply baseball's shills

We kind of like it in New York

April 23, 2003 / 3:46 p.m. ET

New York! New York! Now that Joe Kerr has sung <u>the praises of the French and Paris</u>, people naturally want to sing the praises of New York — especially in post-9/11 times like these. <u>And so they have.</u>

There is in fact a whole book of praise, <u>"Poems of New York,"</u> published not long after 9/11. Its editor, Elizabeth Schmidt, notes that "poets who have written about New York are masters at preserving, and allowing us to cherish, moments of life in this theater of chance and change."

Here, for example, is a sonnet by <u>Edna St. Vincent Millay</u> that captures something very private (yet terribly public) in the life of a subway rider that could happen to anybody. Though <u>published nearly a century ago</u>, in 1917, it feels like it could have been written just yesterday.

If I should learn, in some quite casual way,
That you were gone, not to return again—
Read from the back-page of a paper, say,
Held by a neighbor in a subway train,
How at the corner of this avenue
And such a street (so are the papers filled)
A hurrying man—who happened to be you—
At noon to-day had happened to be killed,
I should not cry aloud—I could not cry
Aloud, or wring my hands in such a place—
I should but watch the station lights rush by
With a more careful interest on my face,

254

Or raise my eyes and read with greater care
Where to store furs and how to treat the hair.

People say that after 9/11 New York has become a friendlier, more caring place. That may be so. But what Millay is speaking of seems so indelible a part of modern life — in this or any city — that even 9/11 will not change it.

April 24, 2003 / 10:31 a.m. ET

Dredging up The Ungloved One: Before "Survivor," before "Fear Factor," before "The Bachelorette" and "Joe Millionaire," before "Mr. Personality," there was the avatar of all TV reality shows — "the trial of the [last] century," starring Mr. Personality himself, O.J. Simpson.

Dredged up from the dim recesses of celebrity memory by The Hollywood Reporter, the Ungloved One was said yesterday to be "preparing for his debut as the star of his own 'Osbournes'-esque reality show." It turned out, thank God, that the Reporter was blowing smoke. Except that everybody was sucking it up.

The story made the rounds until the New York Post, that bastion of truth, reported the real story: "Simpson hasn't been approached by the companies that are planning to create the show." His lawyer told the Post: "They can't have a reality TV show and call it the OJ Simpson TV show without our involvement."

Which sounds exactly like an invitation to be involved, doesn't it? So maybe, at the end of the day (my un-favorite phrase), the story will turn out to be true, that Simpson could indeed "become the star of a new reality television show that would be centered on snippets of his appearances at hip-hop concerts."

Conflating The Ungloved One with hip-hop (as a non-performer no less?) sounds like the ultimate in the fakeness of reality TV. But that wouldn't surprise us, either, and certainly not Eric Olsen, who says it's the American way to turn the news — and reality itself — into money-making fakery.

Olsen is exercised about the Iraq action figures now on the market, like "Saddam Insane," "President G.W.," "Butcher of Baghdad," "British Ally," "Osama is Drag" and the talking "Iraqi Dis-information Minister Action Figure Doll," the former Iraq Information Minister al-Sahaf, whose news conferences were almost worthy of "The Daily Show" with Jon Stewart on Comedy Central.

In the meantime, here's an e-mail from a laser-sharp reader (faithful, too) who's exercised by yours truly and my staff of thousands. She seems to think I've become a kinder, gentler person — and that's unsettling.

Melisa C. M.
Miami, Fla.

"You know, I'm surprised at you. I'm surprised that you haven't yet said anything about the fact that Jennifer Lopez's new video 'I'm Glad' is 'Flash Dance' in the space of 4-odd minutes with the occasional (but mandatory nonetheless) up-look-butt-shot. I would have, by now, expected you to lambaste her lack of originality with this video and what a pathetic figure she makes. Basically, I'm surprised that you and 'your staff of thousands' (LMAO, yea right!) haven't yet found an excuse to bring it up. Oh, and another thing, Ms. Lewinsky in Mr. Personality, hello. This is a topic that is screaming for one of your dissections. Make it good and make it interesting."

Well!

Postscript: People have gone so nuts about Dixie Chick Natalie Maines' anti-Bush remark that we thought we'd remind you: You can sign an online petition supporting her right to dissent. The last time we mentioned it, 2,642 people had signed the petition. That number is up to 7,666 at the moment.

April 25, 2003 / 11:51 a.m. ET

Just what the doctor ordered: O.J. Simpson said he'd consider being a news commentator at Robert Blake's murder rial: "I'd love to do it. I think I have a lot of insight." That's got to be the funniest quote of the day, unless Donald Rumsfeld has scheduled a press conference.

At least Simpson has spared us the pain of seeing him star in a new TV reality series. Or has he? He's says he won't be doing it, but that hasn't seemed to deter the production company from making it without him. "We've got everything done, the reality show is coming," the company's founder says, presumably referring to taped snippets of Simpson.

If only Allen Funt were still around. As Juice reader Mike White reminds me, "Candid Camera" was the real avatar of reality TV, not the Simpson trial — except that Funt caught people unaware and made us laugh at their harmless foibles. Today's reality shows are just the opposite. Everybody is aware of being on camera, and none of the shows are funny.

In the meantime, NBC has pulled the plug on "Just Shoot Me." Frankly, that's not a bad thing. I thought the show was dumb. But it's apparently going to be replaced by various reality-format specials, which are likely to be dumber. Steve Levitan, executive producer of "Just Shoot Me," wants to know, "Where has all the dignity and integrity gone in this business?" He's kidding, right?

April 28, 2003 / 12:58 p.m. ET
Memorializing 9/11 at Ground Zero: Anyone who enters the World Trade Center Site Memorial Competition, which begins today, can rest easy: Maya Lin, whose design for the Vietnam Veterans Memorial in Washington made her famous the world over, won't be competing.

(Officials have posted the rules and registration forms for the competition on their Web site.)

Lin was the star attraction for the press this morning at a news conference across the street from Ground Zero to announce the launch of the competition. Asked if she had any advice for entrants, she reminded them: "You enter a competition not necessarily to win but to express what you believe."

The 43-year-old artist-architect, who's on the jury that will pick the winning design, told me a few days ago it was easy for her to stay out of the contest "because a long time ago I said I wasn't going to do any more memorials. Being on the jury is a way for me to help out."

As we reported earlier, the competition is open to "anyone anywhere in the world" who is 18 years old or older. Entrants have four weeks from today to register (the closing date for registration is May 29) and eight weeks to submit their designs (the closing date for submissions is June 30).

Entrants may register and submit entries online or, for those without Web access, by Fax: 1-800-717-5699. There is a $25 entrant fee. All entries will receive a registration number, so the jury will not know the identity of the entrants. The complete guidelines are available on the Web site in English. (They're also supposed to be posted in abbreviated form in Spanish and Chinese. So far they're not.)

On May 28 the public will be able to express its views about the memorial at an open forum. Five or so finalists will be chosen by the jury and a winner selected in the fall.

April 29, 2003 / 11:56 a.m. ET
Countering a bad impression: The U.S. Central Command hasn't yet issued a deck of cards with most-wanted antiquities to match their cards of most-wanted Iraqis, but a pair of online jokers have. They're not the only ones, though.

Serious art historians and archeologists are putting photos of looted treasures online with a searchable database to help the recovery effort. Lost Treasures from Iraq shows beautiful photos of looted sculptures and statuary, figurines, stone vessels, pottery, jewelry and coins.

Here, for example, are a 5,000-year-old bowl with relief decoration, from Ur, (dating from 3,000 B.C.) and a cast copper statue head from Nineveh, of either King Sargon I or his grandson, Naram-Sin (dating from 2,250 B.C.).

Wired magazine has more details about the Lost Iraqi Heritage project. The Archeological Institute of America also offers a lot of information about its Task Force on the Cultural Heritage of Iraq.

The Department of Defense in Washington and U.S. troops on the ground in Iraq have received so much bad press for turning a blind eye to the looting of Iraqi antiquities that I've been waiting for them to launch a counteroffensive. And yesterday they did.

U.S. Central Command and Gen. Tommy Franks reported that Iraqis are turning in looted antiquities. More than 100 of them! Which leaves roughly 169,900 items still missing, as the antiquities saga continues.

I've been pondering what took CentCom and Franks so long. Could it have been the Frank Rich article lambasting military negligence in his column in the Sunday Arts & Leisure section of The New York Times? (Free registration required.)

Rich was somewhat late, but his piece was powerful nonetheless. Given the platform and timing — his column appeared the day before Gen. Franks made his pitch — I'd say it was one of the sharper points of the spur.

April 30, 2003 / 12:38 p.m. ET

The art of the ridiculous: Deadpan humor has been perfected by The Onion. All it really has to do is take news stories to their logical conclusion — that is, to the ridiculous. The Onion doesn't have to reach far for its material and, in a pinch, would not even have to embellish it.

Here, for example, are five of the funniest, not funniest, tastiest, most peculiar and desperate news stories — all true, or at least actual — just from the past day, none from The Onion.

The funniest — Ex-Iraq Info Minister Gets TV Job Offer: "We want to benefit from the experience of Mr. Sahaf and his analysis of the current situation and the future of Iraq," says Ali al-Hadethi, supervisor of the Dubai-based al-Arabiya satellite channel.

The not funniest — Jack Osbourne Goes to College ... Make That Rehab: The 17-year-old teenager has checked himself into a detox facility with the full support of his parents. "He's doing very well and we're all very proud of him," his sister Kelly Osbourne said.

The tastiest — <u>Strangled Duck Served Here</u>: "Select guests have gathered at a top Paris restaurant to sample the one millionth duck to be snatched from grassy marshland, carefully strangled and ritually cooked with its own blood."

The most peculiar — <u>Graceful Shoplifting Doesn't Work</u>: Attorney Donald Etra said his client was "gratified that she is not being charged with a felony."

The most desperate — <u>Get Me Off This Cruise Ship or I'll Kill You All</u>: "The defendant said that she never wanted to go on this cruise with her family and that she wrote these notes hoping that it would shorten her time on the cruise, thereby allowing her to rejoin her boyfriend in Orange County, California," Edward Kubo Jr., U.S. Attorney for the District of Hawaii, said.

Share your perspective on entertainment and the arts with <u>Jan Herman</u>. MSNBC is not responsible for the content of Internet links.

Jan Herman

Latest entertainment and arts news from the Web

Entries from May 1 to May 30, 2003
(Some links may be nonfunctional.)
Back to 'The Juice'

LATEST UPDATES

May 1, 2003 / 8:31 a.m. ET
   Shocker! Are 'Idol' voters for real? America's youth came to the rescue of its well-earned reputation as tasteless and tone-deaf when it voted front-runner Ruben Studdard one of its two least favorite contestants last night on "American Idol."

   Although Ruben turned out to be safe, advancing over Trenyce to the next round of four finalists, it was even more shocking than last season when voters dropped Tamyra Gray from the show.

   My staff of thousands wants to know: Was the vote rigged for drama? It wouldn't surprise me if we find out one day that it was. And why didn't U.S. Marine Joshua Gracin, who was clearly out-classed, stand up and do the honorable thing (like announce he was taking himself out of the competition)? I have no idea, but I'm not the only one.

   "After reading through [the] judge[s'] comments for both Josh and Ruben, Ryan announces that Ruben is in the bottom two!" recapper David Bloomberg writes for Reality News Online. "The audience boos. Simon mouths, 'What?!' I don't know that I've ever seen him this stunned. Josh drops his head into his hands. He knows he shouldn't still be sitting on the couch while Ruben is in the bottom two."

   And, Bloomberg concludes, "A person with much less singing ability is continuing forward in this competition at the expense of others solely because that person has a huge fan base who continually votes for them [sic] no matter how bad they are."

May 1, 2003 / 8:31 a.m. ET
   Postscript: What's the point of writing about 'Idol' anyway? I might as well write about the World Wrestling Entertainment. Professional wrestling

has more cultural significance when you give it some thought. The other day, for instance, I was talking about the origins of reality TV with my staff of thousands and one of them came up with the provocative notion that for relevance the WWE beats "Candid Camera" or O.J. Simpson's "trial of the [last] century" any day.

"If one wishes to study the true ancestor of today's reality shows," he said, "one must enter the 'squared circle of honor' and look to professional wrestling." (I can't help it if he sounds like that nice twit who sends Ruth Fisher around the bend on "Six Feet Under.") "Same sorts of contrived drama, same sorts of carnival theatrics. The only difference I can see is that the wrestlers don't take themselves as seriously as the reality show participants."

Mr. Twit didn't stop there. "A fan can sit back with a beer and watch professional wrestling and experience every emotion of which he is capable. Joy, sorrow, sympathy, anger. He can laugh at the parodies. He can appreciate the athletic ability of the participants."

Nor did he stop there. "For one's typical fan, professional wrestling is the Wal-Mart of entertainment," he went on. "Indeed, it serves the same market. One's typical fan appreciates professional wrestling and NASCAR races because, when either is on TV, there are no lines at the Wal-Mart. But I digress. For an hour or so, one's typical wrestling fan can forget about making last month's payment on his pickup and lose himself in the world defined by the squared circle of honor."

Mr. Twit summarized the issue this way:

1. Professional wrestling is a morality play, a soap opera, if you will. One has good guys and bad guys and virtuous ladies and tramps. Good choices result in good consequences. Poor choices result in bad consequences.

2. It is all parody and satire anyway. The late comedian Andy Kaufman recognized the satirical nature of the medium and used it to great effect in his wrestling gag. It's all about talking trash and poking fun.

3. Professional wrestlers, no matter what else one thinks, are gifted athletes. Fake falls and all, it takes athletic ability to do what they do.

4. And professional wrestlers are gifted in other ways. Jesse Ventura. Need I say more?

May 1, 2003 / 3:53 p.m. ET

Shocker, part 2! Are 'Idol' voters for real? Everybody has a theory about why Josh Gracin got more votes last night on "American Idol" than Ruben Studdard. Many of the theories I've seen have to do with patriotism and the fact that Gracin is a U.S. Marine.

"What's at play is a bias in favor of a military man in time of war," Eric Olsen writes, "even though, through no fault of his own, Josh Gracin was singing and dancing in Hollywood while his cohorts were in harm's way in the desert halfway around the world."

But I've also read a lot of e-mails saying that Ruben seemed such a shoo-in that his fans didn't bother to vote in the numbers they had earlier. It could be as simple as that. Others say that Gracin's fans found a way to beat the system. If they have, I'm willing to bet the others' have too.

So maybe it's all the above.

As to Gracin's non-deployment to Iraq, I've read lots of denials by the Marine Corps that he was given favored treatment so he could remain on the show. The most detailed piece of I've seen on that subject, Nikke Finke's jeremiad in the Los Angeles Weekly, reports otherwise.

Does any of this make a difference? Probably not. Gracin is likely to be voted off next time. If he's not, "American Idol" has a crisis on its hands.

May 1, 2003 / 7:52 p.m. ET

'It's been said she knocks 'em dead': But what a comedown for Tina Brown. She used to be such a powerhouse — taste-maker, cultural arbiter, editor of The New Yorker, founder of Talk magazine. Now she's just a TV talking head.

Not a good one, either. At least not yet. To put it kindly, Brown has a long way to go. Judging from last night's debut, "Topic [A]," her new show on CNBC, has a long way to go, too. Was anybody really interested in what Barry Diller, one of her guests, had to say about the Internet, when all he had to say is that it's "revolutionary" and "interactive" and "a new medium." Like, duh?

Brown is much better at answering questions than asking them. In today's Times of London, she writes in her column that "successful TV performing requires rapid fire attention deficit disorder simultaneously with intense focus." She certainly has the focus. And her critics have always said her chief shortcoming at The New Yorker was attention deficit disorder. So what's the problem?

Thinking fast on her feet, according to her own postmortem. "There's no time for honing and thumb sucking," she writes. "The rough drafts are on the air. The worst thing about TV is that the next day everyone from the guy in the dry cleaners to old school friends you've taken years to shed offers an opinion."

Poor Tina Brown. Maybe one day, <u>if CNBC lets her hang around</u> long enough, she'll be able to rise to the level of that speedy intellect, Larry King.

May 2, 2003 / 1:43 p.m. ET
On the wings of a non-dove: As television spectaculars go, President Bush's prime-time special last night from the flight deck of the USS Abraham Lincoln was rated a grand success. According to Washington Post TV critic Tom Shales, it evoked <u>memories of both Ronald Reagan and Bob Hope</u>. It's hard to beat that combo for patriotic entertainment.

But Bush went even further with his "Top Gun" heroics before the speech. Landing a jet on an aircraft carrier is something neither Hope nor Reagan tried. It's been trumpeted as the president's Tom Cruise moment, but I like to think of it as his Michael Dukakis moment. (<u>Remember Dukakis "driving" that tank back in '88?</u>) Seems to me Bush busted himself from "commander-in-chief" to "pilot's assistant" (OK, co-pilot). All he had to do was take the bows. My hat's off to the pilot.

May 3, 2003 / 2:32 p.m. ET
Random notes: Here's an enjoyable read: Peter Plagens' <u>"In Defense of High Art,"</u> which does what art critics ought to do more of — explain "high art" without sounding highfalutin. Plagens is not only lucid, he's funny.

A typical paragraph: "High art versus pop culture is no longer a matter of fancy French restaurant cuisine versus mom's home cookin' or a juicy cheeseburger at the corner diner. High art's opponent is the equivalent of 10 billion tons of ersatz potato chips made from a petroleum derivative, flavored with a green 'sour cream and jalapeno' dust manufactured in the same vat as the latest hair regrower, and served in little silver bags through which not one molecule of air will penetrate until 2084."

The art critic for Newsweek, Plagens (who actually retired not long ago, which in corporate-speak makes him its "outsourced" art critic) is also the genuine article — a painter himself. Here's what <u>his own high art</u> looks like.

May 4, 2003 / 2:53 p.m. ET
More random notes: British artist David Hockney has taken aim at the meaning of photography vs. paintings in depicting war. He argues that despite their realistic detail <u>photographs may actually hide what happened</u>, while paintings can interpret events with greater accuracy by probing their deeper significance.

In other words, as Mark Lawson writes in the Guardian, "Send the paintbrush to the frontlines, Hockney appears to be saying, not the Nikon or the Sony."

While that will never happen, Hockney may stimulate a debate in the art world, as he did when he claimed that masters from the 1500s on commonly used lenses and optical devices as tools of their trade to speed their work and improve their draughtsmanship.

But judge Hockney's latest foray for yourself. This time he has made a watercolor called Problems of Depiction (not reproduced well, sorry, but the only image I could find), which is based on Picasso's 1951 painting Massacre in Korea, and he's written a note to explain what motivated him.

May 5, 2003 / 9:58 a.m. ET
Some Internet legends never die: They just keep making the rounds. Take Andrew Marlatt's riff on the "Axis of Evil," supposedly written by John Cleese. It's very funny, and you can understand why people would think the co-creator of Monty Python's Flying Circus had written it.

It begins: "Bitter after being snubbed for membership in the 'Axis of Evil,' Libya, China, and Syria today announced that they had formed the "Axis of Just as Evil," which they said would be more evil than that stupid Iran-Iraq-North Korea axis President Bush warned of in his State of the Union address. Axis of Evil members, however, dismissed the new Axis as having, for starters, a really dumb name." And it goes on for nine more funny paragraphs.

Even the Boston Phoenix's fine, widely quoted media critic Dan Kennedy recently fell for it as an item, Secretary of Sanity John Cleese, in his Weblog. (Scroll down.) But people! It was first published by satirewire.com more than a year ago, on Feb. 1, 2002, and again, 10 days later, under Marlatt's byline in TheWashington Post. Marlatt is also the author of "Economy of Errors." Just thought you'd like to know.

Let's face it, being duped is an occupational hazard for anyone on the Internet. I recall being duped myself about some great haikus just last month. I thought they were "actual Japanese error messages," but they were all published in a Salon.com contest and were no more Japanese than I am.

May 6, 2003 / 10:23 a.m. ET
Counting the losses: The last time I looked 170,000 antiquities had gone missing from Iraq's National Museum. Those were the high estimates. The low estimates came in at 50,000. Now, if you can believe it, the number is down to 38.

Yes, three dozen plus 2. And that number comes not from The Onion or the Borowitz Report, or any other spoof artists, but from the Chicago

Tribune, a real, honest-to-goodness, reputable Windy City newspaper.

Tribune foreign correspondent Christine Spolar reports that contrary to previous estimates, "A total of 38 pieces, not tens of thousands, are now believed to be missing." (Free registration required.) It was the administrative offices of the museum that were ransacked, not the museum itself.

Huh? A new "inventory compiled by a military and civilian team headed by Marine Col. Matthew Bogdanos rejects reports that Iraq's renowned treasures of civilization — up to 170,000 artifacts — had been lost during the U.S.-led war against Iraq," Spolar writes. "It also raises questions about why any of the artifacts were reported missing.

Another question it raises is, can we believe any of the numbers coming out of Iraq?And what about the contradictions? Spolar herself concludes in the same report that the museum basement was ransacked of roughly 5,000 items "not suitable for display." So pick a number. Was it 38, 108, 5,008? 50,008? 170,008?

All the numbers seem fantastic — and that's not counting the $650 million found by U.S. troops in one of Saddam Hussein's palaces. Today comes news that Saddam's son, Qusay, robbed Iraq's Central Bank of $1 billion and had it hauled off in three tractor-trailers. Tomorrow, will it turn out to be $38, $308 million, $3.8 billion or $3.8 trillion?

And how about those missing weapons of mass destruction? Will we find 38 liters of anthrax, 38 tons of mustard gas, 38 mobile bio-warfare labs and 38 about-to-be nuclear bombs? Or will we find 38 nothings? It's anyone's guess. (Free registration required.)

May 6, 2003 / 1:18 p.m. ET
  Changing the subject: Now that Wal-Mart has pulled Maxim, Stuff and FHM from its shelves, deeming them too racy for its customers, I've got to admit I've never given any of these magazines a glance — and I don't even shop at Wal-Mart.

To express my doubts about the giant retail chain, therefore, might seem questionable. So here's Eric Olsen doing it for me: "Does America see its culture defined by Wal-Mart?. Maybe not, but Wal-Mart does, and what Wal-Mart wants, Wal-Mart gets, including a compressed, sanitized, 'family-friendly' culture."

May 7, 2003 / 8:58 a.m. ET
  Morality, bottom line, double standard: Most of the e-mails prompted by yesterday's Wal-Mart item typically approved of the giant retailer's

"morality" in banning racy men's magazines such as Maxim from its shelves.

"Those of you who live in NYC or LA may not shop in Wal-Mart. But for those of us who live in small towns and cities in 'fly over' land, Wal-Mart is a godsend. It offers reasonably priced goods that appeal to people that live on fixed incomes. They are among the few retailers that are willing to take a chance on small town America. It is comforting to know that some retailers set standards on the basis of morality and not just the bottom line." — Larry Heater, DDS, Wolf Point, MT

But some e-mails pointed out that Wal-Mart has invoked a double standard.

"Setting a standard by which items in your store most be measured is fine, but why the one-sided sexist application of this standard? Wal-Mart still sells the female equivalent of Maxim. ...The covers of [these] women's magazines have made me blush while waiting in line with cover stories entitled, '5 oral sex tricks you must learn,' and '58 new ways to make him squeal.' I don't read [them] and don't care whether either of them are sold in Wal Mart but don't have a double standard of reverse sexism."
— Houston Prather, Oak Island, N.C.

I messaged back: "Are those women's magazine story titles real ones, or did you just approximate them?" He replied: "I did not write them down when I saw them but the one I saw specifically used the phrase 'oral sex tricks'."

About that bottom line: Wal-Mart is reportedly the largest private employer in the U.S.; sells 36 percent of all dog food; 32 percent of disposable diapers; 30 percent of photographic film; 26 percent of toothpaste; 21 percent of pain remedies, and 15 percent of single-copy magazine sales. Given those numbers, I'm not as comforted as Larry Heater.

Postscript: Suddenly the tide of e-mails has turned more critical.

"If Wal-Mart is so concerned about promoting a 'family-friendly' culture, why do they sell shotguns? You can't buy an album with a curse word on it, or a magazine with a scantily clad woman, but you're free to go in and buy a shotgun which you can use to blow somebody's head off. Excellent priorities this store has."
—Jessica, Coral Springs

Hey, Jessica — I know Wal-Mart sells rifle gunsights. But does it really sell shotguns? I don't believe it. Please tell me you're wrong.

"Hypocrisy! Wal-Mart won't sell morning-after birth control pills, but it will sell magazines that offer oral sex tricks. What about the guns and cigarettes? These are far more damaging to America's health."
— Merry, Santa Fe, N.M.

May 8, 2003 / 7:34 a.m. ET
The Wal-Mart shotgun question: OK, people — call me naïve! Call me a babe in the woods! Call me dumb! I asked such a foolish question: "Does Wal-Mart really sell shotguns?"

Paul Goode, from Redmond, Wash., set me straight. "Does Wal-Mart sell guns?" he wrote. "Is the Pope Catholic? Was Bambi's mother cute before a hunter did her in? Don't take my word for it, see: USA Today. Note that the USA Today article terms Wal-Mart 'the nation's biggest gun seller.'"

(See also: The Pleasanton Weekly for code violations by a Wal-Mart store that resulted in a suspended license to sell firearms.)

You can't say Wal-Mart has been all bad. Here's KC3 (Kentucky Coaltion to Carry Concealed) urging its members to lobby the retail giant: "Wal-Mart has agreed under pressure from Million Moron March Moms ... NOT to sell guns at a new store in Tampa because it's 'near' a high school! If they knuckle under because they haven't heard from the average Joes and Jills who support them, then this could spread nation-wide!"

And here's a lament that "Wal-Mart quietly ordered its stores to adopt a tougher policy on gun sales that goes beyond the requirements of the federal government."

Goode wasn't the only one to set me straight. Hundreds of other did, too. But some e-mails puzzled me, like this one from Mark (no last name), of Baltimore, Md. "To the people crying about Wal-Mart selling shotguns," he writes, "shotguns are primarly used in hunting (deer not people). Hunting people is what handguns are for and Wal-Mart doesn't sell them."

Now I may be naïve, and I may be a babe in the woods. But I lived for more than five years in the northernmost reaches of Vermont, where deerhunting is a way of life. Among the hunters I knew, anybody who went deer hunting with a shotgun was beyond the pale.

May 8, 2003 / 7:57 a.m. ET
'Idol'-atry in action: The voters on "American Idol" redeemed themselves last night. They shipped the U.S. Marine Josh Gracin home and re-upped Ruben Studdard, Kimberly Locke and Clay Aiken as the show's three finalists. (Smirky host Ryan Seacrest, an official People magazine

"Beautiful Person," claimed there were 22 million votes.)

At least the voters got it right this time. Mr. Nasty — aka judge Simon Cowell — got the voters wrong twice in a row. This week he said Gracin should have been kept on. Last week, when Gracin was kept, he said Gracin should have been voted off. Here's a blow by blow.

Who will be rejected next week? Vote here.

Meantime, all those folks who claimed that 'Idol' voters were motivated by racism and/or bias against fat people when Studdard was nearly dumped last week (I stopped counting those e-mails) will have to bite their tongues.

It was the most appalling, the most ridiculous, the most wrong-headed moment of the season. But my staff of thousands and I were optimists. We said the voters that time around were merely tasteless and tone-deaf. Like Abe Lincoln — make that Thomas Jefferson — we still held some truths to be self-evident.

May 9, 2003 / 9:23 a.m. ET

What celebrity means — Bart vs. Navasky: The difference between a Hollywood intellectual (there actually is such a thing) and a New York intellectual has been defined for me by Peter Bart, editor-in-chief of the show-biz bible Variety, and Victor Navasky, editor of the liberal-left bible The Nation.

At a gathering last night in the Chelsea Hotel's basement bar, the two of them were asked to begin their chat for a group of college graduates interested in the meaning of celebrity in contemporary society with a favorite anecdote about a celebrity.

Bart told a mildly interesting one about Robert Evans (more Hollywood insider than celebrity) that was really all about … Peter Bart … in the course of which we learned that Bart spent 17 years as a studio executive at Paramount, MGM and Lorimar collaborating on important movies with important people after starting out as a reporter for The Wall Street Journal and The New York Times.

Navasky told a very funny anecdote about the late Truman Capote (more celebrity than author) that was really all about … Truman Capote … in the course of which we were entertained by Navasky's sense of humor and the bizarre meaning of celebrity as demonstrated by the insular reality of Capote's life.

I'm still not sure if I know what celebrity means. But now I know the difference between a Hollywood and a New York intellectual. I'd recount Navasky's anecdote for you if it weren't too long to go into. E-mail him at vic@thenation.com and ask him to tell it again. Maybe he will. And come

268

back here later today for a demonstration of what makes Michael Jackson fans on the Web different from Wal-Mart fans and deer hunters.

Postscript: Ellen Cuttler, of Niskayuna, N.Y., writes in an e-mail: "Hi. I don't know what 'celebrity' means, either. But singer Brad Paisley has an interesting perspective which he puts into his song 'Celebrity.' There is a link to the lyrics at the bottom of that home page. It may not help you in your quest, but I think it will make you smile." Sure did.

May 10, 2003 / 12:27 p.m. ET

The pop culture of shotguns: Now that I've received hundreds upon hundreds of e-mails from deer hunters all over the continental United States telling me how dumb I am, let me say this: My ignorance is stunning. But that's what I'm here for — to let people feel they're smarter than at least one person on Earth about their special interest.

That's why, when I've sometimes written about Michael Jackson, his most rabid fans have messaged me, literally by the thousands, to tell me how stupid I was not to appreciate his warmth, talent, kindness, generosity, brilliance, and yes, genius. (It's exhausting to list all the things they love about him.)

But deer hunters are a different breed. For one thing, they're more literate. This may surprise you. It did me. And they're very, very well informed about guns and the laws regulating deer hunting, not to mention the Wal-Mart shotgun question.

I'd written that among the hunters I knew in the northernmost reaches of Vermont — where I once lived and where deer hunting is a way of life — anybody who hunted deer with a shotgun was beyond the pale. It goes to show how little a transplanted city slicker knows (even if he did own a 30.06 rifle).

Billybob set me straight, but at least offered a pinch of vindication: "You're right, in New England hunters primarily hunt with rifles (besides the few nut jobs who insist on hunting with bows, pistols, slingshots, beer cans and Buicks). But out in the Midwest where the terrain is flat and a misplaced rifle shot can keep on going and going . . . hunters use [short-range] shotguns firing lead slugs."

And here's Ed Stoddard, of McKenney, Va.: "In the great North woods [and] in the open West and Rocky Mountain states, rifle hunting is normal and necessary. In many southern states ... shotguns with slugs are used, requiring close-range shots. The density of the population and number of hunters in these areas are the reasons for this difference."

In fact, for just those reasons of safety, many states beyond the South, too — from Illinois, Ohio and Indiana to New York, New Jersey and more — actually outlaw deer hunting with rifles and insist on the use of shotguns with appropriate cartridges instead.   By the way, I sold my 30.06 rifle when I left Vermont, never having shot a deer — and I've never gone deer hunting since.

May 11, 2003 / 1:31 p.m. ET

   Small-town savior or company gulag? I see that David Brooks has caught up to us on the subject of Wal-Mart with a gorgeously clever satire, "No Sex Magazines, Please, We're Wal-Mart Shoppers," in this morning's New York Times. (Free registration required.)

   But, in fact, Brooks' main target is not Wal-Mart or its shoppers. He takes aim at the shibboleths of liberal culture — as he does in his 2001 best-seller "Bobos in Paradise" and in his neoconservative commentaries in The Weekly Standard, where he's a senior editor.

   He tees off beautifully on the social consciousness of Trader Joe's, "the grocery store for people who wouldn't dream of buying free-range chicken broth from a company that didn't take a position against offshore oil drilling."

   The rest of the article is equally funny. But Brooks is unfailingly awed by Wal-Mart's reputation as "patriotic, community oriented, family-centered, rural and religious," and he never once mentions Wal-Mart's spotty record as an employer.

   I've received so many e-mails from people describing their shabby treatment as Wal-Mart employees or former employees that it's unfair to ignore them, as I've done thus far.

   The main complaints are that Wal-Mart discriminates against women employees in compensation and promotion, cheats employees out of fully earned wages and violates the rights of disabled people in its hiring practices. Trusting soul that I am, I believe my e-mailers. But are they really who they say they are? Do they have a personal ax to grind? So, rather than just print a few of their messages, let me offer documented evidence of their claims.

   Here's a report from The New York Times of Feb. 16, 2003, detailing what could become "the largest employment discrimination class action in American history." The suit alleges discrimination against female Wal-Mart employees, claiming they are paid lower wages than men and consistently passed over for promotion.

   The article also states: "More than 40 lawsuits are pending that accuse Wal-Mart of pressuring or forcing employees to work unpaid hours off the

270

clock. Wal-Mart officials deride all these lawsuits, though in December a jury in Oregon found Wal-Mart guilty of forcing 400 employees to work off the clock."

There's no shortage of suits. Here's a 2001 class-action lawsuit brought in New York state on behalf of 80,000 employees. It charges that Wal-Mart has systematically avoided paying them earned overtime wages. Similar cases were pending at the time in Oregon (the one noted above), Washington and Massachusetts.

Here's a 2001 report from the San Francisco Chronicle: "Plaintiff Stephanie Odle of Lubbock, Texas, was in tears as she described an eight-year career that included 11 transfers and working weeks of 70 hours and more in expectation of promotions that were given to men."

Here's a 2002 report of Wal-Mart paying $6.8 million in a consent decree to settle 12 lawsuits for violating for rights of disabled job applicants and former employees. And here's a thread of e-mails about rotten Wal-Mart practices that, if true, make it sound like a company gulag.

May 13, 2003 / 3:26 p.m. ET

Hollywood comes to Broadway: Every year around this time Broadway gets ready for its closeup. The fabulous invalid primps and puffs out its chest, as though the Tony Awards were the equal of the Oscars. The theater producers put on a nationally televised Tony ceremony (June 8 on CBS), in the hope that it will achieve the sort of glamour that makes the Oscars such a draw.

The peculiar thing is that this year it just might. When Broadway looked like it had the deathly pallor of a corpse, cursed by a musicians' strike and the tourist blues of a gloomy, war-time winter, the invalid stood up and walked. Suddenly movie and television stars began treading the boards as though hell-bent to prove they are living, breathing actors, not just celluloid faces or TV celebrities.

Appearing in various Broadway productions right now are Helen Hunt, John Turturro, Antonio Banderas, Marisa Tomei, Al Pacino, David Straithairn, Chita Rivera, Molly Ringwald, Elizabeth Ashley, Dianne Wiest, Philip Seymour Hoffman, Brian Dennehy, Vanessa Redgrave, Robert Sean Leonard, Stanley Tucci, even Eddie Izzard and Bill Maher. And that's not to mention directors Kenneth Branagh and Baz Luhrmann, or perennial Broadway stars Bernadette Peters, Harvey Fierstein and Brian Stokes Mitchell, or Paul Newman's star turn earlier this season.

Nor is it to say that Broadway is bursting with new ideas. Many of the best current offerings are revivals — musical ("Gypsy," "Nine" and "La

271

Boheme") and dramatic ("A Day in the Death of Joe Egg," "Long Day's Journey Into Night.") Moreover, the two entirely new musicals "Hairspray" and "Movin' Out" that dominated the Tony nominations with 13 and 10 nods, respectively, are not exactly new. The smash hit "Hairspray" is a retro look at the 1960s, restyled from John Waters' 1988 non-musical film of the same name. And Twyla Tharp's "Movin' Out" is a wordless, plotless dance tribute to Billy Joel's music, the sort of concept "pioneered" a couple of seasons ago by "Contact."

Meantime, here's another peculiarity: Richard Avedon's photo of Vanessa Redgrave in this week's New Yorker conveys more about her role as Mary Tyrone in "Long Day's Journey into Night" than anything the critics have said in their most fulsome praise. The photo says more even than anything Redgrave herself conveyed on the night I saw her performance from a pretty good seat in the orchestra.

This revival of Eugene O'Neill's classic, the quintessential American play about booze and dope and the self-torment of a tragic family, is four hours l-o-n-g and, from my perspective, somehow packs less emotional punch than it should. Not that you could ever tell from Ben Brantley's rave review in The New York Times (free registration required) or from John Lahr's in The New Yorker, both of which seem like sales pitches from the best used-car salesmen on the lot.

Given an ensemble as powerful as Redgrave, Dennehy, Hoffman and Leonard, I was hoping for something more than a family portrait of clinical dysfunction; I was hoping for a towering revelation, a drama that would leave me dumbstruck, perhaps in tears, certainly in awe. But no such luck.

At the end of the play, after all the booze is drained from the bottles and the morphine haze has settled for what seems like forever over the Tyrone family, I drifted out of the theater with an audience apparently eager to get home. There was no prolonged applause, no standing ovation, no second bows for the cast. The audience — star-studded, too, with Meg Ryan and John Lithgow and other celebrities — filtered into the street and hailed whatever cabs came along, and that was that.

May 14, 2003 / 11:27 p.m. ET
'Idol' chatter: For me the biggest disappointment of "American Idol" was not that Kimberly Locke got the boot, leaving Clay Aiken and Ruben Studdard for next week's sing-off. I'd said the winners should be Aiken and Studdard. And the voters got that right. (I didn't think they would.)

My biggest disappointment was Tamyra Gray, one of last season's finalists. Brought back to fill air-time Wednesday in a typically padded show, she sang "Somewhere Over the Rainbow" — and tanked. Was she just having an off night? I recalled her voice ringing with power. Now it seemed awfully anemic.

Gray looked great, very stylish, like a cabaret sophisticate. But her song arrangement? Ugh. It was so understated Lena Horne couldn't have brought it off. (I've since been informed it was the late, great Eva Cassidy's version from her "Songbird" album.)

But the irony is that Locke had sung "Over the Rainbow" earlier in the competition, and a video clip briefly reprised her performance. If nothing else, it was a reminder that while Locke hadn't found the 'Idol' pot of gold, she knew how to sing that song.

As for last season's No. 2 finalist, pretty boy Justin Guarini, who was brought out to fetishize "Unchained Melody" (a promo for his upcoming CD), all I can say is — Woof!! He could have taken lessons from Aiken, who covered "Unchained Melody" Tuesday night and slammed it home.

So who's going to be next week's winner? Vote here.

One thing really puzzles me: Fans have a couple hours to cast their votes, right? How could there have been more than 19 million votes, as 'Idol' host Ryan Seacrest told us, in that amount of time. For that matter, how could there have been 22 million votes last week?

I'm not the only one asking: "It was impossible to vote on the phone last night. After trying to vote off and on for the allowed two hours, I was never able to get through on the lines. That makes me wonder who did vote? ... Would someone please explain how votes can be tallied from the phone calls if it is impossible to get through? Doesn't this affect who is honestly the winning contestant? Many of us who tried to vote would like to have an answer to that question." — Nancy Houston, Oakland, Calif.

Maybe Sarah [no last name given] has the answer. "Ruben should win," she wrote in an e-mail. "I love him so much that I voted for him 105 times last night." Hey Sarah, how about giving Nancy some speed-dialing tips?

OK, here's the real answer: "The intro of text messaging this season answers your question as to how the accumulation of votes mounted in such a short amount of time.
— Jennifer, Sandston, Va.

Wait a minute!! "Voting 105 times does not count as 105 votes. During last year's 'American Idol,' kids with sophisticated computers had a program to redial over and over. The producers caught on, and now votes are only counted once from one phone number. Sarah, I'm afraid redialing is just a waste, as it will only be counted once.

— Sam Phom, Portland, Oregon

Wait another minute!!! "Sam Phom is wrong. You can vote multiple times for a single contestant (Ryan says it again and again throughout the show). Voting multiple times and using power dialing are two very different things. The power dialing is what producers are monitoring:

"What's being done about power dialing? Production will have in place weekly monitoring procedures designed to prevent individuals from unfairly influencing the outcome of the voting by generating significant blocks of votes using technical enhancements. The producers reserve the right to remove any votes identified by producers as 'power dialing' votes."

— Mary, Philadelphia, Pa.

And in closing (online in real time): "Jan, I find myself having to vent as I watch 'American Idol.' The performances are one-half step up the musical food chain from Muzak. The medley that opened the show was soulless and at best some kind of Up With People regurgitation. If this is what passes for 'American Idol'-atry then I am saddened deeply by the state of music in these United States. I hate to sound like Simon [Cowell] on a bad hair day, but man, that opening number was wretched.

"I realize that I have come to the wrong alter to worship musical creativity and inspiration. I shudder to think what would happen to a contestant with, say, Frank Zappa's stage presence and perspective. It also makes me think back on the musical artists that I admire, such as Joe Jackson, Randy Newman, Andy Partridge and Kate Bush, who would be laughed off the stage in this sort of event.

"Anyway, with all that said, I wish the winner the very best in a musical career which is bound to include numerous stints at Disney World and Vegas. I just hope that I do not have to be subjected to any of the 'original' material that will eventually be all over the airwaves. I detect smidgeons of technical talent in the performances of these contestants, but I have yet to see one iota of creative talent. End of rant. Have a wonderful evening."

— Jeff Bowden, Florence, Kentucky

May 14, 2003 / 12:39 p.m. ET
'Idol'-izing America and Oprah, too: When Oprah gets into the act, as she did the other day with her backstage visit to the set of "American Idol,"

you know the show has more than merely arrived: It rules. But you knew that already, didn't you!

So what don't you know?

That <u>Kimberly Locke</u> was the underdog going into last night's three-way final but was so good she sent the judges into a swoon — even Mr. Nasty, aka Simon Cowell — and could come out a winner tonight?

That <u>Ruben Studdard</u> — as sweet as he smiles and as sweet as he sings and as much as the judges love him — has been sounding too much the same and could come out a loser tonight?

That <u>Clay Aiken</u> faltered momentarily, but then delivered what judge Paula Abdul called the best performance of the competition yet? That the judges have said that before to others?

That the tighter the "Idol" screw is turned, the nicer the judges get in general?

Let's see tonight what the voters decided. Whom would you drop? <u>Vote here.</u>

I hesitate to make a pick myself. I think tonight's winners should be Aiken and Studdard. I think the voters will pick Aiken and Locke. I think the producers would pick Aiken and Locke, too.

May 16, 2003 / 6:27 p.m. ET

Gaming the 'American Idol' system: What I cherish most about "<u>American Idol</u>" is not its sense of fair play — all pretense to fairness notwithstanding — but the idea that 'Idol' voters are gaming the system.

In 'Idol'-land, voters are encouraged to cheat because cheating is not considered cheating; it's just being savvy. Some fans vote hundreds of times for their favorite singer. Thus "American Idol" is not even a popularity contest; it's a speed-dialing, text-messaging competition.

Do all the phone and text-message votes count? <u>It depends on whom you believe.</u> Some say they don't, because the producers are wise to the game and screen out the gamers. Some say all votes count no matter how many times they come from the same source.

One anonymous e-mailer wrote me that he voted 423 times for Kimberly Locke. "Just kept pressing redial, wait six seconds, turn off, on, redial, and at the end of an hour ... counted 423 times I connected." In this case it apparently didn't matter. <u>Locke got the boot anyway</u>

Here's what two other gamers did:

C. Guo, of San Mateo, Calif., writes that he couldn't get through from his land-line home phone. "However, I was able to vote 230 times in the 2-

hour time limit [by] using a cell phone (yes, from AT&T wireless, although I suspect the same can be true for all cell phones). And yes, text messaging works, too (if you're willing to pay the fee.)"

Dana B., of Centreville, Va., writes: "Folks, I don't know about you, but when I voted ... I just kept hitting the redial button. ... In a span of about 10 minutes, I was able to vote 27 times. ... I see no reason why there couldn't have been over 19 million votes. ... So, how about if we cut out the sarcasm and trust that the vote counts are accurate. This isn't Florida."

The ultimate gamers, however, may be the "American Idol" producers themselves. They've assured us they wouldn't manipulate the vote count to favor any particular contestant. That would risk violating federal law. But Whay Jones, of Dallas, Texas, writes: "They still can alter the outcome dramatically and 'legally' by controlling the phone-call influx rate."

His theory is a little complicated. But stick with him. "There were 19 million votes that came in on Tuesday," Jones writes. "That's 53,000 votes per minute per contestant. If one contestant is averaging 90,000 votes per minute while another contestant is averaging 47,000 votes per minute, 'A.I.' can set the allowed influx call rate at 50,000 per contestant per minute."

Were that done, he explains, the difference between contestants would be minimized from 43,000 votes per minute to 3,000. (Over two hours, a difference of five million votes would be minimized to a difference of 360,000 votes.) So the difference in the vote count "can be effectively dropped."

(You may recall that on Wednesday night's show, "Idol" host Ryan Secrest announced there was a mere four percent difference among the votes for Locke, Clay Aiken and Ruben Studdard.)

Jones continues: "I'm not accusing the 'A.I.' producers of committing this fraud; but I want to bring it out into the open, so that someone would catch it if they ever did." And he concludes with a plea to the producers: "Please open all available phone lines" for Tuesday's final sing-off.

I'd bet that Aiken and Studdard want to win fair and square. But they've got to be hoping their fans have speed-dialing savvy and nimble thumbs.

May 17, 2003 / 11:59 a.m. ET

Gaming the 'Idol' system, Part 2: I've no idea whether the producers of "American Idol" have set a phone-call influx rate (see below) or used any other procedure to "adjust" the call-in votes of their sing-off.

But too many "Idol" fans who've e-mailed me — the huge majority, in fact — keep saying that something is wrong. This one is typical of hundreds of e-mails:

"I have two phone lines in my home and a cellular phone and I couldn't get through — not one time. I was getting a recording saying this is not a working number."

— Earlene Matthews, Birmingham, Ala.

To remain above suspicion, the show's producers ought to clarify their procedures before the finale airs. Are they adjusting the vote or not?

In the end it may not matter, just as it doesn't seem to matter that Hollywood's box-office figures are reported as gospel, yet they're not independently verified.

We know, for instance, that "The Matrix Reloaded" opened to blockbuster business on Thursday. Whether or not it set a one-day record and beat the numbers for "Spider-Man, as Warner Bros. contends, has more to do with hype and bragging rights and setting expectations for the rest of the run than with accuracy.

But when the most authoritative, widely quoted, "independent" source of box-office figures admits, "I have no choice but to take the numbers they've given me" — referring to Warner Bros., as Paul Dergarabedian, president of the Los Angeles-based monitoring firm Exhibitor Relations, did this morning in The New York Times — it doesn't build my confidence.

So take your pick — Clay Aiken vs. Ruben Studdard, "The Matrix Reloaded" vs. "Spider-man." It's a gamer's game. The entertainment world, like the real world, has morphed with the times. And the times may not be what they seem.

Postscript: The latest Newsweek says "American Idol" producers, "did install a 'phone cap' that keeps an individual from placing hundreds of votes during the two-hour call-in window." But voters tell us they've gotten through hundreds of times. Perhaps Newsweek means the cap prevents the multiple votes from being counted more than once, as Sam Phom noted here last week, although even that is disputed.

May 19, 2003 / 10:32 a.m. ET

Of ideologues and propagandists: They're still out there in force pushing their agendas. Jon Alvarez, for example, is a relentless promoter of Patriotic Americans Boycotting Anti-American Hollywood (PABAAH). His spam arrives like clockwork. I usually send it straight to the trash bin. But this time, to share the pain and illustrate the derangement of our Dubya days, I thought I'd bring you his latest piece.

This is his current "action item":

"1. Do not pay to see the new Renée Zellweger film "Down With Love" out in theatres this weekend.

"2. Contact Starbucks at info@starbucks.com and let them know how you feel about their use of Sheryl Crow's music at their stores.

"3. Do not rent Hugh Grant's new movie 'Two Weeks Notice.'

"4. Do not rent Ed Norton's 'The 25th Hour.'

"5. Do not pay to see the upcoming Ed Norton film 'The Italian Job' set for release in theatres May 30th.

"6. Do not pay to see the upcoming Matt Damon film 'Stuck On You' set for release in theatres late 2003."

He urges support for "Terminator 3," Arnold Schwarzenegger's upcoming film, Rob Lowe's TV series "The Lyon's Den," to air in the fall; Joe Pantoliano's series "The Handler," also to air in the fall; and Patricia Heaton of "Everybody Loves Raymond.

Alvarez claims that People magazine will publish one of his letters to the editor. "I write them so often," he explains, that he's not sure which letter it will be. "I believe it is about Susan Sarandon and George Clooney being on their 50 Most Beautiful People list. I told People that they should not have made that list, as they are UGLY AMERICANS! At least I hope that's the one they chose to print."

Finally, he's thrilled to report "that MCI has listened" to his sort of humbug "and will no longer use Danny Glover as their spokesperson!" Glover, you may recall, has spoken out against the politics of President Bush.

May 19, 2003 / 10:34 a.m. ET

Wal-Mart wags the culture dog: And we thought the wars of the Reagan and Clinton years were over. How dumb of us. They're still being fought not just by the traditional cultural warriors of the right and the left but by other means, principally the mass-market merchandisers.

Ideologues and propagandists like recently defrocked moralist William Bennett notwithstanding, David D. Kirkpatrick details how it's the big retails chains shaping cultural tastes. (Free registration required.) Wal-Mart is so influential, Kirkpatrick reports, that "the major record labels have satellite offices near [its] headquarters in Bentonville, Ark., to cater to its buyers." Warner Brothers, BMG and EMI have gone so far as to invest in Christian labels because of soaring sales largely due to Wal-Mart.

The chairman of AOL Time Warner's book unit launched a religious imprint "because a book buyer for Wal-Mart told him that more than half its sales were Christian books." Similarly, Crown and Penguin have started conservative imprints. "They have not dictated to us, but we are very smart about servicing that channel the way that they would like to be serviced," the chief executive of HarperCollins told Kirkpatrick.

Corporate "cultural whoredom" such as that goes hand in hand with what has already been called "the media whoredom" of the corporate press. If you're unfamiliar with the term, have a look at mediawhoresonline, "The site that set out to bring the media to its knees, but found they were already there." Or as James Wolcott puts it in his excoriating piece, "Round up the Cattle," in the current Vanity Fair: "They're not prostitutes, they're pushovers." (Sorry, it's not online.)

May 20, 2003 / 12:41 p.m. ET
The 'American Idol' money shot: The term "the money shot" has entered the language through common usage in everything from basketball and billiards to book titles and band names to Paula Abdul's praise for Ruben Studdard's smile. "See those dimples right there?" she remarked. "That's the money shot! That's the money shot!"

Beneath her Al Capone hat, she looked so knowing. She sounded so emphatic. She pointed to her own cheek, like: "Don't you forget it!" It was such an out-there "American Idol" moment that it was replayed on Monday night's special. But frankly my jaw dropped the first time I heard her, and again on the replay.

"Oh dear!" as my maiden aunt likes to say. "What's this world coming to?" Do I know something Abdul doesn't? Do I know something the show's producers don't? I doubt it. Do I know something most "Idol" fans probably don't? Maybe.

That term comes from the porn industry. It's a porn-film term. If you don't believe me, maybe this citation will help: "In 'The Film-Maker's Guide to Pornography,' Stephen Ziplow describes 'the money shot' or 'c - - shot,' as the key moment in the porn production, the one the punters pay to see." (Second paragraph.)

What I'd like to know now is: Will Wal-Mart, which advertises on "American Idol," drop its ads from the show the way it dropped the lad magazines from its shelves? If Ruben Studdard ever makes any CDs in the future, will it stock them if his dimples are showing? Will it stock them if he hides his dimples? Will it stock Paula Abdul's CDs? And since I'm in an asking mode: Did you know where the term "the money shot" came from?

Meantime, whom do you want to win tonight, Big Poppa Ruben, aka The Velvet Teddy Bear, or Baby Clay, The Southern Crooner? Vote here.

Postscript: "I too could NOT believe it when Paula called Ruben's dimples "the money shot!" I thought it was standard knowledge that this was a porn term, and a pretty gross one at that.
—Tee, Saskatoon, Canada

May 20, 2003 / 3:01 p.m. ET

Hypocrisy rules: This just in from Gerald Ball, of Norcross, Ga. in re: Wal-Mart wagging the culture dog: "Look you hypocrite. Ever hear of Bessinger's Barbecue Sauce? Well, it was an extremely popular, high-selling item at Wal-Mart, but they stopped carrying it, even after it's manufacturer sued them. Why? Because Bessinger's Barbecue Sauce has the Confederate battle flag on it's label, and Wal-Mart acted to protect the sensitivities of their black customers.

"You are aware that 'conservative' Wal-Mart stocks a lot of items geared towards black audiences and is the only major retailer that celebrates the black American slavery emancipation holiday Juneteenth. Wal-Mart's founders also run a scholarship program that pays private school tuition for thousands of poor mostly black and Hispanic children.

"Wal-Mart isn't harming anyone by refusing to carry soft-core porn magazines (or barbecue sauce with racist logos) and selling edited CDs and DVDs. People like you are doing the harm by demonizing them for not conforming to your liberal views and trying to pressure them into changing just because you can't tolerate someone out there not thinking like you (or catering to those who don't think like you)."

My staff of a thousand hypocrites wants to take this moment to congratulate Wal-Mart for banning Bessinger's Barbecue Sauce from its shelves. We also want to point out that Wal-Mart was not alone in pulling it. Kroger, Publix, Food Lion, Bi-Lo and Harris Teeter pulled it, too. They also have our congratulations. And if any other congratulations are in order for other corporations doing good deeds, please don't hesitate to let us know. My staff and I prefer to think of ourselves as generous hypocrites.

May 21, 2003 / 7:54 a.m. ET

Hanging a chad: Based on Tuesday night's milquetoast sing-off for Idol in Chief, which has come to seem the highest elected office in the land, I considered it my patriotic duty to abstain.

Yes, I abstained! It's a good thing, too. With less than two percent of the votes separating Clay Aiken and Ruben Studdard the last time, to believe "American Idol" host Ryan Seacrest, I hated to think my vote would be the one that tipped the balance. Because as much as I thought Aiken should be chosen over Studdard, I was too disappointed by both of them to give either one my vote.

When Studdard sang Burt Bacharach's "A House Is Not a Home," and Aiken sang somebody's original "This Is the Night," all I could think was: Ugh! By their second selections — Studdard's version of "Imagine," by John Lennon, and Aiken's version of "Here, There, Everywhere," a Paul McCartney song — I began to feel I would have to give up my 'Idol'-land citizenship.

The judges meantime were doing their best to put a good face on things, saying stuff like, "Very pretty. I think both of you are saving the best for last. I hope so anyway" (Simon Cowell).

Along came the third offerings. Studdard sang Westlife's "Flying Without Wings," and the audience was transported. Paula Abdul said: "This is like a religious experience. It's the church of Ruben." Cowell said: "You saved the best for last. That was fantastic.

Then it was Aiken's turn. He sang the Simon & Garfunkel song "Bridge Over Troubled Water," and the audience erupted. Abdul said: "You gave us chills. You took a classic song and made us feel like we were hearing it for the first time." Cowell began by saying he thought Aiken had an off night but, saving the best for last, wrapped things up with a mother's glowing praise: "I think that performance could win you the competition."

When they announce the results on Wednesday night, it will take two hours. That's not an election, that's a milking. Register your objection here.

May 22, 2003 / 12:17 a.m. ET
'Idol' by the numbers — not! So now we know. Ruben Studdard is Idol in Chief. And Clay Aiken is Idol in Waiting. The smirky, know-it-all host of "American Idol" told us right from the beginning: "You're not going to believe how close this is."

And you know what? He was right. I don't believe it. Nor, I'm sure, do the Clay Aiken "Idol"-ators who've been crying foul for weeks, claiming the producers were loading the dice in Ruben Studdard's favor.

Frankly, it doesn't matter whether they were loaded or not. But it's no help for truth and the American way when the show itself can't get the numbers right. Host Ryan Seacrest announced at the top of Wednesday night's "Idol" capper that only 13,000 votes separated the two contestants out of 24 million. Then, two hours later, he made a correction, telling all of us brain-addled fans that it was, in fact, only 1,335 votes between them.

Man, I thought, not possible. That makes George Bush's election over Al Gore look like a landslide. Then you think of Florida and the U.S.

Supreme Court, and you realize anything is possible.

Trouble is, when you do the math, both of Seacrest's figures were wrong by whopping margins. If, as we were told time and again, Ruben got 50.28 percent of the vote and Aiken got 49.72 percent, the real difference between them was 134,400 votes. Well, an inch is as good as a mile. Besides, confusion over the numbers is fitting. Last night's show seemed like a political convention anyway — including the bombast, the state-by-state vote results, the favorite-son posters, the hometown crowds and the confetti.

FREE VIDEO START ▶

Ryan Seacrest talks with Katie Couric about the final tally that gave Ruben Studdard the win.

If at times the production strutted like it was crossed with a tent revival (complete with gospel choir in a reprise of Tuesday's sing-off) and a Vegas stage show-cum-lounge act (featuring a chorus line of "Idol" finalists practicing for their tour), that was all to the good. The show turned out to be more entertaining than I expected and more than it deserved to be. I'll settle for that, milking and all.

Postscript: O Canada! Gawd save 'em. They're planning a "Canadian Idol," to begin in Toronto on June 11. They've just launched the Web site. I don't even want to think about "American Juniors," the virgin child of "Idol," which premieres June 3. (My staff of thousands has phoned in its vote demanding that I never mention it again.)

May 27, 2003 / 11:23 a.m. ET

Calling Woodward and Bernstein: Nobody ever said "American Idol" was running a democracy, least of all the producers. But given thepeculiar voting arrangements for last week's Ruben Studdard-Clay Aiken showdown, it looks more and more like the version of democracy installed by the U.S. Supreme Court a couple of years ago.

I thought I wasn't going to have to write about "American Idol" again until next season. I've already had my say (too many times for my own sanity) about the show's flawed voting system and was even willing to overlook hundreds upon hundreds of e-mails from Clay Aiken fans that they was robbed.

But now comes unequivocal proof — reported by the Evansville Courier

& Press in Indiana — that Cinergy Communications took 169,382 misdialed phone calls intended for Aiken and 72,114 for Studdard during the three-hour voting period for last Tuesday's finals — all because of a glitch having to do with changed phone keypads.

Cynergy, a telecommunications company in Evansville, provides telephone service throughout the Midwest and the South, according to the newspaper. What's really interesting is that the glitch let an independent observer see a huge swath of 241,496 real votes and revealed an actual voting pattern, something the show's producers have never allowed.

That pattern — more than 2 to 1 in Aiken's favor — throws the show's results into doubt even if the margin for Studdard's win is only narrowed and not overturned from that swath alone, and even if it's not a scientifically weighted poll. But as Courier & Press reporter Rich Davis writes, "If this were a political election instead of an entertainment contest Aiken might seek a recount and call [Cynergy] as a witness ..."

That's being optimistic. Our great democracy has shown that counts and recounts yield doubtful results. Anyway, as they say in "Idol'-land, both finalists are winners all the way, n'est-ce pas?

May 28, 2003 / 11:32 a.m. ET

Last call for 9/11 memorial competition: Today's the day. Officials will be all ears for anyone who wants to put in his or her two cents about the World Trade Center Site Memorial Competition. They're holding an open forum, beginning at 6 p.m. ET, in lower Manhattan. Members of the competition jury will be there, too. And the forum will be Webcast live.

Now why do I say "two cents," as though public opinion doesn't count for much? For three reasons. One is that the Lower Manhattan Development Corp., the agency charged with overseeing the competition, has lowered the profile of the forum.

As much as the LMDC wants to know what the public thinks, it doesn't want the sort of debacle that led to scrapping the original Ground Zero development plans after a "Listening to the City" forum of 4,500 city residents, experts and 9/11 victims' families. Although that turned out to be a good thing in the end, leading to the creation of much more imaginative proposals, it was a huge embarrassment at first and caused unexpected and unwanted delays.

The second reason is that the LMDC now knows from experience that, for all its wisdom, the public can be misguided when it comes to technical issues and pertinent details of such a complex undertaking as Ground Zero redevelopment. This often leaves the debate to lobbying groups with special interests. And while they can move things along by articulating the public's key concerns, they can also mire the debate in narrow, contentious arguments.

The third reason is that, unlike the urban architectural competition, this one will be decided solely by a 13-person jury of experts. The jury has said it is willing to listen to the public in terms of its needs and desires, and there is a representative of the families of the victims of 9/11 on the jury. But it and LMDC officials have also said the jury is not likely to be influenced by the public in terms of aesthetics and how the design fits the ideological meaning of a 9/11 memorial.

In the meantime: It looks like the jury will have plenty of designs to choose from. The LMDC says more than 7,000 people from all 50 states and more than 80 countries have registered for the competition. Tomorrow — May 29 — is the last day to register. (Registration will end at 5 p.m.) The competition is open to "anyone, anywhere in the world, 18 years of age or older, regardless of professional accreditation." The entry fee is $25. Here are the guidelines. The design proposals will be accepted during a three-week period (June 9-30). A winning design will be selected in the fall.

Paramount Pictures

FREE VIDEO START ▶

Bob Hope singing "Thanks for the Memory" in "The Big Broadcast of 1938."

May 30, 2003 / 7:46 a.m. ET

The long life of Bob Who? Now that Bob Hope has turned 100, we can all take a deep breath. Yesterday's fanfare was well deserved. Anyone who lasts that long ought to be congratulated.

I wonder, though, how many movie-goers and couch potatoes under the age of 30 ever gave him much if any thought before yesterday? For all Hope's fame and achievement, it just may be they'd never heard of him.

I took a poll of my staff of thousands. Except for one entertainment nerd who actually saw "Road to Zanzibar," not one had ever seen a movie of Hope's. Only two had ever heard of Dorothy Lamour. The rest said they had heard of Bing Crosby because of the song "White Christmas," but they'd never heard Hope sing his signature tune "Thanks for the Memory."

Ol' Ski Nose doesn't get out much anymore. So he's probably unaware of his decline in popularity. Lucky for him.

So little was made of Katharine Hepburn's recent milestone — she turned 95 on May 7 — you'd never have known she was still alive. Hepburn always was more reclusive than Hope. Certainly more aloof. When she turns 100, if I'm still around, I'll be sure to let you know. She's not regarded as the greatest American screen actress for nothing.

May 30, 2003 / 11:34 a.m. ET

Is Sean Penn mightier than the sword? Sean Penn has taken a full-page stunner of an ad in The New York Times this morning — a real cry from the heart about his trip to Iraq before the war, why he went and what it meant.

Called "Kilroy's Still Here," it's at least 3,500 words by my rough estimate and set in type that will make you go blind. But it's filled with emotion, personal vignettes about himself as a father, about his children, about his father, a decorated soldier in World War II, and most of all with righteous indignation about his country.

Not since the McCarthy era has any actor of his caliber stood up so staunchly and at such length for his principles. (OK, maybe Tim Robbins, except they're not in the same league as actors.) "Kilroy's Still Here" does not have the ring of Lillian Hellman's famous declaration: "I cannot and will not cut my conscience to fit this year's fashions." But while it lacks the vigor of memorable phrase-making, it strikes a powerful note just the same.

Some people will regard the piece as self-serving, partisan screed. But Penn declares: "I'm not a Democrat, not a Republican, not a Green, not aligned with any party. ... I'm an American and I fear that I and our people are on the verge of losing our flag. ... That same flag that took me so long to love, respect and protect, threatens to become a haunting banner of murder, greed, and treason against our principles, honored history, Constitution, and our own mothers and fathers."

And he really lights into the Bush administration: "Our flag has been waving, it seems, in servicing a regime change significantly benefiting US corporations." He continues: "We found that our Secretary of State presented plagiarized evidence of WMD in Iraq to the American people and the world. ... We see Bechtel, we see Halliburton. We see Bush, Cheney, Rumsfeld, Wolfowitz, Powell, Rice, Perle, Ashcroft ...We see no WMD's [weapons of mass destruction]. We see dead young Americans. We see no WMD's. We see dead Iraqi civilians. We see no WMD's. We see chaos in the Baghdad streets. But no WMD's."

(He's not alone in wondering what happened to the weapons that Bush went to war over. Plenty of others are asking the same question: Where are the WMDs?)

Back in December, when Penn came under attack for his trip to Baghdad, I defended him as "a guy with a head on his shoulders." I think that's truer than ever. He's also someone with heart.

I tried to get hold of Penn to find out if he paid for the ad himself. But he's shooting a movie at the moment in northern California. His spokesperson, Mara Buxbaum, says he did pay for it. I was so glad to hear that that I forgot to ask, how much? Meantime, Penn won't be commenting on "Kilroy," she added. "He's going to let the essay speak for itself."

I was fast enough on my feet to ask, What's the movie? Answer: A little indie thing called "The Assassination of Richard Nixon." Uh-oh. Or as they said the other night on "The Daily Show": "Journalists [and I suppose actors] have no role regarding the war in Iraq. The government will tell us what we need to know. People who disagree are 'Hitler-loving queers.'"

Share your perspective on entertainment and the arts with Jan Herman. MSNBC is not responsible for the content of Internet links.

Entries from June 2 to July 7, 2003
(Some links may be nonfunctional.)
Back to 'The Juice'

LATEST UPDATES

June 2, 2003 / 11:34 a.m. ET

Jackson, Streisand, and the NY Phil: I'm nowhere near anybody's Hall of Fame, but I feel like Roger Clemens this morning. (Oh c'mon. The Yankee pitcher who's having trouble clinching his 300th victory.)

Unlike him, though, I've got some really good relief. The sad saga of Michael Jackson is covered in our two-story package that pretty much says it all. And if you want the latest on Barbra Streisand's dumb move, look no further than our commentary on celebrity stupidity.

I suppose I could tell you that the New York Philharmonic is going to leave Lincoln Center (after more than 40 years in residence there) and move back to Carnegie Hall (its former home). The signatures aren't on the dotted line yet and the move won't come for a few years. But it sounds like a done deal. I just received a hasty electronic press release from the chairmen of both Carnegie Hall and the Philharmonic, rushed out to catch up with this morning's front-page story. *(Free registration required.)*

Consider yourself told. Now can I go back to bed and nurse my cough? (Don't worry. It's not SARS. No fever. You can't catch that stuff through a computer, right?)

June 3, 2003 / 8:44 a.m. ET

The bug's got me: Considering the flood of hate mail that's come in about Sean Penn, I don't know if he's mightier than the sword. But I do know the bug I've got is mightier than me. That may be more than you wanted to know. But unless my cough lets up between now and the end of the day, I'll see ya tomorrow.

June 6, 2003 / 11:47 a.m. ET

Much better, thanks: All those get-well messages were greatly appreciated. They and a lot of tea did the trick.

June 6, 2003 / 11:52 a.m. ET

The big bamboozle: You may have noticed by now that I've never once mentioned Jayson Blair, the staff writer who bamboozled The New York Times with a whole lot of bogus reporting. I've steered clear of the subject for many reasons besides the fact that I have friends at The Times.

But so many readers have asked my opinion about the mess Blair made that if I didn't add my two cents to what has become a discussion without end, I'd be shirking my responsibility to this column — something The Juice staff of thousands, which regards me as a veritable Mencken, won't let me do.

Even then I might not have said anything, because what is left to say? The bamboozling has been examined from so many angles — from the decline of ethics, morality and Western civilization, to race and diversity, affirmative action and management issues, let alone the pathology of lying and the decline of journalism — that it seems impossible to say anything fresh.

With the resignation yesterday of the two top editors of The Times, however, there is no choice. I must tell you the one simple thing that nobody has said, at least not that I have seen written anywhere: Blair could have spent less time and energy reporting his stories for real than the time and energy it took to concoct bogus stories and cover his tracks.

For someone in as much of a hurry to make it to the top as he was ... oh, never mind. End of comment. I'm no Mencken (sorry to disillusion you, staff). The lessons to be drawn from this whole sorry episode will be drawn by The Times itself. *(Free registration required.)* It's in the best position to draw them and in the best position to benefit from them.

June 6, 2003 / 11:54 a.m. ET

Equal censorship for all: I see that Wal-Mart has announced a cover-up of all those racy women's magazines — Glamour, Cosmopolitan, Marie Claire and Redbook. The retail giant is bringing out its dreaded "U-shaped blinders" to hide the cover photos and language deemed offensive to its shoppers.

That's only fair. You may recall Wal-Mart took a bunch of racy men's magazines off its shelves last month. You may also recall that we criticized the company as a hypocrite and censor here, here, here, here, and here. It's still a censor, but at least it's being a tad less hypocritical. Nice to know The Juice has so much influence. Now what about all those guns and ammo it's still selling?

June 7, 2003 / 11:43 a.m. ET

The pecksniffery of media pundits: Squawking heads on cable TV are the worst offenders. But few can match the sanctimony of the New York Post on the subject of Howell Raines and The New York Times.

Here's the faux classified ad the Post ran on its front page on Friday, the day after Raines resigned from The Times, under the headline "**Paper of Wreckage**."

HELP WANTED
EXECUTIVE EDITOR
For Manhattan-based
newspaper of record. Lefty
francophile with diversity
obsession and knack for
plugging circulation leaks.
Allergic to Republicans ok.
Tolerance for high taxes a must.
America-basher a plus.
Respect for facts optional.

It's meant as a joke, of course. But all you have to do is reverse the terms, and it's an exact description of the Post itself, a daily rag that could not stand up to an eye-blink of scrutiny when it comes to fairness and factuality in its news columns:

HELP NEEDED
Manhattan-based
tabloid of sleaze. Righty
sycophant with anti-diversity
obsession and knack for
boosting circulation.
Allergic to Democrats a must.
Intolerance for taxes a must,
especially for Post co-chairman
billionaire Rupert Murdoch.

Clinton-bashing required.
Respect for facts?
Never heard of 'em.

June 9, 2003 / 10:47 a.m. ET

The diplomacy of a puppet regime: Kofi Anan, Secretary-General of the United Nations, was asked the other day whether he regards Elmo, of "Sesame Street," as a special U.N. representative. This was asked tongue-in-cheek, but it was not a trick question.

"Absolutely," Anan replied. "He's very special. In fact, I invited him to come and work at the U.N. and he said, 'Sure. Do I get a Nobel Prize?' And I said, 'If you work very hard.' He said, 'How long would it take, three days?' So you see how sharp he is."

The question was not meant to denigrate Anan, diplomats in general, the U.N. or "Sesame Street." It was asked at a benefit dinner for the Sesame Workshop, which was honoring Anan for his efforts in helping children around the world. Their education, particularly for girls, and their welfare are part of the U.N.'s many worthy projects.

We can't resist offering the rest of the exchange.

Question: You don't think it would go to his head in gaining power and setting up his own puppet regime in a country somewhere?

Anan: I think muppets and children don't have those kinds of problems. It's we grown-ups [who do].

Anan, the consummate diplomat, not only proved that he has a wonderful sense of humor but also that he can diffuse what might be seen as a subversive attempt to equate Elmo with Gee Dubya and still make the same point.

June 10, 2003 / 6:43 p.m. ET

Let's all turn the page: Suddenly people are reading books. If it's not Hillary Clinton's pseudo-memoir "Living History," it's Dan Brown's pseudo-thriller "The Da Vinci Code." Both of them are big best sellers.

Why pseudo? Because, if you believe today's devastating review by Michiko Kakutani *(free registration required)*, Clinton's book "has the overprocessed taste of a stump speech [and] the calculated polish of a string of anecdotes to be delivered on a television chat show."

Kakutani writes that this "wildly hyped" memoir is "a mishmash of pious platitudes about policy" and "robotic asides about her official duties in Washington," along with "familiar accounts" of how she went "from Goldwater girl to liberal student activist to high-powered lawyer to first lady

290

to senator from New York" — all pretty much cribbed from two of her earlier books, "It Takes a Village" and "An Invitation to the White House." Kakutani could be wrong, but I doubt it — even if she *is* a critic.

When it comes to "The Da Vinci Code," I can testify from personal experience. I read the book because the reviews raved about it — one even said it was among the greatest thrillers ever written — and then I ran into this smart-looking professor type at the gym who was carrying it around with him. "Any good?" I asked. "Brilliant," he said.

So here's what happened: The first chapter started out well enough, but then the book fell off a cliff. The characters couldn't hold my interest. They might have had they not been so paper-thin. The "fascinating esoterica" about the Catholic Church, ancient secret societies and the meaning of the Holy Grail piqued my curiosity — until all of it became a prop. I pushed on to the end, hoping things would improve. They never did. The prose and the plot belong to a boy's adventure.

Save your money and read the latest *about* "The Da Vinci Code." It's actually more of a mystery than the book.

June 11, 2003 / 12:01 p.m. ET

Puccini in the park: In a reprieve from rain, the skies cleared above Manhattan and roughly 100,000 people came last night to the Great Lawn in Central Park for a free concert performance of the Metropolitan Opera singing Puccini's "Turandot." The lush beauty of the music, the cool breezes and the grandeur of the New York skyline in the distance made the world seem right.

Stretched out on blankets as far as the eye could see, we were more than a band of brothers. We were polyglot humanity. We had gathered there for pleasure, not for combat. It was a huge picnic with a sublime soundtrack under the stars, a reminder that life can be civilized even in a time of turmoil.

The harsh realities of war and terror were not lost on us. Their presence beyond the park underscored our luck. We seemed to have entered a safe zone, where conflict was banished from our minds. Thank you, Puccini. Thank you, Met Opera. Thank you, City of New York.

June 12, 2003 / 9:34 a.m. ET

Where is Kidman when you need her? Nicole Kidman's magic did not rub off on her "Moulin Rouge" director. Baz Luhrmann brought a different kind of musical to Broadway — Puccini's "La Bohème" — and it's closing on June 29 after an eight-month run. That's respectable, but "respectable" is not good enough on Broadway or anywhere else these days. The show will lose roughly $6 million for its investors.

Maybe if Kidman had starred in it — and maybe if Luhrmann had staged it in English instead of the original Italian — it would have become a spectacular hit. The production itself was nothing if not spectacular, and so was the buzz. Luhrmann's idea was to lend his Hollywood style to Broadway and do for the stage what he'd done for movies: Bring an edge to musical theater.

He transplanted the setting of "La Bohème" from 1830s Paris to 1950s Paris and cast young, opera singers who looked sexy. Unlike the smash-hit "Rent," which is a watered-down rock version of "La Bohème," he mounted a real opera, or as real as Broadway can take. The production even had English super-titles.

Unfortunately, Luhrmann's ambition sailed over the heads of middle-brow musical-lovers and beneath the taste of real opera-goers. His biggest mistake, however, was not casting Kidman. So what if she's not an opera singer. She could have lip-synched her arias. Who besides the critics would have minded? The "Mama Mia" crowds?

Meantime the Metropolitan Opera's real Puccini is wowing them for free in New York City's parks. And Luhrmann's "La Bohème" will have a limited run early next year in Los Angeles (Jan. 9-March 7) at the Ahmanson Theatre. It will then move on to London in the spring (May 30-Oct. 30, 2004). Both L.A. and London want the show even without Kidman. How nice.

June 13, 2003 / 11:59 a.m. ET

Peck vs. Heston, fistfight on the prairie: If you had to pick the two movie stars who stood most fiercely at opposite ends of the political spectrum it would be Gregory Peck and Charlton Heston. Peck, who died yesterday , was the epitome of the Hollywood liberal. Heston, who is apparently afflicted by Alzheimer's disease, has been the epitome of the Hollywood conservative.

Of Peck's nearly 60 films, "The Big Country" was the only one he ever made with Heston. It is often overlooked, unfairly, and went unappreciated again in Peck's obituary.

For "A Talent for Trouble," my biography of Willy Wyler, who directed that film, I interviewed both Peck and Heston, and both talked about a particular scene in it that they regarded retrospectively as a vivid commentary on the characters they played, the views they represented, the violence they engendered and, implicitly, their own disagreements.

"The Big Country" was a sprawling, contemporary, anti-macho Western, a huge production in which Peck starred as the prissy-seeming hero from back East. Heston played opposite him as the chief ranch-hand heavy. (Heston wanted to turn down the role. "There's no way to put this without sounding vain," he told me. "But when you're a leading man, the first thing you ask is, 'Is the picture about me?' It wasn't, of course. The picture was about Gregory Peck.")

When the movie premiered in 1958, it received a cool-to-mixed reception from the critics. But the vast Western landscape — photographed in gorgeous color and shown in wide-screen theaters — drew unqualified raves, particularly for its unexpected philosophical implications. Critics pointed out that it dwarfed the people, made them seem puny against the immensity of nature.

This was in keeping with the picture's anti-macho theme, especially a fistfight between Peck and Heston that was meant to debunk the old Western cliché about settling scores. What was unusual about the scene was how it was filmed. Wyler had placed Peck and Heston in the middle of a bare, sun-parched prairie and set up his camera on a high ridge, looking down at them from about 100 yards away.

(Heston recalled thinking: "I don't know what lens he has on, but we can't be larger than ants in that frame." When he tried to spot Wyler and the camera crew, they were barely distinguishable. "I thought, 'He has to be kidding. He's doing this to be mean. He can't use this footage.'")

It took a full day to make the sequence, but it showed how exhausting a fistfight could be and, as Heston later realized, underscored "what really was an overriding theme — the futility of violence." Heston and Peck flail away at each other until they can hardly stand. They're covered with sweat and dust. In medium shots, their blows sound like muffled thumps. In long shots, they can't be heard at all — and the silence is telling. By the end of the fight they're too weak to land any blows. And when they both call it quits, Peck says to Heston: "Now tell me … What did we prove?"

Gregory Peck, rest in peace.

June 15, 2003 / 11:03 a.m. ET

Readers write back: Lots of e-mail in recent days on Gregory Peck and William Wyler's "The Big Country" (a film with a cult following), Charlton Heston, Puccini, opera, Nicole Kidman, Baz Luhrmann and a sex change for yours truly (not for the first time).

Margie
Marshfield, Wisconsin
Nice story.[Peck vs. Heston, fistfight on the prairie.] Thanks. Mr. Peck was my all-time favorite.

Nayanika
New Delhi, India

FREE VIDEO START ▶

NBC's Keith Morrison reports on Gregory Peck's career, which included such classics as "Roman Holiday" and "To Kill a Mockingbird."

Two heavyweights, both of them. May Peck's soul rest in peace. May Heston have strength to brave out Alzheimer's. Wyler is a master craftsman and we miss great directors like him.

John Bundick
Saint Joseph, Mi.
Re: "Peck vs. Heston, fistfight on the prairie": One of your best columns. I appreciate your insight and the straightforward, unbiased approach used to relay these observations. Because of his politics, few entertainment industry observers are able to discuss Mr. Heston in an objective (respectful?) manner.

G. Lustre
Lebanon, Tenn.
What a perfect way to honor both men, in contrasting them and using "The Big Country" to epitomize it — plus remind us all of a great movie.

Walter Mckay
Vancouver, B.C., Canada
Has President Bush seen this movie?

Chuck Hardesty
Chesterfield, Missouri
I'd like to thank you for writing that article. "The Big Country" has long been one of my favorite movies. Another memorable scene that exemplified the character played by Peck was when he rode and broke the horse "Ole Thunder" with no one except the ranch hand Ramon to witness. Peck admonished Ramon to tell no one about it. Later, Ramon unwittingly reveals that secret to Peck's fiancee and her friend and states what I consider to be

one of the most memorable lines of the movie, portraying both Peck and the character he played: "A man like this is very rare."

Debbie Hollingsworth
Jonesboro, Arkansas
I love "The Big Country." It is one of my favorite favorites. It's the whole story. What really makes a man a man? What is love really about? Why do we do the things we do? It answers all of those questions.

(Here are <u>more reader e-mails about Peck, "The Big Country" and Heston</u>.)

Now, about Dan Brown's best-selling thriller "The Da Vinci Code" and Hillary Clinton's best-selling memoir "Living History":
Jen Stelling
Albany N.Y.
I read your column a few times a week (I read it as long as it's not about "American Idol" or reality TV). Glad to see that someone panned "The DaVinci Code." I read so many positive reviews but was overwhelmed by its corny plot and smug hero when I actually tried to read the book. Plus the writing was amateurish and clumsy. I thought perhaps that I had picked up the wrong book, since so many raved.

Steve Berner
Boca Raton, Fla.
Thank heavens for a voice of sanity amid the hype! I have worked in various areas of the "book biz" for most of my life and am still amazed at the way PR can replace quality in so many cases. Hillary's book, whatever its flaws, at least has a certain historical import, but "Da Vinci"??? Come on! How many people are really slogging through a novel that creates "suspense" by the simple trick of withholding even the most basic of "revelations" by digressing for 10 pages of "background" time and time and time again? Anyone wanting to read a book on a similar subject that really does deliver the goods, should hie themselves to their local print purveyor and get Daniel Silva's less-promoted, but infinitely superior "The Confessor."

(Here are <u>more emails about "The Da Vinci Code" and the Catholic Church</u>.)

April
Ocean Park, Maine
If Hillary's book is anything like her mock interview with Barbara Walters, I don't want anything to do with it. I couldn't even force myself to get through the television monologue. That had to be the lowest point in Barbara Walters' career. Hillary was sappy, robotic, contrived, and OVER-REHEARSED with every word she uttered. Gag me! No, gag HER!!! Somebody, PLEASE!!!

(Here are more e-mails about Hillary Clinton and her memoir.)

Changing the subject:

Norman Dishotsky
Palo Alto, Calif.
Dear Juice, Great stuff on Puccini in Central Park. For those of us way out here on the West Coast, it's a delight to be transported by a first-hand report of culture and civility in the heart of New York. Thank you and keep it coming.

Shane Hockin
Tallahassee, Fla.
Wow. Puccini in the Park. That sounds so awesome. Almost makes me wish I lived in good ol' NYC. I wonder if Tallahassee, Florida, has an opera? If so, I wonder if they'll play for free in Kleman Plaza for me? Probably not. Oh well. It was nice hearing about your experience.

Caolainn
Toronto, Ontario, Canada
I journeyed from Toronto Ontario to NYC specifically to see "La Bohème" on Broadway, and I was not disappointed in the least! As a movie, musical and opera afficionado, I saw it as a spectacular fusion of all these arts. The only reason it didn't perform well at the box office was because there are not enough individuals who are fluid in their entertainment choices to attend it.

Joe Burinskas
Denver, Colo.
Are you serious about Nicole Kidman in "La Bohème?" She is as bad an actress as she would be a singer, and is a shining example of all that's wrong

with Hollywood today. As for the Baz-stard's pathetic little attempt at "art," his staging was overblown and unmoving, a clear example of someone with a lot of ambition and very little talent trying to show what he is capable of on Broadway. Good riddance to this spectacular garbage.

No, Joel. I wasn't serious.

And finally:

Joseph M. Frates
Laurel Springs
The main thing about Jan Herman's "The Juice" is that it seems she's usually right on the money when it comes to her summaries, being concise, short and right to the point. She doesn't beat around the proverbial bush with anecdotes and fill-ins, just to lengthen her articles. One (such as I) can scan through and know exactly what she's trying to convey to her readers. Thanks !!!!

Boy, that's nice to hear. I thank you, and my staff of thousands thanks you, and my late mother and father thank you, too. The last time I looked, though, I was still a guy. You're not the first reader who's suggested a sex change. I suppose it would be an adventure. But my wife might object. I'll ask her.

I guess it wasn't finally:

Mohamed
Toronto, Ontario, Canada
I want to say, sir, that your writing, in its eloquent simplicity surpasses its subject matter, and makes us think about all the violence and hatred in the world today. Beyond all the intellectual, financial, religious, and geo-political polemics, we are all just human beings and in the words of Mr. Peck, when we harm each other for any purpose, "Now tell me. What did we prove?" Thank you, once again, sir, for a brilliant and well-written tribute to an artist and social activist who had a positive effect on countless lives over many decades. And will continue to do so.

I asked my staff of thousands not to post this email. It would be boastful, I said. Someone might think poorly of me. I'm really a bashful kind of guy.

But hundreds of the thousands simply out-voted me. What could I do? This is a democracy.

June 17, 2003 / 2:41 p.m. ET

The gunfight at the GZ corral: Nobody ever said rebuilding Ground Zero would be easy. But trouble brewing among the principal players — architect Daniel Libeskind (whose "Memory Foundations" design was chosen as the template for redevelopment), Larry Silverstein (the commercial developer who holds the lease on office space at the site), and the Port Authority of New York and New Jersey (the public agency that owns the site) — has all the earmarks of a gunfight.

Libeskind is reported by the New York Post to be "demanding greater control over key projects" to the consternation of Silverstein and the Port Authority. Since it's the Post doing the reporting, however, you have to read between the lines. Which is not difficult when an unnamed source is prominently quoted as criticizing Libeskind for "overreaching."

In other words, Libeskind's ox is being gored because he wants to be the "lead designer on signature elements" of his redevelopment plan, such as the 1,776-foot Freedom Tower and the underground transportation hub that will also anchor the site. His critics' ostensible beef is that Libeskind has "no experience building office towers or major transportation projects."

The real beef is that Libeskind wants to preserve the integrity of his plan. I can't blame him for trying to keep it from being watered down or "developed" into oblivion by commercial and political interests that seem to have little regard for him, less for the idealism of his plan, and least perhaps for the 9/11 victims' families who have raised their voices in his support.

So he is attacked as a "control freak" in a Post editorial, while his wife, Nina — a strong-willed, square-jawed advocate who does not suffer fools gladly — is attacked in the news columns as a virago.

There are other things at stake besides the integrity of the plan, of course. (Did someone say money? How about oodles of money?) Still, I say "hogwash" to Libeskind's critics.

I guess it's not enough that trouble is brewing in Iraq. Here in New York, where our Bush-styled "homeland" took the biggest hit, we have our own troubles. Except for the fact that Ground Zero has become an American symbol reaching far beyond the precincts of Manhattan, these troubles would be parochial.

June 18, 2003 / 8:13 a.m. ET

Rushdie's 'Fury' vs. Ginsberg's 'Howl': The <u>50th anniversary of City Lights</u>, poet Lawrence Ferlinghetti's landmark bookstore in San Francisco, got me to wondering what makes a piece of writing last. And I don't mean "<u>Harry Potter.</u>"

Sept. 5, 2001 - Author Salman Rushdie talks about "Fury" with Matt Lauer on NBC.

Let us compare mythologies (*pace*, Leonard Cohen): Consider two similarly titled works: Salman Rushdie's novel "<u>Fury</u>" (published in 2001, a week before 9/11, by Random House) and Allen Ginsberg's poem "<u>Howl</u>" (published in 1956 by City Lights, in its Pocket Poets series).

Both take their inspiration from New York City. Rushdie's "Fury" is a formerly up-to-the-minute rant nearer to us by half a century than Ginsberg's "Howl." The contrast between them, however, underscores nothing so much as the difference between facile word-slinging and a cry from the heart, between glibness and desperation.

<u>Allen Ginsberg</u> was a mid-century outsider, a social pariah railing against Mammon. <u>Salman Rushdie</u> is an insider (especially since the fatwah) posing as an outsider who rails against celebrity.

Although Rushdie's frame of reference is global and his intentions large, "Fury" has the sound of self-importance. It demonstrates the emptiness of words tossed off with cynical aplomb. "Howl" glows with the incandescence of deep feelings; it demonstrates the tensile strength of words that five decades on apply more than ever.

\Here is the main character in "Fury" describing what he ironically calls a golden age. The catalogue, though true, is stereotypical and already outdated. The words are cribbed from newsprint and deprived of energy like dull journalistic phrases:

"While the greenback was all-powerful and America bestrode the world, psychological disorders and aberrations of all sorts were having a field day back home. Under the self-satisfied rhetoric of this repackaged, homogenized America, this America with the twenty-two million new jobs and the highest home-owning rate in history, this balanced-budget, low-deficit, stock-owning Mall America, people were stressed-out, cracking up, and talking about it all day long in superstrings of moronic clichés."

Here is Ginsberg in "Howl" describing the stressed-out, cracked-up

299

casualties of a similar if earlier "golden age." The writing feels spontaneous, improvised (though it surely isn't), the words wrenched from life:

"I saw the best minds of my generation destroyed by madness, starving hysterical naked, / dragging themselves through the negro streets at dawn looking for an angry fix, / angelheaded hipsters burning for the ancient heavenly connection to the starry dynamo in the machinery of night, / who poverty and tatters and hollow-eyed and high sat up smoking in the supernatural darkness of cold-water flats floating across the tops of cities contemplating jazz, / who bared their brains to Heaven under the El ..."

Is the difference between "Fury" and "Howl" a matter of sensibility? Of subject? Of focus? Of period? Is it simply a matter of tone? It's certainly not a matter of belief, because Rushdie and Ginsberg both come down on the same side of things. Yet only "Howl," courtesy of City Lights, will be remembered long into the future.

June 19, 2003 / 1:43 p.m. ET

Readers write on Rushdie, Ginsberg: And I thought everyone was a movie critic. Turns out everyone is a literary critic. Who knew? I'll be posting a separate page of e-mails in reply to yesterday's City Lights item . But for now here's a taste of the way the deluge is running:

Alli Smith
Joplin, Mo.
"Rushdie couldn't carry Ginsberg's pencil bag. Yes he is an excellent writer, but there hasn't been and can never be another Ginsberg."

Ashesh Ghose
Mumbai, India
"Way to go Jan. Allen Ginsberg was a genuine poet. Rushdie is a genuine fraud."

Tim Ryback
"I have always been a great fan of 'Howl' and have never understood why — or needed to, for that matter. But thank you for remnding me how remarkable a piece of writing it is, even after a half century, and especially when placed against contemporary competitors who by all rights should hold our attention more easily, but do not."

Mark Fishbein
New York City
"'Howl' is a poem, using the presentation of words and phrases which have an inner music, a beat. 'Fury' is prose, feels and acts like prose. Comparing the two is like comparing a symphony to a string quartet."

Vincent Scorza
Patchogue, N.Y.
"In 50 years will anyone know who the heck Rushdie was?"

Tatiana
Calgary, Canada
"Couldn't agree more. I just read 'Fury,' late I'm sure, and was too disappointed by the fake, almost-bored-sounding writing."

Piotr
Millburn, N.J.
"A well-intentioned article; however, you are giving Rushdie too much credit by even mentioning him alongside Ginsberg. Ginsberg was one of the greatest poets of the last century in any language. He will be read for generations. In this context it is not even important that Rushdie is an opportunist — all that he wrote will disappear from memory very quickly, even 'Harry Potter' will outlast it by a long shot."

Ruby P.
New York City
"I knew Allen Ginsberg's dad. [Ginsberg's] father was an English teacher at Rutgers University and his son absorbed his attitude in life. Also inherited his way with words. ... Allen's work is a piece of literature that makes you think about your world."

Sheila
Denver
"Oh, Jan, your prejudice is showing. I thought Mr. Rushdie's comments very easy to read, quite relevant and an honest observation of America today. I don't necessarily disagree with Ginsberg, [but] his poem is hardly readable *in comparison* to Rushdie's paragraph. Your comparison is such that you are eating a piece of apple pie while discussing your distaste for chocolate cake."

Yes, Sheila. I'm biased. That's what it says at the top of this column: "Arts and culture news with attitude." Something else I should mention by way of full disclosure: Once upon a long time ago, I worked at City Lights Books.

June 20, 2003 / 3:37 p.m. ET

The children who know what they see: In the 13 months I've been posting The Juice, I've written about Ground Zero, Danny Pearl, the Holocaust, Wal-Mart and a lot of other things that prick the conscience. But I've never once mentioned Rwanda. A new photo exhibit reminds me of this. It's called "Through the Eyes of Children: The Rwanda Project."

Normally, you'd have to go see it at Lincoln Center in New York, where the show is running through next Friday. But in fact you can see it online. All you have to do is click on the photo link below, and you will witness something extraordinary: pictures taken by children at the Imbabazi Orphanage in Gisenyi, Rwanda, many of whom were maimed and orphaned by the genocide of 1994.

One more paragraph, and I'll get out of the way: The orphanage is run by Rosamond Halsey Carr, an American who has lived in Rwanda for more than 50 of her 90 years. She introduced the children to David Jiranek, another American, who taught them how to take pictures. You may already know of Carr from her book, "Land of a Thousand Hills," or from her appearance in the movie "Gorillas in the Mist," which was filmed on location in Rwanda and was about her friend Dian Fossey.

Here are the photos. Go to "The Gallery" and click through them. They're listed by the photographers (on the right) with short biographies, too.

My staff of thousands thinks the single best photo in the show is Jacqueline's "Gadi" — an easy call, I'd say. ("Gadi" leads off the online exhibit. It also won First Prize for portraiture in the Camera Arts 2001 Annual Photo Contest.)

It's tougher to choose the best photographer. My overall favorite is Musa, who's 12. Not far behind is Twagira, also 12. Each of Musa's photos shows a stunning gift for mood and lighting ("Sitting on Rail") and for composition ("Bicycle at Wall"), and there isn't a mediocre shot in the bunch. I also love Imanizabayo's portfolio, especially "Man with Bike and Chairs" and "Girl with Tray." Seems to me that Uwamahoro's "Gate Watchman" and Umuhoza's "Watch Sellers" rank among the best individual shots, too. What do you think? Let me know your favorites.

Postscript: Don't overlook the flash-art documentary introduction. And be generous. The site is soliciting <u>contributions for the orphanage</u>. A $100 tax-deductible contribution gets you a 13-inch-by-19-inch print of your choice. A $1,000 contribution gets you 13 prints of the same photo or a single print of a photo by each of the 13 photographers.

June 23, 2003 / 11:54 a.m. ET

Read that book! Stop that door! I'm a "Harry Potter" illiterate. I don't say that with pride. And I don't say that with the shame All I know firsthand of "Harry Potter" is what I've seen in the movies, which I bet is what most people know of "Harry Potter" even if the latest book sold a <u>humongous 5 million copies</u> within a single day.

So "Harry Potter and the Order of the Phoenix" did better in the dollar department than <u>"The Hulk" on its opening weekend</u>? So Rick VanderKnyff, MSNBC.com's Potter specialist, thinks <u>it's a pretty good book</u>? So I'm looking in the rearview mirror at this gonzo pop-culture moment? So sue me.

I don't have enough doors in my house for those door-stoppers. I don't care if "Phoenix" stole the "Hulk's" thunder. I don't care if I'm a "Harry Potter" illiterate. The only adults I know who've read the "Potter" books did it because of their kids, or were in the business of reviewing books.

When I see adults reading a "Potter" on the subway, I wonder about them — the balding businessman in his suit and tie, the stylish secretary with her hair done in corn rows. I wonder: Is it really their "Illiad"? Has it become <u>the organizing myth of their culture</u> ? Or are they just trying to be kids again?

June 24, 2003 / 11:41 a.m. ET

Potterphilia reigneth: My "Harry Potter" illiteracy naturally provoked a ton of e-mail. Not so the item about the children of Rwanda, aka <u>the children who know what they see.</u> Well, we know what you care about.

Most of the Potter mail was thoughtful, (almost all of it touting author J.K. Rowling's brilliance as a storyteller); some of it was delusional and much of it professed pity for my ignorance. Which got me to rethinking yesterday's item, <u>the Rowling doorstop</u>.

Many wondered why I objected to "Harry Potter" being read by adults simply as well-crafted entertainment. I didn't object. I just said I hadn't participated. The "Potter" series is probably no better or worse than <u>"The Sopranos,"</u> or <u>"Band of Brothers,"</u> or Stephen King's novels, or even Tom Clancy's. Some of this stuff has more cachet and some less, but it's all just entertainment.

In the end many more people will have seen "The Hulk" than bought "Order of the Phoenix," even though Rowling's book stole the movie's opening-weekend, box-office thunder. The biggest book in the world still can't touch the latest sorry comic-book movie adaptation, or a season closer for "American Idol."

I'm guessing, though, that a lot of those five million purchased copies of "Phoenix" will be re-read many times over. In 20 years, kids reading the Potter books now will be passing them along to their own children. I don't think "The Hulk" will be handed down with quite the same reverence.

The "Harry Potter" series will be the pop-culture touchstone for a certain generation, if it's not already, in the same way the Beatles were for my generation, or the "Star Wars" movies were for another generation and, maybe, "The Brady Bunch" was for yet another (poor saps).

What was surprising was how many people took the bait and tried to argue for Rowling as the new Homer. Still, I've been persuaded to give "Potter" a try. Who knows, by summer's end I may become Jan Potterphilia Herman. Am I off the hook now?

Postscript: It would have been far more gratifying if as many e-mails had come in for the children of Rwanda as for the adults of Potter.

June 26, 2003 / 3:54 p.m. ET

Generosity begins in Canada: Are Canadians the world's most generous people, or what? I'm beginning to think they are. It's hard to know for sure, but one thing I'm certain of: Pound for pound, they put Americans to shame.

Is that an overstatement? Of course.

The other day, in a moment of despair that had my staff of thousands wringing its many hands, I complained that a flood of e-mail was flowing in about Harry Potter and only a trickle about the children who know what they see, aka "The Rwanda Project."

A disproportionate number of e-mails from Canadians suddenly began to arrive, like these:

Angela
Canada
"I hope your article about the children of Rwanda provoked more donations than it did e-mail. Because of it I decided to donate $100. I really thought some of the pictures were beautiful, and I hope that their talent isn't wasted!"

304

Sandee Johnston
Toronto, Canada

"I thoroughly enjoyed looking at all the pictures and am committed to donating $100 (U.S.) just to be able to get my favourite picture ('Hanging Corn' by Dusingizimana). Whether or not I'll be able to claim the donation through the Canadian tax office, I don't care as long as the monies go to where they should: the children. Rwanda and the genocide in the '90's really hit close to my heart so this was a great thing for me to find, through you. Thanks again.

PS: I'm a huge Harry Potter fan as well, have all 4 of the previous books and will be picking up the newest one tomorrow."

Scott van Leenen
Edmonton, Alberta, Canada (living in Tokyo)

"I am a Potter fan, though I was much more impressed with the Rwanda article. I have to thank you also. If it wasn't for you, I would have missed the site completely — to my loss. I bought a print. I agreed with your assessment — I bought 'Sitting on rail.' I also agree that Musa is the best photographer. The resilience of these kids is remarkable. I will buy more photos as I can afford. I should have sent an e-mail giving my appreciation sooner. I thought of doing so when I was exploring the Rwanda site, but I got distracted by the photos and donating and forgot. Just wanted to let you know that at least one reader was deeply affected, moved, and appreciative of your Rwanda story. Thank you."

Catherine Stojak
Montreal, Quebec, Canada

"Here is something that I want you to know. I took action when I read [about] those wonderful children from Rwanda. I contacted the Director, who replied to me by the next day.

"Here is my plan: I will hold a HUGE fundraiser for these children. I am actively working on raising the awareness of the plight of these children who have seen and experienced way too much. Their story is compelling and hugely emotional for me. Exploring their website, I had to get a hold of myself (I was in my office at the time) as I kept crying. I will do everything I can to get the retailers, salons, and restaurant to support my initiative to help these kids.

Bottom line Jan: I heard it from you. I went to the website because of you. I am doing something because of you. Hope this helps."

Sure does. Meantime, am I saying Americans are not generous? Not if I value my life. In fact, these messages came, too:

Rachel
Spartanburg, S.C.
"I'm not exactly a fan of yours, though I do agree with your opinions. I just thought you would like to know that your item on the children of Rwanda did not go ignored. I went to the site and bought two of the photographs that I found most interesting. 'Gadi' by Jacqueline and 'Boy on Beach' by Musa. My husband wants to get 'Man with Bike and Chairs' by Imanizabayo for his office wall. Thank you for letting me know about such a worthwhile cause."

Shane Hockin
Tallahassee, Fla.
"I can't speak for everyone, but when I read the children of Rwanda website, I got out my checkbook. There did not seem to be anything else to say about it, so I wrote in about Harry."

Here are <u>many more e-mails</u>. But this one you have to see:

John Smith
Heathsville, Va.
"It would be natural for you to love the Canadians. Like you, they belong to the far left of liberal and they hate America. A perfect marriage of fallacious thought. ... America haters stick together, and pat each other on the back for their fascism."

Leftwing fascists, huh? Why not rightwing communists? How about bilateral libertarians? Or ambidextrous freeloaders? I'm open to suggestions.

June 27, 2003 / 11:43 a.m. ET
Making do without Camus: My abiding attraction to French novelist Michel Houellebecq's writing forces me to post a <u>review of his latest book, "Lanzarote,"</u> which hits the scale at a mere 87 pages. That's a tenth the size of the latest <u>"Harry Potter"</u> and, for the right readers I would hope, 10 times more rewarding.

The review, by Rod Liddle in The Spectator, is a peculiar notice — admiring yet not. It begins: "'Slight,' I think, is the adjective I'm looking for here." Liddle goes on to remark that the book gives "terrible value for money" because it's "little more than a blueprint for last year's brilliant 'Platform' but all that notwithstanding, you would not wish to miss it."

I've written about Houellebecq before — when he called Islam "the most stupid religion" and when, after French Muslims brought suit against him, he was cleared of "inciting racial hatred." And I've recommended his books to every one of my friends and even to some of my relatives and neighbors.

Each one, without exception, has come back to me with little enthusiasm. One stopped reading the novel that brought Houellebecq to prominence, "The Elementary Particles," after 75 pages because it was "too depressing." (Here's an excerpt, unfortunately not the best example.) Another admired the direct style in "Platform" and its quickly sketched world, but disliked its characters. Yet another liked the plot and didn't mind the characters, but had no love for either. And none appreciated Houellebecq's misanthropy or the intellectual underpinnings he brings to it.

As Liddle points out, Houellebecq's misanthropy runs deep, yet "can be dispelled every now and again by sexual intercourse, the redemptive powers of which permeate each of his previous books." That is only one reason why I'll be ordering "Lanzarote" from England, where it's just been published in translation from the French. (I'd rather not wait the year or so it's likely to take for an American edition to appear.)

The more important reason is, as Liddle also notes: "There is no other writer like him, at the moment, for wit, acuity or the transparent beauty of his prose. His themes are always big and bravely expounded." Think of "The Stranger" by Albert Camus and you'll get a hint of Houellebecq's mood. It's apparent that Houellebecq has thought of Camus.

June 30, 2003 / 7:43 a.m. ET
Caravaggio and the Soprano mob: I appreciate the need for arts education. My staff of thousands appreciates it. Let's all agree that right-thinking Americans who value the civilized life appreciate it, too. But writing about it is almost as boring as reading about it. I know. I've done my share of both.

Which is why I was floored by the full-page ad sponsored by Americans for the Arts in Sunday's New York Times. This was the headline: **"No wonder people think CARAVAGGIO is a guy on The Sopranos."** Accompanied by a self-portrait of Caravaggio as Bacchus (captioned *"Let's be honest, he wouldn't last 10 minutes on The Sopranos"*), the text began: "Here's a 16th-century Baroque master whose bold naturalistic painting style first created a sensation, then a movement. A guy whose life was filled with the turbulence and excess of a dozen Mario Puzo novels. A guy who, while troubled, ultimately found redemption — and immortality — in his art. But does the kid next door even know who Caravaggio is? Fuhgedaboutit."

Fuhgedabout the kid next door. Are there inner-city rappers and hip-hop artists anywhere who wouldn't want the fame, success and (let's not be cynical) sense of accomplishment that Michelangelo Caravaggio (1573-1610) achieved in his too-short life? Wouldn't they identify with his — forgive the term — self-empowerment?

"He grew up in less than ideal circumstances," the ad continues. "Much of his family perished in the plague, and he spent much of his youth on the notoriously treacherous streets of Rome. As a young man, he labored beneath others much less talented than he and had difficulty making a living. He faced adversity at every turn.…When his legendary temper threatened to get the best of him, he created his most vital masterpieces. … [His] work is not only a great example of the Baroque period, but also a case study in the importance of art as an outlet."

"Outlet" is putting it mildly. Have a look at these paintings, and don't forget to enlarge them: Medusa's Head, Judith Beheading Holofernes and The Sacrifice of Isaac. They give you a sense of Caravaggio's volcanic aggression. In fact, he was always running into trouble with the law for everything from assault and battery to murder. (He killed a tennis opponent over a disputed score.) The truth is, Caravaggio could have held his own with any of the Soprano mobsters. He makes them look like pikers. Imagine if he hadn't been a painter. And all those gangsta rappers? Fuhgedaboutit.

Postscript: A reader writes: "Did they really have tennis then?" The answer is: They did. Tennis is an ancient game, invented at Stonehenge and imported to Italy in the Middle Ages. Nah, just kidding.

The real answer is: Tennis was invented in ancient Greece and was known as "spharistike" ("let's play"). A wound-up piece of leather was batted back and forth over a net with bare hands, no racquet.

June 30, 2003 / 8:34 a.m. ET

Farewell to Katharine Hepburn: Hepburn, 96, died Sunday at her home in Old Saybrook, Conn.. She wasn't called Katharine the Great for nothing. Read Harry Haun's appreciation, and you'll understand why.

FREE VIDEO START ►

The four-time Oscar-winner (for "Morning Glory," 1933; "Guess Who's Coming to Dinner," 1967; "A Lion in Winter," 1968, and "On Golden Pond," 1981) received 12 Oscars nominations during her 60-year career. But that was only the beginning of her accomplishments.

Katherine Hepburn discusses her life with Katie Couric on "Today" in a 1991 interview.

July 3, 2003 / 8:54 a.m. ET

Google helps GWB find WMD: Just in time for the Fourth of July weekend, Google has shown true patriotism with a giggle for the nation and especially for G. Dubya (thanks to Anthony Cox, the Web wit behind the giggle.)

Try this: Go to http://www.google.com/. Type: **weapons of mass destruction** (no quotation marks). Do NOT click Google Search. Instead, click: **I'm Feeling Lucky.** Then read the whole error message carefully. If you're one of those people who have no time for a couple of clicks because you're leaving town now for the holiday, you can go straight to the error message. But it does spoil some of the fun.

July 7, 2003 / 8: 57 a.m. ET

Good-bye to The Juice and all that: Self-importance, the occupational hazard of bloggers, gave rise to the claim that they were responsible for the resignation of Howell Raines, the former executive editor of The New York Times, because they prolonged the life of the Jayson Blair scandal.

Some media observers have pointed out the absurdity of that claim. What's not absurd, though, is the occupational hazard. It grows on bloggers like a fungus. Show me a blogger and I'll show you someone who needs to be fumigated every once in a while. There are exceptions, of course, like yours truly.

But in the interest of staying fungus-free, I will no longer be writing The Juice. I could say it's because MSNBC.com and I are parting ways, which is true. I could say it's because my staff of thousands has fled, which is not true. I could say a lot of things. Regrettably, like Falstaff thinking of the field of battle, I say the better part of valor is discretion.

I thank my staff of thousands (you know who you are) and also you, dear readers. You've been so loyal and so many, you made The Juice far and away the most popular Weblog on MSNBC.com. I've had great fun writing it. After more than a year, though, it's time to move on. Anyone who wants to can reach me personally at my private e-mail address.

'The Juice' archives:
May 2003
April 2003
March 2003
February 2003
January 2003
December 2002
November 2002
October 2002
September 2002
August 2002
July 2002
June 2002
May 2002

Share your perspective on entertainment and the arts with Jan Herman.
MSNBC is not responsible for the content of Internet links.

Printed in Great Britain
by Amazon

10536126R00176